Praise for

IMAGINING THE LAW

"Every lawyer and anyone else with an intellectual interest in the historical development of our American legal system will be educated, challenged, and captivated by Norman Cantor's brilliant, witty, and learned book."

—William D. Zabel, senior partner, Schulte, Roth & Zabel

"I have read *Imagining the Law* with interest and pleasure. It is a learned book in the sense that it shows familiarity with the relevant sources and the literature, and mature reflection, but it is also a well-written text, full of humor and pointers to our own time."

—R. C. van Caenegem, professor emeritus of medieval history and legal history, University of Ghent, Belgium

"[A] fascinating collection of insights about both the common law and legal history itself." —*Jurist*

"[T]his book has much to offer. . . . [Readers] will gain a historical understanding of the fluidity and adaptability of our common law." —*Trial*

ALSO BY NORMAN F. CANTOR

IMAGINING THE LAW

Common Law and the Foundations
of the American Legal System

NORMAN F. CANTOR

HarperPerennial

A Division of HarperCollins*Publishers*

The Library of Congress has catalogued the hardcover edition as follows:

Cantor, Norman F.
    Imagining the law : common law and the foundations of the American legal system / Norman Cantor. — 1st ed.
        p.   cm.
    Includes bibliographical references and index.
    ISBN 0-06-017194-4
      1. Common law—United States. 2. Law—United States—History.
  I. Title.
  KF394.C36   1997
  349.73'09—dc21   97-8766

ISBN 0-06-092953-7 (pbk.)

99 00 01 02 03 ❖/RRD 10 9 8 7 6 5 4 3 2 1

To the memory of
Sir Geoffrey Elton

The law is unknown to him that knoweth not the reason thereof, and the known certainty of the law is the safety of all.

—SIR EDWARD COKE, C. 1630

The huge mass of historical stuff that is now-a-days flowing from the press goes . . . to make the mind of the nation. It is of some moment that mankind should believe what is true, and disbelieve what is false. . . . Literature and art, religion and law, rents and prices, creeds and superstitions have burst the political barrier and are no longer to be expelled. The study of interactions and interdependencies is but just beginning, and no one can foresee the end.

—FREDERIC WILLIAM MAITLAND, 1901

We cannot study separately the institutions and mentality of a people. Only by investigating them side by side, by seeing how certain ideas correspond to certain social arrangements, can both aspects become intelligible.

—BRONISLAW MALINOWSKI, 1915

What a time it has taken us to shake off the shackles of the law—to make a reality of emancipation of history from the lawyers.

—SIR GEOFFREY ELTON, 1984

Contents

Preface

THIS BOOK IS WRITTEN for the layman and the beginning student, although some practicing attorneys may find it interesting and useful. It is an attempt to explain how the legal systems of Britain and the United States and most other English-speaking countries got to be the way they are.

These countries live under English common law, and this book explains the social, political, and cultural factors that shaped the emergence and development of common law and examines the strengths and weaknesses of the common-law system, which has come to play a great role in our lives. There is also a focus on the legal profession, its composition and behavior pattern, which has played a central role in English society from the thirteenth to the mid-twentieth century.

There is a close connection, easy to perceive in the round and at a distance but difficult to articulate in detail and close-up, between the common law and English liberal political institutions. Since English common law was perpetuated after the American Revolution as the basis of the United States legal systems at both the federal and state levels, the constitutional and political significance of the English common-law heritage has been an enduring if complex theme in American history. The same may be said of course for Anglophone Canada, Australia, and several other modern states that were products of the British Empire.

Amazingly, in the United States in the past quarter of a century the legal profession has drawn into itself perhaps half of the best students graduating from American colleges, with important consequences for both the profession and society in general. The common-law culture of the three-quarters of a million U.S. lawyers is explicated in this book.

Another theme of this book is how closely intertwined was the making of common law in England with the development of the social class called gentry—roughly speaking, the rural upper middle class—and how the law in Britain took on the mind-set of the gentry and at the same time molded this dominant class's own culture and behavior. The history of English common law presents a fascinating case study in historical sociology—namely, how a set of institutions and regulatory concepts founded in a rural aristocratic society became adapted (advantageously or not) to the needs of an increasingly commercial and eventually industrial society. Much of the controversy about the common law in early modern England and to some extent still today, in both Britain and the United States, stems from this sociological condition, not unknown elsewhere but existing in a particularly vibrant form in English legal development.

The system of trial by jury—distinctive to Anglo-American common law and a subject of much current debate in the United States—is examined in its development. It will be seen that the strengths and weaknesses of trial by jury have long been prevalent and are not recently emerging characteristics of this central aspect of common law.

Also highlighted is the way theorists have interpreted the common law, pointing to the cultural and intellectual contexts that have conditioned these efforts at theoretical judicial constructions, which have always fallen somewhat short of the dynamic and productive qualities of the common-law system.

This story of the common law is here set in contrast with the other great legal system that developed in the Western world, that of Roman law, which since the later Middle Ages has been the legal system prevailing on the European continent and many overseas areas settled by the continental powers, such as Latin America, or even to some extent Quebec and Louisiana. Roman law was also the basis of the canon law of the Roman Catholic church, which is still operative today.

There are very important differences between common law and Roman, or, as we may also call it, continental law. It has been traditional in accounts of common law to assume its superiority to Roman law. That assumption does not prevail in this book, not only because Roman law was solidified a millennium before common law and the latter owes quite a bit to the former, but because intrinsically, as they currently function, continental law is by no means inferior as a legal system to common law, and in the area of criminal justice, it can be plausibly argued, is actually superior to common law.

I am not a lawyer, but I have taught legal history in various American universities for four decades and for a year in an Israeli university. I was introduced to the study of common law by the greatest of American medieval historians, Joseph R. Strayer, at Princeton in the early 1950s. He also was not a lawyer but had mastered the forms of action at common law and perceived them as part of the rise of the medieval state. Over the years I discussed many of the issues in this book with Sir Geoffrey Elton, who held the chair of constitutional history at Cambridge, although himself not a lawyer. I gained much from these discussions. From 1982 to 1989 I taught English and once American legal history in the New York University School of Law. In that context I also participated in a vigorous legal history seminar conducted by William E. Nelson and learned much from Professor Nelson, and from two other continuing participants, Professor John Philip Reid and Mr. Lawrence Fleischer.

Anyone who undertakes to write legal history stands in the shadow of Frederic William Maitland, who was a law professor at Cambridge at the beginning of the century and was in equal parts a great historian and a pioneering sociologist of the law. A scholar of almost equal stature and influence on the side of American legal history was James Willard Hurst, of the University of Wisconsin Law School, who wrote in the 1950s and 1960s. This book owes much to these giants and to a host of later writers. Among the recent writers on legal history, Brian Simpson, R. C. van Caenegem, Michael Clanchy, and Lawrence Friedman have had perhaps the greatest influence upon me.

It must be noted, however, that legal history as a discipline is in a relatively early stage of development. With very few exceptions professional historians lack the technical capacity to read legal documents, and law schools are rarely and at best marginally interested in appointing and rewarding historians of law. In American law schools a legal historian can only be appointed if he or she can teach one of the basic introductory courses, such as property or liability. In England, aside from less than a handful of chairs, there are virtually no appointments available for legal historians. The continental law schools have almost no interest in history; their approach is structural and philosophical rather than developmental.

Under these circumstances vast areas of legal history remain underresearched and conceptually underdeveloped. Thus there are literally tons of English court records from the period 1300–1500 that have never been looked at since the multilingual court clerks wrote down a near-verbatim record of the cases. American law professors today are quite active in applying literary theory to legal texts, but almost nothing has been done to write legal history in the context of this vanguard humanities theory.

The field of legal history conceptually exhibits a strong parallel to the history of science, which has benefited, as legal history has not, from lavish funding provided by learned foundations and universities. The history of science can be written narrowly and simply as science that takes place in the past; this kind of history of science is highly technical and is concerned mainly with recreating the thought processes of great scientists who happened to live in the past. Another approach to the history of science interprets the development of science interactively with present-day concerns and within the contexts of past culture, society, and politics; it frequently takes a critical attitude to the behavior of scientists. Not surprisingly the latter approach is not popular among scientists and has been condemned as subversive, judgmental, and amateur in its understanding of science.

Similarly writings on legal history can be divided into, first, those that are devoted to close professional study of the law that happened in the past. They are highly technical works and focus on the operations and techniques of the legal profession. A prime example of this genre is J. H. Baker, *Introduction to English Legal History* (London/Boston: Butterworths, 1990), 3d ed. The other group of writings on legal history is similar to the second approach to the history of science, taking a broad cultural, social, and political perspective from present-day concerns.

Mine is the latter approach. It may be called, pejoratively or otherwise, social constructivist or relativist. I prefer to call it the sociological and cultural history of law. Nevertheless I have read closely and tried to understand what the masters of the more narrowly technical approach to legal history have to say, not always an easy task, since frequently they seem to be addressing only London barristers or American law school professors.

Several lawyers and historians accepted my invitation to read an earlier draft of this book and provided valuable criticism: Louis

Knafla, William Nelson, Judith Nolan, Michael Stein, R. C. van Caenegem, and Arthur Williamson. They are of course in no way responsible for any shortcomings or errors in this book.

I wish to thank the staff of the Bobst and Law Libraries of New York University and of the Firestone Library at Princeton University for their unfailing courtesy and cooperation. The Office of the Dean of the Faculty of Arts at NYU funded secretarial assistance.

My secretary, Eloise Jacobs-Brunner, contended with my bad typing and handwriting and through various drafts put the book on computer disk for HarperCollins. Dawn Marie Hayes helped me prepare the bibliography. Sue Llewellyn copyedited the text of the book with her customary intelligence and skill.

I wish to thank my editor at HarperCollins New York, Hugh Van Dusen, and my literary agent, Alexander Hoyt, for their encouragement and patience.

1
Law and Legal History

LAW IS THE SYSTEM of state-enforced rules by which relatively large civil societies and political entities operate. This programmed social functioning is backed up by the exercise of power by a politically sovereign body.

What constitutes law among the behavioral codes by which groups or individuals in society live has been defined by legal philosophers in three different ways. Some say that law is the command of a sovereign power to obey a rule, with a penalty for transgressing it. This view is called legal positivism and has been particularly associated with the nineteenth-century English philosopher John Austin.

On the other side are those who say that law is the application within a state or other community of rules that are derived from universal principles of morality rooted in turn in revealed religion or reason or a kind of ethical communal sensibility. This view is associated with Thomas Aquinas, in the Middle Ages, who articulated it in the form of natural law theory, and with Lon Fuller and Ronald Dworkin, among recent American legal philosophers.

In the 1960s the widely esteemed Oxford philosopher H. L. A. Hart tried to find an intermediate position between these two opposing definitions of law according to positivism and natural law. He argued that there are "rules of recognition" in which the obligation of rule conformity is brought about by "social pressure" and customary social behavior rather than by sovereign command and penalty.

Many stipulations, Hart claimed, are recognizable as law that are pragmatic rules for transactions between private parties and functionally lie outside the sphere of sovereign command and penalty. No sovereign power, no matter how ambitious and aggressive, can enforce more than part of the spectrum of laws we live by. Even the concept of sovereign power is problematic and vulnerable.

Whether Hart really established an intermediate position between the two standard positions in legal philosophy or simply found a new way—subtle, perhaps, or confusing—of associating law with ethics in a context of linguistic analysis and pragmatic theory remains a matter of dispute.

The law is divided into two kinds. There is criminal law, by which peace and security are maintained, and whose violation results in publicly administered punishment of greater or lesser severity and brings upon the transgressor the stigma of moral turpitude. Second, there is civil law, which regulates relationships between individuals, families, and corporations involving other than criminal activities and provides state-enforced techniques for accumulating and distributing property and other forms of wealth. For example, murder and robbery fall within the jurisdiction of criminal law. Contracts, personal liability, and marriage and divorce are within the purview of civil law.

There are instances in which criminal and civil law overlap.

Torts (liability for personal injury; the word "tort" comes from the Norman French for "wrong") can involve criminal prosecution as well as remedy to the injured party in a civil action. Manslaughter may involve civil penalties as well as punishment under criminal law and similarly, tax evasion can be countered by both criminal prosecution and restitution under civil law. But for the most part criminal and civil law are quite distinct, both conceptually and in practice.

All political entities have legal systems and law courts. But law as it has creatively developed in the Western world, from the Roman Empire to the present, has been mostly in large political units and social organizations, covering extensive territories and diverse populations.

There is much less need for law in small groups. Thus while Orthodox Jews live under the halacha, which literally means "law," in practice they are governed by heads of families and one rabbi or handful of rabbis who make ad hoc decisions to sustain the group's social functions and culture, although for authority the rabbi may judicially cite the Bible and prestigious commentaries on it.

The Greek city-states had legal codes, but since they were small populations and territories with participatory democracies or tightly run oligarchies, they needed little written law. Juries of six hundred drawn by lot from the community or a handful of dictators and oligarchs made up the law as needed.

The Germanic peoples of the early Middle Ages and the Icelanders of the thirteenth century drew up law codes, but these codes dealt only with very narrow disputed areas of their social function. Germanic kings and Scandinavian lords arbitrarily made legal decisions when they wanted to, or the community of active warriors met together over a keg of beer and jawboned a consensus.

The modern state of Israel emerged after 1948 with an unusually rich set of legal heritages—rabbinical, English, and Turkish.

But as a matter of fact, not until the 1990s was the judiciary and its determination of the legal system important in Israel. Until economic expansion and increasing size and diversity of the population, due to the Russian immigration of the 1980s, changed the context, Israel's small Jewish population was run by an exotic elite of perhaps two hundred families, and the judiciary drawn in any case from this same elite were mere adjuncts of what was decided in upscale living rooms in Jerusalem and Tel Aviv. Even in the mid–1980s a sophisticated Israeli with a problem did not retain an attorney. He phoned—or had someone else phone—a cabinet minister at home to get the latter's intercession.

This personal approach to problem solving rather than use of a public litigator is generally characteristic of small populations with narrow, powerful elites. Even in now heavily populated wealthy Japan, corporate executives, still bound by the culture of an earlier aristocratic and tribal society, with a small population, are reluctant to resort to litigation, which carries a social stigma.

The early Roman Republic had a similar ad hoc, personally shaped legal system in which a small handful of leaders of prominent families met in the senate and assembly and made sufficient judicial decisions. In the later republic, by 50 B.C., this artful system no longer worked well. The number of people involved were too many, the factional conflicts too fierce, and the entire physical area, covering large stretches of the Roman-ruled imperial Mediterranean coastline, became too expansive for this ad hoc, personal, and in-group approach to law. Therefore the Romans had to develop a formal, public, institutional, state-backed legal system with panels of judges impersonally hearing cases and rendering decisions by the authority of the emperor.

Thus emerged one of the two systems of law in the Western world. The other, English common law, developed in the later Middle Ages because—among other reasons—the territory involved and the number of people affected, even in the "scept'red isle," were too great for personal and family solutions, especially when complicated property disputes and mayhem generated by organized crime were involved. Coming down into the modern world, English common law became much more elaborate and sophisticated as England's wealth and population multiplied and its imperial interests proliferated after 1700.

The most developed, complicated system of law in the world and the locus of the most constant resource to law courts for dispute settlement—and the largest legal profession by far—developed in the twentieth-century United States, especially after the New Deal took hold in 1937, because of the country's size, wealth, population, and international interests. Indeed, law was so necessary in the United States for conflict resolution in regard to almost every conceivable personal aspiration and social function, that a two-tier, federal and state system of courts had to be fully worked out. The tensile relationship between the two systems was in itself another cause of American legal elaboration and much judicial theorizing.

Therefore, when you are thinking about the creative side of the history of law, you are focusing mostly on large societies and major political entities—the Roman Republic and Empire, the medieval English monarchy, the modern European states and their overseas offshoots, and especially commercial, industrial, and imperial Britain and the vast, bicoastal, fiercely challenging United States.

The effort of the Russians to live in their own continental country by oligarchic power—whether of the czars or the commissars—rather than by legal systems did not work well. It resulted in unrestrained and unpunished criminality on the part of the czarist and Communist oligarchies themselves and the inability to provide the necessary legal context for modern industry, high technology, and international corporate economy, contributing to political collapse, first in 1917 and then again in 1990.

*   *   *

Legal history is a good route to understanding the essentials of Roman law and common law because it shows how these systems developed in response to social needs, political conflicts, economic changes, and cultural patterns. It explains judicial institutions and legal principles as outcomes of particular operations in real time and space. Efforts are also made to explain legal systems philosophically as a derivation and extrapolation from ethical and metaphysical concepts, but the result is neither as comprehensible nor as convincing as historical explanation.

In constructing a paradigm of the history of English common law, historians try to enhance clarity of patterning and highlight meaningfulness by applying categories and pursuing historiographical assumptions. That is the way it is done in all fields of history. The good historian operates like a sculptor, selectively molding an image out of an amorphous block of facts.

In recent decades historians of common law have been inclined to employ the distinction between public and private law that has been a favorite of twentieth-century jurisprudence. Public law is the juristic area concerned with the relationship between governments and peoples and therefore between law and politics; this is constitutional history. Private law focuses on relationships at the subgovernmental level, between persons (and juristically a person can be a business corporation). Prime areas of private law are held to be property, torts, contracts, and debt.

Roman law was keenly aware of the distinction between public and private law. The former was the law of the state, the *res publica* (the public thing); the latter the law of persons. A prominent thirteenth-century English legal theorist who had a strong Roman-law background, Henry of Bracton, was aware of the applicability of the conceptual distinction between public and private law to English common law. But the distinction between public and private law had little actual currency in England before the eighteenth century and did not gain significant interest until the early twentieth. A problematic aspect of this distinction was that at least before 1300 English constitutional (public) law was grounded in the law of property and contract, and a clear distinction between public and private law was lacking.

Yet in recent decades, the leaders of the thriving Cambridge University school of legal history, J. H. Baker and S. F. Milsom, have perceived medieval English law through the prism of the distinction between public and private law and they have concentrated their work on private law. Their casebook of medieval and early modern English law comprises exclusively private lawsuits, and Baker's narrative textbook survey has little to say about constitutional history. In taking this provocative stance, the Cambridge dons have matched the inclinations of many legal historians on the faculties of leading American law schools. Private law, it is felt, is the real subject of legal history; constitutional history, at least in the English venue, is boring old stuff that can be left to underpaid faculty in political science and history departments.

Another ingredient in the formation of paradigms has been the interpretative assumptions used by legal historians. There are seven productive and innovative approaches to interpreting and writing legal history, some much more developed than others.

The first—and mainstream—approach follows the assumptions that however imperfectly, belatedly, and perilously, judicial institutions and the legal profession, at least in the Anglo-American world, have provided a large measure of justice and liberty and are integral to an ethically committed civil society. Yet in the shaping of legal institutions and operative mode of the legal profession, the social, political, and cultural context plays a significant role. There is an interactive process between legal ideas and procedures and the societal context. This mainline liberal approach to legal history was propounded by Frederic William Maitland, a Cambridge University professor in England at the beginning of the twentieth century, and further exemplified in the writing of James Willard Hurst, a University of Wisconsin professor, in its middle decades.

The Maitland-Hurst school of mainline liberal interpretation of legal history was, especially in the United States, easily compatible with the temperament of law school teachers, bridging critical reading of texts with moderately progressive ideology, and the mind-set of ambitious, well-trained, and similarly disposed students who emerged from these thriving schools.

The mainline approach took a bifocal view of the common law. It was both celebratory of the moral purposes and outcomes of the law and frankly cognizant of the law's association with landed, corporate, and other privileged interests. It assumed that over time the ethical stratum had come to—and would continue to—prevail over, or at least substantially channel the privileged interests. Departure from the Maitland-Hurst tradition was conditioned by lack of faith in this accommodation between ethics and privilege, or reading of legal texts in some novel manner not normally pursued by law school teachers and their students, or some combination of these two radical discourses.

Second, tangential to but separable from the mainstream approach, is the view that legal systems simply serve as the instruments of dominant classes, since 1800 the industrial and financial bourgeoisie. The most celebrated book on American legal history in the past two decades, by Harvard Law School's Morton Horwitz, takes this strongly Marxist approach.

Disagreement between the first and second approaches turns largely on when, how, and if the common law transcended the shaping effect of class interests and became rooted in an ethical continuum, which could be at some discoverable critical juncture in the past (such as 1215, 1787, or 1937) or in the Marxist view only in a vaguely wished-for future.

A third and more pessimistic paradigm places the law as the instrument of repression that perpetually serves the holders of power at any time and place, whatever their social background. The repressive service of law to power, from this point of view, alters in structure and varies in intensity, but never departs from its basically amoral, domineering character. Judicial reform signifies only new and more sophisticated forms of repressive service to power. This is the view of the French guru Michel Foucault, and it has also seriously influenced feminist legal historiography.

Fourth, some—inspired by the French psychoanalyst Jacques Lacan—give a Freudian twist to this dark vision, somehow connecting judicial and psychosexual forms of repression. Law becomes the visible structure of the Other, grounded in the oedipal father, embedded in the subconscious.

Fifth, there is the anthropology of Claude Lévi-Strauss, in which mind and society—and its institutions, including law—are part of the same universal system, exhibiting common binary structural forms. Both provocatively radical and highly conservative implications can be drawn from this doctrine.

While Lévi-Strauss, who taught in Paris, developed his structuralist theory in the 1940s and 1950s in the last precomputer era, the cognitive basis of computers—the whole mathematics of the computer is based on the binomial theorem—has legitimized his theory. Lévi-Strauss believes that interactive polarity is the building block of mind and society.

Taking up the radical implications of anthropological structuralism, and adding accretions from the third and fourth approaches to legal history (Foucault and Lacan), and given focus by the philosophical and literary disquisitions of Jacques Derrida, is the sixth approach to legal history, that of deconstruction. Not only would deconstruction separate law from ethics now and in the past and forever, but it would view all legal systems as intrinsically fragile and immediately and constantly susceptible to breakdown, contradiction, and alteration. That such a view is viscerally repulsive to the legal profession and outside the bounds of current political discourse does not exclude it from the intellectual arena in which legal history operates.

As has generally been the case in the humanities, the application of the ideas of Lacan, Foucault, and Derrida has within legal thinking resulted in an adversarial position. In a book with a boldly psychoanalytic title—*Oedipus Lex* (Berkeley: University of California Press, 1995)—Peter Goodrich, who holds a prestigious endowed chair in law at the University of London, claims that "there is . . . no real object of legal science but only that fantasm [*sic*] of unity necessary for the maintenance of the profession itself," and, somewhat elusively, that law as an "institution internalizes as its own form of unhappy consciousness the failures upon which its successes were built." We are likewise not surprised to be told by Goodrich that law is psychoanalytically an antagonist and oppressor of women's being.

The seventh approach to legal history follows from the postulates of the Law and Economics group, which emerged principally at the University of Chicago Law School in the 1970s. Influenced by the market economics of Gary Becker and Milton Friedman, ideologically reacting against leftist interpretations, emboldened by the Reaganite political adventure in the 1980s, this school of thought found its most visible spokesman in Richard Posner, now a chief judge on the federal court of appeals. The Law and Economics approach is essentially early-twentieth-century pragmatic liberalism put through the prism of market economics—Maitland and Hurst conjoined with David Ricardo.

The mind-set of the common law is the same as the one that was operative in market capitalism, and the institutions of the common law were instrumental in the rise of capitalism from the fourteenth century onward. Their connection served the interests not of a single selfish class but of society as a whole. That is the historical vision of Law and Economics. It is closely affiliated with the Reaganite and Thatcherite politics of the 1980s and similar conservative political affirmations since then.

The seven valuable approaches to legal history can be categorized thus:

1. Justice and liberty, mainstream
2. Marxist
3. Foucault–feminist power, pessimism
4. Lacanian, psychoanalytic
5. Structuralist
6. Deconstructionist
7. Law and Economics

From about 1925 to 1960 some politically radical and heavily sociological versions of the first approach, as well as all instances of the second, to legal history were known as legal realism. Since the late 1970s varying combinations of approaches 2 through 6 to legal history have been called critical legal studies, or CLS.

Though these appellations are largely marketing devices within legal academia and do not per se contribute to understanding legal history, they are much used and cannot be avoided.

The intellectual problem with the term legal realism is that it embraces both the mushy leftist fringe of approach 1 as well as the more clearcut reductionist approach 2. The term CLS (and "the crits" in law schools who propound it) caused confusion because the term covers such a variety of combinations of approaches 2 through 6. Another problem is that writers in this camp not infrequently sound off without having read or at least understood what the provocative Frenchmen Foucault, Lacan, Lévi-Strauss, and Derrida actually said. Yet French theory is not astrophysics; it is not hard to read and comprehend.

The issue for legal history is productive application of theory to a difficult developmental spectrum. Legal history without interpretive theory is deficient in meaning and significance. However, applying theory so as to generate readable and interesting history is not an easy task. The challenge is not much taken up because most academic historians pursued that discipline as a career choice with the naive assumption that they could avoid theory. It cannot be avoided if good history—in this instance, good legal history—is to be written.

There has been much debate in recent years among those committed to the theory behind approaches 3 through 6 of legal history as to the nature of a legal text. Is a legal text (case or treatise, perhaps also legislation) affected by the same allegedly fragile, unstable deconstructive qualities as a literary text? Or is a legal text intrinsically different from a literary text and does it retain a high component of objectivity, stability, and autonomy and can it therefore be read at face value, or close to face value, as representing the pursuit of justice or reflecting the interests of class and power?

As long as legal theorists cannot agree on whether a legal text is or is not different from a novel or poem as a piece of writing or as a cultural construct or social artifact, the contributions of the theorists drawing on recent literary theory (or making "the linguistic turn," as it is fashionably called) for legal history will be problematical and restricted in value. There is no sign of early consensus on the horizon.

There is a sociological as well as an intellectual side to this ongoing debate that has generated a substantial body of writing. Those who viscerally would like to take a fully deconstructive position and claim that a legal text has the same characteristics as any literary text are obviously bothered by the lurking feeling that they would thereby derogate from the study of law and legal history its most attractive social aspect, its long-standing connection to political power and social privilege.

Whatever the precise nature of a legal text in theory, its academic analysts have always behaved as though they were dealing with something more objective, important, and socially meaningful than their colleagues in the literature departments, and hence deserved more salary and prestige than the humanities professors. Nearly all legal theorists of radical disposition show a reluctance to abandon this privileged position. They are caught between an underlying revolutionary disposition and professional obligations and durable ambition for superior campus status.

This tension reinforces the preexisting intellectually conservative proclivity of legal historians to assume that they are dealing with a body of writing discernibly above and beyond belletristic literature. This tension also explains that while on purely intellectual grounds, applying Lacan or Derrida to legal study is bolder, more innovative, and possibly more fruitful, the radical theorist and historian who has had the most influence on writing of legal history has been Foucault, whose reduction of all institutional and organizational change and cultural departures to being instruments of power has been more widely recognized and imitated. Foucault's radical legal thinking leaves legal texts within the conventional domain of sociological operations rather than psychological phenomena.

In the past, efforts to give a psychoanalytic perspective to legal and judicial functions have not had enduring success. At the time when the American legal realists were flourishing in the 1940s, Jerome Frank in their midst proposed a Freudian approach to interpreting the behavior of magistrates and attorneys. Much was made by Frank of oedipal signification. This view encountered vehement opposition from the mainline legal realists, such as Harvard's Roscoe Pound, partly on intellectual grounds of opposing specious psychologizing to explain behavior, and partly on the ground that psychoanalysis had no applicable use in judicial practice. Indeed, when Frank ascended to the federal bench in New York, he eschewed applying his Freudian theories to his own judgments and courtroom behavior.

At the NYU School of Law today, there is a seminar room outfitted as a shrine to Frank's memory. In the plaque apotheosizing Frank, his quondam radical psychological approach to interpreting legal behavior is not mentioned.

Lacan and Derrida, from somewhat different perspectives, the former from psychiatric analysis, the latter from philosophical and literary analysis, signify the return of the Freudian gambit to the reading of legal texts, and in the case of Derrida at least there has been significant impact. Yet their influence on legal thinking has lagged far behind Foucault's much more easily applicable sociological reductionism.

In the absence of consensus on the prescribed theoretical foundations for legal history, the historian will have to pick his or her way eclectically among the theories as the opportunity arises, instrumentally using one idea or another as the situation offers.

But this is what historians always do, especially the really good ones—they are intellectual scavengers, using shamelessly and conditionally whatever theory helps organize and explain their data to give a composite picture of the past. And narrative maintains its intrinsic interest and intellectual legitmacy. Whatever else the legal historian does, he or she must tell a clear and emotionally satisfying story.

2
Ancient Advocacy: Cicero

IN THEIR FIRST SEMESTER, students at the prestigious NYU School of Law are required to take a course called "Lawyering." This course is taught by a nationally famous professor of judicial practice whom NYU lured away from Stanford Law School at a cost that would make a professional athlete stop and think. It involved a penthouse apartment built to specifications laid down by the demanding professor and his wife and a teaching job for the spouse, also a lawyer, as well as an extraordinary salary, even by bloated law school standards, and sundry other benefits. Of course, the salary looks absurdly modest compared to what a free-agent star quarterback might get, but remember that this is a tenured appointment that will run for several decades, not four or five years, or less if severe athletic injury intervenes.

What is so wonderful about this professor and what he can teach? He can not only instruct the students on all forms of an attorney's behavior, outside as well as inside the courtroom, but viewing TV tapes of students' fledgling efforts, he offers trenchant critiques of their awkward duckling steps into the great role of professional attorneys.

Young women and men under his tutelage are taught the finer points of professional behavior that—along with the deep knowledge of the context of the law they will acquire in other courses—will transform them into effective and affluent advocates of their rich clients.

Many hidden subtleties are involved. One TV-taped exercise exposes the students to some unfortunate person seeking representation who is not worth representing, either because the case is too trivial or the petitioner cannot pay the high fees. The issue is how to discourage the suitor without insulting him and taking up more than a few minutes in a busy day that bills four hundred dollars an hour. This is a crucial problem in a great attorney's life, a lesson to be learned that is as important as the text of some famous Supreme Court decision. The callow young students, either because of lack of social grace or overcome by foolish empathy, often flunk this exercise on the first go-round by talking at length with the improbable client. They are chastised by the professor, who reminds them that this is not the way a prominent attorney behaves. This is not good lawyering.

If the greatest Roman advocate of them all, Marcus Tullius Cicero (106–43 B.C.), could be brought back to teach the NYU course on lawyering, he would do as good a job as the smoothie from Stanford because he was the ancient world's most famous and skillful lawyer. He is also the individual in antiquity we know most about, because more than seven hundred of his letters, many highly personal and intended only for their recipients' (friends or relatives) eyes, and fifty-seven of his greatest orations, most delivered (before his own editing and fleshing out) in the courtroom, have survived.

Furthermore Cicero's Latin rhetoric, complicated but punchy in style, down through the centuries has been regarded as the standard of Latin prose, emulated by humanist scholars and taught to boys in elite prep schools.

Cicero was not the first prominent lawyer in republican Rome. He himself mentions a certain veteran attorney named Hortensius, already successful in practice when Cicero started his own career, who was his losing opponent in the famous case that made Cicero's professional reputation. Cicero carefully observed Hortensius's courtroom style but, he claims, significantly improved on it, Hortensius being prone to stilted argument and to consult his notes too much.

Cicero became the greatest advocate of his day, the man you wanted to represent you in litigation if you could afford it, the winner of a series of sensational cases, some with important political overtones. He was even more flawless, eloquent, and admirable in posthumous reputation down into the mid-twentieth century than he had been in life. His name, his visage, his sentences became etched in marble and set the model for the legal profession in common-law countries, even more than in the Roman-law world.

That is because Roman law, a generation or two after Cicero, accorded overwhelming control in the courtroom to the imperial magistrates—the emperor's judges who restricted the freewheeling aggressive advocacy that Cicero practiced—centering on the heroic silver-throated attorney drawing all attention to himself and talking endlessly about anything that was even remotely connected to the case.

Cicero lived and practiced in the later days of the Roman Republic (it was replaced by Caesarean autocracy just sixteen years after his death). In republican courtrooms the verdict was not rendered, as later, by a small panel of sober, cautious, prosaic, emperor-appointed magistrates who had no taste or time for attorneys' grandstanding, but in the old republican and Greek manner before a large jury—usually around forty senators or other prominent politicians eager for a show and with well-educated ears and eyes attuned to an elaborate or subtle turn of phrase, a handsome face, an elegant gesture of the hand and arm, and a well-cut toga.

In Cicero's day, in the late republic, both civil and criminal actions for upper-class people started when someone made a petition to a political official (resembling a mayor) called a praetor. The latter would then appoint someone experienced in the law to act as presiding judge in a trial. A jury comprising usually 40 to 50 men (but it could be as many as 180) would then decide the case, after an often lengthy trial with presentations by counsel.

How criminal trials of poor people in Cicero's day were conducted in Rome is not known; presumably they received summary justice from a magistrate. The capability of ordinary people to engage in civil suits was limited by the very high cost of such actions, involving not only the hiring of counsel but substantial court costs.

Whether civil or criminal, the trials in which Cicero participated nearly always concerned litigants or defendants from the upper class. Even when he undertook to represent a person of modest circumstances, it is likely that a wealthy interested third party gave him at least a token fee on the side.

The courtroom in which Cicero practiced in his glory days around 60 B.C. was more like the California courtroom of today than the structured, judge-dominated courtroom of imperial Rome, which had fully developed by A.D. 150 and is still the legal practice in Germany, France, and other Western European countries, with their Roman-law heritage.

Furthermore, between about 1300 and 1950, and perhaps still occasionally today in upscale prep schools, the core curriculum for adolescent boys was astonishingly Cicero's own great courtroom orations. When these boys grew up to be practicing lawyers in the common-law courts in London, Boston, or Toronto, they only had to call on their educational experience in their most impressionable adolescent years to know viscerally and spontaneously what great advocacy was. Cicero had shown them the way, and they had under duress of stern schoolmasters absorbed these Ciceronian lessons into the very depths of their consciousness.

Cicero's talent for writing as well as speaking the difficult, cumbersome Latin language has never been equaled by anyone. His Latin prose style became the model for all subsequent masterful writers in Latin, such as the Christian theologian Saint Augustine in early-fifth-century Tunisia, and the Renaissance humanist Petrarch in mid-fourteenth-century Florence. Furthermore Cicero's prose style, with its immensely skillful use of subordinate clauses and rushing, cascading phrases leading to a pithy climax, has been imitated by some modern masters of English prose, notably Edward Gibbon in the eighteenth century and Winston Churchill in the twentieth.

Though it is risky to use this exuberant, richly textured style, it has tremendous impact if done well. Lawyers are not as a rule great prose stylists, and no advocate or attorney has come remotely near challenging Cicero's empyrean position as a writer. With this important but singular exception, he was in every way a typical highly successful lawyer of the Western world, down to the immediate present among English barristers or Wall Street law firms. He fitted fully the pattern of an important lawyer's background, ambitions, behavior, lifestyle, interests, and legal and political philosophy. He was the prototype of the big-time advocate.

Privately Cicero acknowledged that judicial orations were part of his work as a barrister and often did not represent his personal opinion: "Anyone who supposes that in my necessarily forensic speeches he has got my personal views under seal is making a great mistake. . . . We orators are brought in not to say what we personally think but what is required by the situation and the case in hand" (translated by John Cook).

The role and attitude of an attorney in the later English common law (and in the United States today) could not be more succinctly and bluntly stated.

Cicero's role as the typical upscale lawyer is to a limited but still significant degree a matter of his personal impact, through his writings, on subsequent generations. How a great lawyer speaks, writes, behaves, and lives is enshrined in Cicero's voluminous writings. Those who had what we would today call a prep school (that is, humanist secondary) education or immersion in the Latin classics in college, could get immediate inspiration for modeling themselves on the master advocate from Cicero's own communications.

Cicero's place, however, as a typical lawyer of high public image and immense professional success, with attendant behavioral patterns and personal style, can best be explained sociologically rather than by the longitudinal perpetuation of a tradition that he started. Given the work commitments of a litigator in an adversarial kind of courtroom scene—one advocate against another in oral pleading in front of a jury—Cicero's talents, temperament, lifestyle, interests, and philosophy comprised a well-rounded category of public and private persona: the prominent, affluent, influential, and much admired lawyer: "Get me Cicero."

Cicero's class and family background are highly typical of successful lawyers at all times and places. He was not an aristocrat, not from a senatorial family, nor from a clan of great landholders, corporate magnates, and statesmen. He was from the provincial aspiring middle class. His family could afford to give him a very good education; after that he was on his own.

Cicero moved upward socially to become what the Romans aptly called one of the "new men," a millionaire lawyer, a member of the senatorial elite, and for a short time the holder of high political office and a mover and shaker in circles of supreme power.

Cicero's one problem was that he lived in a bad time, the disintegrating, tempestuous, violent later years of the Roman Republic, in which vicious political rivalry among elite political groups, seeking power and booty, spilled over into violence, assassinations, and civil war. This era ended only a few years after his death, when the surviving leader of one party, originally founded by the now assassinated Julius Caesar, made himself dictator by force of arms, ruled powerfully and wisely as Augustus Caesar, and established benign imperial power to replace the disordered, collapsed, and discredited republic.

Cicero was insufficiently adept politically, or lacking in sufficient good fortune, to dance his way through the political maelstrom of late republican Rome. After gaining the pinnacle of office, that of consul in 63 B.C., his political fortunes went into decline. In the end, twenty years later, he was not even allowed to live peacefully in retirement on his beloved country estate, but was cut down by soldiers in the employ of the powerful political gangster, Mark Anthony, the famous lover of Cleopatra, himself soon to be vanquished by the ascending Augustus Caesar.

In his younger days as a lawyer in Rome, Cicero did all the right things to assure professional, fiscal, and political success. He gained public attention by a politically correct judicial onslaught on a corrupt colonial governor, representing the wounded and outraged citizens of Sicily. He won temporary power and popularity by successfully prosecuting for treasonous conspiracy a shadowy aristocrat, Catiline, who had become the leader of a left-wing populist group. Thereby Cicero endeared himself to the conservative majority in the Senate. He closely associated himself with a billionaire businessman and politician named Crassus, and bought a large house from this magnate, going into heavy debt to do so.

Cicero not only had a lavish domicile in the fashionable heart of Rome. He also bought a large country estate, for which he had genuine affection, spending a lot of time there writing. Not only did Cicero jettison his first wife under republican Rome's easy divorce laws to marry into a more influential clan; he could also be persuaded for enough money to represent shady people or members of opposing political parties.

He likewise did what is today in American law called pro bono work, representing for little or no fee a worthy indigent client, carefully choosing (as great attorneys do) such clients to get maximum favorable publicity. Thus Cicero represented an obscure Greek writer, one Archias, in a humble immigration case, getting Archias his permanent residency in Rome. This case enabled Cicero to expound at length on the glories and uses of literature, not ignoring the mundane ("Good literature spends the night with us; accompanies us on our travel").

Since oratorical advocates like Cicero were gentlemen supposedly removed from trade, they, like later English barristers down to the present day, did not directly bill clients. This fiction is meaningless except to give a fake aristocratic aura to the Roman advocate and the English barrister. In both instances a third party collected the fees, and the charges were heavy. Cicero became wealthy from his courtroom work.

Cicero's speeches and letters resonate with two seminal legal ideas that are absolutely integral to English common law, as well as being developed by his less flamboyant successors, the masters of Roman law, beginning in the constitutive era between A.D. 50 and 200.

The first of these ideas may be called the moral "penumbra" effect of judicial finding. Without this idea many of the progressive decisions of the U.S. Supreme Court in the Warren-Burger era and thereafter, between 1954 and 1975, would have been impossible. Ronald Dworkin, holder of chairs of jurisprudence at Oxford and at NYU Law Schools in the 1980s and 1990s, could not have constructed his thick and lengthy liberal judicial essays—many of which initially appeared in the *New York Review of Books*—without the Ciceronian penumbra doctrine. It is a simple idea, but a very important one—namely that law is part of a moral continuum. Or a circle of ethical compulsion surrounds the legal planet and exercises a gravitational pull on it.

Every judicial issue and decision gives off a moral bank of light.

The good attorney and magistrate focus on the moral penumbra and extrapolate from it back on the specific legal point at issue, and advocate and render decisions in accordance with the conditioning ethical ambience. Every lawsuit has moral implications that the good attorney and wise magistrate will select and define.

There is a strong sanction for progressive court findings, rising from the idea of a moral penumbra that surrounds every judicial act. Cicero did not inaugurate this ethical approach to law. It is powerfully rendered in Plato's *Republic* and *Laws* and more moderately and circumspectly in Aristotle's ethical and political writings. It came to Cicero directly from the Stoic philosophers of his day, a group of applied Platonists and aristocratic political pundits.

Yet Cicero's assertions of the penumbra idea were a main channel for its actual transmission unto the judicial culture of the Western world, along with (after 1200 A.D.) direct impact from the Greek philosophers themselves.

Penumbra is not a legal theory that has gone without challenge. Skeptical thinkers, hard-headed realistic ones, called sophists in ancient Greek times and in later times positivists and utilitarians, have dismissed the penumbra as a fog of unknowing, at best a convenient myth, at worst mischievous "nonsense on stilts," as the English legal philosopher Jeremy Bentham said around 1780 A.D. But it has persisted and has had tremendous consequences for the recent history of the U.S. Supreme Court.

The famous U.S. Supreme Court case *Roe* v. *Wade* (1973), which in effect legalized abortions, was decided on the basis of the penumbra theory. The argument was that although the American Bill of Rights (1791), the first ten amendments to the Constitution, did not specifically recognize a right of privacy, the ten amendments taken together radiated such a powerful ethical penumbra that a right of privacy and a woman's right to an abortion in the first trimester of her pregnancy are implicit in the Bill of Rights.

That Ciceronian penumbra still carries weight is indicated by the fame of its prominent and current expounder, Professor Dworkin, who is idolized by mobs of law students on two continents.

If the penumbra idea has had in recent times a liberal progressive ring to it, Cicero's other main judicial doctrine would today be regarded as a highly conservative one, although in medieval or eighteenth-century England it was at times arguably on the progressive side.

The idea is this: Everyone in a country, even aliens, has an equal right to the due process of the law. But this judicially substantive equality does not mean that the law can be used to amend hierarchical class structure and the economic inequality that exist in society. Indeed, the due process of the law signifies not only an equal chance in the law courts for the poor man, but also protection of the rich man's property and privilege.

Cicero hated anything that smacked of what the ancients called "an agrarian law," using law to redistribute property to the poor—that is, socialism. That was morally wrong and politically dysfunctional and would destroy the stability and harmony of the republic. Cicero's bifocal vision—legal equality, social and economic inequality, both confirmed by the law—became central to English common-law culture in the period of formation 1200–1500. It also became the cardinal doctrine of the Whig political party in England and of the American Federalists and their Republican successors.

Cicero's judicial equality conforming to social inequality was not a simple reductive ideological blueprint for making English common law. Common law developed this principle empirically in the first century or so of its development. Then, in the later Middle Ages, well-read people sensed that Cicero had propounded much the same principles back in the closing era of the Roman Republic. This literary discovery strengthened the hold of the common-law idea that emerged initially out of social exigencies and judicial experimentation. It reinforced the notion that the common law was eternal—and eternally correct. The coincidences of Cicero's jurisprudence and the forms of English common law enhanced the Roman advocate's reputation and made his writings all the more valued in the Western literary world.

An obvious question arising from the texts of Cicero's courtroom orations is, How close to the actual oral presentation is the written form that we have? A prominent English lawyer of the early nineteenth century, Henry Brougham, said of one of Cicero's forensic disquisitions that only a sixth of it actually dealt with the issue judicially and that this kind of freewheeling rhetoric would never be allowed in an English court of law.

The inclination therefore is to regard the written texts as much amplified from Cicero's courtroom advocacy and to assume that much humanistic material was inserted after oral delivery. But it should be remembered that Cicero was addressing a jury composed mostly of highly educated and leisured gentlemen. They enjoyed—and expected—a lengthy rhetorical display.

Even in the late first century A.D., orotund oratorical advocacy was still acceptable, if lawyer and state official Pliny the Younger can be believed. Recounting one of his courtroom triumphs, he set this theatrical scene: "There they were, one hundred and eighty jurors. . . . a huge collection of counsel for both plaintiff and defendant, rows and rows of seats in court, and a deep ring of auditors standing up. . . . I piled on every canvas—indignation, rage, distress—and sailed the seas of that tremendous [judicial] action like a ship before the gale" (translated by John Crook). Except for mention of the huge jury, this account could have been written by a prominent London barrister or an American trial lawyer today. A reasonable guess is that while Cicero's forensic orations were indeed embellished by him for publication, they were remarkably not far from the actual oral delivery.

But already in Pliny's time, courtroom fireworks by an attorney must have seemed old-fashioned and by the middle of the second century highly unusual. Roman law became professionalized and bureaucratized, and the focus of the court switched from attorneys to judges. As power was taken into the hands of an autocratic emperor, as the political theory was broadcast and generally accepted that the Roman people had irrevocably surrendered their legislative power to the emperor, Roman courts became much less glamorous and autonomous than in Cicero's or Pliny's day. Unlimited legal power was vested by the emperor in a small group of jurisprudents (experts) and magistrates who tightly supervised court proceedings. They elaborated both civil and criminal law in great detail and began the task of codifying it.

By the third century A.D., a small panel of judges completely controlled court proceedings. Advocates could still make presentations, but they were closely watched and supervised by the judges. The judges no longer had time or patience for expansive oratorical presentations in the Ciceronian mode. The attorneys were now, by A.D. 200, very much officers of the court and were there to help the magistrates as much or more than to represent their clients.

Cicero's orations were now studied for their stylistic content and humanistic value, not as models of lawyering. Cicero's kind of high-profile humanistic advocacy would be much more at home in an American court today than in a Roman court in the later years of the second century A.D. Trying to emulate Cicero's aggressive style of advocacy would therefore bring only stricture and censure in the Roman judicial court that developed in the two centuries after him, as in the legal system that still prevails in Western Europe and is known to us as Roman law.

3
The Justinian Heritage

WE GET OUR WORD "empire" from the Roman word *imperium*, which means "power" or "authority"; hence *imperator* for Augustus Caesar and his successors, who took over authority over the Roman state shortly after the death of Cicero. In the following three centuries the Roman Empire developed the system of Roman law that prevails in continental Europe to this day. But the definitive text of the Roman law comes not from the first Rome on the banks of the Tiber in Italy but from the second, Byzantium. Here was fully developed the legal culture that predated by half a millennium (and to some extent affected the shaping of) English common law. The Emperor Constantine in the early fourth century built a new eastern capital for the Roman Empire, one that would be thoroughly Christian, which the ancient city of Rome was not yet, and from its magnificent site on the Bosphorus would dominate the eastern, more thickly settled, and richer Greek-speaking part of the empire. Constantine named this second Rome after himself.

Since 1453 Constantinople has been part of Muslim Turkey, and since 1930 has been called Istanbul. Its early medieval glories, when it was possibly the largest and wealthiest city in the world, are much subdued now, hidden under the dust of centuries. But its glorious buildings and unparalleled physical location still hark back to its days as Constantinople, Constantine's city, built over the old Greek port of Byzantium and then enduring as the capital of the Eastern Roman, or Byzantine, Empire.

The way Cicero behaved as an attorney and conceived of the law foreshadowed some key aspects of Anglo-American common law as we know it, and in time had some actual marginal influence on it. But the massive and perpetual impact of Roman law on Western Europe, and the imagining and implementation of a system of law that still prevails on the European continent, came directly not from Cicero but from an emperor of Byzantium after the Germanic invasions of Western Europe in the fifth and sixth centuries.

The relationship between English common law and the other system of European law emanating from the Middle Ages, that of Roman law, remains today one of the most vexed issues in legal history. During the seventeenth and eighteenth centuries, conditioned by contemporary political disputes and ideological formulations, there developed a widespread conviction among the lawyers in England that the two systems of law, English common law and Roman continental law, were antagonistic and mutually exclusive. In the past century there has been a significant move away from this paradigm of juristic repulsion and separation. Learned claims have been put forward as to how much English common law in its medieval era of formation owed to Roman judicial traditions and how broadly it integrated Roman law concepts into English judicial culture. Harold Berman of Emory University has been a particularly forceful advocate of this integrative view of legal history.

This is my view of this controversial matter:

In England, one of the German-dominated successor kingdoms to the Roman Empire, a legal system distinct from Roman law emerged. By the twelfth century there was influence on English common law from continental Roman law in visible ways, particularly on some aspects of civil law and in the development of the legal profession. This means that while continental law experienced a massive absorption of Roman law of late antiquity and the Middle Ages, English law to a much lesser but still real degree has to be seen in the context of Roman legal culture and as gaining some derivations from it.

The Byzantine emperor so important in the transmission of a formative Roman-law heritage from late antiquity to the medieval world, and from there into modern times, was Justinian I (527–65), a ruler of tremendous energy and much accomplishment, if not always wise in policy or fortunate in impact, in almost every aspect of life of the Mediterranean world of his day. Justinian surrounded himself with very capable officials and generals. He was much influenced by his vivacious and ambitious wife, Theodora, a former prostitute and cabaret dancer. Justinian made a strenuous effort to recover North Africa and Italy from the German invaders, and had some short-term success. But within a century of his death the reconquered Algeria and Tunisia fell to the Muslim Arabs, as did Sicily. His twenty years of war of reconquest in Italy left that peninsula devastated and impoverished. Most of the Italian territory Justinian regained was soon taken over by a new Germanic invader, whose name is memorialized in the regional term "Lombardy."

The two enduring monuments of Justinian's rule were the vast cathedral of Hagia Sophia (Holy Wisdom) in Constantinople, which after the Turkish conquest of the city in 1453 became a Muslim mosque for half a millennium and is today a somewhat musty and run-down museum; and the definitive codification of Roman law, the *Corpus Juris Civilis,* forever appropriately referred to as the Justinian code.

There is a small confusion in citing the Justinian code by its official title, *The Corpus of the Civil Law*. The term "civil law" has in Anglo-American parlance two quite distinct meanings. Civil law is noncriminal law. But the Roman legists came to refer to their legal system as a whole, including criminal law, as the civil law, the law of society. (In the later Middle Ages experts on Roman law were often called "civilians.") Thus "civil law" is a term for one of the two main branches of law, along with "criminal law." It is also a term synonymous with Roman law and the Justinian code. The unfortunate duplication of term exists, but the distinction in meaning can be readily extrapolated from the context.

In the law schools of continental Europe for at least five centuries after 1100 A.D., the Justinian code—the last literary work of the Byzantine Empire to be written in Latin rather than Greek—was the basic textbook. From these law schools well-trained and highly literate graduates went out to staff the administrations of the emerging European monarchies of the later Middle Ages and the papal bureaucracy in Rome.

Thereby the general mind-set enshrined in the Justinian code—as well as specific juristic doctrines and the institutional legal system it was supposed to facilitate in operation—entered profoundly and perhaps forever inextricably into the judicial and political culture of the European states and the Roman Catholic Church to the present day. "Its abstract and reiterated legal concepts made Roman law ... a mine of precious materials that jurists, as specialists arrogating to themselves a monopoly on the theorization of social relations, could recuperate and reutilize" (Manlio Bellomo).

In modern print the Justinian code runs to some dozen volumes. (An obscure Philadelphia lawyer produced a good English translation of it in the 1930s.) It draws on the imperial legislation and court workings of the Roman Empire, going back five centuries to Augustus Caesar. It owes much to a series of Roman jurisprudents, particularly one Gaius, who wrote around A.D. 200, and to a first effort at codification (A.D. 425) named for the otherwise incompetent Emperor Theodosius II.

Justinian himself took a personal interest in the *Corpus Juris Civilis*. He not only commissioned and funded its preparation, but played some indeterminable role in the actual work of writing and editing. But most of the job was in the hands of a panel of great lawyers headed by Tribonius, about whose personal life we know nothing.

It may be asked why Roman law developed so elaborately in the half millennium between Cicero and Justinian I. Why did the Roman Empire produce this complex yet well-articulated system of law?

It was said at the beginning that law develops creatively in large political entities, and the Roman Empire was the largest contiguous political structure the world had ever seen. At its furthest point by the second century A.D. it stretched from the Scottish border to the frontier of Iran, from the Rhine and Danube to three hundred miles into the Magreb in North Africa—what is today Algeria and Tunisia. Its population was extremely diverse ethnically and culturally, its people were bound together by Roman imperial administration and the Roman law courts, to which all citizens (which by A.D. 212 meant at least 70 percent of the population of the Mediterranean world) had access and to which they were subject. It is no surprise that such a vast multicultural political entity should have developed a legal system to provide for security, peace, and enterprise.

A second reason why the Romans developed their distinctive system of law was the extreme tension, spilling over into civil war, that developed among the elite ruling families in the later years of the republic. A function of the law was to countervail the divisiveness of these debilitating social and political conflicts among families and other groups fighting for command over wealth and power. Roman law supported the emperor in gaining peace and stability. The law enforced imperial authority, and the emperor in return gave legitimacy and force to the law and supported the magistrates who implemented it.

A third reason for the development of Roman law was the high capacity for literacy among the Roman ruling elite. Legal articulation and law codes were a prime outlet for intellectual and literary capability in the later empire.

The existence of an elaborate written text, particularly if it is ostensibly nonfiction, more attractively if it has explicit social and political meaning, most powerfully if it has legitimizing state power behind it, will in time become the focus and fountain of an ongoing culture. Professors, who mainly conceive it their métier to comment on written texts, will explicate it—in the medieval law schools they were called the glossators and postglossators. Students will exhibit their capacities and prepare for remunerative careers by memorizing large chunks of it. Enterprising writers and publishers (in the twelfth century initially scribbling monks, then successful lawyers) will produce textbook summaries of it. Theorists inside and outside universities will emerge who will take up aspects of it, extend and develop one or the other side of the original text, and further activate the ongoing culture by thinking up novel positions rising out of the culture that grew up around the text and among the elite who lived off it.

This is what happened with Roman law as enshrined in the Justinian code, from the late eleventh century to well into the seventeenth. There were persistently in each generation centers of Roman-law study, beginning with Bologna (still going strong today), a professional elite of magistrates and attorneys trained in Roman law and ready to implement it in every conceivable way, students who sought professional careers by mastering it, and theorists who took off from it.

In France, Germany, and Italy this acculturation and socialization of the Justinian code, modernizing and adjustments, accretions, and imitations having been made, can be said still to be going on. It will never stop. The solidification and intensification of the European Union, both in its concept formation and in its fostering of a narrow ruling cosmopolitan professional elite, will make sure of that.

In the United Kingdom, the strange medley of rightist Tories and leftist Labourites who resist Britain's absorption into the European Union are not really sure why they are resisting. They speak with foolish nostalgia of British imperial and populist socialist traditions, which are obsolete and are as superseded as British dominance in soccer or cricket. What they are really resisting but cannot articulate is the melding of Britain, with its cognate but still very much separate common-law ethos, into the pervasive, homogeneous, immensely rich and productive continental Roman-law culture derived from the heavy volumes of the Justinian code.

The fundamental principles of Roman law in the Justinian code are absolutism and rationality. Absolutism is based on the constitutional myth that developed in the early Caesarean empire of the first century A.D. As the code itself says: "Whatever is approved by the sovereign has the force of law, because by the *Lex Regia* [royal law], from whence his power is derived, the people have delegated to him all their jurisdiction and authority."

Long ago legislative sovereignty resided in the Roman people; they have irrevocably surrendered this authority to the emperor. His will is now law. The law resides in his mouth, in his breast.

The emperor is the head of the Greek church; he holds divinely constituted authority. So in the code religious sanction is added to legislative and executive authority, "for what is greater or more sacred than the Imperial Majesty? Nothing in this world."

Going along with this absolute authority by which the emperor dictates the particulars of the civil law, the law of the immediate society he governs, is natural law, the judicial principles that reason perceives as applicable to all peoples, and hence—the code declares—constitutes the *Ius Gentium*, the law of nations.

This idea goes back to the Stoic philosophers and hence was

already suggested by Cicero. It was clearly stated by Gaius around A.D. 200 as the Mediterranean world under Roman rule became more of a homogeneous political unit and Roman citizenship was gained by the majority of people under Roman rule. In the Justinian code, natural law is universalized to the point that it "is not peculiar to the human race, but applies to all creatures which originate in the air, on the earth and on the sea."

In the later centuries, beginning with the thirteenth and blatantly so by the eighteenth century, the idea of natural law would be a liberalizing or even revolutionary vision: A law of the state that offended reason lost its legitimacy. In the Justinian mode, natural law is in fact a highly conservative principle. It gives greater legitimacy and universality to the law of the imperial state. Reason now buttresses the people's surrender of constitutional authority to the emperor.

The laws promulgated by the emperor are given additional force by according with what "natural reason has established among all peoples." There is no ground for questioning let alone nullifying the imperial law or resisting the judgment of the emperor and his magistrates. To do so offends nature and conflicts with reason, and such high treason is worthy of the most dire and immediate punishment.

"The union of male and female" is part of natural law, and the emperor's laws regulate sexual union in marriage. The hierarchic organization of society, including slavery, is also legitimated by natural reason.

The political theory of the Justinian code is very well thought out and fully articulated to prevent any possible resistance to imperial judicial authority. Since the emperor is the head of the church, religious sanction cannot be used against him; indeed, faith supports imperial power. Resistance to imperial law cannot be based on reason and appeals to natural order. Natural reason conditions imperial law and gives it an additional covering of legitimacy.

What is the temperament behind this legal theory? On the one side it is an unlimited lust for power and control, for wealth and dominance, for personal and social mastery. An imperial courtier named Procopius wrote, presumably in secret, a lurid account of the Justinian and Theodora's insatiable appetites, including sexual practices.

This is one side of the psychology behind the Justinian code. Another side is a yearning for peace, security, social harmony, and judicial clarity. "We adorn peace and maintain the Constitution of the State," says the prologue. Alongside this is a desire for efficiency and order. "We have found the entire arrangement of the law which has come down to us . . . to be so confused that it is extended to an infinite length and is not within the grasp of human capacity." The law must be clear, accessible, finite, easily researched, and readily learned. This is the most admirable side of the Justinian system.

In comparison, rationalization and codification of English common law was only attempted in the mid-thirteenth century by Henry of Bracton, a clerical lawyer trained in Roman law; his effort resulted in a mess and had no practical outcome. Codification was talked about in the English revolutionary era of the 1650s; nothing happened. It was called for by liberal reformers in the late eighteenth and early nineteenth centuries; nothing happened. It was officially begun in the 1960s but has made very little progress.

In the United States the codification of federal commercial law carried out in the early 1950s by a Columbia law professor was regarded as well-nigh miraculous.

Codification is improbable in Anglo-American law because, in comparison with Roman law or today's European continental law, the legal profession is too autonomous and there are too many vested interests enjoying benefits from the current infinite and inefficient legal corpus. Justinian overcame such obstacles; his authority could repress the special interests, and the judges and attorneys all worked by his mandate. It is also true that sixth-century Byzantium was a more homogeneous and compact society than Victorian England and late-twentieth-century America.

But Germany today is a complex society, and it has in the Justinian tradition a highly compact and well-articulated legal code put together by law professors and applied by judges thoroughly trained for that purpose. Rationalized codification in the Justinian style and open-ended confusion and disorder in the common-law tradition are the outcome more of a cultural than of a functional polarity.

What made the Roman-law system in its Justinian mode work was a set of magistrates who held judicial power delegated by the emperor and who thoroughly controlled the courtroom and its proceedings. This had been the trend in Roman law since the first century A.D., away from the autonomous courtroom with its huge jury before which Cicero orated. The professionalization, bureaucratization, and centralization of Roman law came to fruition in the world of the Justinian code and in continental Western Europe, which enthusiastically adopted it and rigorously applied its operation.

A small panel of magistrates, usually three or five, now presided over the Roman-law court. In civil actions they received written briefs from the litigants or more usually their attorneys, interrogated the disputants based on these briefs, made whatever further inquiries were necessary, and rendered a decision in written form, which the majesty of the state enforced.

In criminal actions the judges also used written pleading as much as possible. A charge having been laid against a defendant, one or more magistrates conducted—with the aid of state police officials—a thorough investigation of the case. There was no time limit on this investigation, an aspect of Roman law today that shocks and frightens people used to the speedy trial provisions of common-law countries. (Even if those provisions are less and less observed in actual practice, owing to impossibly crowded court calendars and delaying tactics by attorneys and judges.)

Roman law required at least two witnesses against the defendant. One of these witnesses could be, and preferably was, the defendant himself. Far from prohibiting self-incrimination, Roman law sought it. The defendant was "put to the question" under torture.

In course of the long inquiry and questioning of a defendant, the magistrates frequently worked out a plea bargain with the defendant, by which he or she confessed to a lesser charge or was promised a more moderate punishment than otherwise in return for his confession. No less than in common-law criminal actions today, the Roman-law system in its criminal jurisdiction needed plea bargaining to make the wheels of justice turn.

There was no jury in the Justinian-type court, no half dozen or dozen representatives of society to consider the facts of the case and decide on guilt or innocence. In modern times some continental countries added a jury to give more democratic mien to the court system. But the jury deliberates with the magistrates and has none of the independence of the common-law jury. Torture was abolished in Roman-law countries only as late as the eighteenth century. But defendants can still be kept in jail for several years before trial while the magistrates conduct their investigations, a form of nonviolent torture. In films or plays about trials in Roman-law countries, what is often made to appear as the product of fascist inclination or a backward cultural affect is fully within the straight-line Justinian tradition.

Roman law was extremely sophisticated in working out the theory and applications of important aspects of civil law. The Roman law of written contract, property, inheritance, and marriage entered into the mainstream of continental law after A.D. 1100. It was in the area of contract law that Roman law exercised its greatest influence on medieval common law and all modern contract law. "One of the greatest Roman inventions . . . is the consensual contract, a contract that is legally binding simply because of the parties' agreement and requires no formalities for its formation" (Alan Watson). This Roman juristic instrument lies behind the common-law principle of freedom of contract.

The Justinian system required a fairly large body of highly educated, experienced, and well-paid judges. Attorneys for the prosecution and defense appeared in court and participated, but their role was marginal. In comparison with the role of defense attorneys in common law, the defendant's advocate in a Roman-law court was of modest importance.

Yet in civil actions, under Roman law, attorneys were critically important because they prepared the elaborate briefs making the case for their clients. It was on the judge's study of these briefs that the civil action in the case moved. If a brief was not well prepared, the client lost.

There were probably in old Byzantium barely enough qualified magistrates and attorneys to keep the system functioning well. The Justinian system could not be implemented in Western Europe in the early Middle Ages before the growth of law schools after 1100 provided a cohort of trained professional lawyers. It was not until three generations had passed, by the early thirteenth century, that supply of law school graduates caught up with demand and the Roman law system could be widely instituted—in Italy and France by 1250; and in Germany by 1450. What contributed to the proliferation of law schools, usually on university campuses in the late twelfth and thirteenth centuries, was the realization by kings and their chancellors that law school graduates made excellent bureaucrats of any kind and that the authoritarian political theory embedded in the Justinian code could be cited to sustain claims for extravagant royal power.

The first law school, in Bologna, was founded sometime between 1080 and 1110, either to serve the legal needs of north Italian merchants or to serve the papacy, which was engaged in codifying the canon law of the church along Roman-law lines. Possibly Bologna would be of use to both sets of clients. The merchants wanted to recover the law of a commercial society; the papacy, to rest judicial authority within the church in Rome. The great teacher and scholar at Bologna was Irnerius, who died around 1130.

Codifying work on the church's canon law was begun under papal auspices under the ambitious Gregory VII in the 1070s or perhaps a few years earlier, while Gregory was Cardinal Hildebrand and head of the papal administration. The codification of the canon law accorded the pope the position of absolute authority in the church that the Justinian code gave the emperor. Alternative, more collegial traditions in early medieval canon law were shunted aside during codification of canon law in favor of this Romanist position. The first definitive code of canon law was completed by Gratian, an Italian monk and legist around 1140, and subsequent amplifications were issued by popes in the 1170s and 1240s. Gratian was something of a liberal. He "assigned to the jurist ... only the task of evaluating acts, not hidden thoughts" (Manlio Bellomo). Unfortunately his successors among the canon lawyers between 1200 and 1700 did not always make this distinction and in the courts of the Inquisition sometimes sought to probe into thoughts as well as actions.

By 1200 the papal Curia and the College of Cardinals were an international court of appeals for thousands of cases a year. More time was now spent in Rome on legal than on theological or even spiritual matters. All but one of the popes from the mid-twelfth to the early fourteenth century were canon lawyers. The great majority of the cardinals were lawyers. Annulment actions alone took up thousands of hours a year of litigation in the papal courts.

By 1200 a law school graduate with a first-class degree had two career choices: He could go to work in a royal judicial system hoping to become a judge and maybe ultimately a leading royal official. He could be a secular person, get married, and establish a bourgeois family, a dynasty of lawyers from which over the decades or centuries to follow would come further "nobility of the robe."

Or the law school graduate could take a further degree in canon law (becoming a doctor of both kinds of jurisprudence, secular and ecclesiastical), take holy orders, and go to work in Rome or as a judge or attorney for a bishop elsewhere. In the latter case he could not legally marry and raise a family carrying his name; taking a concubine and producing bastard progeny was normally permitted, however. Who would end up as royal chancellor or as pope was the ultimate outcome of a career decision made by a law school graduate around the age of twenty-five. It was not much different from the stark contrast of choices facing an American law school graduate with a first-class degree today.

Roman law worked well when its courts were staffed by well-trained, experienced, and self-confident judges who were not hard pressed by kings or bishops to make specific partisan decisions. The quality of magistrates remained so important to the continental legal systems that in Germany today, law students must choose whether they wish to be trained as attorneys or magistrates. The latter are given different courses and different postgraduate experience than the former.

The Roman-law systems in the Justinian tradition were very good at civil actions and in ordinary criminal cases. They were effective at assuring law and order in society. Their weakness lay in being so judge-centered that inadequate training, corruption, and excessive ambition among the judges to climb even higher in state or church, by making decisions that would please those in authority, eroded the quality of the system.

Put another way the flaw in the Roman-law system was the lack of independence of the judiciary, which became very evident when the defendant in a criminal action or one of the litigants in a civil action was in disfavor with the government for ideological or other reasons. This situation became most infamously known when the papal-established courts of inquisition were set to work against alleged heretics in the thirteenth century. The situation was similar, however, when a king wanted to bring down an obstreperous lord or merchant capitalist. A Roman-law court could easily become an engine of royal policy.

There was one other fundamental problem in Roman law as it developed out of the Justinian code, and that concerned the principle of equity. The purpose of the courts in theory was to assure justice in accordance with abstract principles of natural law and universal reason. The written law was supposed to provide that. But if a case came before the judges in which normal application of the law would fail to provide justice, they had the authority to suspend or go beyond the written law to provide equity or perfect justice.

This was a charming and morally attractive idea, but it gave the judges a degree of discretion that worked against the idea of a codified written law. Since little in the way of actual court records of medieval Roman law trials has survived, it is unknown how extensively equity was actually practiced. Papal inquisitors being rough on dissenters or using their authority to persecute Jews (which they were not supposed to do) can be seen as a kind of reverse equity.

The concept of equity drifted into common law in the fifteenth century and is perpetuated in what are known as chancery or "equity" proceedings in common-law countries. It was supposed to provide special court intervention on behalf of vulnerable groups, like widows and children, through the issuing of injunctive relief from the bench. In the nineteenth and twentieth centuries the injunction was often used to protect big business from the impact of workers going on strike.

Equity was a thin double-edged sword. On the one hand it seemed the highest fulfillment of the Roman-law principle of the exercise of natural reason. On the other it undermined the codifying and clarifying qualities of Roman law—its greatest advantage—and opened the way to idiosyncratic or prejudicial behavior on the part of judges. Equity is the point on which the two main principles of Roman law, authoritarianism and rationalism, came into conflict, and this conflict threatened to unravel the stability of the system.

Many of the lawyers who created the English common law in the first three generations of its development, from 1150 to 1250, were clerics with law degrees from continental law schools. Therefore, although they knew they were developing a different legal system in England, they respected Roman law and made some adaptations of it. But as England developed secular, native law schools in the late thirteenth century, Roman law came to have a bad image in England, even as (or perhaps because) knowledge of its actual ingredients and functions declined there.

The deposition of King Richard II in 1399 (and his subsequent murder) was prominently justified on the grounds that Richard allegedly spouted authoritarian lines from the Justinian code. An English chief justice around 1450 blatantly compared free Englishmen living under common law with the unfortunate peasants of France and "boors" of Germany suffering under Roman law. In the early seventeenth century for an English royal official or churchman to have a degree in Roman law was sufficient for him to be branded a lover of foreign-type tyranny by the common lawyers and the oppositional gentry in the House of Commons.

This hostility to and ignorance of Roman law has continued into the twentieth century. No scholar born in Britain has ever written an important general book on the medieval Justinian tradition. Two American scholars, Harold Berman and James Brundage, have done so, on Roman corporatism and canonical views on sex and marriage, respectively. All other major books in English on the Roman-canonical tradition in the Middle Ages are works by German and Austrian or Russian émigrés.

Harold Berman has not merely demonstrated the impact of Roman law on medieval culture and society. He envisages a distinctive medieval juristic culture, drawing upon Roman law but going beyond it in innovative manner, and embracing Western Europe—in church law as well as secular law, in England as well as on the continent—in a universal judicial mold.

Despite the apparent suggestive and illuminating qualities of Berman's *Law and Revolution* (1984), I cannot share his vision of a universal juristic mold in the later Middle Ages, driven by a high Roman-law content, and involving England as well as continental legal systems. I adhere to the more traditional view that English common law is substantially distinct from continental law and represents an alternative to the Roman-law tradition, while still experiencing significant influence from it. Neither the age-old ideological English view that entirely separates common law from continental law and stresses the superiority of the former over the latter, nor Berman's innovative perception of a common European juristic culture building on Roman law and spanning the English Channel, fits complex historical reality.

Comparing Roman and common law and assessing their intrinsic qualities requires some subtle and nuanced perspectives. The only thoughtful and useful book persuasively comparing common-law and Roman-law traditions was written by R. C. van Caenegem, a Belgian historian.

What happened to the German magistrates under the Nazis—their fulsome implementation of Nazi legislation against the Jews and their use of the courts to remove all opposition to Hitler—is frequently cited as further evidence of the ingrained propensity of the continental judiciary to collaborate with tyranny. The horrible record of English courts in the area of civil liberties during and immediately after World War II—the interning of Jewish refugees during the war, and the forced repatriation of Polish and Russian nationals to certain death in the Soviet Union after the war, all done without trials—and the dreadful role of the American judiciary in the Red scare of the late 1940s and 1950s are not considered as contrary indications that Roman law does not necessarily mean tyranny and common law is not intrinsically equated with freedom.

Nevertheless it can be acknowledged that Roman law was and is a powerful contributor to a continental culture of conformity and regulation and close control over society by a self-perpetuating elite. Though this is not accidental—those were among its prime aims from the beginning of its development—it should not detract from highlighting the good side of Roman law: its effectiveness in dealing with ordinary crime and assuring a peaceful society; its intellectuality, sophistication, and codification; and the professionalism of its magistrates. These are precisely the areas in which common law is at its weakest.

What distinguishes Roman law from Anglo-American common law is that at the bottom they represent two very different cultures. Roman law was a culture of closure. Knowing what was good and right in society, it wanted to create a judicial structure that would confirm this goodness and rightness and make their operations in society easier and more evident. What was useful and applicable about the law had already been discovered and written down. After that, as social and economic change occurred, it was only necessary to make adjustments at the margin within a preexisting system.

The treatment of the Jews is an example of this fundamental character of Roman law. The Theodosian code segregated the Jews from Christian society; they were not to build synagogues without imperial permission; they were not to proselytize; they were to live in designated quarters in cities; they were not to have Christian slaves; they were not to have Christian spouses or concubines, and so on. The Justinian code repeated these ghettoization laws wholesale. An outcome of the Roman-law revival of the Middle Ages was renewed application of these laws against the Jews, contributing to the steady deterioration of their position in Western Europe after 1100. The impact of Roman law on the Jews lived on into the modern world, not being fully dissolved in most countries until the late eighteenth and nineteenth centuries. Once Roman law got hold of something, it stuck with it. Doctrinal persistence is central to Roman law.

The original authoritarianism that was ingrained in the Justinian code was given a further push toward closure and conservatism by the development of most medieval law schools within universities, or at least by incorporating the academic mind-set, today called scholasticism, that prevailed in the universities. The scholastic temperament inclined to deep learning, synthesis, system building, and looking backward. It brought together the texts of Greek philosophy with the Christian Bible and the theology and ethics propounded by the church fathers of the fourth and fifth centuries, primarily Saint Augustine. It used logic to solidify this intellectual pastiche into a vast intellectual system that uttered definitions and theories on everything— metaphysics, natural science, psychology, ethics, politics.

The medieval law professors, the glossators and postglossators, were very much a part of this scholastic humanism, and law was integral to the scholastic world system. To the conservativism that was already imbedded in the Justinian code was added in the medieval law schools a further layer of conservative culture by integrating law and philosophical scholasticism.

Since around 1980 critical legal studies professors in American law schools have exhibited a neoscholastic propensity to integrate the common law with highly sophisticated intellectual systems, very different in character of course from medieval scholasticism. But they exhibit the same temperamental inclination to make law part of a philosophical system as was evident in the medieval schools. The fierce arrogance of the medieval law professors is reincarnated also in the CLS professors. Radical in their own eyes, the CLS people draw no lessons from the association of Roman law and medieval scholasticism, or from the downside of a legal culture integrated with philosophy.

Whatever may be said about common law, "closure" is not a

term easily associated with it. From its beginning in the twelfth century, there was an open-endedness about common law, an ongoing creativity in its character, and a high degree of autonomy on the part of its professional carriers that in composite represents something very different from Roman law.

What were the factors in English society, government, and intellectual life that made common law so different is a historical problem that legal historians in this century have periodically attempted to resolve, starting with Frederic Maitland around 1900 and continuing to the present. Although there is some consensus on what these factors were, the issue is far from being settled.

A metaphor for Roman law would be a mighty stream flowing in a deep channel between high banks, whose progress is controlled by an elaborate set of carefully manipulated dams and locks. The metaphor for common law would be the headwaters from which streams flow in all sorts of directions. Although only one or two main rivers come out of this turbulent body, and despite the efforts made to control them, the initial wildness and disorder recur like stretches of whitewater, from time to time, as for instance, in seventeenth-century England or the United States from 1954 to 1980.

The origins of Roman law and its development are not hard to determine, and the place of law in a continental society is predictable. Common law by contrast is messy and even mysterious in origin, hard to depict in its course of development, and indeterminable with regard to its precise place in society. The primordial headwaters occasionally emerge again, seemingly fed by some mysterious underground spring, and the common-law waters rush through society, overwhelming fixed sites and creating havoc.

Common law from time to time threatens to take over society and transform its institutions. From this kind of revolutionary eruption—from this quality of volatility, mystery, and unpredictability—Roman law spares us.

From the perspective of the present a prominent difference

between Roman and English common law (and also derivative American law, particularly in the eastern United States until the late nineteenth century) was the treatment of women. Put simply, Roman law gave women a very high degree of equality, both to inherit and administer property and to make contracts. Common law placed very severe limitations on women's rights in this aspect of civil law, which were not fully removed until very late in the nineteenth century.

The cause of the difference in attitude to women is that Roman law originated as a system of relationships among a highly literate and mostly peaceful aristocracy, living in the generous and relaxed urban environment of the Mediterranean ambit, while common law developed between 1000 and 1300 among an intensely competitive military aristocracy in an almost entirely rural society.

After 1066 a fierce group of colonial conquerors from Normandy in France replaced the native English landlord class and tried to maximize their yield from control over the subjugated people. In this tense and harsh situation, even women of the Anglo-Norman nobility had to endure status deprivation so that their fathers, brothers, and sons could most fully exploit this rich but overwhelmingly rural country.

Essentially, in the urban town house of the Roman nobility, there was room for a high degree of legal equality for women, but in the fortresses, castles, and manor houses of the medieval lords who ruled England, women's judicial equality was severely restricted, and reflections of this adverse situation continued in common law far into modern times.

It is ironic and significant of a peculiar side of English culture that all those who through many centuries propounded the identification of common law with freedom and of Roman law with authoritarianism did not stop to ponder how much greater privilege women of the propertied classes enjoyed under Roman than under common law.

4
Glanville's World

LATE IN THE AFTERNOON of the first Monday in October of the year 1180, there was a great commotion in the town of Colchester, the county seat of Essex, lying sixty miles northeast of London. In the dust stirred up by their heavy horses' hooves, three royal justices; two laymen wearing their chain-mail tunics, breastplates, and long cloaks and carrying swords; and a cleric dressed in simple dark woolen cloth, accompanied by a bodyguard of four heavily armored knights, rode into town waving a royal banner.

This imposing group took up their reserved rooms at an abbey on the edge of town and went to the best inn in the heart of Colchester, where they refreshed themselves with a high-protein venison dinner washed down by several tankards of strong beer. The next morning at dawn, after a breakfast of bread and beer, the justices and their bodyguards rode into the center of town and walked quickly through the silver-encrusted oak doors of the headquarters of the wool merchants' guild. This would be their courtroom for the next ten days, until they moved on to the neighboring county of Suffolk.

In the large hall of the merchant guild, the justices sat at a long table on a raised dais. A wooden bar was hastily erected a few yards below to keep back the crowd of litigants and onlookers. A monastic clerk recruited ad hoc sat at one end of the table with pens, ink, vellum, and a huge gob of sealing wax at the ready to make a record of the court proceedings. He had to be trilingual, since—while the court record was set down in a simple Latin style that Cicero would have condemned—pleadings could also be in French, the language of the nobility and wealthier gentry, or English, the language of the lower classes.

The justices read out their royal commission, which mandated them to hear the pleas of the Crown in the county of Essex. In England there were some thirty counties or shires, the prime unit of provincial administration and law. Varied in size, many could be ridden across in a hard day in the saddle, while others would take two or three days to get across. For many centuries there had been monthly meetings of the shire courts, at which the magnates who held land in the county were normally present, along with a fluctuating number of free peasants who had business at the county court of one kind or another, or who attended simply out of curiosity and a wish to make themselves known to the magnates, the lay and ecclesiastical lords. In the year 1180 each county court met twice a year under the presidency of the king's itinerant justices. During the ten days the justices would be in Colchester, the monthly Essex shire court became a royal court, and all business was conducted under the king's seal.

The shire court was now a "court of record," whose proceedings could be appealed to a central court in Westminster in London. Such appeals and the sending of the trial records to Westminster were actually rare at this time, partly because convicted murderers or robbers were usually put to death immediately, and partly because even when a costly appeal—normally in a civil action involving substantial property—was heard in London, the judges who heard the appeal in Westminster would be very likely to include one or more of the very same circuit judges sent out to hear the pleas of the Crown in Essex.

A new legal term was coming into use in 1180. The judges were there not only to hear the pleas of the Crown, a generic term for all lawsuits under royal supervision. They were now specifically said to be in the county town "to hold the assizes," a term coming to mean any civil or criminal suit involving a jury in some way.

From this time until 1297, the circuit of itinerant justices, traveling from three to five county seats in succession to preside over trials, were also said to go out on "general eyre." That meant they would not only hear pleas and hold assizes but in the congested ten days, working from dawn to sometimes well past sunset, deal with a host of administrative (that is, money) matters in which the king had an interest. They would collect back taxes from wealthy delinquents, sardonically brushing aside the cries of churchmen that they wanted to appeal to Rome. They would seize property that had come into the king's hand by judicial forfeiture, or royal wardship over an unmarried woman or underage male in the landed class or a widowed baroness. They were to make sure that anyone owing debts to Jewish bankers, who conducted their loan business under exclusive royal license, paid the balance directly to the Crown in case a convenient pogrom had carried off the Jewish banker.

No wonder that local churchmen and gentry complained that the general eyres were impoverishing the countryside. No wonder that in frontier shires like Cornwall whole villages of people disappeared into the woods or bogs when the itinerant royal justices put in their appearance at least every six months. It was like finding yourself in the clutches of the FBI, the IRS, and a predatory Wall Street law firm all at the same time.

If one could take a confidential poll among the many dozens of people who crowded into the guildhall each day for business before the court (producing a tremendous shortage of beds at the local inns and of stalls in the barns) as to what the litigants and their families thought they were witnessing, at least half would not say the birth of English freedom but rather the imposition of royal tyranny by a tough and resourceful ruler. Henry II (who reigned from 1154 to 1189) would not seem any different than the king of France or the emperor of Germany, except for his peculiar judicial methods, and the fact that he was even more demanding than these other rulers.

This, however, is not the way the head of the three-judge panel, the chief justice of England himself, Ranulf de Glanville, or the clerical member of the trio, Glanville's nephew, Hubert Walter, later to become archbishop of Canterbury, would see it. They thought they were in the vanguard of legal progress. Nor would the third judge, the severe and wily Richard Fitz Neal, the head of the Exchequer, the accounting and judicial division of the royal treasury, somewhat reluctantly pressed into service as a circuit judge. Fitz Neal was polishing a manuscript in his room at the abbey each evening, a breakthrough book on royal financial administration. Glanville and Hubert in their few leisurely moments also talked about collaborating on a book depicting the new assizes system and hailing its beneficence for the people. Ranulf would certainly need Hubert's help in getting the treatise into readable and persuasive Latin form.

There were two reasons for the great crush of litigants at the county court of Essex in that October week. First, while pleading in the royal court was supposed to be confined to "freemen," excluding members of manorial serf families bound to the land in perpetuity, the royal justices were so liberal in enforcing this rule that even in 1180 probably close to three-quarters of the population fell under the judicial purview of the shire court when it met under the presidency of the royal itinerant justices.

Indeed, this was a prime way for a serf to obtain legal status as a freeman—be a litigant in some case in the royal court. Of course, if landlords were really keen on preserving serfdom, the justices would have been much more restrictive. But serfdom was the product of a rural economy where there was a shortage of labor, which was still true even in the eleventh century. The idea was to keep peasant families bound to the manorial village so they would share their crops and field work with the lord of the village. Now that the population was rising rapidly in the late twelfth century, many lords found that the land, pasturage, and other benefits they had to give to serfs were no longer fiscally feasible. It was cheaper to give serfs their freedom, threaten them with eviction, and then hire them back at competitive short-term wages— like IBM firing a computer programmer and hiring him or her back the next day as a temporary worker without benefits.

The other reason why the court calendar was crowded was that the holding of assizes to settle disputes about possession of land was found advantageous to the landed classes, especially the gentry and the upper stratum of peasants. The higher nobility had extrajudicial ways of protecting and holding land, but even they could often see an advantage in litigation in the royal courts. Coming out of a lawsuit would be frequently certification of possession of a landed estate through registration in a "final concord" giving the result of the litigation. Three copies of this settlement were made, one copy for the royal chancery as well as copies for the two litigants.

In any case there was the court record to appeal to. Certainly the wealthier and more ambitious gentry, the rural upper middle class, assiduous in protecting and adding to their family landed wealth, could agree with Glanville that this aspect of the new royal assizes was a good thing.

The assizes jury in civil actions relied on the memory of twelve prominent men of the neighborhood in which the disputed land lay. They were sworn to recognize the truth, and hence they were called a jury of recognition. The word "jury" comes from the

Latin *iurare*, to swear. The jury was impaneled by the sheriff to meet together before the justices got to the county seat on their circuit to "view the land" (make sure they knew which piece of land they were talking about, if necessary by walking around its perimeter) and to agree unanimously, ready to so instruct the circuit judges, who was the rightful possessor of the land, or whether the claimant was indeed the legitimate heir of the recent possessor.

Yet, much more than admiration for the prodigious memory of the jury, it was getting the court's judgment written down in a royal document that appealed to the landed class. Written record meant more to them than memory because a written record legitimated in some way by the Crown was a shield to protect their landholding and to secure new properties when gained, through purchase, or marriage, or litigation, or gift from a magnate.

England in the late twelfth century was in transition from being an oral to a literate society. The royal court's written records or the documents it stimulated showed that literacy was almost as invaluable for a landlord as it was for his younger brother, who was intensely educated and sent to get a university degree at Paris or, most recently, Oxford, and to prepare for a career as a churchman.

The term "assizes" was originally just a French word for a law—something that was judicially "set down." But in 1166 an important new set of laws, the Assizes of Clarendon, was promulgated by King Henry II after meeting with the lay and ecclesiastical nobility, some hundred of them, at the royal hunting lodge at Clarendon. Sleepless nights among the king, his counselors and judges had preceded the Clarendon assembly as the legal changes were agreed on in royal circles. Holding important meetings with his barons at his Clarendon hunting lodge was a favorite tactic of the king, like conferences at golf resorts for American corporate magnates. Besides, his barn at Clarendon had the largest floor space in all England for holding meetings as well as boarding horses. Ten years later another important assize was proclaimed at Northampton.

At both assizes or sets of laws, the most important provisions concerned the use of juries in both civil and criminal cases. And so the meaning of the word "assize" was transposed to signify use of the jury. In the assize of *novel disseisin*, a jury was used to resolve this most common form of property dispute. A jury of the *vicinage*, or neighborhood, where the disputed land lay was put on oath to swear unanimously whether the claim made by the complainant or plaintiff of his recent wrongful dispossession was valid. If the assizes jury testified to the truth of that complaint in the shire court presided over by the royal judges, then the plaintiff was restored to possession of the land by the sheriff acting to carry out the judgment of the court.

Additional "petty" or possessory assizes were *mort d'ancestor* (rightful inheritance of possession); and *utrum*, whether a piece of land was a feudal tenure—that is, subject to normal rents and taxes—or a "free alms" tenure, a charitable status to which rents and taxes did not apply.

Yet another possessory assizes decided by jury testimony was *darein presentment*. This arose out of a dispute between two lords over which of them had made the "last presentment" or appointment of a priest to a church. The litigants were disputing not merely this honorable right of appointment but who was the lord of the land on which the local church was built, since traditionally in northern Europe including England the lord who had endowed a church with "living" property to support the priest also held the right of advowson, the appointment of the priest. It was the assize jury's task to scratch their heads and try to remember who had made the most recent clerical appointment in the neighborhood; the last appointer had a prescriptive right to do it again. Amazingly, a third of the parish churches in the Church of England are still today in advowson, still subject to a patron's right of appointment. In the 1960s Peter Sellers made a hilarious movie, *Heavens Above*, about confusions arising from advowson. Given that parish priests were important people in medieval localities, and that continuing patronage over the local church in its property was attractive to the landed class, the assizes of *darein presentment* was not over unimportant kind of property disputes to be decided by the assize jury.

The whole assizes action started with the issuing of a writ from the royal chancery on petition of the plaintiff or complainant and his payment of a relatively modest fee—two shillings, equivalent in 1997 to about one thousand U.S. dollars—for issuing the writ. Known as a writ of course, it was automatically issued on payment of the fee.

The writ went from the royal chancery to the sheriff, telling him to impanel the jury in preparation for the next holding of the assizes in the shire court. If the plaintiff lost his case, that is, the testimony of the jury went against him, he had to pay an additional fine of anywhere up to the equivalent of twenty thousand dollars for wrongfully bringing suit, although normally he was fined a relatively nominal amount, roughly equivalent to the thousand dollars he paid for setting the assize action in motion. In the Middle Ages (and well into the twentieth century) indigent people could not afford to engage in civil actions; these were for the middle and upper classes.

Getting the jury of twelve to turn up at the trial was a chore for the sheriff and the plaintiff. Another problem was a hung jury. Henry II's judges had little patience with the latter. The judges pressed the jury, depriving them of food, to think again and come up with a unanimous testimony (decision). If they were still recalcitrant, the judge might declare a mistrial and instruct a sheriff to summon a new jury for six months hence, when they would be back in the same court on circuit. Or the judges might pile the jury into a cart and drag them along as the judges rode off to their next court date in a neighboring shire, harassing the twelve recognitors until they rendered unanimous testimony in the landholding dispute.

The assize actions in property disputes moved slowly if that was the wish, as it often was, of the defendant. He was allowed three formal (always accepted) *essoins*, excuses why he could not appear before his case was declared forfeit. English law traditionally hated to condemn someone to lose his property in his own absence from court. And in that society there were plenty of good reasons for nonappearance—including illness, bad roads, bandits, and visitations by the Virgin Mary. There is some indication that the king and judges in developing the assize actions wanted to prohibit *essoins* and get speedy justice for aggrieved landholders and deprived heirs. But the way it worked out was the slow turning of the wheels of common-law justice.

How slow was variable. If a defendant sent word on the first day of the ten-day court session that he couldn't appear because he was ill or the roads were washed out by a rainstorm, the judges might get him to appear by the last day. But very often the filing of an *essoin* meant the case would be postponed for another six months. A wily and recalcitrant defendant could therefore use the slowness of the system to hold onto land unjustly for up to eighteen months. Of course, he might thereby incur the judge's wrath and get slapped with a huge fine at the end.

If we could turn a TV camera on the Essex trials presided over by Glanville, Walter, and Fitz Neal, we would find the most peculiar feature of the assize juries to be that the jury was a self-informing rather than a trial-informing one, as has been the case since around 1500. The medieval jury was supposed to find out as much as it could about the facts of the case before the court met.

How was the figure of twelve for the jury arrived at? Medieval people, like lottery players today, believed in the magic of numbers. Twelve was a very lucky number. Jesus had twelve apostles and if twelve was good enough for the Lord, it was good enough for a medieval law court. In addition, if you took the four points of the compass surrounding the neighborhood the jury came from—north, south, east, and west—and multiplied them by the persons of the Holy Trinity, you got twelve.

Since land constituted 90 percent of the wealth of England in 1180, the use of the assize juries to settle all property disputes in the shire court was a momentous change. Hitherto one had to petition the king personally for the privilege of a jury trial in a property dispute, and it was a big deal and a special benefit reserved for a crony or relative of the king or some bigshot bishop or abbot.

Jury trials in property disputes in this very limited usage go back at least to William the Conqueror's reign, a hundred years before the Essex trials of 1180, and there is at least one documented use of a jury in a land dispute in 1053, almost a quarter of a century before the Norman Conquest. But by now all property disputes in the shire court used the jury if a litigant was willing to buy the issuance of royal writ to impanel the jury. This form of action became central to ongoing legal process.

There was, however, a ceiling on the value of land litigated this way in the county court. Unless both defendants agreed to hear the case in the shire court irrespective of the value of the disputed land, cases involving an estate worth in feudal jargon more "than half a knight's fee" were heard directly in a central court in Westminster, although it too would usually summon a jury from the countryside to London. How much is half a knight's fee worth in 1997 U.S. dollars? Somewhere around half a million.

The litigants might, however, agree to litigate a piece of land worth much more than this initially in the shire court, with the understanding that the loser would then appeal to the central court located in Westminster. The reason for doing it this way would be either the trouble and expense of getting the litigants and the jury to London (and the horrendous expense of keeping them there for a few days), or each party's curiosity as to which side the jury would favor before further negotiation and litigation. This two-tier approach to litigation is still a standard lawyer's tactic in New York State today. The really important trial is at the second level, but meanwhile you have gained some additional information on the strength of your case.

Strictly speaking, holding the assizes referred to civil (property) cases involving an inquest or a jury of twelve men of the neighborhood in which the disputed land lay, who were required to swear before the judges the truth on some aspect of the rightful possession of the land. The jury members were not paid; their expenses were supposed to be—but often were not—reimbursed by the Crown. The word "assize" soon also came to imply a grand jury action of presentment or indictment in criminal cases and in common parlance, a legal action before the royal judges involving some kind of jury.

Clarendon and Northampton legislations mandated the use of another jury—a grand jury of twenty-four or thirty-six "lawful"—that is, rich and reputable—men to deliver a collective indictment of malefactors and perpetrators since the royal justices had last presided over the shire court, usually six months earlier. A criminal case could still be started in customary, age-old fashion with a personal "appeal," calling someone to respond to an accusation in court ("I accuse Robert of killing my brother Thomas three days after Michaelmas on the high road to Nottingham"). But often the necessary accusation didn't get made—the accuser was frightened off or got stuck on the roads and didn't make it to court. Now there was a grand jury as well, more systematically and persuasively available to "present," or indict, defendants for a serious crime before the justices.

The grand jury was certainly not a new idea when Henry II mandated its use in the 1160s and 1170s. The novelty was its use in the royal courts presided over by the king's itinerant justices. As long ago as the year 1000, King Athelstan had enjoined at least some of his county courts to use panels of "twelve leading thegns" (ordinary lords) to make sure the malefactors were accused and to accuse no innocent man. After the Norman Conquest of 1066, the grand jury lingered on in shadowy, unofficial existence in the shire courts until it was newly legitimated by Henry II.

The grand jury was not only a judicial system. It was also a system of social cleansing. In view of pressure on the grand juries to find a defendant for every serious crime, someone who was poor, unemployed, obnoxious—such as the town drunkard or an obvious heretic—was very likely going to get indicted sometime in his life, and then convicted, thereby cleansing local society of the unwanted or very unpopular. Considering that the only welfare system was charity dispensed irregularly at church or monastic doors, using criminal justice to get rid of the unwanted, the misfits, and the unpopular was a rational if cruel system that neoconservatives today would certainly approve.

When it came to criminal law, medieval people were—like us, but even more so—extremely class biased. The higher nobility—the lay and ecclesiastical magnates and their families, who held their lands directly as the king's personal vassals—were not indictable by grand juries. These magnates were an exclusive social club of bluebloods. They had a right to trial by peers, their social equals, but some people were more equal than others. They therefore had a right to be tried by what was later called "the peerage" or the House of Lords, and in 1180 was the *curia regis*, the council or court of magnates that feasted with the king and conducted criminal trials for the magnates in the king's presence.

A complication was that Henry II was out of the country for half his reign, usually fighting in France or governing his huge possessions there, acquired through descent from William the Conqueror and also through his highborn and immensely rich French wife. This meant that trials of great magnates could get postponed for several years, or a large contingent of lords packed up and joined the king in France for a few days (advantageously closer to the source of the red Bordeaux wine, or "claret," they loved so much), or the chancellor or chief justiciar presided in the king's absence.

Peasants who were still clearly in the legal status of serfdom were also not indictable by the grand jury; they were dealt with—roughly—close to home in the lord's manorial court, presided over by the lord's tough-minded land steward. Wealthy gentry, the upper middle class, could and were sometimes indicted by a grand jury in whose panels they themselves stood out as socially the ideal grand jurymen. Usually they negotiated or bribed their way out of an indictment.

In addition there were several protected groups—we might call them affirmative-action populations—who usually didn't get indicted in the county courts by the grand jury, and if indicted were let off by the judges and didn't get tried, and if tried and convicted would get off with a royal pardon often arranged by the judges themselves.

Heading the affirmative-action list were all members of the clergy from priests and monks and sometimes as low as deacon on up to bishops and abbots—about 5 percent of the adult population. They had "benefit of clergy"—that is, a cleric accused of a crime had the privilege of being tried in the bishop's court by the latter's chief judicial official, the archdeacon. Grand juries were sometimes used in these ecclesiastical courts, which were notorious for their laxity and corruption to even blatantly guilty criminal defendants ("The sentence is to make a pilgrimage to the shrine of Santiago de Compostela in Spain, walking the last one hundred miles barefoot"—less strenuous than playing tennis for two weeks in Florida). The Courts Christian, as they were euphemistically called, could not per se carry out capital punishment; they could hand over the convicted ecclesiastical felon to a royal court for capital punishment but they very rarely did so, unless the convicted person was a heretic, in which case he would just as likely be burned as hanged.

The peculiar institution of benefit of clergy was the outcome of the long and noisy row between Henry II and his former friend and fellow carouser, Saint Thomas Becket, archbishop of Canterbury, who insisted on this judicial privilege as part of the nebulous doctrine of liberty of the church. After Becket was murdered in 1170 by four royal knights who attended the king, thinking—probably not erroneously—that Henry had said he wanted to be rid of the "turbulent priest," the king had to make up with the pope. Henry's main concession in order to be received back into the spiritual fold was to grant judicial benefit of clergy, which Becket had wanted (the pope, a great canon lawyer, never specifically said he agreed with Becket).

In reality benefit of clergy never worked quite as smoothly as Henry's concession seemed to promise. The accused cleric had to produce a letter from a bishop confirming his clerical status. This was sometimes difficult to obtain on time. By the time the episcopal letter arrived in the shire court, the "criminous clerk" might have been indicted, convicted, and hanged. Yet soft treatment of clerical criminals remained the norm.

Benefit of clergy lasted until the eighteenth century, by which time generous treatment for other protected groups in the royal criminal courts was often subsumed under the term "pleading their clergy," even though the group might be laymen or even female.

Late medieval court records show that the other affirmative-action groups in criminal law were children under the age of fourteen; young women, especially unmarried ones (on the other hand, mature women, married or widowed, might be convicted for witchcraft and get burned as punishment); physically challenged old people; soldiers on their way to join the royal army overseas; and lunatics (insanity was a defense in the old medieval common law).

Those who got indicted by a grand jury and were required to defend themselves in a criminal trial were adult males of the middle and lower classes. The latter, unless they were soldiers called up to join the king's armies, were assumed to be a steady recruiting ground for the criminal class, so there was plenty of work for criminal justice to do in Glanville's time.

The problem in 1180 was that having gotten an indictment by the grand jury (and after 1215 any personal accusation had to be endorsed by a grand jury to make it valid), the judges lacked a good method of proof of innocence or guilt (something that remains a problem in some parts of the United States). In 1180 Glanville and his colleagues were frustrated that for methods of proof to determine guilt or innocence after a grand jury indictment, they had a choice of applying the old unsatisfactory ones that had been in use since long before the Norman Conquest. These were compurgation and ordeals, which had in fact been in use for a half a millennium, since the German invaders landed on Britain's shores. Following indictment defendants had "to make their law" by one of these two methods.

Compurgation was organized lying. Acquittal rates were high, and therefore it was something of a privilege for the justices to award this method of proof to a defendant. Compurgation meant that the defendant was regarded as innocent, or was a rich landholder, merchant, favored churchman, or attractive young woman.

In compurgation, or, to use its English term, oath-helping, the defendant swore on the Bible—or, better still, holy relics (saints' bones)—that he didn't do it. Then he brought in oath helpers in numbers and prominence designated by the justices to swear that his oath was "clean," that he couldn't possibly have committed, say, murder or armed robbery. It was a kind of character witnessing but was taken seriously by the court and hence was sparingly awarded by the judges. In spite of lavish warnings by attending clergy that perjury meant a thousand extra years in purgatory or worse, lying was common in compurgation.

The enterprising Anglo-Saxons thought up a remedy as early as

A.D. 1000, an amended system called "suit of witnesses." The compurgators had to be chosen from a court-designated list of blue-ribbon oath helpers, not just the defendant's raunchy brothers-in-law. It helped a little, but not much. The awkward compurgation system lingered on into the sixteenth century among big-city merchants for less than hanging crimes. It is still in use among Orthodox Jews in the diamond trade in New York City today in their community courts: "Reb Mendele couldn't have stolen that diamond; he is a Hasid."

The other method of proof, used 80 percent of the time, and weighted against the defendant as compurgation favored him, was the hoary Germanic ordeal. In the parlance of the court record, an indicted defendant sent to the ordeal was required "to make his law" by ordeal. The motto here was not "We'll lie through our teeth" but "Leave it up to God to show if the defendant is guilty."

More often than not the Lord said: "Guilty." Perhaps that is why thirteenth-century sentimental stories had defendants and condemned criminals usually praying to the Virgin Mary, Mother of God, to help them. Her son, Jesus, was apparently on the side of grand juries.

Henry II and his judges so distrusted the ordeal when it freed someone as not guilty that they stipulated in legislation that anyone indicted by a grand jury but cleared by the ordeal had to leave the country (or in practice pay a huge fine).

There were no less than five kinds of ordeals: cold water, hot iron, hot water, holy wafer, and battle. The ordeal of cold water was the most commonly used in England because it required a pond or stream of significant depth, of which there are plenty in that wet isle. The defendant was bound hand and foot and thrown into the water. If he sank he was innocent—a rope was tied to him to pull him out (before he drowned, it was to be hoped). If he floated he was declared guilty because water—being one of the holy elements in nature—would not receive a guilty person. It was so believed scientifically and so taught in the universities.

In the ordeal of hot iron, a piece of metal was heated red-hot in a fire. The defendant had to grasp it and walk a prescribed number of steps—how many determined by the judges in accordance with the defendant's reputation, bad or very bad. His hand was bound up and it was examined in three days. If the burn wound seemed to be healing, he was innocent; otherwise, guilty and he was mercifully hanged before he died of gangrene.

In the ordeal of hot water a stone was placed at the bottom of a cauldron of boiling water. The defendant had to put in his hand and arm (whether the water was up to his elbow or shoulder again depended on his reputation with the court). As in the ordeal of hot iron, his hand and arm were bound up and in three days reexamined.

The ordeal of holy wafer was reserved for accused clergymen, the famous criminous clerks of the Becket controversy. In the ordeal the accused cleric had to try to swallow a dry holy wafer from the sacrament of the Mass. If he choked on it, he was guilty; otherwise, innocent and could go home to his wife and children. In the twelfth century, despite the papacy's mandating of clerical celibacy, most parish priests still had families.

Was there any rationale to these barbarities, which were carried out in front of the judges and grand juries in the shire courts annually in many thousands of cases? A little. Before going to the ordeal, the accused was subjected to ecclesiastical brainwashing. He had to swear his innocence on the Bible or holy relics. He was admonished by the priest to confess his guilt if he was guilty as charged so as not to perjure himself and endanger his soul (the actual severity of alleged endangerment would take the theologians in the schools months to debate—and come to no firm conclusion). Whether this brainwashing was effective, from the meager quantity of criminal trial records surviving from before abolition of the ordeals, is highly doubtful. Medieval people thought of lying as a part of life, even if they had their hand on a saint's collarbone.

Ordeal by battle came in with the French knights and the Norman Conquest. At the beginning it was simply the privilege of the conquerors in a colonial society. If a French soldier was accused of a crime, he had the privilege of fighting his accuser. (So much for justice if the accuser was an Englishman set to fight an armored French knight—and on horseback yet.) Not many FitzHughs got accused by Ælfwigs under these circumstances.

By the time of Glanville, trial by battle could be used in criminal cases when one member of the knightly class (who by now was often of mixed French-English lineage) was accused by another. Trial by battle in criminal actions was only used if there was a personal accusation and both parties wanted this form of ordeal (the accused knight did not fight the foreman of the grand jury that indicted him). A new twist was added to overcome the problem of the two combatants being unmatched. Either side could designate a "champion," a fighter to take the field (*champ*) of battle on his behalf.

To prevent someone from simply hiring a Mike Tyson or a Dallas Cowboys linebacker to fight for him, the champion was supposed to be someone with an interest in the case—a blood relative or a vassal (legal dependent) of the litigant. The system still seems to have allowed opportunity for unequal combat, however. There was also one kind of civil action—a property dispute about ultimate title—in which battle was sometimes used, down into the 1170s.

In spite of the appeal of trial by battle to the imagination and plotlines of Victorian novels and Hollywood films, it was an uncommon event. Yet as late as 1817 a wealthy eccentric gentleman accused of a crime chose to defend his honor by trial by battle, at which point it was retroactively abolished by act of Parliament.

The other, more standard ordeals were not officially abolished but were abandoned when news arrived in England in 1217 that two years earlier, at papal behest, the participation of clergy in ordeals had thenceforth been prohibited by the Fourth Lateran Council in Rome. This eliminated the ecclesiastical brainwashing, its only rational ingredient. Even as they hastily and awkwardly tried to find a substitute method of proof, the judges who were Glanville's immediate successors must have heaved a quiet sigh of relief at being rid of the abominable ordeals. Allowing compurgation to everyone wouldn't have been the solution. It was too soft. The judges came up with the second jury, variously called the petty (from the French *petit*, or "small") jury or the jury of verdict, to decide on guilt or innocence of the defendant indicted by the first, or grand, jury.

Historians have speculated on why the papacy in effect abolished the ordeals. The official reason was that clergy were not supposed to participate in actions that led to the shedding of blood—that is, capital punishment. Considering that the lifestyle of three-quarters of the clergy was exactly the same as the peasants from whose ranks they came and to whom they ministered, this pious claim was a joke, but so were a lot of the claims that came out of the papacy. Another and better reason was that Pope Innocent III, a voracious reformer of church discipline, did not want clergy to use up time hanging around secular law courts when they should be studying Saint Augustine or at least sweeping out the village church. But the best explanation is that the austere, learned, aristocratic Roman lawyer Innocent III thought it high time that this Germanic barbarity of the ordeals was abandoned. Good thinking.

Once the English people get something good, they tend to stay with it. They are still drinking tea every afternoon, as they have since it became an upper-class fashion in the eighteenth century. The grand jury lasted in England down into the 1930s. After that it was replaced by a simpler system: A Crown prosecutor presented enough evidence to a magistrate to have the defendant "bound over" for trial. California has the same system, although the prosecution there may still choose sometimes to use a grand jury. In judicially conservative New York State, the grand jury flourishes as splendidly as in the age of Glanville, and as the saying goes, the Manhattan district attorney could get a grand jury to indict a ham sandwich.

In England the itinerant assizes/circuit judge system lasted until 1971, at which point it was at last decided to let each county have its own set of permanent, noncirculating judges. It was a glorious tradition while it lasted. In the early 1850s an obscure Illinois lawyer, Abe Lincoln, rose to wealth and prominence by following the circuit judges around the state, taking on all manner of clients, but especially the Illinois Central Railroad, which he defended against liability suits for the mayhem it inflicted on its passengers (until the invention of the Westinghouse air brake in the 1880s, it was hard to stop trains).

In thinly populated outlying provinces of the once resplendent British Empire, judges of assize still go out on circuit. In Winnipeg, Manitoba, Canada, along with endless hockey and curling scores, the newspapers still announce that Judge Bass is going out to hold the assizes in Portage la Prairie or Neepawa.

Except in libel and defamation cases, the English stopped using the jury in civil actions after World War II. It is still heavily used in the United States in such actions, especially in liability suits, in which juries award horrific damages and make the lawyers as well as the plaintiffs very rich.

The extensive use of the jury in property disputes (civil actions) was a big step forward. The universal use of the grand jury and the replacing of ordeals by the petty jury, or jury of verdict, was also progress—although in the latter instance a debatable one. Judges of Glanville's generation and two succeeding ones down to 1240 fully integrated the jury into English law. It became the hallmark of common law and is so enshrined in the American Constitution. The obvious historical questions are,

Why and how did the jury become central to English law? What factors caused the emergence of distinctive English common law?

There is no consensus among historians in answering these questions partly because court records from before Glanville's generation are very sparse. They were either not kept in writing or have been lost. Research and writing of English legal history suffer from too little documentation before 1180 and too much after 1300. Another reason for the lack of consensus on what used to be called "the origin of the common law" is that questions like this have all sorts of ideological implications, which not unnaturally encourage highly diverse answers.

Furthermore, since around 1965, historians have gotten used to not answering longitudinal questions like the one about the origins of the common law. Especially in England it is professionally wise for an academic not to attempt big questions but to concentrate on narrow issues on which he or she can display learning and wit and not become vulnerable to angry reviewers who may want his or her job or seek to prevent him or her from getting one.

There are three standard explanations for the twelfth-century legal revolution and the establishment of the common law. The popular Victorian thesis, brilliantly expounded by Oxford's William Stubbs (later a bishop) around 1870, was, in the nineteenth-century mode, dialectical. Anglo-Saxon institutions were strongly popular and communal, allowing a high degree of autonomy for local societies. Authoritarianism and centralization came with the French conquest in 1066. The rise of the common law, and especially the proliferation of the jury system, represented the resurgence of the popular element in the constitution—the political system that Stubbs believed was tantamount to the establishment of the common law—and was followed by popular legislation in the thirteenth-century Parliaments, but now in the advantageous framework of effective peace and order. This cheerful thesis may sound ridiculously simple-minded and naive but isn't. As a paradigm of medieval English constitutional and legal history, it has never been superseded—just made obsolete by nondialectical and more functional thinking. (Just present Stubbs's thesis to a bright college class: They will eat it up. The Victorians in some way knew their market.)

The second view is Frederic Maitland's, around 1900. The common law had little or nothing to do with the Anglo-Saxon heritage, which was at best murky and didn't continue beyond 1066 except for the shire court and writs. The jury is a French invention. What happened in the reign of Henry II and his sons was that the common law and the jury system served the interests of both kings and the landed class, especially the gentry. So the common law was functionally brought into existence. But it was for a long time always fragile, being heavily grounded in custom and social consensus, and didn't have to turn out the way it did. Stubbs was a confident Tory, Maitland a worried liberal, convinced that the price of freedom is eternal vigilance and good luck.

A third explanation, not well articulated, was propounded by Cambridge's S. F. Milsom in the 1970s and 1980s: The king had very little to do with it, the higher nobility a great deal. It was in their interest to develop a new system for litigating land disputes. The common law was an aristocratic invention, in Milsom's view.

Milsom and the other doyen of the Cambridge school of English legal historians, J. H. Baker, have no interest in public or constitutional law, the common law's relationship to politics and government, or in criminal law. They are only interested in private law, mainly property, liability, and family.

Milsom's depoliticized version of the emergence of the common law fits the general approach to legal history of the Cambridge school headed by himself and Baker. If legal history is concerned only with private law, then the rise of the common law is only explicable within a paradigm grounded in private law. This means that the important institutions of the common law in the thirteenth century reflected the interests and behavior of the higher nobility, and the royal government played little or no role.

As Milsom himself stressed, this view is a significant departure from Maitland's.

Maitland's interpretation of the emergence of the common law partially departs from the overwhelmingly political and constitutional thesis propounded by Stubbs. Milsom almost entirely departs from the Victorian political and constitutional view. His work can be seen historiographically as a reflection of the general disenchantment with the English liberal heritage that characterized British historians after 1950.

Milsom does win some points against his Cambridge predecessor, Maitland, by showing how well the common law in property actions suited the family interests not only of the wealthier gentry but also of the great landed families of the nobility, who wielded enormous power in 1180. In his pithy, elliptical manner, Milsom wrote in 1976: "The lord's interest was not a problem. Certainly not a problem for the king's court. . . . Great things happened; but the *only* intention behind [the assize writs] was to make the seignorial structure work according to its own assumptions."

Stubbs and Maitland, from different standpoints, the one ideological and dialectical, the other laboriously functional and sociological, argued the opposite. The royal judges on the one side, the gentry landholders and jurymen on the other, collaborated from the 1170s on through the next century to undermine the judicial powers of the great lords and their "seignorial structure." In Milsom's view, the lords tried in the late twelfth century to improve civil actions to suit their own interests. In so doing they created a kind of benign Frankenstein monster that eventually, perhaps around 1300, got away from them and left them with a vast economic but greatly diminished judicial power.

Milsom tells us that the treatise on the *Laws of Customs of the Kingdom of England,* customarily called simply *Glanville,* was an important source of his 1976 book *The Legal Framework of English Feudalism.*

The *Laws and Customs* is the book that Glanville and his

nephew, Walter, talked about while they were on circuit and began to write down in the mid–1180s. (Some historians believe that *Glanville* was actually written by the clerical son of another chief justice—Richard de Lucy. But there is no good reason not to attribute the treatise to Glanville and Walter.) Walter was a likely coauthor of the work, which is regarded as the first of the four classic treatises on the premodern common law. The others, named after their authors, are: Bracton, around 1250; Coke in the 1620s; and Blackstone in the 1760s, from the last of which Abe Lincoln in the 1830s is alleged to have learned common law.

There is some indication that Glanville and Walter never quite finished their treatise. Perhaps they ran out of time or interest. After a detailed discussion of the civil assizes and writs, the section of the book on criminal law seems cursory, rushed, and not well informed.

But Glanville's discussion of the civil assizes and writs nonetheless gives us much information that does not come from other sources. It shows the self-awareness of Henry II's judges that they had done something important, that they had laid the foundations for a distinct legal system. It owed something to the Roman law flourishing on the Continent (Walter had studied at Bologna). But common law was going off in another direction from Roman law. The hallmark of the English system were the assize juries in the shire courts, impaneled by royal writs—this is the main theme of Glanville, and this in Glanville's view is the heart of English law. Now landholding was litigated by actions that "from a beneficial constitution of the kingdom called an assize are generally settled by recognition"—that is, by juries.

Unlike his nephew, Walter, Glanville was a layman. Though literate in French, he was not fully Latinate; he was not educated in the universities. He stemmed from the middling gentry. He entered early into royal service, fought as a soldier against the Scots, did a variety of demanding administrative jobs including that of sheriff, and rose through the ranks to become a circuit judge and then chief justiciar of the realm, an important political as well as judicial position.

Glanville learned his law empirically on the bench, sitting at Westminster (and in the saddle, so to speak, on circuit). He had a very different life experience from that of the law professors in Bologna or Paris, steeped in scholastic humanism, which they applied to explicating the Justinian code.

An empirical man, a man close to the soil and the people, this Glanville was also passionately dedicated to the king and his purposes. England would see many great lawyers like him in centuries to come. He was their prototype.

Of the four classic treatises on the common law, *Glanville* is the most prosaic, the most inclined to see legal institutions as an outcome of mundane problem solving for rural society. In Glanville's eyes the common law is rooted in process; doctrine and history have almost nothing to do with it.

None of his three successors would have this persistent empirical attitude. They would bring to explaining the common law much theory and learning, even though two of them, Bracton and Coke, also had much experience as judges and lawyers. Glanville kept it simple. Walter may have had a different perception, derived from Roman law, but in collaborating on the treatise with his uncle, he kept this deep culture quarantined from the imagining of the law of England.

Glanville was present at the creation, and he communicated what was meaningful to him. Henry II would have stated it differently, and from another perspective the austere Walter probably could have done so also, but he kept quiet as far as the professional treatise known as *Glanville* was concerned. He helped his uncle turn his ideas into passable Latin prose and did not attempt to put a philosophical gloss on the work. Common law is process. Common law is writs that inaugurate forms of actions and juries that effectively conclude these judicial cases. That is all you really need to know.

It may seem a simple way of understanding the law, and compared to the Justinian code and its edifice of Roman law shot through with theory, it assuredly is. But at least half the time of first-year law students in American law schools today is still spent studying actions—that is, cases. Glanville wouldn't be surprised at what he would find if he were to sit in on a class on property in a law school today. It is still his common law.

5
Englishmen and Frenchmen

MUCH OF EUROPEAN HISTORY in the early Middle Ages turns on conflicts between peoples who fought, like the Romans, on foot and those who fought on horseback. The latter had made their fateful appearance among Asiatics who invaded the Roman Empire in the fifth century and played a principal role in its downfall. In the successor kingdoms that followed the Roman Empire in Western Europe, especially in what became France, the innovative method of fighting was adapted and improved upon.

In the Battle of Hastings in October 1066, fought between the forces of Anglo-Saxon king Harold II Godwinson and an invading army of Frenchmen led by Duke William the Bastard of Normandy, the English defenders were still on foot and not in the saddle. They encountered the invading armored French knights on horseback. Despite their technological backwardness, the English put up a good fight, and William and his horse soldiers won the field only after a long day's fighting.

Most of William's army were lords and peasants from Normandy. The forefathers of William and these Norman French had come into the area around Rouen in the early tenth century from Scandinavia as fearsome heathen Vikings in their longboats. Hence they were known as *Normanni*, the Northmen. Nominally subject to the feckless king in Paris but in practice independent, the Norman duke and his followers rapidly adapted French language, religion, and culture and the French way of fighting on horseback. The land and climate were unsuitable for grapes, so instead they planted apple orchards and from the applejack they made a brandy now called (after a local bishopric, still there) Calvados, the brown lightning of the medieval world.

For a century the Norman warriors spent their time in drunken brawling among themselves, but eventually the duke got firm control over them. Making use of clerical administrators trained in Roman and canon law and imported from as far away as northern Italy, the duke created a highly effective central administration in his territory.

The eleventh-century Norman nobility were fecund. By the second decade of the eleventh century some of the surplus Norman nobility had gone off on their own in a freebooting expedition to conquer Sicily from the Arabs and Greeks. Their great Cathedral of Mount Royal can still be seen in its pristine grandeur just outside of Palermo. William the Bastard thought this overseas adventuring a political waste. He decided to use the ample military prowess of the baby-booming Norman nobility for his own purpose. With the addition of mercenaries gathered from neighboring French provinces he planned and executed the conquest of 1066 that abruptly terminated the venerable English monarchy.

The Anglo-Saxon kings (A.D. 600–1066) were fond of issuing "dooms" or law codes. These are relatively short documents, usually written in Old English, although the clerical scribe who wrote them down for the king, after the latter had consulted with a very small group—perhaps a dozen, perhaps two dozen—of lay and ecclesiastical magnates, was bilingual and could have written down the laws in either English or Latin.

English was chosen for the Anglo-Saxon kings' law codes because when a copy was sent to a shire court or a monastery to be proclaimed through reading it out loud, many more people could understand the English than the Latin.

The law codes were not a summary of all existing law. They were statements only of confusing or disputed points in the law. The greater part of the law remained oral and was never written down. It was retained in the memory of the older magnates at the shire courts, who were therefore called "doomsmen," men who knew the law. Sometimes the dooms issued by the kings contained a rhetorical flourish to communicate the king's concern for the law, his wish that the courts meet and do justice, that the laws be clear and comprehensible, and that the laws be enforced.

There was always in Anglo-Saxon law, which prevailed before the Norman Conquest of England in 1066, the intimation that the law was something the king endorsed but did not control, that the law was something he had a fondness for, a concern about, but that he did not master it. The law was something that lay like a nourishing rain over the English countryside, benefiting society, both king and peasant.

The Anglo-Saxons wanted to settle things, to resolve disputes, to reach consensus. This was the point of the law. It was not to make anyone strong or rich. It was the means of maintaining harmony among clans, among families, between groups, between individuals. "Where a thegn," says a royal doom around A.D. 1000, "has two choices, love or law, and he chooses love, it shall be as binding as judgement." What this means is that agreement, consensus on a disputed matter, shall be as binding as if the litigants went to court and a trial was held. This penchant for love, for consensus, and a resort to trial only if consensus cannot be reached after much jawboning, runs right through the northern medieval world, from Scandinavia to Iceland. There are lawsuits and trials in the wonderful thirteenth-century Icelandic sagas, but only when face-to-face discussion, strenuous efforts to reach agreement, and much eloquent phrasemaking around the campfire over kegs of beer have led to no resolution. Litigation and trials, and decisions by courts, came about only when love is gone, and there is regret that things have come to such an unhappy pass, and that the bird of peace has flown away.

English courts before the fierce Frenchmen took over in 1066 used whatever means they could think of to process a trial. The courts established lists of wergilds, monetary compensation to kin for death of a family member, or to individuals for loss of a limb. They used compurgation, including panels of blue-ribbon oath helpers, "suits of witnesses," and ordeals, as means of proof in trials. They divided the populace in the countryside into groups of ten, hence called a tithing, and made nine of the group responsible for bringing a tenth who broke the peace to justice (a system that was later called frankpledge).

The Anglo-Saxons used the accusing jury of twelve leading thegns of the county to bring in collective accusations against alleged criminals. In civil disputes about landholding they occasionally employed a jury of recognition to testify in court as to who the rightful landholder was.

Always, the impression from the legal records of the Anglo-Saxon era remains that these judicial instruments were wielded almost reluctantly, that no one relished litigation or flexed their power by use of judicial process. They preferred love to law, consensus to trial, interpersonal agreement to judgment imposed by the court. There were much more important things in life than law—poetry, art, faith.

The Anglo-Saxons appear to have been satisfied with their legal system. It worked well enough; it cost virtually nothing to operate; it didn't require teams of specially trained, high-priced experts. If something went wrong in the functioning of the legal system, if a shire court failed to meet at the new moon or to consider someone's case, or to do justice, the king called in a clerical scribe and told him to send a writ to the men of the particular shire court to pull up their socks and rectify the situation.

The royal writ was a few lines penned on a narrow strip of vellum or parchment—bleached sheepskin. It was folded up, and over the fold was placed a piece of beeswax with the king's seal embossed on it. If the royal messenger was intercepted by an enemy of the king who wanted to read the message, the messenger could swallow the writ—no harder on the tummy than swallowing a piece of chewing gum.

Hard cases make law. What this means is that, over time, novel disputes occur that seem complex and frustrate the prevailing legal thinking and the processes used to apply the ideas. Something complicated emerges, something awkward, something novel, something that pushes those knowledgeable in the law to the limits of their conventional thinking, and challenges them to go beyond.

That is why since the 1880s at the flagship Harvard University Law School, and within fifty years at all reputable American law schools, students have been educated in the law not by copying down and memorizing the pronouncements of law professors as in Roman law schools, but by the case method, by studying the records of hard cases and trying to replicate in their own minds the thinking of lawyers and judges when confronted by these conundrums. That is why the common law is held to be based on "legal reasoning."

Sometimes it is said that hard cases make bad law—that these very difficult disputes constitute puzzles that are so complex that they are really judicial outriders beyond the normal body of the law and therefore don't matter much. But it is in confronting the challenge of hard cases that legal thinking moves—hopefully forward, often messily and awkwardly.

The hard cases that challenged the judicial imagination of the

Anglo-Saxons arose in the area of inheritance and transfer of land, which comprised at least 95 percent of their wealth. Real estate and its transfer are still an important segment of law today—what is called "conveyancing" in England.

Normally there was no problem about landholding. The landlord held it and enjoyed it, and when he died, the land passed to his eldest son by "folkright," the customary law of the folk.

Folkright by 900—which applied everywhere except in the county of Kent, in the southeast—thus favored primogeniture, in which the eldest son gets nearly everything, so that the family's influence and visibility can be maintained. Parage, dividing up the land among male siblings, which obtained in some parts of France, would immediately or within a couple of generations have eroded the family's power and influence by steadily splitting up the land in each new generation.

Only in Kent was parage practiced—and this is because the people of Kent were culturally different from the rest of the country. They were neither Angles nor Saxons, but Jutes, coming from much farther east in the Germanic homeland than the rest of the English people. Parage in Kent was called gavelkind.

Primogeniture wasn't quite as tough on younger sons or daughters as it might seem on the surface, but it was tough enough. The daughters had two choices as they grew up—marriage or a nunnery. The cost to Daddy was about the same. To marry off a daughter, the landed father had to provide a dowry, which could be either money or land. To place a daughter in a convent of holy sisters would usually cost the same in the form of a gift to the nunnery's endowment (nunneries in this Benedictine era were only for wealthy women; women of modest circumstances could feel privileged to slave away as servants to the socially upscale nuns).

A lord might prefer a younger son to his eldest son and heir. The eldest son might be mentally disturbed, physically disabled, or gay and unlikely to marry and continue the family line. But there was nothing under the folkright of primogeniture that a lord could do, short of improbably persuading his eldest son to become a monk and therefore a nonperson in property inheritance. The lord while he was alive could make a modest gift of family land to a younger son, but folkright prevented giving him more than this.

One younger son, at most two, could be provided for in this way. No more than 10 percent of the lord's land—less if a highly attractive estate was involved—could be disposed of in this way and not descend through primogeniture. The shire court, where the heads of leading county families and the king's sheriff were present, along with the bishop, would jealously guard the inheritance of the eldest son through folkright and prevent the lord from giving away more than a slice of the family lands to a second son.

If there was more than one younger son, he was normally sent to a monastic school to become lettered and trained to gain a career in the church. Any other sons received military training, were equipped by their father to be soldiers, and prepared for careers as mercenaries. In the case of the higher nobility, the earls and suchlike, folkright's preservation of the family lands assured that the heir would succeed his father at the king's *witan*—the council of wise magnates—would feast with the king several times a year and then offer him whatever counsel he sought.

Folkright's guarding of the integrity of a family's lands was buttressed by a provision in the law codes that lands alienated to a younger son could not further be given away or sold but must stay in the younger son's family. Behind this provision was the hope that the younger son's line might eventually die out, and then the land could revert back to the family main line, stemming from the eldest son as heir.

The hard cases that arose in the English law of inheritance were of two kinds. The first involved the legal instrument by which there was a record of land being given to a younger son. The second hard case, never satisfactorily resolved, had to do with land given away by the landlord to an ecclesiastical institution.

The Anglo-Saxons had three kinds of legal documents. The first was the writ, normally issued by the king, telling a court to meet and do justice. The second was a will, which was commonly used. But unlike the will in Roman law, it could not—before the sixteenth century—dispose of land but only of movable property—jewels, swords, horses, artworks and so on. The lord could not reach out from beyond the grave and through a will deprive his eldest son of what came to him by the customary law of folkright's support of primogeniture in the shire court. Wills were thus restricted in their dispository capacity until the mid-sixteenth century.

Clerics taught the Anglo-Saxons about a third legal document, which was already widely used on the Continent, the charter (*carta* in Latin), called the "book" (document) in English. It was the charter that testified to the alienation of land by the lord before his death to someone (his younger son, or an ecclesiastical institution) other than the normal heir by folkright. Land so alienated was therefore called bookland—land held by document rather than folkright. Not folkland, but bookland.

The format of the charter was borrowed from France. Unlike the skimpy writ, the charter was a big, imposing Latin document, meant to overawe any challenger and impress any court. It was written on vellum in the best inks, sometimes with an illuminated initial at the top left-hand corner. (Such illustrations are now considered important examples of Anglo-Saxon art.)

The standard charter had five parts. First, the greeting: "I, Edward, by the grace of God King of the English, to the sheriff and all freemen of Hampshire," or, wherever the land being transmitted lay. Second, the harangue, boilerplate usually copied out of a formula book imported from France, giving the reason for the gift of land ("Out of love for my good son Robert . . . "). Third, specification of the actual estate granted. Since central land registration did not exist before the eighteenth century, if the land in question was not a well-known estate ("the king's hunting park at Abingdon"), it was necessary to spell out the circumference of the estate carefully: "from the rear door of the cathedral two hundred paces to the great oak tree, then two miles to the old mill at Ipswich, then one mile to the covered bridge over the River Isis . . ."

Fourth, came the curse, the sanction clause. Anyone who violated the grant was not only braving the king's wrath but endangering his soul. If the recipient was a church, the curse was elaborate, and involved more boilerplate from a formulary. Finally, at the bottom of the sheepskin came the witness list, the names of those allegedly present at the act of transfer of ownership of the land, their Xs next to their names and their embossed wax seals hanging from strips of parchment pushed through holes sliced in the bottom of the charter with a sharp knife. Sometimes there are more names than seals, possibly indicating imagination or fraud on the part of the scribe, or possibly accounted for by the fact that many wax seals turned to dust over the centuries. That is why the wily and rich popes used lead seals (bulls).

A hard case for the shire court, involving transfer of land to a younger son against the presumptive folkright of primogeniture, could come about in one of two ways. First the charter in law only witnessed a dispositary act; it was not the act of transfer itself. The transfer legally occurred by voice and gesture in front of witnesses whose names and seals were supposed to appear at the bottom of the document; transfer could not be by document alone. Parchment does not make a land transfer, was the medieval rule. In this predominantly oral society, the grantor had to vocalize his grant; and just as important, the recipient of the gift had physically to take possession of the land, preferably by riding around the estate's perimeter, making a noise, and having someone read from the charter. Innumerable lawsuits in medieval land law centered on the issue of—while there was an existing document—whether oral disposition and physical possession had actually occurred.

The second hard case arising from a father's alienation of land to a younger son focused on the document itself, as the years and decades passed and lives and memories of witnesses faded. Insofar as the charter was witness to the transaction, was the document produced in court authentic, or was it a forgery, manufactured by a compliant cleric for a fee? Since clerical institutions frequently forged charters on their own behalf, it was not hard to find a bribable scribe to generate a document supportive of the claim of a younger son or one of his progeny. The courts had no sure way of authenticating documents, especially if they looked appropriately old, the ink was not bright and fresh, and a plausible number of witnesses' seals hung from the parchment.

These hard cases in land law forced courts to confront complicated issues and to engage in a measure of judicial reasoning. It was in contemplating and debating these conundrums, more often than in royal legislation, that the shape of the land law emerged.

The hardest case of all involving landed wealth, extremely frustrating for Anglo-Saxon heirs and later heirs in this society, was the alienation of family land to the church. When it passed into that "dead hand" of the church, it was irrecoverable by the family because while priests, bishops, and abbots came and went, their ecclesiastical institutions endured to the end of earthly time. The grant was to the church, to the clerical community, not to an individual cleric. The recipient of the grant in fact was usually the saint after which the ecclesiastical community was officially named: "to the Cathedral of Saint Mary in York," or "to the community of Saint Gregory at Ipswich."

Ever since Catholic missionaries had landed in England in the sixth century, first from Ireland and then more dominantly from

Rome, the clerics had sought special treatment. First they insisted that their bodies, possessions, and buildings be taken into the king's *mundyburd*, his area of personal protection, previously reserved for his family, his domestic stockade, and his feasting halls. Eventually so many churches dotting the countryside came under the king's protection that the king's protective shadow was generalized in the idea of the king's *frith*, the king's peace, and covered the whole country.

Then the churchmen insisted the king endow them with lands, often from his own family possessions. Waiting endlessly for meager remittances from Rome or squeezing the peasants for tithes couldn't do the job of funding the ambitious building, droves of monks, and great libraries and art workshops the churchmen aimed for.

Mutual benefit, however, was involved. If the king would alienate a succulent family estate to a cathedral or abbey, the priests and monks would pray for his soul, which then would be speeded through purgatory (virtually no one got assigned to hell in this populist religion) and lifted up to heaven. Kings took this offer seriously, as did other great lords who proffered benefactions to the church.

Medieval heirs did not think this quid pro quo—sharply reduced time in purgatory in return for real estate—was nonsense. They believed in this religious system too, and would in time seek their own exchange with the church. But enough was enough. As the old king or earl began to fail (forty was the onset of old age in this medicineless society), he was closely watched by potential heirs. Sons were glad to allow fathers as many concubines as they wanted. They got nervous when priests, confessors, and persuasive bishops and abbots came calling.

There were no legal means of preventing faltering fathers from richly endowing churches. This conundrum could not be legally overcome. Society felt, however, that there was a limit to invasion of folkright, and a king or earl would not be able to find appropriate witnesses to append their seals to unreasonable alienation. Yet munficent giving did occur. That is how Westminster Abbey got started—with a huge endowment by King Edward the Confessor.

"The Confessor" means "saint." King Edward didn't need much persuasion around 1060 to make his endowment gift to the abbey. He had once been a monk, and himself neglected the king's number one duty to produce progeny, preferably male. He retained his monastic vow of celibacy and never had sex with his wife. His death in 1065 therefore produced a succession crisis. There was a survivor of good King Alfred's line, the House of Wessex, from which the Confessor stemmed, off in distant Hungary. He was ignored. The House of Wessex was deemed extinct and the earls and other top lords met and exercised their right to elect a king, choosing the wealthiest earl, Harold Godwinson. But in Normandy, across the English Channel, the French duke William the Bastard had a claim by inheritance to the English throne; his great-aunt was from the House of Wessex. He also got the pope to endorse his invasion of England by cynically promising to bring the English church more closely under papal rule.

In October 1066, William put together an army of eight hundred mounted knights, some of them mercenaries from outside Normandy, and transported his army with their horses and another thousand infantry, in a vast fleet of little boats each no bigger than a tennis court. William got a favorable wind after two weeks' waiting. Harold had just defeated the invading Norwegians up in the north, near York, when he got word that the Bastard's fleet was on its way, daring something that Napoleon and Hitler were later afraid to attempt, a seaborne invasion of England.

Harold marched his exhausted army the length of the country, losing many on the way (medieval soldiers thought one big battle a year was enough risk). Even then his army, while it fought only on foot against French cavalry, probably outnumbered William's forces at the Battle of Hastings. A close daylong struggle ended when a French arrow went through Harold's eye and his army fled at their fair king's death.

William, now the Conqueror, stood on the dank battlefield of Hastings in the onsetting dusk of an autumn afternoon and claimed England as his own, to do with as he wished by right of conquest and inheritance and papal blessing. In the next five years he squashed all resistance—many English lords were either killed, pushed down into the ranks of the peasantry, or fled overseas to offer themselves to the emperor in Constantinople for mercenary service in the imperial bodyguard.

What had occurred was the naked colonial conquest of a rich country by a small group of fierce soldiers from overseas, headed by a determined and clever ruler. It was similar to the British conquest of India in the eighteenth and nineteenth centuries.

But the British left half of the Indian princes in place. William the Conqueror removed all the English landlords, both secular and (with one exception—Wulfstan of Worcester—who was reputed to be a saint) all the bishops, and nearly all the abbots. The removal of the leaders of the English church was facilitated by the papacy's push to enforce sacerdotal celibacy (no sex for churchmen because it was claimed that they were already married to the church, the metaphysical bride of Christ). This old idea in canon law had never hitherto been enforced, and nearly all English ecclesiastics, from bishop down to parish priest, had concubines and families. Now the sex card could cynically be played to remove the top ecclesiastics in England for violating canon law and replace them with Frenchmen.

William I enjoyed a reign in England of twenty-one years. He spent half his time fighting and administering on the Continent. For this reason as well as the more general one of operating a strong government and making some significant political and social changes, he needed a capable, energetic, and absolutely loyal head of his administrative staff, which comprised a group of about thirty clerics and lay lords. By 1072 the king had brought over Lanfranc from a Norman abbey and installed him as archbishop of Canterbury.

Lanfranc was the king's chief of administration. He had been a close associate of the Conqueror in his Norman French duchy. In origin Lanfranc was a middle-class Roman lawyer from northern Italy who made a career switch to a life of learning. He moved to Normandy and entered monastic life in order to become a theologian and canon lawyer, and ultimately he became an ecclesiastical administrator as well. An austere, ambitious, and politically clever man, Lanfranc was of immense use to the king in pacifying the conquered country, in settling in a new French aristocracy on its expropriated lands, and in developing instruments for maximizing the drawing of wealth from rich agricultural land of one million people, 90 percent of whom lived in the southern half of the country. "That rich man," a French king's chief minister said enviously of William, "a buyer and seller of knights."

In practice the Norman settlement meant the granting of land and offices to about one hundred French higher nobility and fifty ecclesiastical lords, and below this ruling class to perhaps another thousand French knights and two hundred clerics of more modest social stature.

Lanfranc no less than William was fearless and skillful in dealing with higher nobility. In a series of protracted lawsuits, Lanfranc challenged the king's half-brother, who was a bishop in Normandy and an earl in England before he himself took over as archbishop. He won all lawsuits, getting the testimony he wanted from peasant juries and the judgments from Anglo-French aristocrats, who dominated the special courts set up to hear these great lawsuits. He won his lawsuits partly by using forged charters.

Just as the later English conquerors, the raj, took advantage of the best India had to offer—madras cotton, tea, chutney, mulligatawny soup, curry, and until around 1850, Indian women—

William and Lanfranc perpetuated most of Anglo-Saxon law, making adjustments and additions that were functionally useful to the king and the new landed class.

Anglo-Norman law perpetuated the written instruments of Anglo-Saxon law—the writ, the charter, and the will. The shire court continued as the provincial court, now also using the French appellation of county court. The king's main official in the shire, the sheriff ("shire reeve," or county agent), was also perpetuated. Now known sometimes as the viscount, his status and importance were upgraded. He not only presided at the county court, he was responsible for collecting royal taxes in the county. This made him more powerful and usually wealthier than previously, and the office of sheriff was much in demand among second-echelon French lords, those below the great nobility of 150 lay and ecclesiastical magnates.

From the very early years of the twelfth century, the county courts were presided over by a panel of itinerant justices. It was realized a sheriff was often too busy, not sufficiently learned in the law, and too enmeshed in county politics to make a good judge. But he was still important to shire courts' operations. He made sure that litigants were present and that judgments were carried out. If a jury was summoned in civil (land) disputes to recognize the truth before the court, it was the sheriff who impaneled the jury of recognition and made sure it was present when the case was called.

In the decades following the Norman Conquest, juries of recognition were more frequently used than in the Anglo-Saxon period. This was partly because the institution was identical to inquests used in Normandy, and these French inquests appear to have been ultimately derived from Roman law. So juries of recognition or inquests were frequently called to investigate and testify before the shire court in landholding disputes. They were still summoned by writs of grace—writs issued by the king as a special privilege for litigants—rather than by writs of course. But during the reign of William and the immediate royal successors from his family (1066–1154), there was certainly more use of juries than in the Anglo-Saxon era.

The jury of recognition functioned well enough for it to be the most important source of information in the compiling of Domesday Book, a vast inquiry into landholding for taxation and judicial purposes that William ordained and that was nearly completed when he died in 1087. In every village a panel of peasants was sworn and asked who held the land in 1065, in 1066, and presently, and what kind of people worked the land, and what else was on the piece of land, from cattle and horses to mills and fishponds. No other European state before 1700 was capable of such a thorough inquiry into landed wealth, which was summarized in two huge folio volumes. The sweeping use of the jury in this way in every village of the realm imprinted it on the consciousness of all ranks of society as a central institution of judicial and administrative life.

The use of the grand jury of indictment in the shire court presided over by a royal official was not continued after the Norman Conquest. Yet grand juries were probably still used in courts not assembled under royal mandate; familiarity with this institution of criminal law was not lost, and it was revived in the 1160s.

William and Lanfranc abandoned the grand jury because for many decades the new ruling French families constituted a thin stratum of elite in society. They often did not have time to serve on grand juries, and there would not have been enough of the French elite to staff the juries. If grand juries had continued after 1066, they would have been heavily made up of Englishmen, and the French invaders would not want to be in a position of being indicted by English-dominated juries.

The revival of the grand jury—which took about a century— had to await a time when intermarriage and social fusion between French and English was extensive, and when a new class of middling county landholders had emerged. Whether French or English in ancestry or, as often products of ethnic mixture, this class—later called the gentry—lacked ethnic consciousness and could be relied on to bring in criminal indictments free from prejudice. By the 1160s this social and ethnic transformation had occurred, and the grand jury, whose use in nonroyal courts had continued, could be brought back into the shire courts to interact with the royal circuit judges.

At the most local level, in the villages, in a society that lacked a publicly supported peace system, the Anglo-Saxon self-help tithing unit, now called frankpledge, was continued.

When the itinerant justices began to go out on circuit in the early years of the twelfth century, they added two judicial functions aimed at peacekeeping. There had to be an accusation for every violent death or the county court would be assessed a *murdrum* (murder) fine. In every violent death, the shire court had to show through "presentment of Englishry" that the deceased was not a Frenchman, a politically incorrect death that would require extraordinary scrutiny. Well into the thirteenth century, the itinerant justices were still assessing *murdrum* fines if the grand juries failed to indict someone for every violent crime. By then "presentment of Englishry" was obsolete.

Henry I, William the Conqueror's third son and second successor on the English throne, married in 1102 an English princess descended from the House of Wessex to bolster his claim to the throne, thereby politically legitimating intermarriage between French and English. The higher nobility in the thirteenth century might still pride themselves on the purity of their French lineage but the ethnic distinction between the two nations had lapsed. Presentment of Englishry in the thirteenth century was a legal archaism by which the circuit judges could harass a shire court that had annoyed them in some way.

In addition to the shire court as the main provincial court, there were two other local courts, both perpetuated from pre-

Conquest times. The hundred court was a township court; there could be several dozen hundreds within a county. It dealt with minor, noncapital crimes and negotiated disputes among the peasantry arising from their agricultural work.

The hundred court confusingly overlapped with the manorial, or leet, court, whose jurisdiction was over a manorial village's peasant serfs. Presided over by the manorial lord's land steward and using juries, at least informally, it too resolved disputes arising from agricultural labor. But the lord also had the right to exercise "high justice" over his serfs—hang them high for murder and armed robbery. Insofar as the members of the hundred court were free peasants, not serfs, they could not be tried for capital crimes other than in the shire court.

Sometimes the area of jurisdiction of the hundred and manorial court was the same, and the two courts were then combined into one. The confusion arose when the jurisdiction of a hundred court embraced larger or smaller parts of several manorial villages.

At the local level there was one additional mechanism of criminal justice—the "hue and the cry." When a peasant witnessed a serious crime he was supposed to yell "Hue, hue" (a cry still used at hog-calling contests in the southern and midwestern United States), and others who were in earshot were supposed to take up the cry, and they were supposed to try to apprehend the malefactor, pursuing him to the borders of the hundred, where the peasants in the next hundred were supposed to take over.

At all levels of criminal-law jurisdiction, a sentence of outlawry could be imposed by the court. Someone who had resisted a court jurisdiction and fled before trial, or escaped punishment after being convicted, was declared an outlaw. Now he or she "wore the horns of the stag" and could be shot down by anyone's arrow on sight. This institution was perpetuated from the Anglo-Saxon era.

In the towns, which included only 10 percent of the population, shire and hundred courts also operated. The bourgeoisie often paid the king for the privilege of choosing their own sheriff and police officials. Jews imported into England from Rouen to build up trade and start a credit system were under the king's special jurisdiction and protection. Their loan activity was conducted under royal license. The itinerant justices registered the Jewish bankers' loans and helped them collect from debtors, and anyone killing a Jew would have to answer to the sheriff and the royal judges.

All merchants, Christian and Jewish, traveling on the roads were supposed to sound a trumpet periodically to indicate that while they were strangers in the countryside, they were engaged in peaceful activity. Merchant horn sounding was also an Anglo-Saxon practice.

The local mechanisms of criminal justice and self-help policing were effective in maintaining law and order for a king in Anglo-Saxon England. You were less likely to get mugged traveling through rural England in 1120 than in some parts of New York, Detroit, or Los Angeles today. Violence was more often spontaneous than malicious. Everyone, at least all adult males, carried a weapon. Everyone drank strong beer or mead (fermented honey), also very potent. Drunken brawls were frequent. Personal mayhem rather than organized crime was the problem before the thirteenth century. After that organized rural crime became endemic.

At least 90 percent of the judicial system that was in operation a half century after the Norman Conquest was in existence before fierce Duke William stood triumphant on the battlefield of Hastings. If a thegn who had taken a leading part in his shire's court in 1010 turned up in the same county court a hundred years later, he would find little that he was unfamiliar with or miss little that he was familiar with, and the differences were easily explicable.

The visible changes were that the grand jury of indictment was not being used because it could have been employed by resentful Englishmen against the French elite, and the court twice a year was presided over by a panel of circuit judges sent out by the king. There also appeared to be more frequent—but still only occasional—use of the inquest jury of recognition in civil land disputes. One new form of ordeal, trial by battle, had been added. But it was essentially still the same legal system in respect to shire court structure and functions.

At the most local judicial level, the hundred and manorial courts, and the village self-help peace system, nothing had changed. Yet two major changes had come about to affect the development of the common law. These were in the nature of the judicial culture and in the social structure and theory within which the legal system operated. These two cultural and social contexts were affecting the common law's development and slowly pushing it toward further changes.

The ideology of kingship and the structure of feudalism were forces that shaped English law in the twelfth century, impelling change toward the world of Glanville.

The geographical setup of England also played a part in driving the development of the common law. The population of England around 1150 was approaching a million and a half people. This doesn't seem like much, but only 20 percent lived in the northeastern half of the country—an area unsuitable for grain growing and thus a land whose verdant hills were huge sheep and cattle ranges. Similarly, the southwestern extremity of the country, in Cornwall and nearby, was rocky and swampy and was thinly settled even in the nineteenth century.

Close to 80 percent of England's population in the twelfth century was crowded into the lush crop-raising south central rectangle of the country, lying between Kent in the southeast up to a little beyond Cambridge and a bit north of the modern city of Birmingham, across to near the Welsh border, down to Southampton on the Channel coast, and back across to Kent.

This was the "champaign" (field-crop) country of densely settled agricultural villages, small towns, and rich fields of grain cereals. It was a land of lords and peasants.

There was little need for law in the northeast and the southwest—those were patriarchal worlds of traditional dominance by a handful of great tribal families, their kin, and their servants and dependents. But in the champaign meadowlands of the great English south central plain, law was needed to control crime and resolve endless disputes about the retention, inheritance, and transference of valuable land titles. Here in only 40 percent of the total area of medieval England was the classic land of common-law institutions, where legal processes were needed for general welfare. Thus did geography and topography drive the early history of the common law.

And the king's government by 1100 was set up to drain the wealth of the champaign country. The sweetest word that the king ever heard was "escheat." This meant that the lineage of a royal baron's family had died out, given the unhealthy diet and lifestyle of the higher nobility; in any given decade 10 percent of such aristocratic families expired. Then the land reverted back to the king's hand by feudal law of escheat, but now it was richly developed land with thousands of peasant serfs generating rich crops.

6
Kings, Lords, and Lawyers

VIEWED FROM A DISTANCE, most of the judicial system of the Anglo-Saxon era was perpetuated in the Norman
French monarchy after 1066. Yet there was a different and critically important cultural and intellectual ambience in which the
law in England now functioned. There was a different attitude on
the part of the king and his officials toward the law that altered
the place of law in its political and social context and also
impelled legal development toward the framework of the recognizable common law that took shape by the time of Glanville in
the late twelfth century.

The Anglo-Saxon kings had mostly stood aside from the law.
Besides urging that the community courts headed by the shire
courts meet and do justice, and issuing little law codes on dis-
puted points, the legal culture was something tangential to the
Anglo-Saxon king's well-being and ambition. Beginning with
William the Conqueror, the Norman French kings and their

Angevin (or Plantagenet) descendants and successors after 1154 viewed themselves as heads of the legal system, as intimately responsible for the functioning and improvement of law. Importantly for the development of common law, the Norman and Plantagenet kings saw law as an instrument of royal power, as a weapon to assert their control over society, as a way of making their aura and administrative impact felt among great landed families and humble peasant villages alike, and as one means of siphoning wealth from society.

The ambitious involvement of the Anglo-Norman and Angevin rulers of the late eleventh and twelfth centuries in the making of the common law stemmed from their ideology of kingship. The Anglo-Saxon kings too had regarded their office as making themselves God's representative over the people. But the post-Conquest rulers regarded their anointing and crowning to the holy office of kingship as an opportunity and responsibility to be cultivated, more than as a blessing simply to be enjoyed.

Furthermore these Frenchmen bore with them the grandeur and hauteur of the high French aristocracy—members of a restless class who felt they were out on earth to dominate and enhance their status and resources. This aggressiveness was reflected in the ambitious stone buildings they erected, replacing the wooden stockades in which the Anglo-Saxon kings had been content to dwell. It was reflected in the elaborate taxation systems they operated; in the elaborate histories and biographies of themselves they commissioned from skillful, compliant narrative writers; and also in care about the structure and operation of the law. Post-Conquest law, especially for William the Conqueror, his son Henry I, and his great-grandson Henry II, was a matrix that was affected by the high-toned ambitious, activist character of the Anglo-French dynasty that now ruled England (and whose direct descendant still sits on the English throne, even if the bloodline has long become effete and attenuated).

That in the first century after the Norman Conquest there was a tincture of Roman-law ideology in this royal perception of the law is evident. Lanfranc, William the Conqueror's chief minister and effective head of the royal government during the long stretches of time when the king was away fighting on the Continent, was a Roman and canon lawyer with all the authoritarian ideological overtones implied by such a background. In the government of Henry I in the first decades of the twelfth century, particularly in his chancery (document office), there worked a group of clerics steeped in the Roman law tradition. They tried to produce a law code, to be called "The Laws of Henry I," that synthesized indigenous judicial traditions and practices within a Roman-law framework. They did not get far into this work because they soon realized that the synthesis of disparate legal traditions and conflicting judicial cultures could not be accomplished.

What survived of their work is mainly ideological fragments that communicate the authoritarian Roman disposition of their high ambitions. As part of their plan of the Romanization of law in England, they hoped to appoint a resident justice for each county. The lack of sufficient trained lawyers in a country with no native law school (and where none would exist until the late thirteenth century), as well as the prohibitive costs of such a system, requiring three dozen law school graduates, forced them to abandon this type of legal system in favor of the panels of circuit judges, the justices in eyre, a system that could operate with only a half-dozen law school graduates.

But as to where their hearts lay, what these royal clerks of the early years of the twelfth century wanted if they had had the resources, there can be no doubt—it was the imposition of the Justinian heritage on England. That they had to settle for cheaper alternative operations built up out of existing materials made the common law possible. Yet a conventional authoritarian sensibility existed at the core of royal government. At least until the rise of native law schools and a legal profession consciously separate from and hostile to continental law emerged in the late thirteenth century, these royal clerics' Romanist temperament from time to time came to the fore and had a passing impact on the actual shaping of the common law.

As late as the 1140s, Vacarius, one of the leading teachers of Roman law in Bologna, was brought over by Roman-inclined royal clerical officials to coach them on the niceties of the Justinian system then beginning to radiate northward into France and Germany.

The Bolognan visitation came at a particularly unpropitious time for implementation of the Roman system in England. After the death of Henry I in 1135, there was a protracted civil war over the throne between his unpopular daughter Mathilda and his feckless French nephew, Stephen. The long stalemate in this desultory but destructive struggle inevitably weakened royal power and diminished royal wealth. It was no time for Romanization of English law. The perilous political situation countervailed that possibility and threatened the continuation of the strong and wealthy monarchy established by William the Conqueror.

As a result of a compromise peace between the royal claimants, Mathilda's son by the count of Anjou came to the throne as Henry II (Plantagenet) in 1154. The legal issue he faced was how to build on the old institutions of English law, modestly amended after the Norman Conquest, so as to create an indigenous system of civil law and criminal justice that would be at the same time cheap and effective in serving the needs of society and enhancing restored royal power.

Henry II's judges had to give special attention to the legitimacy of land tenure. In order to gain political support within the aristocratic community, Mathilda and Stephen had been lavish in making new grants of lands and attendant privileges from the royal demesne—the lands still in the king's hands at the death of Henry I. Some of these grants by the two contenders for the throne overlapped, and a decision had to be made between rival claimants. In addition, in the two decades of feudal civil war (1135–54)—which Victorian historians called "the Anarchy"—lords both great and small had used the confusion of the time to usurp lands from their more vulnerable neighbors. Now there had to be a systematic effort to establish the rights to disputed tenures, making use of inquests as well as other recourses of the royal judiciary.

The system over which Chief Justice Glanville proudly presided in the 1180s was the ingenious response to this challenge. Yet a kind of visceral Roman palimpsest was still prevalent in royal judicial circles, not trying now for the importation of Roman law (as was then occurring in the Kingdom of France), but rather manipulation of the common law in Henry II's reign (1154–89) in the direction of a fierce royal power. This was an empirical, only vaguely ideological absolutism, as was persuasively demonstrated in the 1950s in a now-much-neglected book, *Angevin Kingship*, by the venerable Oxford don and constitutional historian J. E. Jolliffe.

This trend toward judicial absolutism, parallel to but not specifically imitative of Roman law, reached its peak in the first decade of the thirteenth century in the reign of John (1199–1216), the second son of Henry II to succeed him. A brilliant administrator and intransigently greedy for wealth and power, John ran into two obstacles (aside from spillover from the diplomatic and military alliance of the pope and the ascending French monarchy against him) to his use of common law as an instrument of irresistible royal power. One was the emergence of an ideological party committed consciously to what we would recognize as constitutional liberalism and was known in the thirteenth century as an aspect of philosophical Thomism—the intellectual system developed by Saint Thomas Aquinas at the University of Paris. The other was the distinctive system and concept of landholding in England, which derived from the circumstances of the Norman colonial settlement.

The intricacies of this system of gaining, retaining, inheriting, and transferring land were such that it generated a social and political structure and a derivative judicial culture that operated contrary to authoritarian Roman dispositions. Embedded in England's rich land—productive of grain in the south and supportive of vast sheep and cattle ranches in the north—was a system of social relations that fostered common-law institutions and resisted ideological traditions of Roman absolutism.

Seisin (possession, or tenure) was the key word in the system of landholding that prevailed in England after the Norman Conquest. It lay at the center of civil law, since land and its possession and exploitation were the source of 90 percent of wealth, for four centuries or more after 1066.

Seisin was the application in England of the feudal system of landholding that prevailed in northern France, whence the French settlers of the Norman Conquest stemmed. But because William claimed all of England in 1066 as *terra regis, seisin* and feudal tenure took on distinctive qualities in England that became the platform for developing of the common law of property and generally for the processes and concept of English civil law.

Roman law allowed for absolute ownership of land—private property, *ius in re* (right in the thing), or alod (from the Latin *alodium*). As a result of the colonial conquest of England, only the king fully owned the land. Everyone else who enjoyed and exploited land, in theory at any rate, only possessed it. It was not held absolutely but conditionally. It was possessed, not owned outright. It was held by feudal tenure, not the full ownership of private property.

Those great lords—some one hundred lay magnates and fifty or so ecclesiastical ones—who received land directly from the king and were therefore the king's tenants in chief (also known as the king's barons, the higher nobility, or the aristocracy)—held their munificent lands, the base of their family's or ecclesiastical institution's affluence and influence, in return for service to the king. If they failed to fulfill their obligations, to carry out the terms of "service owed," they were charged with felony, feudal treason. If convicted by their peers (the other tenants in chief) in the king's court, they would lose their lands and with it their status as well as their wealth. "Felony" (which later was used for any capital crime) was therefore the most feared word in the lexicon of a great baron.

William the Conqueror in the first decade of his reign distributed land on *seisin*, conditional tenure, at first mostly to the ecclesiastical magnates. They could be relied on to be more steadfastly loyal to him, and he could use the knights settled on their lands as part of his royal army to keep the lay baronial settlers in hand. Then William started to distribute land to the lay magnates, taking care to distribute a great fief (feudal estate) or honor in two or three blocks in different counties so that one lord would not dominate a whole county.

An exception was made along the Scottish and Welsh frontiers, where the "marcher," or frontier, lords did receive the privilege of single very large blocks of land in return for the onerous task of defending the contiguous borders. As a result separatist traditions developed in the frontier marches, and rebellion in the next five centuries usually began in these regions.

At the time of William's death in 1087, nearly 50 percent of the land was still in the royal demesne. By 1154 only 20 percent was still royal demesne, Mathilda and Stephen having bought support by lavish distribution of land to the great magnates during their conflict over the throne. By 1300 only 10 percent of the country was still in the king's private possession as royal demesne. After that the size of the royal demesne waxed and waned over the centuries. Today 3 percent of England and Wales and perhaps 5 percent of Scotland are in the royal demesne, making Elizabeth II the richest woman by far in the world and the richest person in the United Kingdom.

To receive his feudal estate (fief or honor) in *seisin*, a lord had to become the king's feudal vassal (sworn, loyal follower). In a solemn ceremony he knelt before the king, and the king and the vassal engaged in a two-fisted handshake. This was the act of homage or loyalty by which the vassal became the king's "man." Then the vassal swore fealty (loyalty) to the king, charmingly promising to love what the king loved and hate what the king hated. The king then promised to honor and maintain his vassal.

This maintenance could mean simply keeping the vassal in the royal household and giving him food, military equipment, and spending money. In the late twelfth century there were still hundreds of such royal household knights. But what the magnate wanted was to become a tenant in chief of the king, to get a big land allotment on *seisin* and go out on his own. That is what the game was all about for the lordly family—land tenure—not free beer and steaks in the king's dining hall.

The king "enfiefed" his vassal. He gave him a fief or honor (a very big combination of estates), after the oaths of homage and fealty, which were frequently sealed with a kiss of peace on the mouth. Homoerotic implications were significant in this ceremony, the binding of man to man.

The king handed over a knife to the vassal, signifying that the latter would fight for the king when summoned to do so, and a stalk of grain, signifying the land to be given out on conditional tenure. Then the clerks were called in, and they memorialized the transaction in elaborate charters, after which the royal vassal or tenant in chief took physical possession of the land, built a great house or several such on the land he had received, and prepared to strut high in county and national society as a result of this feudal *seisin*.

The military service owed was for the king's vassal to bring himself and a designated number of armed, trained, and mounted knights (normally stated in multiples of five, up to sixty) to the king's feudal army when the king issued a summons. The length of service was forty days a year, which seems modest until one realizes that in the eleventh and twelfth centuries, armies led by self-indulgent nobility normally fought only during good weather, from mid-June to mid-September, and that medieval soldiers, at least those from the nobility, believed wisely that one big battle a year was sufficient risk to life and limb.

What was important for English development was not William's institution of these rules of military service by tenants in chief in return for lands. Such rules also prevailed in the northern part of France. It was his immediate departure from them. He had already used mercenaries—as much as a third of his army at Hastings. Now in fighting on the Continent, he preferred not to risk again transporting a large number of mounted cavalry in rickety little sailing boats across the hazardous English Channel. He always personally took with him on his continental campaigns between ten and thirty of his lay vassals to serve as his military commanders. The rest of the royal lay vassals stayed home, as did all the bishops and abbots in the ranks of the higher nobility, in return for substantial lump-sum payments to the king and nearly all of their own vassals.

The military service of cavalry contingents that the tenants in chiefs owed King William and his successors was commuted to a money payment of so much per soldier. This was called scutage, "shield money," and with it the king purchased the services of mercenaries on the Continent. Flanders and Brittany as well as Normandy produced a surplus of competent, forever underemployed cavalry.

The complete freedom from personal military service accorded many lay vassals—those who weren't the king's favorite commanders—and the staying at home of nearly all the knightly contingents of the great vassals had enormous social, political, and judicial consequences. Since they did not go to war, many of the higher nobility retained only modest military skills, making them soft and malleable in the face of royal power; and of the five thousand knights of all ranks in England by 1100, the great majority never engaged in professional military conflict in their lifetime. Their armor and swords rusted. They stayed home, put roots into the county, and within two or three generations had become transformed from feudal knights into the gentry of the shire, the local landlords who staffed the juries and did other unpaid legal work for the Crown.

There were two other kinds of service owed in the feudal contract of *seisin*: "suit of court," counseling and judging and legal duties; and various kinds of onerous feudal taxes (besides scutage, which strictly speaking was commutation of military service, not a tax). Three times a year the king held a great feast (resembling the *witan*) in London or in his hunting lodge at Clarendon. The 150 or so tenants in chief were supposed to appear and participate in the festivities, which might include jousting (war games) and listening to minstrels declaim *The Song of Roland* or the King Arthur stories and other epic and romantic poems celebrating the loves and values of the aristocracy. At this time the same group transformed itself into the Great Council of the realm, which approved of legislation desired by the king and advised the king about policy, mainly matters of war and peace. Then the same group, still groggy with strong beer and red meat, became the *curia regis*, the king's court, the venue for trials of the great nobility for felony, breach of feudal contract.

We have an almost word-for-word stenographic record of a felony trial in the king's court from 1088, the first year of the reign of the Conqueror's fierce, gay son William II Rufus. Through a baronial spokesman acting as prosecutor, while the king relaxed on his throne and examined the handsome legs of the secular nobility, a charge of felony was brought against the frontier bishop of Durham, the wily, energetic, and aesthetically advanced Frenchman, William of St. Calais. He planned and began the building of the huge Cathedral of Durham. Built in the Norman perpendicular—a transitional style between Romanesque and Gothic—it is still in use.

Bishop William was guilty as sin. He did not convincingly deny the charge. Instead he claimed the right to go to Rome and be tried for felony treason by the pope. "We are not judging you as a bishop," said Lanfranc sternly, "but as a vassal of the king." The verdict by consensus of the assembled nobility—after suitable jaw-boning—was guilty as charged. Bishop William was stripped of his land and his ecclesiastical office as well and exiled to France, from where a few years later he begged the king to be allowed to come back. As so often happened after a noisy judicial confrontation in the highest ranks of medieval feudal society, the bishop of Durham was forgiven and was restored to his position and possessions.

The trials for felony of the king's great vassals in the *curia regis* were the direct predecessor of trials by peers in the House of Lords after 1300; this privilege continued for the higher nobility until 1925, when a drunken lord committed manslaughter by automobile, insisted on the primordial right of trial by his social equals, and was acquitted, generating democratic outrage and legislative abolition of this hoary judicial privilege.

Technically fiefs were not inheritable and returned into the king's hand on death of the vassal. Since such reversion produced tremendous instability and the threat of downward mobility in the lives of the great landed families, however—upsetting as well the order and routine of the county courts, which were dominated by those families—in practice fiefs and honors became inheritable not later than 1100. *Raoul de Cambrai*, a French poem of around that time, much prized in aristocratic circles, has as its plot an aristocratic heir who is denied inheritance of his patrimony by an obtuse ruler and goes berserk—justifiably, the poet indicates to the approving audience.

Women of the higher nobility could not fight, nor even participate in the bonhommie of the *curia regis*. Nevertheless, if a male line died out, a woman—the eldest daughter or sister or, these lacking, a widow—could inherit lands and the aristocratic title from her father or sibling or husband, if she was married. Her husband, lucky guy, got the woman's body, her lands, and her family title to go with his own, and a summons to the royal court cum council cum feasting hall.

Feudal law recognized that all heirs, including women, could automatically inherit if they paid an inheritance tax called relief—"relieving," or returning, the family lands back from the king's hand. A relief was normally equal to a half year's income from the lords' estate. Since the estate could be generating income of as much as a billion dollars a year in current U.S. money, this levy was substantial. Aristocratic families commonly didn't have so much cash on hand; they were mighty consumers and lavish spenders, not savers. To get the cash to pay a relief, they commonly mortgaged the land to a banker—which is where the Jewish moneylender came in.

The family could usually handle its situation except that if a family had two additional deaths within a decade of the senior landholder's, its inherited tax debt would become unwieldy. The head of the family might have to go on a Crusade to keep from defaulting on his debts and losing a large segment of the family lands—a Crusader's lands were protected by the pope, and a moratorium on Crusaders' debt payments was declared. But this too was awkward. There had to be an ongoing Crusade to join, and those Arabs weren't soft; they had a nasty habit of killing Frenchmen, as they called all Crusaders.

In the same category of tax burden on the king's vassals was feudal wardship. If the heir was an underage male (not yet sixteen) or an underage female (not yet fourteen), or unmarried at any age, or a widow, the king became their guardian. Royal service as guardian of his vassals' heirs was not looked on benignly by the great landed families.

"Wardship" was almost as dirty a word as "felony" among the higher nobility. This was because while the lands were in royal wardship, the king usually sent in agents who rustled the cattle, extorted money from the peasants, and stole the furniture and artwork. Then the king, as guardian, could marry off the ward to anyone he wanted. He was not supposed to "disparage" his wards by marrying them to social inferiors, but in return for a bribe or as political patronage, tough kings like William Rufus and John did just that. The fair flowers of the French aristocracy found themselves hitched to a robber baron or a rough but rich frontier lord of doubtful lineage.

Feudal wardship was not finally abolished until King Charles II in 1662 gave his assent to parliamentary legislation doing just that. Charles had to promise to abolishing wardship before the landed families would let him back into England to claim his beheaded father's throne.

A final form of feudal taxation that fell under the rubric of service owed for lands under *seisin* was aids. There were two kinds—regular and gracious aids. Regular aids belonged to the king as part of his reserved status; they followed from the royal prerogative. When a king knighted his eldest son—that is, recognized his maturity—around age sixteen, married off his eldest daughter for the first time, or was captured and held for ransom, the great nobility had to cough up huge gifts of money, roughly proportional to the income from their estates. The ransom provision actually became operative in the 1190s. The blockheaded giant (he was six feet two in a time when normal male stature was five feet four) Richard I the Lionhearted managed to get captured and held for ransom by the German emperor. Two-thirds of the huge ransom was collected and paid to get Richard home. The balance was never paid.

Gracious aids meant they were freely given by the nobility assembled in the Great Council. The king had to have a purpose for the money, and war against France was the favorite. The higher nobility felt that such extraordinary aid by consent should not be given, or indeed even asked for, more than once every five years—well, maybe three if the king was tough or popular.

Constitutional historians see the feudal gracious aid as the direct predecessor of the Parliament-granted tax of the late thirteenth century and after, called a subsidy. It was indeed a legal precedent, but the subsidy would have developed in any case for various political and economic reasons.

Onerous as were the obligations of royal tenants in chief to the king, nobody ever regarded such status as anything but the best thing under heaven. Not only were they greatly enriched by the landed endowment from the king, but royal vassals enjoyed their position as leaders of both national and county society, with all the political influence, good marriages, and deference from all other ranks of society that went with it.

Each tenant in chief of the king distributed on feudal contract, or "subinfeudated," a substantial portion of the lands he received from the king. So the king's barons had barons or vassals of their own, with precisely the same obligations to themselves as the lord that they, the king's tenants in chief, each owed to the king. A great magnate could have dozens of vassals or "knights" of his own, to whom he had distributed land, who had sworn homage and fealty to him, and who owed him all the ingredients of feudal service including relief, wardship, and attendance at the lord's own baronial court.

Then each of these subvassals or knights could and often did turn around and subinfeudate vassals of their own, generating yet another level in the feudal hierarchy of subtenants, or "mesne tenants," until the lowest level of knight, called *vavasor*, was reached, who either had no infeudated lands and was merely a household knight, or whose fief was a modest piece of land that generated income not much greater than that obtained by the top stratum of peasantry.

While this whole structure and machinery of feudal hierarchy operated, from tenant in chief of the king down three or four levels of subinfeudation to the lowly *vavasor*, the land was toiled and the herds were raised diurnally by the million peasants in

England, who varied greatly in wealth from prosperity to penury. They were enmeshed in a variety of legal statuses, the big distinction being a manorial serf bound to the land and a free peasant who was mobile and who could negotiate in allegedly advantageous circumstances with the lord or his land steward for whatever deals the labor market allowed.

In France subinfeudation implied political weakness for the king in Paris. The great French dukes and counts were nominally the Parisian monarch's vassals, including the duke of Normandy, count of Anjou, and duke of Aquitaine (titles held simultaneously by the fortunate and aggressive Henry II), but such titular lordship meant little because the subvassals owed loyalty to the duke or count, not to the French king. William the Conqueror, who as duke of Normandy was aware of the political weakness inherent in the French system—he nominally gave homage to the French king but spent much of his time fighting him—tried to prevent this situation being replicated in English feudalism.

William and his successors on the throne insisted that they were the "liege lord"—overlord—not only of their immediate tenants in chief but of every subvassal, down to the lowliest and loneliest *vavasor* in the realm. There is a story that as he aged, and two years before he died, William gathered every vassal in the whole feudal hierarchy in a huge field in central England and had them all swear loyalty to him, an act of homage that would prevail over their loyalty to their immediate lords.

Such dramatic oath swearing wouldn't mean much unless the king was strong and awesome and his administration effective in reaching down into county society. Generally this long arm of the monarchy was effective, and in this regard the emergence of the circuit judge system in the early twelfth century and its intensification in the age of Glanville was politically important. If twice a year the royal judges presided over the county court and all sorts of judicial and administrative business got done under the itinerant justices' aegis, that was a powerful and repeated reminder of the king's liege lordship. Also effective in casting the long royal shadow was the impaneling of juries of recognition by royal writ in civil actions, and the royal mandate for the forming of grand juries and the indictment of malefactors before the king's itinerant justices.

With regard to deployment of the shire courts as emblems and instruments of royal power over society, there was, however, at the beginning of Henry II's reign a limitation in royal jurisdiction. Each baron had the right to set up a feudal court, a court baron, a miniature replication of the *curia regis*, and preside over disputes over landholding between his own immediate vassals. Around 1120, perhaps in a weak political moment when he was justifiably worried whether the magnates would allow his unpopular daughter, Mathilda, to succeed him, Henry I had issued a law confirming this important jurisdiction of the baronial courts over land disputes between two vassals of the same lord.

In the eighty or so years following the onset of the Angevin legal revolution in the 1160s, the key segments of judicial action were transferred out of the baronial courts into the royal courts, to the shire courts under the itinerant justices, and to central royal courts in Westminster. By the fourth decade of the thirteenth century, the baronial courts had little or no judicial business—all cases of civil action, all land disputes, irrespective of the prevailing lordship over the litigants, were now in the royal courts. The baronial courts became "courtly"—social occasions during which romantic poetry was recited and dances were held; they were no longer law courts.

This drawing of all land disputes into the royal courts between 1165 and 1240 had more to do with the practical imposition of royal authority over the subvassals than with the swearing of mighty oaths of liege lordship. No matter who your lord was, the litigation on which maintenance and enhancement of your family's wealth depended was now under royal judicial jurisdiction. Nothing could be more important than this juristic expansion in enhancing royal power, in bringing down the shadow of royal government onto the daily life of every member of landed society, from earl and bishop to ordinary gentry and obscure *vavasor*. And by the royal judges liberally allowing any peasant who wanted to, or who could afford it, access to the shire court, the mass of peasantry as well was absorbed into royal law, which by the mid-thirteenth century constituted a national law.

There were three kinds of judicial action by which cases were transferred from the baronial to the royal courts, eventually nullifying the legal operations of the baronial courts. First was the writ *praecipe*, employed by Henry II's government, by which the sheriff was simply ordered to stop a case from being litigated in a baronial court and to transfer it to the county court under royal judges. This writ had no place in feudal tradition nor was it created by legislation of the Great Council of magnates. It had no sanction; it was arbitrary. It wounded the pride as well as undermined the legal privileges of barons over their vassals. It was abolished by Magna Carta in 1215 and stayed abolished in the final, official version of Magna Carta, issued in 1225.

The second way of transferring a case to the royal from a baronial court was by a writ of right, which was an appeal mechanism. A case having been tried in a baronial court, the losing party got a royal writ of right on grounds of "default of justice"—a nominal claim, a formality of expression—and the case was heard over again in a royal court, and the decision in the baronial court could be overruled.

In the three decades after Magna Carta of 1215, the royal courts also accepted writs of entry as a way of nullifying baronial judicial jurisdiction. Writs of entry had the same effect as *praecipe* but they were legal; they had sanction. A writ of entry was an examination of long-term title to land and not merely recent possession—what Glanville and the judges of the 1180s called a "grand assizes" (long-term claim to title) as compared to a "petty assizes" (recent possession). The royal courts, because of the need to engage in scrutiny of charters and to consult royal administrative and legal records, asserted a monopoly of inquiry into ultimate title so that "perfect equity," as Glanville optimistically called it, could be achieved, even if the litigants were subvassals of the same lord.

A grand assize under a writ of entry precipitated an expensive and often lengthy piece of litigation, involving searching for title, that could go back several decades beyond the memory of juries, and regular examination of puzzling written records. The case might never come to a conclusion, frustrating Glanville's triumphant heralding of the grand assizes as a breakthrough in judicial structuring.

But in the decades following Magna Carta's abolition of *praecipe*, a writ of entry was also used as a legal fiction to gain the same purpose as *praecipe*. Ostensibly searching for title, the case could actually involve only recent possession, not long-term title. It was in this instance a legal subterfuge to get the case from a baronial to the royal court.

The motivation behind the drawing of all land disputes into royal courts, which was completed by around 1240, and the nullifying of the baronial courts as legal entities—a key development in the making of the common law—has been much debated by historians. The classical interpretation, already proposed by Stubbs in 1870, was propounded by Maitland around 1900 in his magisterial history of the rise of the common law. According to Maitland's exposition, the factors involved were a combination of the political ambitions of the monarchy; the intention of the royal judges to create a rational and national system of civil law separate from but in effect parallel to Roman law; and the family and personal interests especially of the gentry, who felt more sure of justice in land litigation in royal rather than in baronial courts, where a lord's prejudices could shape the decision.

Milsom in the 1970s offered a depoliticized alternative, much applauded by historians resident in law schools. As such legal historians prefer, Milsom vested the change tightly within judicial functions and almost entirely outside the framework of political ambitions and royal policy. The complexity of litigation over landholding within the intricate system of feudal relationships was such that the baronial courts could not handle these actions, in Milsom's account. The pressure of litigation and the complexity of process was such that the great barons themselves recognized that their modest baronial courts were incapable of resolving this ever expanding, ever more sophisticated block of civil actions. Only the royal courts had the judges, the records, the evidentiary juries, the legal consultants, and finally the authority to enforce judgments that could satisfy the needs of great families and ordinary gentry alike.

Thus in the Milsom thesis the transformation of landed actions and the transference of cases from the baronial to royal courts arose out of the integral circumstances of the land law itself and the judicial and economic needs of all classes, led by the great lords themselves.

Which interpretation you follow, Maitland's or Milsom's, depends heavily on the documents you read. If you read both political and legal documents, you will be inclined to agree with Maitland. But, following the canons of recent legal history, if you write legal history entirely from judicial records, you will view the advance of the dominance of royal courts in land law as generated by pressures inside judicial actions and the instinctive needs of interested parties, particularly the higher nobility, with their initiative in recognizing the dysfunctional character of their own baronial courts and their need for the process that only royal courts could provide.

The dispute between Maitland and Milsom is grounded in whether you see legal institutions changing in the context of broad political, social, and cultural factors or within the purview only of legal mechanisms, the needs of litigants, and the artful devices of judges and lawyers. While in the period 1920 to 1970, legal historians situated in law schools—in the heyday of legal realism and its totalizing proclivity to sociology and sympathy for Marxism—hailed Maitland, in recent decades a positivist narrowing of focus to the confines of professional boundaries has generated the view that only lawyers make law, a dogma presumably flattering to law students and their teachers.

Thus the useful way of perceiving the Maitland-Milsom controversy is to look at the genre of available documentation for the Angevin legal revolution. If you think that contemporary writers who were working in the legal system, such as Roger of Howden, a clerical chronicler who was also a royal justice and therefore Glanville's colleague; or who were not lawyers but still courtiers, like Walter Map and Gerald of Wales, retailing gossip about the king and his ministers, whom they knew "up close and personal"; or humanistic writers on political theory like John of Salisbury, who was for many years the chief secretary of the archbishop of Canterbury—if you think these kinds of writers were misinformed or mischievous, you will probably come out on Milsom's side.

If Maitland's is a sociological approach to explaining the emergence of the common law, and Milsom's a strictly judicial one, a third and distinctive perception arises from Michael Clanchy's seminal *From Memory to Written Record* (1979, extensively revised edition 1993).

Clanchy's approach may be viewed as essentially anthropological in character. From reading his innovative and insightful book, one perceives that the development of English law in the twelfth century was occurring precisely at the time that England was in the process of transition from an oral to a literate culture, from one in which memory was the exclusive or main repository of legal knowledge to one in which written documents such as writs, charters, and innovatively records of litigation were playing an increasingly important role, although facets of memory such as the juries' recollections about landholding and crimes were also crucial. Written records were coming to play key roles in litigation, but oral pleading in court remained important.

Theorists like Walter Ong and Marshall McLuhan in the 1960s and 1970s made the polarity between oral and literate cultures the critical fulcrum of all human history, and in the 1980s and 1990s the orality/literary paradigm became immensely popular among critics of medieval belletristic literature. Without engaging in this level of grand theory, or trying to define precisely the tenuous difference between an oral and written culture or whether such a naked polarity ever actually existed in the medieval world, it can be recognized that Clanchy has made an important contribution in pointing to the need to perceive the rise of common law in this anthropological context.

There is no question that the latter half of the twelfth century saw an explosive escalation in the facets of written culture, exemplified by a vast outpouring of all kinds of written materials and the rapid multiplication of highly literate people, mostly males, among whom were well-trained products of the new universities. Given the available forms of written communication, the written instruments of social conditioning and political control, and the ambitions of the university graduates for employment and power, a drastic alteration in legal processes was bound to occur in England.

In fact the use of written records in law as in other facets of English royal administration itself impressed on society the importance and utility of literate communication. The English shift from orality to literacy was led by government officials rather than poets. When a royal writ started a lawsuit that could mean enrichment or impoverishment for a gentry family, when a record in a court case had a measure of finality that was difficult and expensive or impossible to modify or expunge, the fearful meaning of literacy and its social and personal consequences was brought home to provincial and local society. It meant that access to literacy or to experts who could use its power on behalf of clients and petitioners in the law courts was brilliantly advertised.

Viewed in this way, as occurring somewhere on the fault line between oral and literate cultures, there was bound to be a legal revolution, and this judicial upheaval was bound to generate in time a legal profession, which in turn would promote further modification and sophistication in the law.

The oral/literate polarity can be drawn upon to provide one explanation of why England rejected Roman law. There is no more intriguing question in all of legal history than why England did not follow the continental pattern and adopt Roman law in the time of its strong state building in the twelfth century. Why at the time when the German emperor was endorsing the Justinian code (at least for his Italian domains) and in the late twelfth century the Roman-law graduates were eagerly hired by the newly energetic French monarchy, did the Angevin legal revolution go in a different direction, to what we know as the common law?

The answer given by Stubbs in the nineteenth century, that the heavy carryover of Anglo-Saxon legal institutions impeded Roman penetration, remains generally rejected as smacking of Victorian organic determinism, even though R. C. van Caenegem has provided persuasive empirical evidence of Anglo-Saxon judicial continuity into the twelfth century.

The view held by both Maitland substantially and Milsom exclusively is that *seisin*, a system of conditional tenures arising from Anglo-Norman feudalism, was critically different than the Roman idea of property or full private ownership of land. Given the central importance of the land law in shaping all of English civil law, *seisin* was the determining force in English legal culture and drove English law away from Roman law. There is much weight to this argument, although like Stubbs's Anglo-Saxon freedom it is reductionist. Its specific weakness is that as all fiefs became inheritable, land tenure remained formally conditional, but in practice over time it became steadily more difficult to terminate *seisin* judicially. By the fourteenth century *seisin* had turned into freehold ("fee simple"), which was close to Roman private property.

Three fortuitous circumstances also played a greater or lesser role in separating common law from Roman law. Henry II and his judges in the first decade of his reign already found in operation a fragmentary legal system, using unpaid juries and panels of itinerant justices rather than resident county judges. This incomplete system was cheap to operate, much more so than the professionally staffed Roman system would have been, and Henry II and his officials built on this base. Common law was thus a judicial cost-saving venture.

The common law as it functioned in the late twelfth century represented an income-bearing item in the balance sheet of a greedy monarchy, needing to siphon ever larger funding from society to meet the costs of the elaborate royal lifestyle and the king's ambitious foreign policy. The profits of justice were something the king and his officials readily visualized when they contemplated the judicial system.

Five percent of the income of the Angevin crown came from the profits of justice. On the civil side the common law produced steady income by the fees paid to the chancery for the issuing of writs to start legal actions, or to secure recording of settlements and judgment in land disputes. On the criminal side, the chattels (movable property) of executed murderers and robbers belonged to the Crown. These were normally humble items—a cow, a bed, a plow—but seized by assiduous sheriffs and their assistants, the income mounted up. Even a farm animal that by mischance had caused a death—an ox that killed a child—belonged to the Crown.

When the king and his officials thought about the profits of justice around 1180, they realized that introduction of a Roman-law system such as was at that time proliferating in the territory of the Parisian monarchy would sharply reduce the profits of justice, since Roman law meant a cohort of highly trained judges and the sophisticated law schools to train them. Common law may have seemed amateurish and jerry-built in some respects compared to Roman law, but it was much more profitable for the crown.

A second adventitious circumstance was that in the period of the Angevin legal revolution there were no Roman law schools in England. The new University of Oxford devoted itself to the humanities and theology, not law. If Oxford had established a Roman-law school around 1160, the outcome for English law would have been different. When England got native law schools in the late thirteenth century they not only taught common law exclusively. They were ideologically as well as empirically hostile to Roman law. The impact of law schools on judicial development cannot be underestimated, as witness Bologna's importance for the European continent in the twelfth century, or Harvard Law School's impact on American law from the 1890s to the 1930s.

A third fortuitous circumstance was church-state relations in England. Henry II was determined to perpetuate his predecessors' policy of asserting royal authority over the church in England and to keep the papacy from interference. To this end he not only precipitated the murder of Archbishop Thomas Becket. He also prohibited papal inquisitors from landing on English shores to pursue heretics. Popular heresy was not the problem in England that it was in France, perhaps because England was less urbanized than France, and Henry II's government tried and burned the handful of heretics there (mostly Oxford graduate students) on its own, without aid of the papal inquisition. The courts of the latter were staffed with canon lawyers trained in the Roman tradition, used the techniques and processes of Roman law courts, and helped to familiarize areas where they operated with the Roman-canonical tradition. That influence was lacking in England. No papal inquisitions in England meant no Roman law. Anyone who has read Umberto Eco's novel, *The Name of the Rose*, or seen the film based on it, which depicts an inquistorial court at work, will see the strength of this argument.

To these explanations of why England developed its own common-law system may be added two perceptions arising from Clanchy's identification of twelfth-century England as undergoing transition from an oral to a literate society.

The first perception is that common law combines ingredients of both oral and written law and perfectly reflects the conditions of a transition from one culture to another. The second perception is that the fault line between oral and literate cultures releases dynamic and innovative cultural forces and is conducive to fresh thinking and experimentation, which are reflected in the Angevin legal revolution from about 1165 to about 1235.

Yet another way of looking at the making of the common law arises from reflecting on the implications of two recent books—Richard Southern's *Scholastic Humanism and the Unification of Europe*, vol. 1 (1995), and Robert Bartlett's study of medieval frontier societies, *The Making of Europe* (1993)—buttressed perhaps by a cultural version of American historical sciologist Immanuel Wallerstein's world-historical Marxist paradigm of core and periphery societies.

In the twelfth century a richly textured hegemonic culture—what Southern calls scholastic humanism—centered in the cathedral schools and the universities that grew out of them was in the process of emergence and solidification. Roman legal study, using the same dialectical exposition as exhibited in philosophy and theology, was very much a part of this doctrinaire scholastic culture, exemplified for Southern in Gratian's codification of the canon law in 1140 along Romanist lines.

England was an economically rich, politically advanced society but nevertheless a frontier one, a periphery culture compared to the core scholastic culture that gestated in northern France, the Rhineland, and northern Italy. It was a place where the propensity of scholastic humanism toward the imposition of rationality and learned tradition on social operations was exhibited, but only marginally so. Given England's frontier and periphery status, it developed its own legal system separate from the Continent and found a unique solution to the problem of imposing learned intelligence on society.

7
Bracton's Courtroom

IN THE 1250S, JUST three-quarters of a century after *Glanville* was written by two royal judges, another royal judge, Henry of Bracton, was working assiduously on his treatise on the common law.

Bracton was, like the authors of *Glanville*, a middle-class lawyer with many decades of service to the Crown. His treatise, however, *The Laws and Customs of England*, was more learned, ambitious, and theoretical than its predecessor. Written when the Angevin legal revolution was coming to fruition in the concluding phase of the initial creative era of the common law, it reflected this judicial context of satisfaction and optimism.

Bracton's treatise, written in Latin, is a long work, running about 450 pages in modern type. Its textual history has been peculiar. Whether Bracton would have considered that he had finished the treatise when he died in 1268, we do not know. Since there are no extant copies from his own day, it may be concluded that he never finished it and never published it by sending multiple copies out to be deposited in important libraries, the method of publication in manuscript in the days before printing began at the end of the fifteenth century.

In the fourteenth century, when, for mainly political reasons, Bracton was popular in some influential circles and copies of the treatise were in demand, a manuscript copyist conflated Bracton's original text with some detailed commentaries that had been written about the treatise in the century after Bracton wrote. Some of these expanded on points that Bracton made. Some appear to have tried to deemphasize the Roman-law references that appear frequently in the text, and at least one strongly denied the political theory that distinguishes the treatise. All these commentaries were then incorporated into the original text, without appropriate distinction and set-asides, making the treatise confusingly jumbled in places, and Bracton appear to be self-contradictory in his political theory of law.

It is this conflated text that is the prime manuscript tradition coming down from the later Middle Ages to modern readers. Two American legal historians—George Woodbine at Yale and Samuel Thorne at Harvard, in the 1920s and 1930s and the 1950s and 1960s, respectively—devoted the major part of their scholarly careers to restoring Bracton's original text, and finally such a reliable version became available in the 1970s, with an excellent translation from not easy Latin provided by Samuel Thorne, who in the course of his long and arduous labors trained all the legal historians produced by Harvard Law School during more than three decades.

Henry of Bracton was the last of the great English ecclesiastical lawyers of the Middle Ages. He wrote just before the establishment of purely secular professional law schools in London. He belonged to a generation in which an eager middle-class young man, seeking to become learned in the law in more than just an empirical training-on-the-job manner, would make his way to the

Continent, in Bracton's case to the University of Paris, and study Roman and canon law there.

Not only was Bracton deeply learned in the Roman-canonical tradition, but he was greatly influenced in his outlook by the rising philosophy and general intellectual movement in Paris, which came to be called Thomism after its most memorable exponent, Saint Thomas Aquinas. When Bracton studied at Paris in the 1220s, Thomas of Aquino, a Dominican friar from an aristocratic Neapolitan family, was still just a graduate student there, in the classroom of Albert the German (also known as Albert the Great) another Dominican friar. But the political and legal ideas, stressing restraint of power, the rule of law, and a consensual view of institutions, was already in the radical academic air of the Left Bank. Indeed, the founder of this movement of philosophical and judicial liberalism was probably a clerical professor from England, Stephen Langton, who taught at Paris in the first decade of the thirteenth century, went on to work in the papal government in Rome, and ended up as a highly controversial and politically activist archbishop of Canterbury.

Langton, Albert the German, and Aquinas were in the full sense of the term churchmen; Bracton was not. To be a student at Paris in the thirteenth century you had to be in holy orders—that is, nominally a churchman—but Bracton's ambition and interest focused not on serving the church, but rather on working as a lawyer in the royal administration. In temperament he was a secular lawyer. Pursuing that inclination, he had a very successful career, becoming the leading royal judge of his time. Notes that he made on cases while on circuit—which he studied intensively while writing his treatise—have survived, and the judicial records of the time also show him working very hard, presiding over panels of circuit judges and hearing both civil and criminal cases. His treatise shows that he was particularly interested in contract law, the exposition of which in his treatise makes extensive use of Roman law. But Bracton also appears to have been fascinated by criminal trials and to have reflected much on the developing jury-of-verdict system.

Bracton's legal interests were also centered on constitutional law, arising from the relationship between royal government and judicial operations. It is in this latter capacity, that of judicial theorist, that he attracted the attention of later generations and was still quoted by constitutional liberals in the nineteenth century.

What pushed this immensely successful lawyer and judge in the direction of constitutional doctrine was the proto-Thomist philosophy he imbibed at Paris; his own empirical efforts as a judge in trying to balance the centralizing power of the royal courts with a determination to do justice in particular cases; and his continued association into the 1250s with what can be termed the political left in England of his day, led by a faction in the high aristocracy, by a prominent bishop, and by the head of the new Franciscan order of friars in England.

Bracton appeals to modern writers and thinkers about jurisprudence because he combined great success at the bar and on the bench with keen attention to the liberal philosophical and political trends of his day. He stands at the head of a long English tradition of political liberalism, asserting the rule of law over strong government.

It is not anachronistic to see Bracton as a kind of medieval Holmes or Brandeis. It is not surprising that Yale and Harvard Law Schools devoted so much expensive professorial time to producing a genuine text of his treatise. Though also well aware of the laborious textual restoration that needed to be done, legal scholars in modern England did not want to devote their careers to the task.

Bracton's early judicial career was spent as a protégé and junior colleague of an eminent judge, Walter Ralegh. Some scholars have recently seen Ralegh as the major author of the treatise that bears Bracton's name, but there is no reason to sustain this hypothesis. The treatise that bears Bracton's name is the work of a man learned in Roman law derived from clerical and continental traditions, as well as a master of the procedures and ideas of the common law. For Ralegh to be the author of the Bracton treatise, the work would have had to be written before 1240. The text of the treatise reflects, however, the maturing of the common law in the expanded jury system and the liberal ideas imported from Paris that were eventually to be identified with Thomism.

These qualities point to the version of the treatise that we know to have been written in the 1250s and 1260s. This signifying content of the treatise, as well as the knowledgeable attributions in medieval manuscripts, definitively point to Henry of Bracton as the author of the treatise that bears his name, although what he learned as Ralegh's protégé and colleague could naturally have entered into the composition of written work as it took shape under his pen in the fifties and sixties.

Bracton was a Devonshire man, from the southwest of England. This is where King Arthur's Camelot is believed to have been located. It is also the locale of "Wessex," where Thomas Hardy's novels are set and where Hardy lived most of his life. This part of England lies apart from the main road system stretching northwest and northeast from London, and in the Middle Ages it was therefore a region somewhat isolated from the rest of the country.

Devonshire people are supposed to be quiet, unconventional, and inner-directed, with an intense love of their somewhat rocky and bleak land. We can picture Bracton fitting into this stereotype. We can picture him on the southwest circuit as a native returned to his beautiful and isolated homeland, thinking deeply about what the common law was doing to break down regional isolation and to bring Devonshire, as elsewhere, into a generalized legal and political culture.

He probably had mixed feelings about this development. He was enthusiastic about the law, but he was sensitive to its leveling effect. (He would probably have liked Thomas Hardy's novels and could have seen himself as a secondary character in *Far from the Madding Crowd* and *The Return of the Native*.)

In the last two decades of his life Bracton was chancellor of Exeter Cathedral, located in his homeland. This does not, however, mean he was committed to the church as an institution. In the Middle Ages, giving senior bureaucrats sinecures in the church was a way of rewarding them with a lavish supplementary income and pension. The chancellor of a cathedral was the chief judicial official for a bishop. Bracton would have followed standard practice and hired a canon lawyer to perform the normal responsibility of the office. Possibly he took off two or three weeks a year to visit Exeter and consult with the bishop and his own surrogate and handle an important case in the bishop's court. But his heart and mind lay with the common law.

Bracton was proud of the way the law was developing, and he had reason to be. In the seventy years since Glanville wrote, the edifice of the common law erected on the foundations of the circuit judge system, the jury, and the law of *seisin* was being topped off, and, most important, the adversarial shape and rhythm of pleading—trials in court—were clarified and intensified.

In one of his more brilliant discussions, Maitland pointed to the exception, or "special plea," as the narrow gateway toward the complex thicket of a more recognizably modern kind of litigation. This meant not rushing through a case in a few minutes with the outcome predetermined by the testimony of the jury or inquest in a civil dispute, or the indictment and verdict by juries in a criminal trial, but slowing down the breakneck speed of Angevin trials to consider specific issues in court, in the presence of the judges that the jury had not previously agreed upon before the court met. It meant the judges turning to a jury and asking them now to consider an issue they had not previously considered—here is the slim forecasting of modern trial by jury, the beginning of the transition over the next two hundred and fifty years or so from the self-informing medieval jury to the trial-informing modern jury.

Maitland saw the exception, or special plea (the former is from the Latin term, found in Roman law; the latter is the English term commonly used by the fifteenth century), as the key that turned the lock in the making of common law trial process. With it judicial thinking in general became more sophisticated and more prone to examine minutely the facts of the case.

When exceptions began to be pleaded at the end of the twelfth century, at the assize trials, the older generation of judges must have been unhappy that they could not rush through every trial and be at the local inn by late in the afternoon. By Bracton's day the judges accepted with equanimity this slowing down of trial procedure because better decisions and a higher content of justice would be rendered.

Incidentally the legitimation of the exception also made resort to counsel in civil actions more necessary and contributed mightily to the development and enrichment of a legal profession headed by professional experts.

In an exception, or special plea, the defendant did *not* make a formal or simple denial: "I did not kill William three days after Michaelmas." The defendant responded in some special way that was not a simple negative: "The jury was impaneled under the wrong assize writ"; "I plead benefit of clergy." As we examine the plea rolls—the summary Latin record of court proceeding on the case and the judgment rendered, which begin for us in the mid–1190s—we see the exceptions slowly but steadily increasing in number and with these special pleas the length and complexity of cases increasing.

This was much more true of civil than of criminal actions, partly because judges were not inclined to interrupt the condemnation falling on a defendant's head from the combined rendering of two sworn panels of neighbors, the grand jury indictment, and the petty jury's verdict; and partly because attorneys in criminal cases before the seventeenth century were not allowed to speak in court except in treason cases, although presumably a lawyer could stand behind the defendant and whisper advice to him.

But attorneys (the term is from Roman law) could by Bracton's day actively and fully represent a client in court in a civil action. To use their expertise, to win a case and elevate their fees, they made as great a use of the exceptions as judges would allow if their clients' cases were inherently vulnerable.

As a result any landowner who went to court in an assize land case or to a central court in Westminster without an attorney was either very foolish or too poor to afford one. Law cases now became much more technical and the pleading back and forth more incisive and subtle. You had little chance without counsel, unless your case was so blatantly strong that a jury would support you vehemently and unflinchingly without counsel.

The cases in land law over which Bracton presided by 1250 were like those tennis matches that were now the rage at the vanguard French aristocratic social courts: back and forth, back and forth, the attorneys trying to get the judge to frame the case for the jury, resulting from pleading of exceptions, and denials of such so that the jury would focus on an issue in such a way that a lawyer's client would be favored.

This adversarial clash had a name that sounded like a tennis match: it was called a "traverse." An ordinary negative plea by a defendant was a general (that is, standard) traverse; the exception was often called a special traverse. The attorney aimed swift dispatch of the judicial ball into the far corner of the opponent's territory. Game, set, and match. It required great experience, wit, and forensic skills to triumph in this fast-paced litigation—as it does today, which is why 80 percent of lawyers never dare set foot in a common-law courtroom but leave litigation to experts.

It worried Bracton, so ethical in his temperament, so committed to achieving justice in society, that the common law—especially in civil actions about possession of land—was steadily becoming more complex and that it was very hard to proceed without knowledge of the intricate processes of the land law. Even deciding which writ to seek from the king's chancery to start a case was a worrisome challenge. Get the wrong writ and your case could be thrown out on a claim of exception even before trial had started.

We have seen that there were four possessory assizes: *novel disseisin* (recent dispossession, the simplest judicially); *mort d'ancestor* (inheritance from recent possessor); *utrum* (whether a piece of land was under regular feudal tenure owing rents and taxes, or "free alms," that is, charitable tenure given sometimes to an ecclesiastical institution); and *darein presentment* (who had been the last appointer of a priest to his "advowson," the land attached to the church, which helped to support him, and therefore which landlord ultimately owned this land).

Cases emerged in which it was not easy to see which writ best fitted the case. Make a wrong decision in the eyes of the judges when it came to trial, and you would lose your suit. Then there was a problem whether land came under petty assizes, or by writ of entry of the grand assizes, involving title going back decades. The latter gave greater security of tenure if you won your case, but grand assizes often led to no decision—the land had been granted in the past beyond the memory of living jurors of the neighborhood, and there was no extant documentation, or there was a charter but its genuineness was moot. Another hard choice; better hire the best lawyer you could afford and hope that he would know what to do.

These complexities and ambiguities frustrated judges too. Their easy in-and-out-of-town schedules to hold the assizes was changing. Not only as the population rose steadily were there more litigants, but cases could now take longer, involve very subtle issues, and require close attention on the part of the judges and exercise of rather high levels of legal reasoning. Being a royal judge had always been demanding. Now it was becoming even more difficult.

It was a good thing that the judges of Bracton's day were well rewarded. They got a salary roughly equivalent to that of a U.S. Supreme Court justice today. If, like Bracton, they picked up a government or church sinecure on the side, that made them affluent and was a hedge against old age. In addition in important cases, involving a rich piece of land, it was customary for both litigants to tip the judges beforehand. If the gifts of both parties were of approximately equal value, that was not considered bribery.

By Bracton's day, there was a shortage of lawyers in England. The lawyers were mostly former judges, and a judge in harness could serve as an attorney on a case not in his own court. There was a great need in Bracton's day for native law schools, focusing on the civil side of the common law, the complex world of *seisin*. By the last decade of the thirteenth century, there were four such schools in London, the Inns of Court, annually graduating lawyers. They are still training barristers today—some might say with a cast of mind stuck in the fourteenth century.

Another advance in the common law in Bracton's day was the further development of the jury of verdict in criminal trials. Its replacement of ordeals, and for the most part of compurgation, had been done by the judges acting on their own review of what was needed. The jury of verdict was never legislated. The defendant therefore had to formally accept a jury verdict—he had "to put himself on the country." Most defendants went along; some were pressured or tricked by judges into doing so.

Recalcitrants were subjected to *peine forte et dure*, the only action approaching Roman-law torture in English common law. The defendant was placed on the ground and stones were piled on his chest until he either expired or groaned, "Country, country," indicating his acceptance of the jury of verdict. There are plenty of instances in the plea rolls where it is noted that the defendant would not put himself on the country. Rather than judicial torture, the judges simply went ahead and got the guilty verdict and hanged the defendant anyway. Dead men make no appeals, was their valid assumption. By 1325 the jury of verdict was an integral part of the trial, and defendants were no longer asked to put themselves on the country.

Bracton and his colleagues had fun with the size of the jury of verdict. The jury of verdict in its early days numbered twelve, or twenty-four, or thirty-six, or forty-eight. Finally the cost and the complexities of getting larger numbers than the minimum twelve into court led to the standardization at twelve. The grand jury was usually twenty-four, so the jury of indictment was indeed grand numerically and the jury of verdict truly petty in comparison.

In the time between Glanville and Bracton the central court system at Westminster in London (essentially unchanged until 1873 and still substantially in existence) was elaborated and defined. It was decided what were the central courts and, given the maddening medieval love of overlapping confusion, what were the differences in jurisdiction among the central courts and what were the routes of appeal from the shire or assizes court to the central courts.

To illustrate the development of the central courts in Westminster, historians used to draw boxes. There was one big box called *curia regis*, the king's court, and then projecting from this central box were three smaller boxes called Exchequer, King's Bench (originally in Latin *coram regis*, "in the presence of the king"), and Common Pleas (originally "common bench," *de banco*). This diagram is not wrong. It does in a way depict the development of the central courts from around 1120 to Bracton's day in the mid-thirteenth century. But it gives too much rigidity to a fluid situation and a somewhat misleading impression of the functional relationships existing in the central court system.

In the first place, by way of correction, it should be noted that this first projection out of the amorphous mass of the *curia regis*, the king's central court, was the Chancery, the writing office under the chancellor, where three or four clerks in 1120, perhaps a dozen in Bracton's day, sat daily and prepared judicial documents at long benches, illuminating the room with smoky candles, scribbling with pens on vellum.

The Chancery clerks produced charters and writs of grace, and later the vast streams of writs of course that automatically set up, through the sheriff of the county, the assize juries. They drafted charters and all sorts of other royal documents, some open and formal with a seal at the bottom (hence "letters patent," open letters) and many other slim administrative memoranda or pithy royal commands, folded over and sealed (hence "letters close," enclosed letters).

The Chancery was crucial for the operation of all other courts, but it did not itself develop as a court until the mid-fifteenth century, when the chancellor received petitions from protected classes and took swift action to protect widows, wards, and lunatics. Until then the Chancery made all the engines of the judicial system operate in a support position, an absolutely critical documentary service division of royal government and law, incidentally impressing on all of landed society the value and distinctiveness of written communications and record keeping.

The first specialized court to emerge from the *curia regis* was the Exchequer court. It was in operation by 1120. It relied on the Exchequer's neat and detailed tax records, called Pipe Rolls.

Using an abacus system for doing accounts, the senior officials of the Exchequer set up a tax court to hear cases of delinquency on the part of tenants in chief and sheriffs who were supposed to deliver their "farms" to the treasury twice a year—the farms being funds derived from the royal demesne in their counties—along with the profits of justice—fines and expropriations of various kinds. Well into modern times the judges who sat in the upper branch of the Exchequer, the tax court, were still called not justices or judges, but "barons," which was what they were called and who they were in the 1120s.

The rationality and thoroughness of the Exchequer was exemplified in its relationship with the Jewish community in England.

By the late twelfth century there may have been two thousand Jews in England, concentrated in three cities: London, Lincoln, and York. Their banking and credit activities (what the medievals called usury) were so successful, under royal protection and license, that the special taxes that the monarchy in turn imposed on the Jews returned 20 percent of the annual income of the crown. The Angevin government set up a separate branch of the treasury, the Exchequer of the Jews, to keep track of this income.

Thereby the Angevin Exchequer could hit a great nobleman with a double whammy. Not only was he subject to a variety of taxes imposed by the Crown, but after he got into debt, as most lords did because of their extravagant lifestyle, the Exchequer collected from the Jewish bankers the greater part of the income they had previously derived from making loans to the nobleman.

Nothing hurts more than paying taxes, and nothing is more humiliating than being pressed to pay back taxes or pay up on loans. The Exchequer constantly pressed aristocrats as well as others to pay up their back taxes, and the royal officials helped the Jewish bankers to collect on their loans to the nobility. Everywhere a great lord looked, the treasury officials and their tax court were on his heels. No wonder that John of Salisbury depicted the administrators of twelfth-century England as a dark force of tyranny. He reflected the wounded exasperation of his ecclesiastical and aristocratic patrons.

The successful work of the Exchequer courts, its success in going after tax delinquents, demonstrated the advantage of having courts in Westminster with specified purposes. After much experimentation and confusion, by the early thirteenth century, two new central courts had been developed—King's Bench and Common Pleas. They are still in existence.

King's Bench dealt with lawsuits between the king and one of his subjects, usually about royal lands or privileges such as his monopoly over wild game in his million-acre hunting preserves. Cases of feudal treason were not heard in King's Bench. The requirement of trial by peers meant that such high felony by a great vassal of the king could only be heard in the old *curia regis*. After about 1350 this meant in practice the House of Lords, the aristocratic upper house of Parliament.

King's Bench was also the court of appeal for criminal cases from the shire courts. But it infrequently functioned in this way for the simple reason that appeal was only by grace of the circuit judges in the shire courts. If they proceeded to hang the defendant after conviction from a stout oak tree at the edge of the county town, there was no possibility of appeal. If there was appeal from a conviction in a hanging offense, it was because the assize judges allowed it.

The Court of Common Pleas was the busiest court in Westminster, and while King's Bench initially had greater prestige, in time Common Pleas became the premier central court, which it remains today. Bracton was a chief of Common Pleas. When in the early seventeenth century Sir Edward Coke was transferred by the Crown from being chief justice of Common Pleas to the same position in King's Bench, he thought he was being demoted by an angry king, and he was.

Common Pleas was the court of first jurisdiction for all lawsuits about rich pieces of land—estates worth more than "half a knight's fee"—unless the parties agreed to try the case, for tactical reasons, initially in the shire court. Common Pleas was also a very busy appeals court from the shire courts in all civil actions. It was the court that determined the fate of gentry families and where even great magnates experienced important triumphs or defeats. It decided on the outcome of all the great land cases.

One would like to say "decided finally," but this was not strictly true, since it was still possible to appeal to the king directly as the fount of justice from a land law decision in Common Pleas. The king would often seek the chancellor's advice on whether to hear such appeals. The records show that appeals above Common Pleas to the king were rarely allowed in practice. If you lost in common pleas, the odds were 50 to 1 that you lost. Go home, tell your anxious family that a disaster for them all has occurred. Common Pleas is where the great barristers strutted and exclaimed and collected huge fees for their critically important work.

There was still another central court developing in Bracton's day, but it was an ad hoc operation and met very rarely. Once in a while a large panel of justices, perhaps a dozen in all, drawn from all the great central courts, plus possibly the chancellor, would sit at special appeals court to deal with some very important and usually complicated civil action. This omnibus court was called the Exchequer Chamber. It lasted until 1873.

The courts thus had well-defined separate functions, with some overlap. But looking at the way the courts operated both in terms of personnel and location, leads one to be cautious about drawing enclosed boxes. During the Middle Ages there was one community of judges at Westminster. Judges were not assigned exclusively to one central court, although they might spend more time on the bench at one court rather than the others. Today in Common Pleas, tomorrow in King's Bench, next week in Exchequer—this was common practice.

Furthermore, when the circuit judges got back to Westminster after arduously presiding over the assizes in three or four counties, they immediately went back to work in one or another central court until they were sent out again to another circuit of county courts. One week in Shropshire, the next in Common Pleas. Being a royal judge was prestigious and well paid, but a very demanding job. There were few days off.

This intense use of judicial personnel was certainly a cost-saving strategy. It also had the intrinsic judicial advantage of making the judges experienced in all sorts of cases, from poaching in the royal hunting preserve to inheritance squabbles among the gentry to tax delinquencies, and enhanced the judges' capacity to handle a wide variety of cases skillfully and with dispatch.

Medieval common-law judges were thus extremely versatile. They were closely watched by the king and the chancellor and if they could not perform adequately they were let out to pasture, sent off to be sheriff of Nottingham and hunt bootlessly for Robin Hood or simply sent back to their family lands with a small pension.

The fluidity of the central court operation was also demonstrated by their location all together in Westminister in one great hall the size of half a football field. Each of the courts had their allotted space in this cavernous, noisy, smoky, smelly hall. The judges sat in parallel rows at the head of the space allotted to each court, a wooden bar separating each set of judges, lawyers, clerks, and current litigants from the crowd milling about further back in the hall.

There were not separate rooms or even fixed partitions for each of the courts. There were simply three parallel rows of judicial action going on at the same time. Toward the back of the great hall there were food and drink stands and stalls selling pens, ink, and parchment pieces (after 1400, also paper), not to speak of the ubiquitous medieval whores also offering their wares. The scene at Westminster looked more like a three-ring circus than the decorous, quiet, modern courtroom, yet it endured until the Victorian law courts were built around 1840.

This peculiar physical setup was again partly cost saving in purpose. But there were judicial functional reasons for it as well, and good ones. Judges could skip quickly from one court to another as they were needed, the always busy Common Pleas drawing on down-time in King's Bench or Exchequer. Lawyers with cases pending in more than one court could move over a few paces when a case was called in another court from the one where they were sitting. This was a reason why lawyers by the late thirteenth century always appeared with a colleague or at least a junior backup, still a common practice today.

There were no hiatuses in the old common-law courts. It was a long day's work for every successful lawyer, often in two or even three courts on the same day.

The medieval judges' "uniform" was the coif, a white silk scarf. Wigs were not worn until the late seventeenth century, introduced from Paris by the Francophile King Charles II.

More than anything else it was the proliferation of records both in the shire courts and the central courts in the age of Bracton that impelled the further development of the common law. The case records were getting steadily longer and more detailed in the mid-thirteenth century. From being pithy summaries in the age of Glanville, they were getting close to stenographic detail by Bracton's time. The court clerk was no longer a monk borrowed from a neighboring monastery. He was a paid, highly skilled, multilingual royal official. Illustrations of court proceedings in the later Middle Ages always show the clerks in the center of the picture, sitting just below the judges.

The three languages of Latin, French, and English competed with one another in the developing courts in the late thirteenth and fourteenth centuries. Latin remained the language in which the pleadings in Bracton's Court of Common Pleas was written down until the end of the eighteenth century, even though in Bracton's time and for another two centuries, most of the actual discourse in the court was in a jargon law French. After Chaucer and other poets made English a literary language in the late fourteenth century, not only peasant litigants would normally speak English during trials. By the late fifteenth century even the august justices and the formidable barristers normally spoke English with Latin and French phrases sprinkled in to stress the dignity and arcane learning of the law. The trilingual clerks took it all in and wrote it down in Latin.

By Bracton's day the detail provided in the shire court records meant that on appeal it was often not necessary to bring a jury all the way to London to testify before the Court of Common Pleas. Their testimony was in the record that the appeals court examined.

The central court indicated its willingness to hear an appeal from the county court by certifying its demand to examine the record of the assizes trial. It issued a bench writ of *certiorari* for this purpose. Today, when the U.S. Supreme Court indicates its willingness—in only about 3 percent of filed appeals—to reconsider a decision from a lower federal court, it too issues a writ of *certiorari*, the sweetest word a lawyer practicing before the U.S. Supreme Court ever hears, aside from actually winning a case.

In the time of Henry II, when an indicted criminal was apprehended after the itinerant justices had moved on to another shire, the judges, on being informed by the sheriff of the county from which they had just traveled, could order the malefactor brought to them for trial in the neighboring county court. But in that instance, two members of the grand jury had to bring the record to the justices on the neighboring county court in order to testify to the authenticity of the recorded indictment. The Victorian constitutional historian William Stubbs thought this bringing of the record by two grand jurymen from one county court to another was an important precedent for parliamentary representation of county courts in the thirteenth century. Legal representation led to political representation, went the famous Stubbs thesis.

Be that as it may, the most significant issue was actually the change of attitude to court records over a hundred years. In Henry II's time court records moved from court to court had to be certified personally by authors of the record, in this instance the grand jury. By Bracton's time there was sufficient confidence in the authenticity of records that a certifying demand by an appeals court in Westminster was enough to get the record transferred; jurymen did not have to put in a personal appearance to authenticate the record. English law was moving into an era grounded in literacy and the validity of written records.

While English common law gave much more centrality to oral pleading than did Roman law—what counted most in civil litigation was the adversarial traverse between the parties or their attorneys in the presence of judges and juries—there was by the age of Bracton a deep respect for the value of court records. They could be cited; they could be appealed to; they could be referred to.

In the late thirteenth century judges began to cite a record of a decision in a previous case in Westminster as revelation of a point of law that could be applied in the cases now before them. This was the doctrine of *stare decisis*, of standing on a previous decision authenticated in the court record as a source for law.

Before the nineteenth century in England, *stare decisis*, a component of what was later called judicial review, became—more than legislation—the source of law applied in the courts. Judges made law by their decision in a particular case. Then this decision was cited by analogical reasoning as precedent for the legal point to be applied in a similar case. This process became central to lawmaking in the common-law tradition.

Activist legislation by modern English Parliaments in the nineteenth and twentieth centuries has overwhelmingly predominated over *stare decisis*—judicial review through precedent citing—but in the United States the medieval tradition of finding law in the record of a previous case lives on, and since the 1930s has taken on immense if controversial proportions.

The respect for written record and the doctrine of *stare decisis* that came with it was the capstone in the development of judicial operations that began in the 1160s. In a century the main structure of the common law had been erected, and it was this structure that Bracton proudly presided over and tried to articulate in his treatise, with the help of citations from the plea rolls.

At the same time Bracton was keenly aware of ideological and political controversy involving the common law and its place in society. He entered frequently and courageously into these ideological and political debates, drawing upon his Parisian proto-Thomistic education to define his views on these difficult matters.

He would probably be surprised to learn that it is this theoretical formulation, this theory of law and politics, that established his posthumous fame, and that it was statements he made in that ideological part of his treatise—only a few pages among hundreds—that got him quoted and admired down the centuries.

Bracton prided himself on his work as chief justice of the Common Pleas, and in his writing for careful discussions of courtroom procedure derived from cases that he presided over and took notes on, as well as from his reading widely in other cases in the court records of his time. He would have regarded his lengthy discussion of written contracts along the lines of Roman law as a significant feature of his treatise. Instead it is for his place in the emergence of judicial liberalism and English constitutionalism that Bracton is now principally remembered.

The overwhelming success of the common-law system in the 1270s was signaled by its comparative relationship to other kinds of courts. The baronial courts, without being expressly legislated out of existence, virtually disappeared as judicial institutions because all members of feudal society, even the high aristocracy, recognized the superiority of justice for themselves in royal courts. Meanwhile the manorial courts, held in the peasant villages under the leadership of landlords' stewards and involving the local peasantry, nominally unfree serfs but also in actuality now often embracing the underclass of free peasantry, became more active as vehicles to resolve land disputes among rural working-class families and to help to enforce peace codes at the most local level.

Since the standard of justice was what the royal courts provided, the busy manorial courts by the late thirteenth century imitated common-law procedure. They started to keep detailed records, which are a goldmine of information for modern historians of the medieval peasantry and their families. The manorial courts introduced decisions by juries (often involving all the villagers present at the court) as well as using compurgation. By

1270 the royally sponsored common-law courts for the middle and upper strata of society were being backstopped by the thriving manorial courts for the ordinary peasantry. These manorial courts' legitimacy was enhanced by their spontaneously imitating common-law procedure without normal intervention by officers of the crown. Common-law procedures by the late thirteenth century, as explicated in Bracton's treatise, were identified with justice, and the manorial courts were impelled, as best they could, to imitate common-law procedures in the settling of property disputes and the suppression of crime in the overpopulated agricultural villages of that era.

8
The Advent of Liberalism

THEORY IN ANY FIELD is inspired by three motivations: First, it is an effort at synthesis, an attempt to encompass varieties of data and experiences and establish a fixed relationship among them. Theory integrates disparate experiences. It is a behavioral code.

Second, there is a psychological motivation behind the formulation of theory. It is an effort to give comfort to the formulator and articulator of the theory, to establish a safe cocoon around him- or herself. What preconscious or unconscious springs are driving this search for comfort depends on the psychology you believe in. Strict Freudians might say that theory is a way of resolving oedipal problems. Jungians could say that theory is a way of establishing reciprocal connection with universal archetypes. Lacanism would say it is a way of articulating "the name of the father"—that is, coming to terms with the concept of the father.

A third motive behind theory is to protect familiar behavior patterns and intellectual traditions against menacing innovative shapes on the cultural and social horizon. Theory is thereby driven by anxiety about, possibly by fear of, destructive forces glimpsed on the horizon. Theory attempts to forestall the expansion and dominance of these frightening shapes and to keep them from controlling the future. In this perspective theory is fearful and conservative.

All these factors can be used to explain Bracton's urge to theorize about government and public law. He did not advance this theory to gain professional advancement. On the contrary, his theory could have hurt his career as a royal judge for being too liberal. Bracton was propounding the essentials of the liberal theory that law is higher than monarchy and restrains political power. He proposed the embedding of royal law in a moral continuum and the imposition of moral constraints on power. He went further and asserted that such rule of law and dominance of morality over power is in imitation of Christ's self-sacrificing life, thereby giving a religious as well as ethical cast to his doctrine.

There were groups in English society in Bracton's day who welcomed this assertion of liberal theory; some churchmen, particularly the new and very popular Franciscan Order; the radical bishop of Lincoln, Robert Grosseteste; and an oppositional faction in the high nobility, led by King Henry III's ambitious brother-in-law, Simon de Montfort, earl of Leicester, who had distinguished Parisian lineage.

But the king and his ministers were probably not enthusiastic about Bracton's theory:

> [The Justinian code says] what has pleased the prince is law. This is not what had been rashly presumed to be the *personal* will of the king, but what has been rightly defined by the counsel and council of the king's magnates.

Bracton here bifurcates the king into two wills—his personal and his public will. The latter is exercised only through the council of magnates, what will soon be called Parliament. Later on there will be talk of the king's two bodies, his natural and his political body. This is the same idea as Bracton's two royal wills. "Sovereignty" (a word not invented until the sixteenth century) resides only in the king's political body or will, not his natural body or personal will. He has authority to make law but only by consent of the magnates representing the people or, as the thirteenth-century barons said, "the community of the realm."

Here is the essence of English constitutional liberalism. Bracton expresses it in an explicit polemical manner: "The king has no other power . . . except that alone which he derives from the law. . . . The law makes the king. . . . There is no king where arbitrary will dominates and not law."

This statement by Bracton will echo down the centuries to be quoted again and again by oppositional forces. The law has been raised, in Bracton's theory, from a set of royal instruments to a substance higher than the king, and his power is held to be derivative from law.

The historian Ernst Kantorowicz, writing in the 1950s, and his many disciples have claimed plausibly that the origin of the English constitutional idea of the king's two bodies is similar to the earlier bifurcation of the personality of a medieval bishop. As an ecclesiastic the bishop owed loyalty to the pope. As a member of the highest nobility he was a vassal of the king and owed loyalty to the king.

Bracton would have been fully aware of this episcopal bifurcation, which was clearly articulated in a celebrated case in the royal court in 1088 and had already made its appearance in land law litigation a dozen years before. Therefore the idea of a bishop's two bodies became in time the king's two bodies, and Bracton played a significant role in this intellectual transition, according to the Kantorowicz thesis.

Beyond doubt Bracton's studies in Paris early in the thirteenth century gave him intellectual tools to formulate this doctrine. It owes something to Roman traditions of natural law and mirrors Cicero's moral penumbra around the law. It owes even more to the group of young radical professors at Paris, originally led by Langton, later by the Dominican philosopher Albert the German, and then by Albert's student Thomas Aquinas.

The theory of law and government in Aquinas's *Summa Theologica*, which he was propounding at Paris at the time Bracton wrote in the 1250s, is very similar to Bracton's theory. Bracton was caught up in a liberal culture within the Western Church in the first half of the thirteenth century.

Another source of Bracton's theory is Magna Carta, the Great Charter. Clause 39 of the text of 1215 was incorporated into the official deradicalized version of that document when in 1225 it was reissued by the royal government and came to be regarded as the first of the statutes of the realm and as a sort of fundamental law: "No free man shall be arrested or imprisoned or disseized or outlawed or exiled or in any way victimized, neither will we attack him or send anyone to attack him, except by the lawful judgement of his peers and by the law of the land."

Here King John promised not to rule otherwise than by the law of the land. In the fifteenth century, there would be talk of following due process of the law. This is the same idea.

The theory of judicial liberalism signaled in Magna Carta of 1215 and clearly articulated by Bracton four decades later was hailed as the critical point in the history of the medieval common law by William Stubbs. Stubbs's work was still being assigned as a textbook to students at Cambridge and Harvard Universities in the 1950s by at least one prominent teacher at these institutions, Helen Maude Cam. (In a now forgotten postwar British film comedy, *Passport to Pimlico*, Margaret Rutherford did a sensational imitation of the formidable Dr. Cam under a full head of steam, explicating medieval texts.)

But already in the 1950s, George O. Sayles, a learned British medievalist, was furiously attacking the holdover of the Victorian triumphalist view of medieval legal and constitutional history, in which all intellectual roads led up to and away from Bracton's doctrine of judicial liberalism. Indeed, Maitland had raised caution around 1900. It is not difficult to point to intellectual weaknesses in Bracton's theory.

First, there is a degree of falsification and denial of experience in the claim that the law makes the king. The progressive and innovative parts of the law that Bracton himself administered were heavily a royal creation, and without an energetic and prosperous monarchy, the legal system would erode and malfunction. The law contributed to the authority of kingship, but so did many other factors—*seisin*, historical tradition, ceremony, religious doctrine, personal charisma. The king did much more to cast his aura of majesty on the law and gain for the law credibility and a touch of majesty, it can be argued, than the law did to sustain the king. Empirically it would be much more accurate to say that the king makes the law than that the law makes the king.

Second, Bracton's theory is confusing about where sovereignty resides in England. On the one side it is in the legislative authority of king and magnates (soon king and Parliament). On the other side it is in the rule of law. How can this be? How can the rule of law be compatible with sovereign legislative authority?

No one has ever answered this question, certainly not the Victorian liberal theorists like A. V. Dicey, who wrote an interminable book on the rule of law. Lest it be thought that this effective contradiction between legislative authority and the rule of law was not apparent to medieval people, it is the prime theme of a book by another Parisian philosopher, Marsilio of Padua's *The Defender of the Peace*, published in 1324. The peace of men in civil society requires one definitive legislative authority, argued Marsilio, starting the long procession of positivist and pragmatic antiliberal theorists.

Third, what is this law that Bracton enshrines in moral guise? It is actually a set of procedures that favor the rich and the well connected, that disadvantage the poor and the humble. Given the common-law's class bias, where does it get its moral sanction to overrule the king? The law provides formal judicial equality, but in practice it was an elaborate mechanism to secure the property and privileges of the rich. The law did not attack the bastions of landed wealth and power; it embraced and protected them.

Are only modern Marxists aware of the class bias of the common law? Not at all. When peasant rebellion occurred in the late medieval England, the rebels went after some of the bishops and abbots, but always also judges and lawyers. "The first thing we do, let's kill all the lawyers," says Shakespeare's fifteenth-century proletarian rebel, accurately enough. On the other side, the peasant rebels always treated the king with respect and avowed their loyalty to him. That was a prime reason why it was relatively easy for the royal government and the lords to suppress and punish the rebels.

The final argument against Bracton—and modern liberal theory—is that he propounds an ethical doctrine, not a legal theory at all. He talks about a substance called law, but he does not deal with judicial operations in this theory. It is not derived from the judicial culture with which he was intensely familiar, but from the theological and political culture. Bracton in fact in his treatise writes at great length about the judicial system, particularly the law of contract and the jury. But his high theory is not extrapolated inductively from the ingredients of law but is imposed from certain political, ethical, and religious traditions extraneous to the common law.

Magna Carta and the thirteenth-century tradition of judicial liberalism endure perhaps even more vibrantly in the United States than in England. The American Bar Association in the 1980s once held its annual meeting in London, not just to get a succulent tax write-off, but to celebrate an anniversary of Magna

Carta. On the faculty of every prominent American law school two or three professors, at least, devote most of their time to teaching and writing about the strength of the tradition of judicial liberalism, going back to Magna Carta and Bracton. Sometimes what they have to say, as in the cases of Lon Fuller and Ronald Dworkin, is at least marginally interesting.

However, pointing to putative weaknesses in the Bractonian/ Thomist liberal tradition is in a sense bootless. For whatever reasons, despite its intellectual weakness, it flourished, was perpetuated, and eventually in the seventeenth century, if not before, came to have momentous political consequences.

Therefore it is worth considering how the theory of liberalism emerged in thirteenth-century England and what lies immediately behind Magna Carta.

Bracton's liberal theory was the product of a critical juncture in the medieval world—Parisian academic culture facing an immensely powerful and at times arbitrary monarchy. This was the situation in England in 1214 when after endless pressure from the pope, King John finally accepted Stephen Langton, a leader of Parisian academic culture, as archbishop of Canterbury. Langton found a large faction of the high nobility extremely discontented with a king whom they thought had overtaxed them and had manipulated the law courts to hurt their families.

Furthermore, this was a king who had lost ancestral lands in Normandy and Anjou to the rising French monarchy in Paris in 1204. This political and military disaster was costly to many baronial families who still held lands in northern France. It was doubly costly to King John, not only losing territories belonging to his ancestors William the Conqueror and Henry II, but suffering a severe deflation in prestige.

Then, in 1214, John's effort to recoup his losses by joining in an alliance with the German emperor against the French king and his papal ally came to naught on the battlefields of France and Belgium. Langton felt that the time was now propitious to put his liberal political ideas into action. He joined with the discontented barons—perhaps half of the higher nobility, among whom the northern frontier barons with great military resources were prominent—to force John to accept Magna Carta.

The idea of the king issuing a great charter of liberties goes back to 1100, when Henry I issued a coronation charter of benign promises because his claim to the throne was weak.

Magna Carta's sixty-three clauses listed mainly financial complaints. It insisted, for instance, that if the king was going to use scutage as a regular tax, by levying it almost every year, he had to impose it with the consent of the magnates. Magna Carta sought the support of the merchant class of London by specifying that they could only be taxed with their own consent, and were not subject to tallage, or arbitrary taxation.

Magna Carta also dealt with some judicial matters. The writ *praecipe* should be canceled, since this taking of cases arbitrarily from baronial to royal courts had no legislative sanctions. The writs of right and writs of entry achieved the same purpose, but the barons won an important victory in principle with abolition of *praecipe*. Magna Carta also stipulated that the shire courts should meet as royal courts under the itinerant justices more often than twice a year—a change, convenient to the landed classes and their incessant civil actions, that was not implemented because of the cost to the Crown.

There was the famous generic clause about protection of all free men by the law of the land. There was a cognate general provision: "To no one will we sell, to no one will we refuse or delay right or justice." This did not mean that the common law would become cheap, but that the king would not intervene to corrupt the legal processes in his own interest.

Finally Magna Carta stipulated that all criminal cases in a royal court must start with a grand jury indictment.

These legal clauses in Magna Carta confirm how central to the way of life of the landed class the common law had become.

Magna Carta indicated that they looked upon the law as their bulwark against excessive and arbitrary royal power. The common law is what protected their property and social status. At the same time there is an ethical edge to these judicial clauses as Langton is covering the class and family judicial interests of landlords great and small with the universalizing theory of Parisian academic culture.

The final clause of Magna Carta stipulated a legal right of rebellion by the nobility against the king, an idea talked about among the Parisian intellectuals and later enshrined in Aquinas's writings. A committee of twenty-five barons is set up to monitor the king's keeping of Magna Carta. If he breaks his agreement to follow the provisions of the Great Charter, the baronial committee will declare a feudal *diffidatio*, a disavowal of homage and fealty, against him and declare war on him.

This clause was soon put into play, as John got from the pope approval of his right to disavow Magna Carta as being forced upon him, and England was plunged into civil war. Fortunately for the country, John died suddenly, leaving a minor heir. The most respected of the barons (one who had not supported Langton and the rebels in 1215), the great earl William Marshal, a man whose life so fitted the aristocratic ideal that his family hired a French poet to write Marshal's life in rhyming verse, became regent for the child Henry III. It was William Marshal's government that in 1225 reissued Magna Carta in truncated and less controversial form, thereby inaugurating its history as a symbol of the fundamental law of the kingdom, even though at any time the king and legislature could in fact rescind it.

Innocent III, the pope who released King John from observing Magna Carta, thought, from his Roman-law perspective, that it violated the political order of the world set down in Roman law. If kings could be so circumscribed in their power, couldn't popes also be subject to consensual restraint? Indeed, such a liberalization of papal government was talked about in Parisian academic circles, and was later to become visibly active in the conciliar movement in the church.

The struggle between Roman-canonical traditions of papal absolutism and liberal conciliarists wanting to make the pope responsible to elected general councils of the church continues to the present day. In the early 1960s (as in the early fifteenth century) the conciliarists seemed to be winning, only to be again overcome by the papal Romanists.

Pope Innocent III was furious that his own protégé and nominee to the archbishopric of Canterbury had taken the radical position and given leadership to the baronial party. Langton was suspended from office and died in ecclesiastical disgrace shortly thereafter. Never again in the Middle Ages was such a doctrinaire liberal to hold the primacy of the English church.

To understand the significance of Bracton's liberal theory, we have to put him into the context of his generation. He was the product of a high academic culture, centered in Paris, that in the face of the rising power of the monarchy and centralization of the church in Rome, and drawing on ethical strains in classical culture, was asserting and glorifying a substance called law that would limit power and authority in both state and church.

This universalizing legal substance would protect communities from despotism and individuals from unfair and arbitrary treatment. This liberal movement in academic culture was also affected by the extreme religious idealism and ethical activism that shaped the Franciscan Order, of which only good things could be said in the early thirteenth century.

Someone brushed by this academic culture would always carry its intellectual imprint. This was the case with Bracton. He was a bifurcated man, at the same time an immensely successful and well-rewarded royal justice and a liberal idealist with oppositional tendencies. If the two cultures to which he belonged did not mesh well—the one moralistic, altruistic, and rhetorical; the other empirical, demanding, and mechanical—that did not dissuade him from putting forth his liberal theory at the same time as he was discussing the institutional procedures of common law.

Bracton is like those radical graduate students of the late 1960s who bear with them forever the stamp of leftist ideology and the activist yearning of those years even as they advance to high positions in the academic hierarchy and are familiar with plenty of data that challenge the New Left philosophy. These people can't help themselves. Something warm and beautiful and magical has penetrated deeply into their psyches, and it always affects their minds and behaviors.

Theory means very little or nothing unless it appeals to the interests of a social group and is taken up by the leaders of that group and is transformed into an ideological instrument of their class purposes. Bracton's theory was first of all a product of the liberal culture of Parisian Thomistic scholasticism. Second, and much less forcefully. it can be regarded as reflective of Bracton's experience as a judge. He witnessed the common law becoming a distinctive code of social behavior and a political substance arguably recognizable as distinctive from the ideals and policy of monarchy.

The latter base of his theory was too tenuous and remote to impress anyone except Bracton himself and possibly three or four other judges. The first base of his theory, its rooting in French scholasticism, had greater potential for social impact, since it was connected to an intellectual and heavily academic movement that had cosmopolitan reach. But this source of his theory and this academic cultural base would have had very little impact in England if his doctrine of the rule of law had not been serviceable to the interests of the significant political classes, the political nation, the aristocracy in the thirteenth century and the rural upper middle class, the gentry, in the following centuries.

The aristocracy, the higher nobility, the magnates—some fifty families of distinctive lineage and enormous landed wealth and constant companionated influence with the king and the Plantagent royal family—were the important political class in thirteenth-century England. This was not unique in Europe. North of the Alps, in Western Europe, from Poland to Scotland, that was also the situation. The thirteenth-century European aristocracy was highly literate and very much involved in politics.

This was partly for defensive purposes, the more so in England with its high degree of royal centralization of the realm. In response to royal power, the great lords had to come off their estates, mitigate pursuit of family and regional interests, and engage in national politics in order to restrain the accelerating engine of royal administration and law.

The political activities of the thirteenth-century aristocracy were also motivated by more positive factors. They had developed a sense of their blue-bloodedness, of their superior biological makeup setting them apart from the rest of society (even though the higher nobility were not an entirely closed caste; there was some recruitment from the top stratum of the gentry, although this was becoming increasingly rare). Inspired by the romantic chivalric literature that was sung and recited nightly as entertainment in their great halls by professional poets, these higher nobility were also developing an intense consciousness of their social roles, both their privileges and responsibilities.

Thomist philosophy recognized and legitimated this special quality of the great nobility. In their hands, according to scholastic doctrine emanating from Paris and slowly being taken up at Oxford University, lay the grave right of rebellion against monarchy when it had turned tyrannical and was afflicting the people.

In normal circumstances thirteenth-century aristocratic political ideology stressed the necessity of the king governing through estates, representative assemblies, of which the aristocracy of course comprised the first and dominant estate. Aristocratic activists talked of the king's ministers being responsible to the estates. They envisioned in critical times putting the royal government in the care of a commission of prominent magnates who would use their exalted beings to rectify imbalances and malfunctions.

Whenever a king was physically weak or doing a poor administrative job or was distracted by private interests, rule through estates and putting the royal administration into commission was much talked about.

Henry III (1216–72) was a victimized king on all grounds. He had no taste for war, and his one effort to halt the spread of French royal territory under his glamorous brother-in-law Saint Louis IX of France ended in miserable defeat. He was no administrator and made a financial mess of royal government. He was distracted by getting involved in papal projects in Sicily and by his commitment to art and building. (Westminster Abbey—after he had Edward the Confessor's church on the site torn down—today is his monument.)

Under these circumstances the higher nobility, led by another brother-in-law of the king, Simon de Montfort, earl of Leicester, put forth the characteristic aristocratic vehicles for reforming royal government between 1258 and 1265. The estates were made more active, and the council of magnates was supplemented (an expedient already envisioned by King John) by representatives of the county knights (gentry) and town burghers. This augmented assembly was called Parliament.

A clause in Magna Carta had already stipulated that the higher nobility would be summoned to royal councils by individual writs and the knights of the county courts by general writs addressed to the sheriff, mandating the choosing of two representatives from each county court. Now, in addition, the autocratic mayors and town councils chose the bourgeois representatives.

The purpose of Parliament in the eyes of Earl Simon and his party was to get sanction for putting the royal administration into the hands of a commission of great lords. This baronial reform plan worked well enough for a few years but fell apart—as all such aristocratic efforts did in the Middle Ages—for two reasons. First, the great lords soon began to lose interest in the boring intricacies of bureaucracy and inevitably quarreled about distribution of power.

Second, the Plantagenet family would not tolerate this humiliation and declension of power if they could help it. In 1265, three years after Bracton's death, Prince Edward, the heir to the throne (Edward I, reigned 1272–1307), raised an army and defeated and killed Earl Simon at the Battle of Evesham.

A dirge written by the English Franciscan friars, vehement supporters of Earl Simon (and of any radical measure of the time), bewailed this great loss for English society. Perhaps Bracton would have felt the same. As a royal judge he was in an awkward position in the struggle between the Plantagenets and the earls, but he certainly was cooperative with the reform party. They embraced his doctrine of the rule of law and the limitation of the king's personal will by the larger body politic of the kingdom.

Bracton was also on good terms with the oppositional bishop of Lincoln, Robert Grosseteste, who had risen from the depths of society through study at the new University of Cambridge and service as a tutor to the young Henry III. Grosseteste, now remembered as a pioneering experimental scientist, was intellectually embedded in the scholastic culture of the early thirteenth century, although in his antipapalism he stood well to the left of Aquinas.

At one point, at the beginning of the 1250s, Grosseteste, Simon de Montfort, Bracton, and the head of the Franciscan Order in England, Adam Marsh, were in dialogue as the possible nucleus of a liberal party in England, and between 1258 and 1265 Montfort put some of their ideas into practice. By 1265 all but Marsh were dead, and the Franciscans were left to sing dirges for what might have been and to turn toward making Oxford the focus of avant-garde philosophy and science in Europe for the next fifty years.

Now the awesome figure of Edward I stood triumphant over the English scene, and soon, by his conquest of Wales and near-successful invasion of Scotland, over the whole British isle.

The huge stone castles that Edward built in Wales to secure his pacification of the countryside—one of which, at Caernarvon, survives in good shape—were emblematic of the determination and ambition of his rule.

At times Edward I seemed to be replicating the policy of his Parisian cousin, the awesome Philip IV the Fair of France, namely to use legal institutions and judicial practices to harass subjects, even aristocratic ones, and instill fear in society.

This tactic comes through most evidently in the royal government's *quo warranto* ("by what warrant") proceedings in the 1280s. For a century there had existed a judicial procedure and a writ by which any lord could demand of an underling to show by what right the latter held particular lands and privileges, to demonstrate a warrant of legitimacy, and preclude usurpation of the land or privileges.

The difference in Edward I's *quo warranto* proceedings were their systematic scope, rolling steadily across the country and directed at the higher nobility. Thereby fear and panic were sown among the great families of the land. As Edward and his officials expected beforehand, many great lay lords could not produce documentation showing precisely how they had come into the wealth on which their status depended.

Charters documenting royal grants were regarded in common law as testamentary, not dispositary (they merely witnessed a royal grant, which was done physically and orally), and therefore not of critical importance. Unlike the religious houses, the lay nobility had previously been sloppy about holding on to written records. A contemporary story tells how a frustrated earl produced a rusty old sword for the royal commissioners, claiming that it had belonged to the founding ancestor of the family, a companion of

William the Conqueror. That sword supposedly symbolized his right to his estates.

There was great resentment against the *quo warranto* proceedings. Characteristically Edward then backed off and offered a compromise. A statute of *quo warranto* of 1290 stipulated that the accession to the throne of Richard the Lionhearted in 1189 was "the limit of living memory." No documentation was necessary to back up customary possession of lands gained from the Crown before that time, thereby protecting most of the great estates of the nobility.

This was precisely the kind of concession that Philip the Fair and his Roman lawyers in Paris would not have made. Similarly Philip the Fair summoned the estates-general of France only once in his reign, and that was simply to serve as the backdrop for a propaganda war against the pope. For Edward the meeting of the English estates in Parliament was an opportunity to get important business done.

Edward was a supreme pragmatist who would use any vehicle to enhance his wealth and power regardless of long-term implication. Therefore he made extensive use of Parliament. By the end of his reign, legislation through estates was integrally fixed in English political practice.

Coming back to England in 1273 from glamorous (puffed up by his PR people) exploits as a Crusader in the Middle East, Edward summoned a Parliament in 1275. He secured legislation that established for the first time a national customs system—the Magna Custuma. The export tax on millions of pounds of raw wool shipped annually from Yorkshire ranches to the textile towns of Flanders (Belgium), and the import tax on hundreds of thousands of barrels of red wine ("claret") imported each year from Bordeaux (then a separate possession of the king, somewhat like the Channel Islands today), gave a tremendous annual boost to the royal treasury, producing by the 1290s a fifth of the yearly income of the Crown. A century later, due to lax administration and large-scale smuggling, the income from the customs had declined in value but was still producing a tenth of annual royal income.

There was a time, especially in the 1950s, when medievalists sharply debated the nature of Parliament in the late thirteenth and early fourteenth centuries. Was it a legislative and tax-levying body, or was it principally a high court, the highest of the realm? Until the later seventeenth century, the estates in England were officially called "the king's high court of parliament." The functions of the old *curia regis* remained with it. It was a place for trials of the great lords by their peers. It was an occasion when the king through his chancellor received petitions (essentially judicial instruments) and responded to them—or didn't. It was the highest court of appeal in the realm, although it rarely heard an appeal unless the appellant was a great lord.

There were meetings of Parliament, as in 1306, when no legislative business was done and no approval for a Parliament–authorized tax (called a subsidy, a development out of the feudal gracious aid) on income and movable property was sought. The knights of the shire and burgesses were never present for the whole length of a Parliament, which could run for as long as three weeks. They were sent home within a week, their expenses paid (until the county representatives made it a sign of their landed wealth and upscale dignity not to collect expenses, and the practice of paying the commoners lapsed until the early twentieth century). Much judicial business was done after the knights and burgesses were sent home.

So Parliament was in a sense a judicial organism (the French *parlement*, dating from the same era was entirely so; French national assemblies, which rarely met, were called estates-generals). After around 1340, when the lords on the one side and the knights and burgesses on the other comprised two distinct "houses," Lords and Commons, the House of Lords retained its judicial functions. It remains today the supreme court of

England, the ultimate court of appeal. Of course the legal work is now done by twenty-five lawyers, made "law lords" for life.

Yet the legislative and tax-approving functions of the early Parliaments are as remarkable as their judicial ones. The writs summoning the knights and burgesses even in the reign of Edward I stipulated that representatives of the commons must have full power (*ploena potestas*) of attorneyship to speak for the county court. Indisputably validating the commons' approval of subsidies and customs taxes was obviously in mind.

In the early Parliaments not only did bishops sit in the House of Lords, where they still sit, but the ecclesiastical lords were instructed that before they set out for Parliament at Westminster they were first to summon (*praemunientes*) representatives of the lower clergy, who were much involved in the production of that agricultural wealth the king wanted to tax. After around 1330 the summoning of the lower clergy to Parliament was stopped because it was discovered that they were so moved by Franciscan and other varieties of clerical radicalism that they were infecting the middle-class representatives; the lower clergy were struck off to their own peculiar assembly, called convocation, which still meets and still generates a radical ambience.

The sweeping changes in the land law in Edward I's reign, instituted at the behest of the wealthier gentry families, were implemented by the mechanism of parliamentary legislation. From the 1290s stem the statute rolls, in which new laws passed by Parliament and approved by the king were inscribed. The 1225 modified version of Magna Carta was retrospectively honored as a parliamentary statute and placed first in the statute roll.

The tumultuous events of the year 1297, when Edward faced a political crisis that threatened his hold on the royal government, demonstrated that Parliament was not regarded as only a normal judicial operation. It had come to be imagined ideologically as the institution that realized Bracton's theory of the rule of law and the political as against the natural will of the king, and the aristocratic consensual political vision to which Bracton's theory became tied.

In 1296 Edward I went to war on land and sea against the French monarchy, which had become enormously strong, wealthy, and ambitious. Edward's Anglo-French conflict was a prologue to and rehearsal for the Hundred Years' War between the mid-fourteenth and mid-fifteenth centuries, which eventually brought ruin on both monarchies.

These wars were naked imperial conflicts, although often disguised by rhetorical claims drawn from dynastic lineages. The two great European kingdoms were now contending over which would control and exploit two very wealthy regions on the flanks of the expanding French kingdom—the wine-growing region of Bordeaux, still under English rule, and the county of Flanders with its prosperous textiles cities; Flanders was nominally under French lordship but was actually independent.

When Edward's invasion of Scotland turned difficult and expensive, he found himself in a ruinous two-front conflict (the French were in fact to seize upon this vulnerable situation and ally with the Scots) that was beyond the resources of even his efficient government. He resorted to every conceivable scheme to force money out of English society. One of his expedients was exiling the Jews from the country in order to seize the assets of the Jewish bankers (which were no longer very substantial, as Italian and native English bankers had been taking over the Jewish banking business during the thirteenth century). The Jews were not readmitted to England until 1653.

Of course the landed classes in the 1290s had no sympathy for the Jews. They were outraged by the royal government's extorting money from the great families by questioning the validity of their land titles or by trying to get the merchants to assent to an increase in the export customs tax on wool, which would be passed on to the wool growers in the landed society.

By 1297 the aristocracy was again on the verge of rebellion, this time with substantial support from the gentry and the merchant class. The great barons signaled their opposition by exhibiting reluctance to serve in France under their feudal contracts. Then they began to hold conspiratorial meetings that issued inflammatory documents expressing such principles as "Tallage will not be paid." The idea here was that the king was subjecting the realm to tallage, to arbitrary taxation suitable only for peasants and serfs, and that parliamentary approval of subsidies and increases in the customs rate were not being sought. Edward's effort to get a separate assembly of merchants to agree to a new customs rate was immediately rebuffed, and his efforts to impose an increased customs rate was denounced as a "maltote," an evil tax.

Faced with a national rebellion, Edward, always the pragmatist, backed down. He began the late medieval royal practice of paying for an ongoing war with deficit financing, with loans extorted from foreign and native bankers and farming of the customs as the dubious security for these loans. He reissued Magna Carta in 1297, symbolizing by this confirmation of the now obsolete document his willingness to abide by the rule of law.

He made an additional big concession by ending the general eyre by which the circuit judges enforced tax collection as well as held assizes. Instead the itinerant justices were now given only judicial commissions of *jail delivery* (criminal pleas), *nisi prius* (civil actions), and a more general mandate (*oyer and terminer*) to hear the pleas of the Crown.

Undoubtedly Bracton would have been happy to see this recognition of his liberal theory by the monarchy. It set a strong precedent for the future. Judicial liberalism owed something to the operation of the common law, the latter in the late thirteenth century a large self-sustaining judicial system with its own administration, distinctive procedures, and the special services it could render to the social elite. But judicial liberalism in the age of Bracton was also perhaps more strongly rooted in aristocratic politics and a Parisian academic culture that was communally and consensually oriented.

Liberalism found in Magna Carta a symbolic document it could rally around, and Bracton's courageous expounding of the notion that the law had more power than the personal will of the king was a condensed expression of the essence of liberal theory.

Edward I's confirmation of Magna Carta in 1297, treating it as representative of a kind of fundamental law, and the expanding use of Parliament by the king and gentry alike provided a strong beginning for judicial liberalism, which has a continuous history to the present day. It is most passionately believed in in the United States—not surprisingly because the American Revolution was justified as an effort to maintain the rule of law and due process of the law against alleged tyranny, and also because the United States has three times the number of lawyers per capita as any other country.

By the end of the reign of Edward I in 1307, an idea was current in powerful circles in England that the king was constrained by the prevailing law of the land and was supposed to give suitable recognition to this law and the processes of its implementation. The king may not have liked this principle, which lies at the center of juristic liberalism, and his administrators and even judges may have often ignored it in their daily work, but judges, barristers, some university professors, some bishops, and thousands of gentry and high bourgeoisie found it meaningful, took it seriously, and in moments of political anxiety would dredge it up and articulate it.

Furthermore, while no one believed that a parliamentary statute was the only way to make new law, the idea of due process of law and the supremacy of the law over the king was already loosely connected to Parliament, and this association would be firmed up in the century after Edward I.

Where this liberalism came from is a complex story. The view held from the mid-seventeenth down into the early twentieth century offered an explanatory dialectical paradigm: There had been Anglo-Saxon freedom; there was Norman French authoritarianism and indeed tyranny. In this view the principle of liberalism that developed into the thirteenth century was the result of interaction between and conjoining of these two political and judicial polarities.

Contrary to what has usually been said in the past half century, this dialectical paradigm—which reached its canonical form in Stubbs's three-volume *Constitutional History of England*—was not nonsense. It was a legitimate way of encapsulating what happened and of explaining the origins of liberalism insofar as it existed in 1300.

But some historians today would point to an entirely different source of an important contribution—not only to scholastic philosophy but also to Roman-canonical legal traditions. In this Romanist-judicial culture was centered a belief in society organized in a series of corporations, semiautonomous units within the panoply of church and state. Each of these units had a strong identity, a legal bind within itself, a commitment to distinctive group behavior, a leadership with certain prescribed powers and resources to implement them.

These corporate units were first recognized as taking the form of religious orders within the church. Then this corporate identity was applied elsewhere—to merchant and craft guilds and the learned professions. Then it was applied to estates, distinctive social groups represented in legislative assemblies.

The corporatist thesis originated principally in German medieval scholarship around 1900 with Heinrich Denifle and Ernst Sackur. Then in the 1950s it was disseminated in the English-speaking world by émigré scholars like Kantorowicz and Walter Ullman. It was given sharper focus in *Law and Revolution* (1984) by Emory University Law School professor Harold Berman, which has gone through eight printings since its publication and been given a prize by the American Bar Association.

Corporatism in theory and practice placed a series of judicial and practical barriers to the centralizing and authoritarian tendencies of the thirteenth-century state everywhere. In England this corporatism was intermixed with other legal and social traditions—the shire courts and the juries, a highly centralized and spatially homogenized judicial system, aristocratic culture, the consensual quality involved in the king as feudal lord ruling with the consent and participation of his great vassals, and Thomist philosophy. All these diverse elements were involved in the advent of liberalism. The impact of Roman-canonical corporatism played at least a secondary role in that development.

For Americans perhaps even more than for British people, the advent of judicial liberalism in the thirteenth century—as signaled in Magna Carta, articulated by Bracton, and integrated into political behavior by the reconfirmation of Magna Carta in 1297—is a subject of persistent, crucial importance. That is because the Bill of Rights of 1791, and the Fourteenth Amendment of 1868, enshrined the idea of due process and equality of the law into the federal Constitution, and in the 1960s the Supreme Court imposed this liberalism on the states and on all individuals resident in the United States.

So why and how liberal theory emerged in the thirteenth century is of direct relevance to the American political experience, whereas the English still have the monarchy, Parliament, the established church, and the distinctive instutionalized life of the gentry and other upper-middle-class people to bind that small country together. Take away the Bill of Rights, the Fourteenth Amendment, and the Supreme Court activism of the 1960s and the American system would implode and the people of the United States would fall apart into myriad warring factions.

If the spirit of Bracton does not endure in the United States, then the republic does not stand. Perhaps that is why law and the legal profession are more important in the United States than in any other country, including England, the birthplace and nursery of the common law. Bracton lives in America, and he has to live if America is to endure.

9
Gentrification

A SOCIAL CLASS IS a large group of people, resident in a particular political territory, with a common set of material endowments, a similar set of family and individual ambitions, a distinctive behavior pattern, and an identifiable intellectual culture. The special group in England called knights in the thirteenth century and gentry by the fifteenth fits this definition of a social class very closely.

The gentry were the rural middle class of late medieval and early modern England. They comprised around 10 percent of the population. They had common material endowments in land, mainly for cereal agriculture in the southern half of the country (where at least three-quarters of them lived), and mainly for sheep and cattle ranching in the northern part of the realm.

The gentry's main interest from 1200 to the mid-fourteenth century was in the accumulation of additional land as well as protection of what they already held. During this period of population boom, there was a steady inflation in the value of land and a scarcity of easy access to augmenting holdings. Marginal land, later abandoned, was brought under the plow.

After the Black Death (bubonic plague and possibly also a rare humanoid strain of murrain) of the mid-fourteenth century, preceded in the second decade of the century by unusual morbidity from crop failure and famine and followed by recurring flare-ups of plague in the fifteenth century, brought about the catastrophic diminution of the population—from as high as six million in 1300 to not more than three million in 1400, a level that stayed the same until 1600—the ambition of the gentry was modified. Because of the labor shortage, there was now less accumulation of new holdings for direct exploitation, although good opportunities were always viscerally pursued. Between 1350 and 1500 the gentry maximized their resources by various management strategies, particularly leasing out land rather than cultivating it directly under their own management and trying to hold down labor costs with the controversial assistance of government legislation.

The common behavior pattern of the gentry was always marked by ambiguity and a certain kind of marginality, which found an outlet in litigation and piety and, after 1550, in political activism.

In the later Middle Ages the gentry were still on the margin of political power, expressed in county and local officeholding and sitting on juries, but before 1500 never as a group significantly gaining political power at the national level, although some individual careerists from this class did gain high royal preferment.

The gentry smelled of the field, the barn, and their constant companions, horses. They drank heavily in beer and overindulged in an increasingly expensive red-meat diet. But they were slowly coming to appreciate more refined living, reflected in heavy investment in good, strong housing and improved domestic comforts.

They were credulous in religious matters, especially with

regard to anything in this medicineless world connected to faith healing, while at the same time critical and jealous of clerical privilege, which they nevertheless sought eagerly for some of their own progeny.

The gentry were literate among males and usually so among females, but never as a group intrinsically interested in cultivating literature and the arts and developing a high level of humanistic learning and intellectuality, although again a very small handful of individuals from this group pursued facets of intellectual culture, mainly poetry. *Pearl*, one of the finest English poems of the late Middle Ages, was written by an obscure country gentleman near Oxford around 1380.

In the crowded rural England of 1300 there were probably close to half a million gentry (including all members of the gentry families) and in the much diminished population of 1400 probably still around three hundred thousand.

There was a broad spectrum of wealth among the gentry from millionaire landlords down to small freeholders with incomes of some fifty thousand dollars annually (in 1997 U.S. currency).

The gentry are divisible into two main groups: wealthy families who were rural capitalists and dominant in the county courts and as MPs in the House of Commons; and small-time local landlords who were comfortable but without capital and had no political involvement even at the county level.

Borrowing a recondite term from military feudalism, the less wealthy and politically influential gentry during the later Middle Ages were sometimes referred to as "esquires" while the term "knights" in this usage was reserved for the powerful and affluent gentry elite, the leadership cohort in the upper middle class of county society. In chivalric imagery esquires were wellborn attendants on the battalion knights and were often young warriors in training. By 1400 "esquires" were just a somewhat vague subset of the gentry class, which was commonly designated by the generic term "knights." "Esquires" became a social rather than a military term, meaning the less wealthy and prominent gentry. Lawyers in common-law countries still frequently use the appellation "John Smyth, Esq."

The top level of the wealthy gentry could sometimes make marriages with titled aristocracy and move themselves and their progeny into the rank of the nobility, although remarkably few did so. Just as rarely did they intermarry with an urban mercantile family of bourgeois capitalists.

In the fifteenth century at the bottom level of the ordinary gentry, there was little to distinguish gentry from the wealthier and ambitious peasantry called the yeomen, except that a gentry family already had a history of landed status and reception of local deference, while the yeomanry were newly arrived in wealth and status.

In the fifteenth century there was much greater bleeding of class lines at the lowest than at the highest stratum of the gentry. Intermarriage between impecunious gentry and affluent rising yeomanry was much more common than between very wealthy gentry and the aristocracy.

As in all premodern societies going back to ancient Greece, the gentry families of the later Middle Ages conformed to the nuclear rather than the extended-family model. Surviving children departed early, the females either to marriage or a nunnery by age eighteen, the sons by twenty-two to getting married and setting up their own establishments on lands given by their father, or to a learned profession or military service. The eldest son, favored by primogeniture, after a good marriage in light of his high expectations, would live well off his wife's dowry while he awaited the great windfall from his father's death. (He would not have to wait long. Life expectancy of males averaged in the low forties because of lack of therapeutic medicine and because of an unhealthy high-cholesterol diet.)

In view of domestic servants and one or two stewards (estate managers) who might be allowed at the dinner table, and possibly a household cleric, ordinary gentry had households larger than their immediate family. The top stratum of the wealthy gentry imitated the aristocracy in sustaining large and very expensive households—a myriad of retainers, guests, a priest to staff the family chapel, plus chefs, wine stewards, grooms, entertainers, and secretaries. The family itself was nuclear but multimillionaire gentry could command a household of many dozens of people, a practice that prevailed in the great English country houses until World War II and was beautifully illustrated in the novel and film, *The Remains of the Day*.

Faithful household servants—and family lawyers—were often compensated by gifts of a small estate under "serjeanty tenure" (household service tenure) which was rent free.

Gentry was a social class, not a titular distinction. Perhaps a third of the gentry families' male heads were officially knighted and called "Sir" (and their wives came to be called "Lady") but being gentry was not per se a titular privilege. "Sir Roger Smyth" was certainly gentry, but there were many prosperous gentry families without a knightly title. Being a "belted" (designated) knight could entail extra political and social expenses and was often avoided by shrewd families. There were relatively poor "sirs" (who might try to upgrade their fortunes dramatically by service in what they hoped would be the king's booty-producing French wars) and there were very substantial gentry families who—if they could, because the royal government sometimes pressured them to take the knightly title—avoided the costly privilege of being Sir and Lady.

In addition to the cultivation, management, and accumulation of land, the building of imposing country houses, the raising and riding of horses, and the complicated negotiations for marriage making—the gentry prized higher education, although (like the American upper middle class today, in contrast to the high bourgeoisie of Renaissance Florence or Victorian England) for strictly utilitarian purposes. An Oxford University degree—less so for a downscale Cambridge degree before 1550—was an avenue for younger sons to gain a good clerical position and possibly move on from there to the exalted and extremely remunerative ranks of bishops or abbots or higher level royal governmental service.

Education at the national law schools, the Inns of Court in London, was always useful for the information it inculcated on the land law and other forms of judicial action. Those who persevered at the Inns of Court and were called to the bar had very good career prospects as barristers and judges, and from there also royal government service.

Getting a university degree or completing the course of study in the Inns of Court in 1450 was expensive. Annual student fees and cost of living at Oxford or an Inn of Court was about the same as studying at an Ivy League university today. Normally the pursuit of higher education was a privilege only of the wealthier, upper stratum of the gentry—as it remained until World War II. Before 1945 access to lucrative career-generating higher education was another hallmark of a well-established and affluent social class.

Glanville and Bracton had written treatises on something called "the law of England." But by the end of the thirteenth century English law was called "the common law." The origin of the term is not certainly known. It may—wishfully and dramatically—refer to the law common to the whole realm. But in medieval Europe, however, secular or nonchurch law was frequently called common law anywhere, and this humdrum rationale may be the origin of the appellation "common law" for English law: It wasn't canon law.

Whatever the derivation of the term, English common law became identified with the interests, attitudes, and behavior patterns of the gentry. It was regarded by them as the bulwark of defense of their endowment and their status. It was central to their well-being and world-view. It was the instrument to satisfy their acquisitive instincts.

Whether we follow Maitland and Stubbs in thinking that the common law during the Angevin legal revolution was already identified with gentry needs and ambitions, or whether we follow Milsom in seeing the magnates' primary role in the fashioning of common-law procedure and principles, with the common law becoming especially identified with the gentry only at some point in the later thirteenth century, the connection between the law and the gentry way of life and thought had occurred by the advent of the reign of Edward I in 1272, if not a century or a half century earlier.

To know the intricate processes of the land law, to find and retain suitable counsel in key cases, to be constantly involved in litigation either to defend or acquire land in an inflationary, land-hungry era, to work out complicated and advantageous leases after 1350, to generate the students for the Inns of Court and the personnel for the legal profession both as attorneys and judges— this was the gentry's self-chosen destiny by the later thirteenth century.

The identification of gentry and law at the same time further shaped the outlook and behavior of the gentry and deeply affected the direction of the development of common law.

The way litigation in land law was central to gentry life in the 1280s as the inflationary cycle in real estate reached its peak is exemplified by the case of *Mortimer* v. *Whelton*, the appeals record of which in *certiorari* has been made available for us by the research of Robert C. Palmer.

This case involved the rich manor of Whilton in the county of Northampton. The value of this estate would be around five million U.S. dollars today. Normally a piece of land of this high value was too expensive to be litigated in a county court in first instance. But as often happened, the contending parties agreed to litigate first in the county court because it was cheaper than to go straight to Common Pleas in Westminster, with a jury awkwardly transported from the countryside; and the counsels for the litigants wanted to feel out the opposition's case before the final and decisive round in appeal on *certiorari* in Westminster.

The contending parties were Felicia Whelton and Joyce la Zouche Mortimer (jointly with her husband, since married women could not litigate alone; Felicia was unmarried at the time of the case).

What lawyers called the "narrative" of events, the story behind the case, ran this way: Back in the late 1260s William of Whelton, a multimillionaire member of the top stratum of the gentry, enfiefed (granted) his younger son, Nicholas, the succulent manor of Whilton by charter (land deed) because William liked his younger son and wanted to enrich him before he died and his elder son got all his property by primogeniture; and also because William was afraid he and his family would lose the manor anyway if he didn't take this evasive action because of an impending felonious judgment against him.

William of Whelton was one of the rich gentry who had rashly taken Simon de Montfort's ultimately losing side in the Barons' War against Henry III. Now that the future Edward I had restored royal power, William of Whelton was about to become (like the historical Robin Hood) one of the "disinherited" gentry.

Nicholas agreed to lease the land back to his father during the rest of William's lifetime. William could then claim, when the avenging royal justices came around, that he could not be "*disseised*" by royal court judgment because Nicholas now owned the land. (This ploy is still used in common law, for example by a tax evader signing over all his property to his wife before the government can sue him for back taxes.) Felicia, one of the two principal litigants in the 1280s, was the daughter of Nicholas Whelton.

William of Whelton was indeed dispossessed of his great manor (and all his other property) by judgment for felonious treason. The king then enfiefed the manor of Whilton to another ambitious member of the top stratum of the gentry, William de la Zouche. Joyce la Zouche Mortimer, the other litigant in this great land-law case, was the daughter and heiress of William la Zouche and inherited the estate of Whilton from him.

Joyce was married to Robert Mortimer. The Mortimers were a large, wealthy, ruthlessly ambitious, and politically well-connected Anglo-Welsh family. The political factor was an important subtext in how the case turned out.

The thorny legal issues that were endlessly disputed by the opposing attorneys in the case were: (*a*) Did Nicholas ever have real physical *seisin* of the land from his father or was it a phony parchment transaction? (*b*) Felicia having lost her claim to the land by inheritance from Nicholas, did the court take affirmative recognition of the fact that she was a minor at the time, as they were supposed to do, and give her unusual attention and consideration, and if they did not take this affirmative action on behalf of a female minor, was the judgment against her therefore invalid?

The case was heard in the 1280s, with Joyce initially in possession of the manor, before three successive juries and panels of circuit judges in the county court of Northampton, after Felicia opened litigation by obtaining a writ of *novel disseisin*. The resulting first jury, consisting of gentry sympathetic to the Whelton family and its historical traditions in the neighborhood and therefore loyal to Felicia, found for her.

Then, before another panel of circuit judges, Joyce and her husband got the land back on testimony of a second, double-size jury, no doubt hand-picked by a compliant sheriff to comprise those not beholden to the Whelton family. Forestalling further litigation by Felicia, the Mortimers had the decision of this second augmented jury (and its "impeachment," or condemnation of the first, pro-Felicia jury) registered in the Court of Common Pleas in London.

But Felicia's capable attorneys were not finished. Before yet a third jury in the county of Northampton, they played the affirmative-action card and claimed that Felicia's status as a minor was not recognized when the land was originally taken by the la Zouche/Mortimer family. The Mortimers refused to respond directly to this new claim, citing the testimony of the second, augmented jury and the registration in London of the pro-Mortimer judgment of the second trial. They claimed *stare decisis*; they stood upon the record. The circuit judges in this third county trial then declared the land forfeited to Felicia because the Mortimers had failed to respond to her suit. Obviously judge shopping was important in this case.

It was time to play the political card of Mortimer influence with the royal government. Joyce's attorneys coolly filed a petition with the chancellor, representing the king as the fount of justice, to quash the recent judgment on behalf of Felicia and to restore the second trial's judgment based on the testimony of the augmented jury and the registration of judgment for Joyce with the Court of Common Pleas.

At this point either the Court of Common Pleas or the all-star Exchequer Chamber with judges from all the central courts (the record is not clear) responding to the chancellor's request for final and equitable action, called for the complete record of the case on a bench writ of *certiorari*. After gravely considering the long record of three county court trials, the high court returned the land to the Mortimers, where for judicial (as well as political) reasons it belonged.

But land law was reluctant ever to close the books on a dispute involving rich gentry land. Judgment was rendered not *sine die* (without a day—closing the case forever) but "without prejudice" to Felicia reopening the case at some future time, she having conveniently announced to the court, when she appeared to be losing her case, her engagement to marry. The Whilton dispute was not finally settled until several decades later, when the surviving claimants, the descendants of Felicia and Joyce, married each other.

The sophisticated strategies used by the litigants in the 1280s could not have been thought up and employed in court without highly skilled, expensive and experienced counsel. It was because of a shortage of such reputable litigators that the legal profession felt it necessary at the time that *Mortimer* v. *Whelton* was being argued to begin to establish secular national law schools in London, the Inns of Court for the training of barristers. By 1310 there were (and still are) four of them: Gray's Inn, Lincoln's Inn, the Middle Temple, and the Inner Temple.

Since the law students needed room and board in crowded, boisterous, expensive London, the judges and attorneys who comprised the leadership of the bar took over four failing or vacant inns (the latter two belonged to the Order of the Templars, disbanded by the papacy in the early years of the fourteenth century after allegations of sodomy and heresy against the order were made by the French king, who coveted their bank in Paris). It is as if the leading law schools in New York City today were called Hilton, Sheraton, Ramada, and Marriott.

The Inns of Court were set up to train litigators, called "pleaders" in the fourteenth century and later (as today) barristers. The lawyers who did the parchment or paperwork of law as well as prepared the cases for the barristers to litigate in court—called simply attorneys in the fourteenth century and later (as today) solicitors—were not provided with training schools. They were trained on the apprenticeship system, like shoemakers and carpenters. They put in many years of service and cheap labor for a solicitor, learning how to prepare documents and ultimately write briefs and finally on demonstrating professional mastery could go out on their own.

To prepare to be a barrister and be admitted to one of the Inns of Court it was (and is) necessary to be "admitted to chambers," in effect to find an internship in a barrister's office. Since there were (and are) always more applications than places, this was an effective way of screening out those who did not come from suitable families (and even when women were admitted to the

English bar in the late nineteenth century, to prevent all but a very few of them from studying at the Inns of Court before the 1960s—things are different now).

The Inns of Court combined functions that are divided among three different agencies in the United States—they are law schools, they are fraternities for barristers and provide club-houses for them, and they admit graduates to the bar. It is a comfortable in-group arrangement.

In the Middle Ages and well into the nineteenth century, studying at the Inns of Court was an alternative to a university education, not something that (as today) followed graduation from university. Students entered young—as early as sixteen—and grew up within the walls of an Inn of Court, taking as long as a dozen years to be admitted to the bar.

An Inn of Court provided lectures, simple and pedestrian in content, on main points of the law. By chance a written bar exam (there was probably also an oral one) of around the year 1500 has recently turned up. It is very easy, consisting entirely of the requirement to comment on some standard land laws from the time of Edward I—answers that could be learned by rote.

It was how the novice did in chambers and his social background that principally determined his entry to the barristers' profession, not a high level of legal learning. Barristers spent years, possibly decades in a junior position to a prominent barrister, before achieving independent seniority and substantial income.

This was another screening device—you had to have (and until very recently still had to have) a wealthy family behind you if you wanted to be an English barrister, because you were going to make very little money in your first ten years in the profession.

By 1400 barristers and solicitors belonged to absolutely different kinds of lawyerly professions. Barristers did not create documents and relied heavily on solicitors briefing them on cases. In modern times some famous criminal-law barristers prided themselves on never talking personally to their clients. And as gentle-men, English barristers did and do not—like Cicero and Roman advocates— send bills. This is as in Cicero's time a mere charade, of course. The solicitors billed on the barrister's behalf and passed the payment on, which in the instance of a senior barrister would be a hefty sum.

Being a senior barrister was and is a highly lucrative as well as socially elite profession. The British TV series, *Rumpole of the Bailey*, written by John Mortimer—as distinguished a barrister as he is a dramatist—devotes one of its episodes to Rumpole (not the most aristocratic of barristers but very plebeian—that is the running joke) spending lots of time fussing because a solicitor has failed to pass along to him his fee with suitable dispatch.

In the American colonies in the eighteenth century, the absolute distinction prevailing in England between barristers and solicitors broke down because of a shortage of any kind of quali-fied lawyer. Yet a functional difference does exist today in American legal practice. Being a litigator is in practice a special branch of the American bar, and 80 percent of American lawyers never appear in court for a trial.

In the early 1980s Prime Minister Margaret Thatcher, trying to sweep the cobwebs out of English society, proposed abolishing the absolute distinction between barristers and solicitors, but the former wouldn't hear of it. What was good enough for the four-teenth century was still good for them. Since 1960 good law schools on university campuses for training solicitors in Britain have developed, and the profession of solicitor has thus generally experienced a rise in status and effectiveness. It is also one in which women are well represented.

The greatest privilege that barristers had (and didn't want the Iron Lady to take away) was filling the ranks of the judges of the central courts. Solicitors today can be local magistrates but still not superior court judges like those in Common Pleas and King's Bench. Judges were and are chosen by the chancellor from among the more prominent senior barristers—called serjeants of law in the Middle Ages and, since the nineteenth century, King's or Queen's Counsel. The chancellor's selection inevitably was and is influenced by political factors as well as records of judicial performance.

The serjeants and QCs were awarded a uniform, a silk gown, to signify their exalted status as leaders of the legal profession. Hence the modern term "taking the silk," to mean becoming a QC.

The QCs—and other barristers—also appear in court as counsel representing the Crown. One of the distinctive aspects of the English as compared to the American version of common law is the very small number of official Crown prosecutors in England as compared to the large bureaucratic cohort in the United States, at the municipal, state, and federal levels, particularly committed to criminal prosecution. Instead of a salaried staff of Crown attorneys, the English system, coming out of the fourteenth century and still in place, is for a serjeant, QC, or some other barrister to be hired ad hoc to appear in court on behalf of the Crown. This explains one of the more puzzling episodes—to some Americans—in *Rumpole of the Bailey,* when Rumpole faces as the Crown prosecutor another barrister from the very same chamber (office) that he occupies.

The conventional explanation for the English system of ad hoc representation of the Crown by independent civilian barristers is that the English love of liberty precludes the establishment of a large and menacing body of salaried government attorneys such as prevails in the United States and is also a prominent feature of Roman law. This explanation is plausibly rooted in ultraliberal, antistatist ideological concerns of the eighteenth and nineteenth centuries. But the practice of retaining barristers to represent the Crown goes back to the thirteenth and fourteenth centuries and was obviously intended to assure more well-paid business for the masters of the Inns of Court.

The English system of ad hoc representation of the Crown,

even in criminal cases, as compared to the American bureaucratic system of large staffs of state prosecutors, has both its up- and downsides. In the positive sense it reduces the possibility of famous, wealthy, highly experienced defense attorneys overwhelming young, low-paid, inexperienced, and self-conscious state prosecutors.

On the downside the English system allows prosecutors and defense counsel—even if not from the same chambers, but always just from the same clubby little world of the Inns of Court—to be too friendly and courteous to one another.

The English system mitigates the fierceness of the adversarial attitude exhibited by the best of the criminal defense bar in the United States. Considering that the judges are also promoted barristers, the bench and opposing counsel in an English trial are all members of the same closed elite world. This makes for orderly trials but not for the best representation of unpopular defendants, as the faulty prosecution and conviction of alleged Irish Republican Army terrorists in the 1970s and early 1980s demonstrated.

But an ingredient of English law was always more concern for removal of unpopular people from the circle of society, rather than passionate effort to establish guilt or innocence.

Another major difference between English barristers and American litigators is that barristers do not work out of corporate law firms. There are indeed no English firms of barristers in the American sense of a number of lawyers—as many as three hundred—who are corporate partners sharing annual "yields" or profits (very rarely losses) from the firm's practice as a whole. A half dozen London barristers (usually less, rarely more) may share chambers (offices) with common secretarial and research support paid for by all the resident barristers. But each barrister in the tradition of the gentry is an independent contractor pursuing his own practice and personally billing a client through the facade of a cooperating solicitor.

The maturing of the profession of barrister and the establishment of the Inns of Court as law schools led to the beginning around 1300 of the production of a series of volumes that comprised selections of significant points in trials during the year. These annual anthologies of the high points of litigation were called the *Year Books*. They were unofficial publications of about four hundred pages each (in modern print) of turning points or innovations in litigation taken from the records of court cases and intended for perusal by practicing lawyers, especially barristers, and by law students in barristers' chambers preparing for their law exams and their call to the bar.

The *Year Book*s are written in law French. They do not normally give an extensive record of a case, and rarely do they include the ultimate jury decision and judgment of the court, although most of the time the outcome of the trial can be surmised from the key part of the case that is extracted from the court roll. The *Year Book* anthologists, probably senior barristers teaching in the Inns of Court, particularly wanted to show determinations by judges in response to barristers' tactics—what was accepted, what wasn't. The *Year Books* are keen to exhibit the traverse, the back and forth adversarial flow between the attorneys, or at least the exciting part showing one attorney getting the better of his adversary.

The *Year Books* are quick to pick up on the judges' resort to analogical reasoning from a similar case—that is, *stare decisis*, or precedent. There are endless examples in the *Year Book* cases of the judges' proclivity to formalism, to sticking to the letter of the law; for example, that thirty minutes of *seisin* is not *de minimis* (too trivial to be legally recognizable) but is still possession; or that crossing into your neighbor's land, while you are trimming a tree on the edge of your own property, to pick up a fallen bough is still a nominal injury to your neighbor.

The *Year Books* also show the judges quick to cite the "parole evidence rule," still today an important principle in the law of written contracts. If a written contract exists setting forth the mutual obligations of the parties, anything said before signing the contract by one or other of the contending parties (orally, "parole") has no force or standing. Again this is a kind of formalism; the written contract is the entire agreement, and no oral promises marginal to the text have validity.

The *Year Books* continued to be produced laboriously by manuscript until the age of printing began around 1500, and then slowly were made more accessible in printed form. Somewhere around 1560 they stopped being produced, to be succeeded beginning about a decade later—eventually under the special aegis of Sir Edward Coke—by the *English Reports*, near-complete texts of important trials, not just anthologized extracts. The *Reports*—products of the legal profession but again not official texts—were in English, not law French. They continued until around 1800, when they were succeeded by modern printing of all official texts of court cases.

Limited as the *Year Books*' annual anthologies of common law's greatest hits were, they are still a gold mine for the historian of the common law. Therefore Maitland around 1885 established an endowment, the Selden Society (named after John Selden, a seventeenth-century antiquarian), to publish the 250 manuscript volumes (in French before 1450) in handsome editions with English translations on facing pages. About seventy of such modern published volumes have by now appeared. There is much more information in their texts of the *Year Books* than legal historians have yet brought to light. The still-unpublished manuscripts of the *Year Books* are in the Public Record Office in Chancery Lane in London, near the high courts and the Inns of Court.

Maitland's two-volume history of the common law (second edition, 1898, always cited as "Pollock and Maitland," even though Frederick Pollock, the jewel of the Edwardian English bar and under a fictitious name the hero of Terence Rattigan's 1948 play *The Winslow Boy*, ended up writing less than 1 percent and unsuccessfully begged the Cambridge University Press to remove his name from Maitland's work) ends in 1272 with the beginning of the reign of Edward I. In researching and editing the *Year Books*, Maitland was preparing also to write about the succeeding two centuries of English law, but he died prematurely at the age of fifty-six from diabetes and pneumonia in the Canary Islands, where he is buried.

Lacking Maitland to show them the way, historians dispute the nature of the driving force shaping the development of English law from 1272 until 1485, the date usually given as the end of the English Middle Ages, with the accession of the postmedieval Tudor dynasty (although a better line of demarcation is 1534, the advent of the English Reformation).

There are four theses on the main currents in transforming the common law from 1272 to 1485. Stubbs in the 1870s proposed an organic and teleological view in the third volume of his masterly *Constitutional History of England*: The impetus to liberty inherited from the Anglo-Saxons, and blended with Norman and Plantagenet efficiency, continued to work itself out and surfaced in the mid-fifteenth century in the "Lancastrian Constitution," what Stubbs saw as the proto-modern liberal ideology upheld by the Lancastrian dynasty who ruled England in the first six decades of the fifteenth century, further molding the common law.

Milsom, in *Historical Foundations of the Common Law* (2nd edition, 1981) and other works, placed the motive force in legal change in the legal profession itself, expanding by its professional skill and use of legal reasoning the principles and processes of the land law into other, novel fields of law, such as liability, debt, and oral contract. The Milsom view is that the legal profession modified and extended the common law on its own in the later Middle Ages.

The prolific American historian of the common law, Robert Palmer, in his *English Law in the Age of the Black Death* (1993), strongly dissented from Milsom's view of an autonomous legal profession working things out by itself. Palmer contended that after the demographic disaster of the Black Death in the mid-fourteenth century, it was royal policy of Edward III's energetic government to restore social discipline by bringing in important legislation that moved the law in new directions. Though there is much to reflect on in Palmer's argument, its weakness is that the common law had already undergone some major changes in the seventy years before the Black Death, and continued to be modified in the fifteenth, after the shock of the Black Death had passed.

Unquestionably Stubbs, Milsom, and Palmer each pointed to important forces shaping late medieval English law and pushing it in some important new directions. But what is persistent throughout the period from 1272 to 1485 and beyond, into the sixteenth century, is the use of the law by the strong gentry class in its own interests. This social factor is the fourth explanation for legal transformation between 1272 and 1485. Through judicial review and autonomous ventures of the legal profession—affected by legislation stemming in part from royal policy in some key areas, and at least vaguely subscribing consistently to a kind of constitutional liberalism—the gentry modified the law to serve its class interests.

The aristocracy did not need the law; they used their incredibly vast material and human resources and their prominence in war and politics to get what they wanted. The peasants had no voice aside from one or two violent but short-lived rebellions. The urban mercantile class was off in its own enclosed bourgeois world. It was left to the gentry to make the common law its prized possession and use it for its class interests.

The main focus of the royal government in the fourteenth century was the imperial struggle against France, and through much of the fifteenth century the focus was on internal squabbles within the royal family over the throne. In this ambience royal policy was only fitfully free to attend to legal change.

In the fourteen and fifteenth centuries there also existed a social and political disposition to leave changes in the law to the legal profession, to the barristers and the judges who rose from the ranks of the barristers. This was the late medieval guild system applied to common law.

The later Middle Ages were the golden era of the merchant and craft guilds. Much of trade and industrial regulation was in the hands of corporate, self-governing guilds. They had a high degree of autonomy, under sporadic and vague Crown monitoring, in organizing and regulating the export of wool and the importation of wine—the principal commodities of English external commerce. In the towns the craft guilds regulated the production and sale of goods manufactured in the shops of master artisans.

The pervasive guild culture, by which economic regulation was assigned to corporate elites in trade and industry, affected the way in which the need for new law was identified and its content imagined and elaborated. There were occasional significant pieces of parliamentary legislation, but less innovation occurred through statute than through the law finding and law making by the legal profession itself acting as a guild parallel to the wool merchants and master shoemakers in their spheres. Behind late medieval lawmaking through judicial review, of legal reasoning from the bench, of innovative argument from the Inns of Court, lies a guild mentality. And since the legal profession articulated the interests of the gentry from whom the profession was recruited, and on whose behalf it functioned, lawmaking by the legal profession meant shaping of the common law in the class interests of the wealthier gentry families.

Throughout all this time in the more than two centuries after 1272, the gentry—forever conscious of their wealth and key position in English society, ambitious to extend and secure their status and wealth, producing the personnel for the legal profession—wanted further changes in the law to serve their immediate interests.

A common-law culture had been created in the long centuries before 1272. It was sufficiently functional by the late thirteenth century to operate integrally in the life of the rural middle class, which staffed its juries, provided the judges and sheriffs who administered it, and sent its sons to the Inns of Court to be well educated there in its judicial processes and hopefully to train some of their progeny for lucrative and socially elevated careers at the bar. The force for change in the common law in the later Middle Ages lies above all in the interests and attitudes and concept formations and behavior patterns of the gentry.

The structuralist semiotics (analysis of signs) of Claude Lévi-Strauss and his disciples provide another insight into the gentrification of late medieval common law. Semiotic theory claims that people fully integrated into a culture see a text produced by that culture differently than do those who stand outside the culture. The latter read the text in a fragmented, isolated, particularized way. Those from within the culture read the text in relation to many other texts generated by the same culture. These semiotic insiders get signification from certain words and phrases that the outsiders do not pick up on. The cultural insiders see the text within a broad perspective of other cultural significations and evaluate its importance in a way the outsider is incapable of.

This is the way it was for the late medieval gentry as they picked up on particular pieces of legislation or innovations produced by judicial review. They put it into a perspective of a legal culture in which they were integrated participants, and they understood these changes as signs of cultural modalities that are not easy now for the historian to recapture.

Perhaps that is why accounts of late medieval common law bog down so readily in a maze of mysterious and not infrequently obscure technicalities. We must struggle to see these technical processes as part of a holistic gentry culture and to try to read the signs as they did. There is an anthropological challenge here that legal historians rarely respond to.

Another way of gauging the significance of the gentrification of the common law is to put it in the context of the long duration of English history.

In a prizewinning two-volume economic history, *British Imperialism* (1993), P. J. Cain and A. G. Hopkins have argued that the driving force and leadership in the rise, development, and perpetuation of British imperialism lay in "gentlemanly capitalism," the combination of the old landed elite with the institutions of London banking and other financial services that emerged around 1700.

This gentry elite, it is claimed, rather than the industrial bourgeoisie or ideological supremacists, consistently determined the course of modern British history and persist in the post-Thatcherite London of today, within the City, to exercise a determining leadership role through international financial services, even though the political empire has disappeared.

If there is merit in the Cain-Hopkins thesis of rooting British imperialism in gentlemanly capitalism, then the pre-modern gentrification of the common law becomes all the more important in the long perspective of English history.

The common law shaped the mind-set and behavior pattern of the landed elite and prepared them to offer creative leadership in the critically important financial service side of modern capitalism. This gentlemanly capitalist ethos was grounded in the interaction between the gentry and the common law in the four centuries after 1272.

Appendix to Chapter 9

A CIVIL ACTION IN 1306 — *A land law case in Common Pleas from the year 1306, from the* Year Books.

The original text, at times pithy and technical, has here been paraphrased and extrapolated in modern language (as well as translated from law French).

Wandrages v. *Bradstroke*

NARRATIVE: Two ecclesiastical magnates, Prior Bradstroke and Prior Wandrages, had traded lands in an even exchange thirty years before. The lands Bradstroke received were out of the country [probably in France]. A charter was drawn witnessing the exchange, and the English king also issued a charter sanctioning the exchange. When Bradstroke entered the lands, he discovered that they were not in free alms tenure [charitable tenure for which no rent or taxes were due] as he expected, but ordinary freehold land owing plenty of taxes and rent. Bradstroke had been cheated, he felt, and sought to cancel the exchange. His counsel had the problem of getting the case into court. He used the petty assize of writ of *utrum*, which was designed to determine by jury whether a piece of land was free alms (charitable) or regular freehold land—a question to which the counsel already knew the answer, because that is why the suit was being brought, but he needed to get the case before a jury and then make special pleas to get the exchange canceled. He ran up against a good counsel for the defendant and a tough and unsympathetic judge.

TOUDEBY *(counsel for the plaintiff)*:

The charter indicates by itself that it was made out of the realm, and therefore we claim it is invalid, having no standing in an English court, and the exchange of lands should be canceled.

MALMESTHORP *(counsel for the defendant)*:

You cannot deny the validity of the exchange because the King also issued a document validating the first charter and thereby bringing the exchange within English legal jurisdiction.

BEREFORD, JUSTICE:

I agree with the counsel for the defendant. Further, we can apply *stare decisis* [precedent] here: There was recently a case in a trial between the king of Scotland and B. In this case the charter also was made outside the kingdom, but it was ratified by the charter of the English king, and therefore the first charter was held to be validated in English law. This is the same issue.

TOUDEBY:

When the exchanges were made, my client Bradstroke acted in good faith and offered a long series of documents going back to William the Conqueror, showing specifically the value and status of the land he offered. The other side didn't provide this kind of verifiable documentation about the land it offered in exchange. That is when the trouble started.

BEREFORD, J.:

That is your client's own foolishness. *Caveat emptor* [let the buyer beware].

TOUDEBY:

When the exchanges were made thirty years ago, in the time of King Henry III, the defendant made an oral promise that the lands were held under charitable tenure. His oral statement was later found to be fraudulent, and therefore the exchange should be canceled.

WARR *(another counsel for the defendant)*:
We cite the parole evidence rule. When there is a written contract, the terms of the contract are entirely within the written text, and any oral statement made at the time has no standing.

BEREFORD, J.:
I agree.

The *Year Book* extract does not say the defendant won, but obviously he did so, as the judge had nothing to instruct the jury on except to look at the text of the original charter which by itself provided no grounds for cancellation.

What was a student or junior barrister supposed to learn by studying this case?

A. You have somehow to get the case into court before a jury, and for that purpose use whatever writ will best get you there, even if it does not really apply.

B. *Caveat emptor*: Provided there is a written contract, a bad deal, once entered into, is almost impossible to cancel.

C. *Stare decisis*: precedent by way of analogical reasoning.

D. Parole evidence rule. If there is a written contract, sidebar and oral promises have no validity.

E. Even very good lawyers lose cases.

F. The issue that the judge allows to be presented to the jury is all-important. If an issue favorable to the plaintiff cannot get put before the jury, the plaintiff will obviously lose. Therefore who presides, especially in a civil trial, can be important for the outcome of the case. What one judge will allow to be put before the jury may be excluded by another. Judge shopping, if possible, should therefore be considered. Justice Bereford was known to be hell on wheels (even Edward I eventually became fed up with him). A plaintiff would have to have a very strong case when appearing in Bereford's court if he hoped to win.

G. Bradstroke was doubly foolish—he made a bad deal and then used up a lot of money in a lawsuit he was likely to lose.

10
Deep Structure

IF TWENTIETH-CENTURY SOCIOLOGY and social anthropology teach one lesson about history, it is simply this:

All systems reach a point in their formative stage when the compelling ideas and social relations attain a centrality of power that is expressed in a deep structure. After that, short of physical destruction by invasion (for example, Germany and Japan in 1945) or internal revolution (for example, France in 1789 or Russia in 1917), the structure will proliferate through all aspects of culture, politics, gender relations, and social stratification and exhibit ever-more-elaborate institutional forms, ideological exemplifications, adapting to and pulling into itself any and all outcomes from historical change.

The point of deep inauguration of the common law had been reached by the start of the reign of Edward I in 1272 and significant judicial growth and adaptation continued to the end of the reign of Henry VIII (1509–47).

For almost three centuries the common law was able to draw on its original discursive expressions and technical formulations between around 1000 and 1272, and driven above all by the needs, interests, and ambitions of the gentry, to absorb all other aspects of social and cultural change into an elaborate articulation of the common law.

The period between 1272 and 1547 was marked by dramatic macrosocial changes: a biomedical and demographic disaster that reduced the population of England and Wales by at least 33 and possibly closer to 50 percent; two centuries of endemic and incredibly expensive warfare with the Parisian monarchy for imperial control of western France and Belgium, ending with total English defeat and almost complete expulsion from the Continent by the mid-fifteenth century; vibrant proliferation of religious individualism in the form of institutionalized faith-healing on an aggravated scale of biblical fundamentalism, theological dissent, and separatist spiritual communities, resulting in disarray of the church's traditional leadership in society and the connected trend to nationalization of the church's material and human resources under royal authority. The era also featured the unprecedented ascension of aristocratic political power between 1320 and 1470 and then its rapid diminution and near-extinction by 1520; the abolition of the vestiges of serfdom and the restlessness and occasional rebellion of rural peasantry buffeted by an unstable labor market; radical and unchecked exercise of the protomodern business cycle, highlighted by long agricultural and trade depression between 1280 and 1480, and then by resurgent prosperity and steep inflation.

Also occurring were the rise of a nativist English-language literate culture after 1350 and its blending in upper- and middle-class consciousness with Renaissance classical humanism and the latter's well-defined and innovative secondary school system; internal conflict and in the fifteenth century intermittent civil war within the long-reigning Plantagenet dynasty, leading to its replacement by the arriviste Tudors in 1485.

Through all these changes and upheavals, the common law continued to articulate its deep structure, absorbing and adapting the impact of these macrohistorical forces into microjudicial actions and cognate ideological formulations, to the persistent advantage especially of the wealthier gentry and its professional cohort in the legal profession.

The making of the common law did not end in the mid-sixteenth century. But the articulation of its deep structure made huge advances between Edward I and Henry VIII. Common law's characteristic ways of facilitating and shaping behavior—its contours as a cultural, social system, polity, and ideology—were mostly in place by the mid-sixteenth century. The characteristics of the legal profession, its consciousness, ambition, reward system, and social role were elaborately constructed by then.

A London barrister of 1540, quick-frozen and revived in New York today, would only need a year's brush-up course at NYU School of Law to begin civil practice as a partner in a midtown or Wall Street corporate-law firm. Because of the stunted nature of the criminal justice side of common law as compared to its elaborate articulation on the civil side, two months of continuing education would suffice for the resurrected sixteenth-century barrister to start practice as a prosecutor or in the defense criminal bar today.

This astonishing fact of how close the common law of 1547 is to that of today, in New York as well as London, possibly tells some key things about English legal history: how rich and creative was its development down to the time of Henry VIII, and how relatively narrow was the margin of opportunity and need for further development thereafter in response to social and cultural change; and how relatively conservative was the common law as a system of dispute resolution and peacekeeping, property and status securing, and how relatively deficient in response to social change it became after reaching the elaboration of its deep structure between 1272 and 1547. One can look up to the old lawyers with admiration and awe or express disappointment and resentment about their modern professional heirs; these are alternative judgmental choices.

But the historical fact of common-law history can be looked at in another, nonjudgmental way. A particular culture or social system reaches its structural formulation, after which any further changes are relatively modest accretions and marginal adjustments.

Think of the history of physics from Einstein to today—its intellectual firmament and professional organization was predominantly the work of two generations from 1910 to 1960. Think of Greek philosophy, fully developed in the age of Plato and Aristotle and only marginally adjusted thereafter. Think of Renaissance Italian art, whose achievements aesthetically, intellectually, and organizationally could be nearly all narrated by Vasari around 1540, looking back only a century or so. Or finally, think of modern medicine grounded in microbiology; it came into existence on a gray day in 1938 on South Parks Road in Oxford, England, when Ernest Chain synthesized penicillin for the first time, and has reached by 1990s the point at which its further development beyond the grandiose accomplishments of the past half century is seemingly too expensive for society to sustain.

It is commonly imagined that a cultural and social system, a discourse, slowly and almost evenly evolves over time. Far more often, however, the discourse is a product of a relatively short period of intense creativity, and once established in behavior, concept, and intricate structure, with attendant group carriers and interested beneficiaries, the system remains fixed with only relatively marginal adjustments.

When Christopher Langdell, the first active dean of Harvard Law School and fomenter in the 1880s of American legal education, introduced the case system still universally in use in American law schools, he intuitively recognized the truism about the solidity of a cultural discourse and social system as expressed in common law. Students spent a great deal of time reading very old English law cases because, in Langdell's view, the conceptual relations embedded in these classic cases were still operative in American law. Fifteenth-century liability was still liability in the nineteenth century even if injury inflicted by railroads was now more devastating and widespread than the havoc committed by oxcarts.

Brian Simpson's delightful *Leading Cases in the Common Law* (1995) raises doubts about this case approach to legal education. He points out that over time what the classic case was actually about gets glossed over for pedagogical purposes, and what students are supposed to learn from the text of the case is shaped by a retrospective glaze put upon it by law teachers.

With this salutary warning about misreading the past for the convenience of the present, it is still possible to see the deep structure of the common law coming together by the mid-sixteenth century. Like all such deep structures, however interpreted by later generations for their convenience, it became very hard to deconstruct, dismantle, supersede, or even radically modify it once it was in place. Neither the shock of the English Civil War of the 1640s—in spite of some momentary rumblings—nor the drastic political rupture of the American Revolution, in spite of the sloganeering about "the new order of the world," effectively dislodged the deep structure of the common law as it coalesced between 1272 and 1547 on the basis of the previous era of creation from 1000 to 1272.

"The common law of England is not to be taken in *all* respects to be that of America," wrote U.S. Supreme Court Justice (and Harvard Law professor) Joseph Story in an 1829 decision. True enough. But Story went on to acknowledge: "Our ancestors brought with them the common law's general principles and claimed it as their birthright."

Whether this is a good thing—whether in English-speaking countries at the end of the twentieth century, lives should be regulated and disputes rendered by immersion in a judicial culture and legal system that was articulated during the Hundred Years' War, whether the common law should be regarded as our birthright or our albatross—is a critically important and increasingly debated issue.

The most obvious taking of sides in this debate falls between those who believe that the common law is grounded in legal reasoning whose outcome has universal and persistent validity, and those relativists and historicists exemplified in legal realism and critical legal studies, who see the common law as the product of a particular time and place and therefore more burdensome than helpful in this postmodernist and high-technology era—symbolically, wigs, coifs, and gowns looking absurdly irrelevant and obsolete in the age of the Internet, space travel, and Prozac.

With some recent American trials, imposed on our sensibility by the ruthless media, the utility and effectiveness of the jury are a flashpoint in the ongoing debate between the judicial rationalists and conservative universalists (who dominate the bar associations and the law school faculties) on the one side, and the relativists and radical reformers on the other.

Between 1300 and 1500 the English jury was modernized. It turned from the self-informing to the trial-informing jury. Whether in criminal or civil actions, originally a jury of the neighborhood where the case lay was supposed to arrive at trial in the county court having previously investigated the case and unanimously made up their minds on a point they could testify to before the judges: "John is guilty of having murdered William on the high road to Nottingham the day after Michaelmas"; "John did recently dispossess William of his rightful tenement." By 1300 this clean and simple use of the jury was being eroded; by 1500 the old jury was gone.

In civil actions what happened was that the opening up of

adversarial procedure ("the traverse") in the trial by pleading of exceptions and making special pleas rather than stipulating simple denials, frustrated the value of the self-informing jury's preparation for testifying to a point at the trial. The decision finally expected of the jury was very often not what they had prepared themselves to relate to the court. The jury was faced with questions rising out of the exceptions or special pleas that they had not previously considered, or even if briefly considered in passing had reached no decision on.

By 1350 the jury in a civil action stood mutely and impatiently in court, shifting their feet, while the opposing barristers battled before the judge (as they do today) to get a question put to the jury that would render the outcome of the trial favorable to their client. The jury had to listen to the traverse and respond to the question put to them by the judge.

In effect the self-informing jury was eliding into the trial-informing jury in civil cases. It was how attorneys presented the issue in the case and how judges responded to this presentation and instructed the jury that was far more important now than what the jury had naively agreed to back in the neighborhood tavern when they initially met, on orders from the sheriff, to reach agreement on the case. That issue was often superseded in the course of the trial and the jury's consensus back in the village tavern was now as useful as stale beer.

If the jury's self-informing original determination was no longer the issue that the judge put before them, at the behest of one of the attorneys, why bother to empanel the neighborhood jury in the first place? It was easier, when the case was called—in civil actions, normally after at least three postponements—to get twelve miscellaneous men together who had nothing previously to do with the case or the neighborhood where the dispute lay, let them listen to the arguments of the attorneys, and respond to the judge's instruction to the jury of the issue he wanted them to give a verdict on. The modern jury in civil actions (in England itself only until the early twentieth century, when the jury was dropped in all civil cases except libel actions as being unable to fathom the technical complications of a case) had come into being.

Why the shift in the nature of the jury from self-informing to trial-informing occurred between 1300 and 1500 in criminal cases seems to have had principally to do with trials in London. London by the end of the fifteenth century was fast becoming the great wen of humanity, with a population climbing toward 150,000, 5 percent of the English population, and spreading out to occupy an area the size of a small county. Half of the gross domestic product of the country was in some way connected to London's commerce and industry. The city remained the center of royal administration and law and the seat of parliamentary politics. The great city's importance was such that it could no longer be allowed to run its own autonomous judicial system along the lines of hoary twelfth-century ideas of municipal liberty.

This meant that the Court of King's Bench became more active as London's criminal court of first instance, as well as serving as an appeals court for criminal matters from the shires. There was an urban peace problem with political overtones; a need for order so that valuable commerce, often in the hands of foreign merchants from Italy, Holland, or Germany, could be pursued; and a steady stream of criminal cases rising from deviant behavior among the tumultuous city masses. In spite of the large number of protected groups "pleading their clergy" (getting special deals), there were plenty of young adult males available to be indicted by grand juries and placed on trial.

The judges in King's Bench were not keen to rely on juries of neighbors of the adult males unprotected by affirmative action. Such self-informing juries from the wards could turn out to be too friendly toward the defendants, or too afraid of their families, or even prone to use a criminal trial to send a message of hostility toward the Crown and its agents. By 1500 judges were instructing court bailiffs to go out in the streets of Westminster and into its taverns and hand-pick juries who could be relied on to do the court bidding and help cleanse society of deviant adult males indicted for murder or robbery.

Now the jury was ignorant of the facts of the criminal case to start with. They had to listen to sworn testimony, giving a narrative of the case, and respond to rudimentary presentation of prosecution witnesses and other evidence. However, not until 1700 could attorneys for the defense, except in treason trials, actually speak in court, and not until after 1800 could they cross-examine prosecution witnesses. The criminal trials were heavily weighted against the defense, and the juries knew what their job was. If common law was remarkably protective of certain groups, it was very tough on young adult males: But this was good sociology, since this was (and still remains) the main social background of the criminal class.

The sixteenth-century jury system left two issues unresolved that are still pressing today, especially in the United States. These may be called blue-ribbon juries and jury nullification of the law.

First, should juries be carefully selected and not democratically picked at random from the general population? Should there be trials by juries of "betters" rather than peers? Unequivocally the common law said it wanted carefully selected "blue-ribbon" juries (as these were called in the twentieth century). In civil actions it wanted men of property, in criminal cases at least men of solid reputation. It never wanted women before the late nineteenth century. In both England and the United States blue-ribbon juries were abandoned around 1950. The gain was for democracy, but not for the quality of verdicts. In civil actions in American courts, where juries are still used, the juries have difficulty understanding highly technical disputes or are prone to make decisions biased against corporations and insurance companies with their deep pockets.

In criminal cases, juries increasingly engaged in jury nullification of the law—that is, found a defendant not guilty in apparent contradiction of the facts of the case presented to them. They refused to have regard for application of prevailing law. This was not a new problem. In the fourteenth century there were already instances of jury nullification when a defendant in a county court appeared in a sympathetic light to the jury. They then decided he had acted in self-defense or was after all a lunatic.

Down to the 1670s furious judges punished nullifying juries with fines and short-term imprisonment as a warning to later juries to avoid such aberrant behavior. But in the 1670s *Bushell's Case* changed all that. Bushell was foreman of the jury who had found the Quaker leader William Penn not guilty of preaching in London without a license even though Penn freely acknowledged, in defiance of the government, that he had done so. When the Penn jury was punished, an appeal struck down the bench's power to punish a jury for nullification.

Whenever political, racial, or religious issues enter a case, nullification is bound to escalate, as has happened recently in high-profile cases in New York and Los Angeles. It is a continuing flaw in the criminal-jury system.

The blatant weaknesses of the jury system inspired Jeffrey Abramson to write a well-received book, *We the Jury* (1994, revised 1995), defending the jury system and pointing out how it might be improved. Among the law professors who lavishly praised Abramson's book was one of the leading defense counsels in the O. J. Simpson case, not surprisingly.

The problem with replacing the jury with the continental system, in which verdicts reside in a panel of judges (with sometimes a token but totally powerless six-person jury thrown in for democratic show, as in France), is not only constitutional and ideological impediments. If the bench is going to make the verdicts, the judges have to be specifically recruited and trained for that responsibility, as in Germany today, where a career as a judge is chosen in law school, and the candidate for the bench given different training and a unique professional experience apart from that of attorneys. As long as judges are jumped-up attorneys as in the common-law tradition, with political factors furthermore weighing heavily in their appointments, the Roman-law system cannot be introduced in English-speaking countries.

The jury system prevails and we are left with Abramson's proposed remedies: "Permit jurors to submit questions. . . . Let jurors take notes. . . . Allow jurors to discuss the evidence during the trial. . . . Preinstruct juries [during the trial]. . . . provide comprehensible, written instructions [from judge to jury]." These remedies will help, although they may provide grounds for appeal on claim that the judge was manipulating the jury. Abramson's remedies do not forestall jury nullification of the law—but nothing will, short of return to blue-ribbon juries, and that is now politically impossible.

The ideal juror in the State Supreme Court (court of first instance) in New York City today is a single mother with only a high school diploma who works in the post office. Anyone with a doctoral degree or high status in a profession will be normally challenged off the jury because attorneys fear she or he will lead the undereducated majority of the jury.

The jury is an imperfect system, but it has been imperfect since it assumed its modern form in the sixteenth century. Bar associations and law schools do not emphasize the problem with the jury system because the criminal defense bar and the civil liability bar offer extremely lucrative practices and because the upscale law school faculties are dominated by ideological populists who see the jury as the bulwark of democracy. So did the authors of the U.S. Constitution, although they would have said the jury was an expression of "republican virtue." Of course they were thinking of blue-ribbon juries. Madison's and Jefferson's ideal juryman was an independent, modestly prosperous farmer well read in Cicero and English history.

Like so much that happens under the banner of democratization, what seems at the time a necessary moral and political advance brings with it institutional degradation that is ignored. A jury of post office workers, nurse's aides, janitors, and fast-food clerks may operate quite differently than one comprising Jefferson's and Madison's sturdy, well-read farmers, but no one wants to address this problem lest they be branded reactionary snobs and neoconservative ideologues.

Certainly law school faculties, prone to congenital populism, are not going to put the viability of jury trial in the democratic context of undereducated urban populations high on their agenda. A lengthy study of jury operations conducted by Justice Judith Kaye, chief administrative judge of New York State, and a distinguished alumna of the now defunct night-school division of NYU Law School, concluded in 1995 with Justice Kaye trying perfunctorily to limit attorneys' preemptory challenges and recommending cleaner bathrooms for citizens on jury duty.

Occasionally when a jury in a civil trial makes some unusually bizarre finding or a jury in a criminal trial does not seem at all interested in the evidence elaborately presented to them, there is a momentary media cry for reconsideration of the jury as a viable institution. But this attention evaporates in the face of next week's media sensation.

The jury of verdict, which came into being without legislation or forethought in the early thirteenth century in response to a pressing need immediately to find a new method of proof, and again fundamentally changed in character around 1500 without any public debate, is perhaps the hallmark institution of the common law. But it has never received much careful consideration. In the past three decades there has been only one book of importance on the history of the English jury, by Tom Green of the University of Michigan Law School. The only close scrutiny of contemporary jury operation in recent years—in the American courts—has come from consultants who advise the criminal defense bar how potential jury members are likely to vote in light of their background. When an institution slides into degradation and dysfunction, fixers and dealers will have new career opportunities.

Alongside the critically important switch from the self-informing to the trial-informing jury was a set of major changes in the land law in the later Middle Ages.

What the gentry wanted early in the reign of Edward I, at a time of population boom and hysterical escalation of real estate prices, were four things: blockage of alienation of family land to the "dead hand" (*mortmain*) of the church, from which the family could never recover it, a complaint as old as Anglo-Saxon bookland; the liberation of the capitalist land market from vestiges of restraint imposed by outmoded feudal obligations, so that speculative buying and selling of real estate could be pursued without legal or political impediments, but only under market conditions; a legal mechanism by which a great family could retain its estates perpetually as a block inheritance, only adding to it but never subtracting from it, and thereby not only secure the economic base of the family wealth forever intact but preserve indefinitely the family's status and influence in county society, which depended mostly on its landholdings; and finally a quicker and easier way to deal with usurpations and evictions by landowners than afforded by old assizes, such as *novel disseisin*.

The gentry got the first three desiderata by parliamentary class legislation put through by Edward I's government in the last quarter of the thirteenth century, at a time when gentry support was crucial for the Crown for new taxes or increased tax rates to fund Edward's imperialist venture in Wales, Scotland, and France. Like all reforming legislation it did not always achieve 100 percent satisfaction of its proponents' wishes, but on the whole it was a big boost for the gentry, and it molded land law for many centuries to come. The improved legal mechanism for protection against ejection from landholdings came by way of judicial initiative in the Court of King's Bench around 1500.

The parliamentary statute of *Mortmain* of 1277 prohibited alienation of land to the church without license from the Crown. This had the effect of slowing down gifts to the church in protection of landlord's heirs. It also provided a new source of income to the royal treasury, with the selling of licenses to allow gifts to the "dead hand" of the church.

Partly because of *Mortmain* and partly because of shifts in religious sensibility toward a more personal kind of piety—in which, furthermore, the whole of a gentry or merchant family participated together—it became fashionable by the late fifteenth century to establish chantries, small family churches staffed by a priest or friar on retainer from the family, either on the family land or nearby.

The higher nobility had always had their splendid private chapels in their elaborate domiciles. Now through the proliferation of these chantries, or pocket family chapels, the practice spread to the middle class, caused in part by *Mortmain*'s limitation on outright gifts of land to the church.

The proliferation of chantries represented a kind of democratization of religious practice, a more personal participation of the gentry in the sacraments. It became common to emphasize Christ's body, and the church festival of Corpus Christi became extremely popular in gentry and merchant-class circles. All this made middle-class people feel more integrated into church life and more personally involved in sacramental Catholicism.

Historians thirty years ago would have said that this more personal and democratic religiosity in chantries helped to bring on the Reformation of the sixteenth century. The middle class came to regard sacramental Catholicism as its personal possession and to be with as it wanted, it was claimed.

More recently a younger generation of historians, now hostile to the Reformation, such as Eamon Duffy, see the Reformation as a reaction against the democratic spirituality of the fifteenth century, as an intellectually and politically elitist effort to deprive the middle class of its populist takeover of medieval spirituality.

The Statute of *Quia Emptores* (from the first words of the statute, "because purchasers") of 1290 opened up the capitalist land market in freehold property. Embedded in all sorts of boilerplate caveats, it nevertheless specifically said that "it is lawful for each free man to sell at will his land or tenement or part thereof." Nothing could be clearer than that. Feudalism as a system of landholding through subinfeudation was effectively abolished. The fief became a piece of land held in "fee simple," which meant it could be bought and sold at will. Capitalism was endorsed.

Of course to get this piece of blatant class legislation, at the behest of the gentry, through Parliament, there had to be included long-winded obfuscating clauses about saving the rights and privileges of the eventual top lord, whose family had once given out the freehold on feudal contract that was now sold on the open market. In practice this meant little or nothing, and the drafters of the legislation and the Crown officials knew it. The legislation provided no specific mechanism for enforcing the overlord's alleged rights or sanctions if they were ignored. The only way to enforce such a claim was by litigation—difficult, slow, and expensive.

The great lords, the higher nobility, were multimillionaires who already had vast holdings that in the 1290s were rapidly inflating in value. They could expand their estates by marriage, by favor from the king, and by booty acquired in serving as generals in the king's wars. There was little to be gained by insisting on the old feudal services and taxes, although that could still be pursued against a new "fiefee," or buyer of land originally granted out on feudal contract, if the protracted litigation was worth it (as it rarely was).

Quia Emptores was a bold, revolutionary piece of legislation. It confirmed a trend already strongly under way, but it clarified the legal context of this trend and sharply accelerated it. Professors in American law schools who in the Langdell tradition still begin their course on property by explicating *Quia Emptores* are doing the right thing—here is where modern postfeudal, free market land law begins. *Quia Emptores* contributed more to modernizing liberation than Magna Carta did.

In the two centuries after *Quia Emptores*, the consequence of its impact on English society and the structure of landholding was the flattening of the old feudal pyramid. In fact, by the early sixteenth century there *was* no longer a feudal pyramid. The king was now not just the liege or ultimate lord of all landholders; he was the *only* lord, the only exerciser of legal authority, over all the landholders in the country.

In the sixteenth century there were great landholders and enjoyers of aristocratic titles, and of course such grandees because of their wealth, enterprise, and family connections loomed large in national politics and local society. But thanks to the effects of *Quia Emptores*'s dissolution of feudalism, the magnates had no vassals. These billionaire landholders had dependents, followers, and bootlickers, but they had no status of enduring contractual and judicial authority over such clients. This was the great difference between pre–1290 feudalism and post–1500 society. At first sight this difference may seem only technical and unimportant, but in politics and the structure of county society it was a functional and meaningful one.

Having been legally emancipated by *Quia Emptores* to buy more land on the open market, the corollary aim of a gentry family was to keep all the family estates and never sell them off. The idea of the gentry family was one of kin extending through time, and at no point should the lot of primogeniture allow an heir, for whatever reason, to divest himself of family property and reduce the family's long-standing capital resources and its attendant social and political status in the county.

To achieve this end, the statute *De Donis* (Westminster II), dating from within a few years of *Quia Emptores*, established the system of fee entail. The French word *entail* means "to cut." Any land that has been entailed, in an elaborate judicial instrument pursuant to the statute, was cut off from alienation, from being sold. The entail system separated the family's capital property from the income that the property generated. Thus the heir had the income from the land for life (Sir Edward Coke in the seventeenth century, who disliked entails, called an entail a "lease for life"). But the heir could not sell off any of the land, could not put it up as security for a loan with any hope of the creditor getting the land, and could not mortgage it. In a particular generation an heir might be feckless, improvident, a bad manager; the value of land might rise and fall, but the entailed land remained with the family forever and was passed on intact to the heir in the next generation, who hopefully would recoup family fortunes or encounter a resurgent land market.

And so by 1350 there were two kinds of gentry lands, those in fee simple, which could freely be bought and sold; and those in fee tail, or entail, which were frozen in the family's possession forever. Setting up the legal instruments of entail under *De Donis* was a special and extremely lucrative branch of conveyancing, or land-law practice. And devising ways to break an entail also brought huge incomes to capable attorneys.

The favorite way of breaking an entail was called common recovery. It was an act of collusion between the landholder and a prospective buyer or his agent. The latter brought a writ of entry claiming old title to the land in question; the landholder did not appear to defend his suit and was eventually deemed in default; and the plaintiff gained the land and quietly paid off the landholder, who had become the seller.

Common recovery required not only sly attorneys but a compliant (or bribed) judge who would not be curious as to why the defendant failed to appear. However, the greatest obstacle to breaking an entail in this manner, and the reason it was not an easy or frequent occurrence, was that the heir in waiting for inheriting the land might notice what was going on, and he (or his guardian or attorney) would enter the case and block the transaction. Obviously common recovery worked best when the prospective heir was an underage son of a father holding tight control over the entailed land. If the heir was of age, or was a nephew, or for some reason had a guardian not his father or uncle, or had an attorney already appointed to represent him, it wouldn't work.

By the mid-sixteenth century, when there was a sudden and huge increase in gentry holdings because of the royal dissolution of the Catholic monasteries and the selling off of the church lands to the gentry at knockdown prices, close to half of gentry lands were entailed. With the rise of the modern novel in the eighteenth and early nineteenth centuries, the idiosyncratic impact of entails on fortunes of individuals was a favorite plot device, as in Jane Austen's *Sense and Sensibility* and *Pride and Prejudice*.

Around 1680 judicial review amended the system of entails. Citing the progressive doctrine against perpetuities—that a legal instrument cannot bind future generations indefinitely—entails as legal instruments were limited to one succeeding generation, father to son, and then had to be renewed. Entails per se were abolished by act of Parliament in 1833, as part of the movement begun by the Great Reform Bill.

But by then another instrument, called a strict settlement, was being used to achieve much of the same results. The strict settlement was an arrangement entered into at time of marriage and was designed principally to protect the lands of an heiress as she entered marriage, restricting or prohibiting her husband from selling off the lands she brought to the marriage bed and keeping her lands for the heirs of her body. The prenuptial agreement could also limit the husband's freedom to alienate his own property.

The strict settlement was therefore a prenuptial agreement that placed lands in a kind of entail, at least for one generation, and as such it can still be entered into today. But in the 1920s in England, with the introduction of high death duties and the plunging of land values between the wars (and before recovery of the real estate market in the post–1950 suburban boom), gentry families had to retain freedom to sell off lands to remain solvent, and the echoes of the entail system in the strict settlement faded out. After six centuries *Quia Emptores* then triumphed over *De Donis.*

With the vast increase in land transactions from the great inflation of the late thirteenth century to the absorption of monastic lands into the open market in the mid-sixteenth century, it was inevitable that enterprising gentry would become dissatisfied with *novel dissesin* and the other old possessory assizes as being too slow, expensive, and cumbersome for resolution of disputes in landed property litigation. Around 1400 a new and quicker form of land litigation began to develop, in the process called a bill of ejectment.

By 1400, as a result of the Black Death and the catastrophic decline in population and the sharp increase in farm laborers' wages, landlords found themselves with millions of acres of arable or ranchlands that they could not directly exploit themselves. Thousands of peasant communities, located on the more marginal land, were simply abandoned, becoming "the lost villages of England," to cite the title of a book on the subject by Maurice Beresford, and never reconstituted.

But for the better land, which enhanced labor costs now made too expensive to exploit directly, landowners sought a return by leasing ("devising") it out for a long term of years. Another word for leasing was letting the land out to "farm," and that is how a legal term (farmer-leaseholder) became an agricultural one. By the mid-fifteenth century, possibly a quarter of the agricultural land in England was held on long-term leases.

Ejectment was a legal procedure designed to protect leasehold-ers from dispossession without having to resort to the slow and expensive assizes, and leaseholding would thereby appear a more attractive and viable undertaking. The ejected leaseholder simply filed a petition or "bill," usually with the Court of King's Bench because the latter was short of business and was willing to respond immediately—seeking restoration of the land for the bal-ance of the term of the written lease shown to the court.

These bills of ejectment provided such quick and relatively cheap remedy that litigants over title to fee simple (ownership, not leasing) also sought the same remedy, and the court came to allow it. Through elaborate legal fictions by the "consent rule" entered into by the litigants, bills of ejectment were used to deter-mine title as well as the securing of leases. By the late seventeenth century nearly all land disputes that had been litigated by the old assizes were now pursued by the ejectment procedure. If you look at the records of land litigation in Virginia in the early eighteenth century, *novel disseisin* seems to be unknown; the cases proceeded by bill of ejectment.

What happened in this development of the land law contra-dicts those who see the common law evolving by the intrinsic application of reasoning within the legal profession. Rather it was accommodation of the law to social change, and the need to drive new procedural avenues through the old common law to serve gentry interests (followed by sharp attorneys finding ways to manipulate the inherited system), that made up the force for spe-cific institutional change.

The same—service to class interests—may be said of the devel-opment of a whole new side to the common law, that of personal actions as distinct from real actions, the land law whose mecha-nism, procedures, and judicial assumptions had driven the found-ing of the common law.

By the fourteenth century it was not merely the buying, selling, securing, and inheriting of land that shaped the lives of middle-class people, although that remained, and was to remain at least until the nineteenth century, the main concern and activity of the affluent classes and the political nation. Now in a more mobile and commercial society, matters involving personal liability for injury, debt, and recovery of loans, and not only traditional written but also oral contracts were important in group operations and individual behavior.

Disputes in these more private areas of conduct were placed before the judges for resolution, and with some hesitancy and initial reluctance, the courts received such cases and between 1350 and 1550 worked out by judicial review, with little or no legislation, principles and procedures to deal with these interpersonal matters.

The emergence of personal actions in common law also represented a kind of judicial democratization, since it brought before the courts in both rural and urban areas people of modest circumstances, whose landed wealth was negligible or nonexistent and who were therefore outside the circumference of land litigation. The development of personal actions greatly enhanced the involvement of the lower middle class and the working class in litigation. In many instances they were too poor to retain an attorney and found themselves standing lonely and unattended before the majesty of the bench. For such ordinary people involvement for the first time in litigation could be a bewildering and frightening experience. But the positive side of personal actions outweighed the negative experience.

On the whole, for the emerging lower middle class, the yeoman farmer and small leaseholders, the urban craftsmen and shopkeepers, personal actions of liability (tort), debts, and oral contracts were a big help in doing business and stabilizing their lives. This expression of private, interpersonal law represented for these kinds of people as valuable a support mechanism from the law as *Quia Emptores* and entails did for the wealthier gentry.

By the end of the thirteenth century, the common law had not only expanded vertically to serve the interests of the English lower middle class and some of the working class, it had also expanded horizontally and moved outward from England to Wales, the lowlands of Scotland, and pockets of English hegemony in eastern Ireland, carried to all these places by the lords and Crown officials engaged in imperialist English efforts of conquest and settlement. English land law and the assizes system penetrated into these areas of an ideologically conceived British ecumene to serve the interests of lordship and ambitious royal administration radiating outward from London.

In Wales and in areas of English ascendancy in Ireland, the expansion and impress of the common law was permanent. It did not entirely obliterate older Celtic legal traditions but overlaid them and prevailed to serve the interests of the colonial ruling elite. This imperializing judicial process was to be repeated in the British Empire of the nineteenth and twentieth centuries, leaving, after the colonial withdrawal of the mid-twentieth century, major ingredients of common law in post-imperial India, Israel, and many other countries that were under British rule.

For political reasons Scotland followed a different road. By the mid-fourteenth century English rule over the Scottish lowlands had been repulsed, and Scotland entered into an alliance with England's enemy, France. This led to the intrusion of Frenchified Roman law into the University of Edinburgh in the later Middle Ages and to the consequent heavy impress of Roman law on Scottish judicial institutions. The whole process was partly reversed in the seventeenth and eighteenth centuries, after London and Edinburgh had a common ruler from a Scottish royal family, and especially after the Union of Scotland and England in 1707, which meant Scottish representation in the now united British Parliament and the extension of royal administration seated in London into Scotland. Even then, modern Scottish law is a hybrid of Roman and English common law, with the Roman-law impress being predominant.

11
Judicial Frontiers

THE ELABORATION OF THE common law into its
deep structure between 1272 and 1547 was accompanied by the
reaching out of the common law to encounter a wide array of
social, political, and interpersonal issues.

From being the relatively narrow stream of land law, criminal
justice, and constitutional law from 900 to 1272, the common law
during the unfolding of its deep structure in the following three
centuries became a veritable flood sweeping over just about every
contour of the social terrain, resulting in the articulation of private law, such as personal actions; novel approaches to criminal
justice and peacekeeping; much more ambitious constitutional
and administrative law; the raising of issues of freedom of the
press and free speech; the establishment of new kinds of courts;
and the delineation of the rudiments of labor and poverty law.

The roiling waters of the common law penetrated many hitherto remote inlets of group and individual behavior and adum-

brated judicial ways of addressing these aspects of society and politics.

Like the United States in the later twentieth century, England from 1272 to 1547 exhibited a tendency to judicialization of society, to a widespread belief that there could be a judicial remedy for every personal wrong and social ailment, that the legal profession could find a judicial instrument for problem solving on a very wide spectrum.

This tendency stimulated legal innovation and enhanced the prestige and wealth of the legal profession and its powerful role in society. As the English people, in spite of their fervent piety and propensity to various kinds of faith healing, lost confidence in the integrity and credibility of the clergy, and inclined to popular anticlericalism, they came to place ever greater reliance on the bar and the bench as helpers and saviors.

The priesthood was being superseded by the lawyers as the most respected of the learned professions. The lawyers imitated the clergy's conviction that they could find remedies for everyone's discontent and frustration. The propensity for social judicialization in the late-twentieth-century United States has come to be ambivalently depicted in American fiction and film, and denounced in the early 1990s in a bestselling book by a New York lawyer, Phillip Howard. Social judicialization was also the trend in the era of the elaboration of the common law's deep structure between 1272 and 1547, and it certainly contributed to the innovation in legal institutions in that period.

The maturing common law left some problems unresolved and still to be debated for later centuries, as well as offering immediate melioration of social operations and help to individuals and families. Marvelously creative on the one side but incomplete and conflicted on the other—this was the general condition of the common law that the era of unfolding of deep structure from 1272 to 1547 left to the following two centuries and beyond.

Some of these issues, made even more intractable and complicated by the circumstances of modern industrial and post-industrial society, are still contended today. The common law's creativity and the intellectual capacity and energy of the legal profession failed to resolve some critical problems for four reasons: First, much of the progress of the common law, such as the development of personal actions like liability, were effected by judicial review rather than by open political debate leading to definitive legislation; the result was messy and unfinished.

Second, the common law tried to offer a judicial solution to an immense array of social problems. Some of these would have been better approached by nonjudicial means of conflict resolution. Some were too fluid and volatile for easy encapsulation in judicial processes.

Third, the world did not stand still, not even in insular little England of the sixteenth and seventeenth centuries. Cultural upheavals, social disturbances, political crises, and ecological modification affected the context in which the law functioned, and presented stern challenges to judicial thinking and the capability of the bar to take into account this ever-shifting context.

Fourth, the tightly in-group, socially conservative, and intensely hierarchical character of the legal profession, and its constant collaboration with wealth and power, posed intellectual limitations when it tried to engage unresolved problems on the intellectual edges of judicial consciousness. The imagining of the nature and operation of the law in the minds of seventeenth- and early-eighteenth-century lawyers was shaped by the facets of high culture of the day, which contained inherent limits to a creative response to unresolved problems along the frontier of the common law.

The legal profession by 1400 had a set of procedures, principles, and word formations that had been determined over the previous centuries. Faced with certain class interests, social needs, and political circumstances, the lawyers adapted what they knew and worked outward from this existing strong base in the old common law toward resolution of new problems.

At no time did the legal profession contemplate starting anew in erecting a judicial structure. They were not separated from the thick culture that had already come into existence. They did not engage in systems analysis. They did not say, Here we have a set of social problems; how can we conceivably best resolve them? They said, How can we adapt and apply the judicial language and processes already at our command in these areas to meet the needs of today's society?

This meant that they moved slowly and carefully, searching out the path to be followed. It also meant that their conceptualization of novel areas of the law was relatively constricted and short of functional maximization of problem solving. The legal profession in the United States and Britain today still operates in this way, which is central to common-law culture.

It is also in the nature of all learned professions to operate in this way. The scientific basis of American medicine was fundamentally changed by the introduction of antibiotics in the 1940s and 1950s. But the previous structure and modus operandi of the American medical profession were preserved intact in the novel context of revolutionized biomedical science, with stresses and anxieties that are evident today.

Similarly the social and economic circumstances of the American academic profession were fundamentally changed by the quadrupling of the student population in the 1960s and 1970s and the overnight establishment of vast numbers of new or greatly expanded campuses. Yet the structure of academia—its recruitment, training, certification, promotion patterns, and pedagogy—remained essentially the same as before in the face of a demographic revolution, with many adverse consequences visible today.

Thus the conservative behavior of the common-law bar, its propensity to add on from the previous base of ideas and operations, its determination of the content of new areas of judicial activity within the intellectual and institutional structure of the inherited common law—whatever may have been additional motivations to this kind of advancement by accretion rather than through innovation—is central to the sociology of any learned profession.

That is why nineteenth-century populists, such as American Jacksonian democrats and English Victorian radicals, hated the learned professions, and that is why the citadels of wealth and power in the twentieth century have spontaneously regarded the learned professions as their natural allies.

From both Roman and feudal sources the fourteenth-century common law inherited a well-articulated system of written contracts. The additional demand in the fourteenth century was for the central Court of Common Pleas and county courts to recognize and enforce *oral* contracts.

This is the kind of problem involved in oral contract: Henry orally solicits John the carpenter to repair his roof. They agree on the price, and Henry gives John a third of the fee as a deposit. John the carpenter never begins the job, or begins it and never finishes it, or does a bad job and the roof leaks. What is John's remedy in law, without a written contract?

The common-law courts were long reluctant to get involved in the morass of these trivial disputes where the evidence was slim or doubtful or amounted entirely to the conflicting word of the two parties.

But in the late fifteenth century the courts came to accept cases of oral contract, using the doctrine of *assumpsit*. When Henry gave a deposit to John the carpenter, the latter "assumed" an obligation in return for the "consideration" (usually money) he had received, said the judges. John the plaintiff had a right to the return of his money and nominal damages, or at least to have the job done.

Assumpsit cases involved artisans and shopkeepers, or laborers and small farmers. It was a lower-middle-class and working-class world over which the common law was extending its civil sway. It was petty transactions of everyday life that the courts now stooped to scrutinize and enforce.

Why enter judicially into this thicket of petit bourgeois business affairs? Three reasons can be given: First, there was the courts' propensity to offer judicial remedy for every wrong and refuse no business. Second, there was involved in *assumpsit* the demotic recognition that the majesty of the law should serve the interests of the common people as well as the affluent, of the petit bourgeois and working class as well as the gentry. There was a current of democratic conscience in late medieval culture. Assumpsit was a positive response to these popular tendencies.

Third, as argued by Robert C. Palmer, after the social catastrophe of the Black Death of the mid-fourteenth century, *assumpsit* law was part of the Crown's determination to instill countervailing social discipline in all classes in an enervated country. *Assumpsit* was a form of imposing needed social discipline on artisans and shopkeepers.

Of course, *assumpsit* never worked very well because so much depended on the word of the contending litigants. These trivial cases clogged up Common Pleas and in the sixteenth century were shunted off to a small claims court, the Court of Requests, whose decisions were often held by losing litigants to be unfair and arbitrary. Consequently the Court of Requests was abolished by act of Parliament in the 1640s.

Anyone familiar with the consumer law and small claims today knows the fragility of oral contract law—how much the old, weak, ignorant suffer in this area of common law. A persistent problem is that hiring an attorney to press a claim of oral contract usually costs more than the yield of the claim, but it is very difficult for most ordinary people to represent themselves effectively in litigation. This is an area in which the old jury of the neighborhood would have been an advantage, or the citizens' panels once prominent in Communist countries (if they weren't so readily politicized) would be more effective than litigation. *Assumpsit* is a prime example of the downside of social judicialization, of trying to solve real but petty social problems by the overmighty mechanism of adversarial litigation.

Alongside the personal action of *assumpsit* for oral contract, there developed in the fourteenth century a variety of writs for recovery of debt.

Whether you call it "capitalism," as Max Weber and R. H. Tawney did in the early twentieth century, associating it with Protestantism (Weber: Protestantism, by teaching postponed gratification, inculcated saving and made capitalism possible; Tawney: Protestantism was the bad ideological tool of capitalism); or "possessive individualism," as the Toronto Marxist C. B. MacPherson did in the 1960s; or simply "English individualism," as the Cambridge anthropologist Alan Macfarlane did in the 1970s, the rise of a market economy and various facets of capitalist enterprise were a feature of the era from 1350 to 1600.

The common law forthwith tried to service a capitalist economy in which credit arrangements and debt for consumption and investment purposes were facilitated by developing judicial mechanisms for recovery of debt.

The writ of *debt* per se was designed to recover an unpaid loan. It is what you are still subject to when you don't pay your credit card bill. The writ of *detinue* was to regain an artifact that had been borrowed and not returned after many entreaties. Charmingly, one of the earliest uses of writ of *detinue* in the mid-fourteenth century was to recover a copy of a book of Arthurian tales about the Holy Grail that a priest had borrowed and neglected to return, perhaps too entranced by the stories about Parsifal and Lancelot to notice. The writ of *trover* was designed to recover a piece of your lost property that someone had found and not returned to you.

As in any capitalist and consumer society, actions for debt were a much-used judicial instrument by 1550. Before the modern law of bankruptcy came in, during only the past century, the problem was what to do with people who were clearly indebted but who couldn't pay up. The heinous solution of the common law until the mid-nineteenth century was enforced detention or imprisonment in slimy holding pens, where food had to be provided by the anguished families until the debtor somehow payed up or made some alleviating arrangement with his creditor, who was wielding the draconian majesty of the law.

Before the very end of the eighteenth century, prisons were not normally used as places for punishing (and hopefully reforming) convicted felons. They were either forced abodes for indicted perpetrators before trial or awaiting (not for long) executions; or detention cells for debtors. The eighteenth-century critic Samuel Johnson regarded imprisonment for a debt as a form of legalized extortion. Indeed, the debtor's prison featured prominently in eighteenth- and nineteenth-century English novels, especially those of Charles Dickens, whose father was held in a debtor's prison while Dickens was a boy, a humiliation that scarred his psyche forever.

Essentially the development of debt procedure was another example of the common law's ready provision of a judicial solution to an emerging social problem, but only a halfway solution. Modern bankruptcy laws presented a big advance in this area of law. But given the almost unlimited proliferation of debt in our consumer society, it is not a problem we have fully gotten a handle on even now. I borrow, you demand payment; I don't pay, you sue; with the court's approval I declare bankruptcy, humiliating my dependents and ruining my credit rating—that is better than imprisonment for debt in the old common law 1400–1850, but not much.

Consumer debt and small business debt, like substance abuse, are a social and psychological as well as a judicial problem. Again the adversarial mechanism of the common law is only a partial and crude solution.

The late-medieval law of debt spawned a writ, that of *replevin*, which came to be valuable for more than debt recovery. *Replevin* was a writ you used if you were imprisoned for debt and wanted to be brought out of jail before the judges and have your case reconsidered. It came to be used as a legal fiction, by anyone sitting in jail without indictment or speedy trial, for debt or whatever reason.

As such *replevin* was a predecessor of *habeas corpus*, a writ of grace (specific privilege) issued by the bench to get you out of a holding jail and before them so that you (or, better, your attorney) could demand of a sheriff or prison warden why you were being held.

Around 1680, by parliamentary statute, habeas corpus became a writ of course. If a session of the Court of King's Bench or the assizes went by and you were still being held without indictment or trial ("jail delivery"), you had a right to have the judges issue the writ bringing you before them, and the prosecuting officials would have to show why you were being held.

Roman law knows nothing like habeas corpus; you can be held indefinitely in a continental law court while the investigating magistrates leisurely go about their work. The makers of a 1980s film about Americans suffering in a filthy prison—being held indefinitely for alleged drug pushing without indictment or trial in a Turkish court—did not know that this was plain old Roman law. Blame it on Justinian, not the Muslims.

The third kind of personal action pushing the judicial envelope between 1272 and 1547, along with oral contract and debt, was personal liability (personal injury, tort), what the English called "trespass." There are case references to it in the closing decades of the thirteenth century, just as the Inns of Court were being established. There was still some carryover to the bench and bar of continental Roman legal education, before the

English legal profession became an entirely indigenous one, with only obscure ecclesiastical lawyers trained in the civil law at Oxford preserving a connection with Justinian tradition. This is another way of saying that English trespass may owe a slim debt to the Roman law of liability, but it is almost entirely a native product worked out by bench and bar in the fourteenth and fifteenth centuries by judicial review, without legislation, and with little Roman borrowing.

Judges were probably somewhat reluctant at the start to get involved in defining a whole new area of private law. But by 1400 they had realized the tremendous market for judicial services in this vigorous branch of private law, and after that there was no holding them back. They loved to pontificate their opinions on this highly active but intellectually slippery segment of common law. The more commercial and industrial a society England became, the broader its middle-class demographic base, the more litigation there was on liability of various kinds.

Today in New York City, at least a quarter of the lawyers make their living—often splendidly—from liability law. Indeed, personal-injury litigation is much more active in the United States than in England for two reasons: In a U.S. liability action, the loser normally does not have to pay the winner's legal fees; in modern English law the loser always pays both sides' legal fees and "court costs," which can also be formidable. So if you stumble drunk off the subway platform and get hit by a train, you or your survivor in Manhattan might as well take a shot and sue the city and the overburdened taxpayers of New York City.

You can do this cheaply for the second difference between the English and American law of tort. In the United States you don't have to pay your attorney anything; usually he or she will represent you (indeed "the ambulance chaser" may very well have approached you and aroused your litigious instincts to start with) for one-third of the proceeds of the case. This contingent representation (you don't pay anything unless you win the case) is strictly prohibited in modern England and if practiced will result in disbarment.

Another difference between modern English and American liability law is that the English have wisely abandoned the jury in such cases except sometimes for libel actions, while the liability bar in the United States counts on the populist instincts, ethnic and class prejudices, and ignorance and confusion of juries to sock it to the governments, corporations, and insurance companies.

Since English judges belong to the same clubs as the executives of government, corporations, and insurance companies, they are not prone to impose huge judgments even if the plaintiffs win, and often they do not in London. The drunkard who fell onto the subway tracks: in an English court that is his fault and he got what he deserved under the screeching wheels of the train, the bum.

Given the propensity of the common law to remedy all sorts of wrongs and of the courts to find new business, the development of trespass was probably inevitable. But it was given a big boost by the erosion of feudal connections and by the effective abolition of subinfeudation by *Quia Emptores*.

In the old feudal world, subtenants, the knights, the gentry who suffered a personal injury of some kind (aside from being evicted from their land) would turn to their overlord to intervene with the perpetrator or his lord and to obtain some kind of satisfaction. In the street language of today, for gentry who were dissed, violent response being prohibited by the king's peace, they would hopefully get their lord to restore respect for them. But when the gentry became free agents, private contractors, individual entrepreneurs, which happened by 1300, honor and dignity, loyalty and mutual aid were henceforth only to be read about nostalgically in Arthurian romances. The age of chivalry— except for aristocrats and their entourage of hired sword slingers—was dead. Now when you suffered trespass on your dignity and honor, on your body as well as on your own land, you turned to the courts for restitution and compensation.

Between 1300 and the sixteenth century, three actions for trespass (that is, for liability, or tort or personal injury) were developed by the English legal profession through judicial review in case law.

The first liability action to develop was "trespass with force and arms" (also called *quare impedit*, from the first two words of the writ used to start the action). This was battery, infliction of bodily harm on the plaintiff. Given common law's propensity to formalization, use of "force and arms" came to be claimed even when that was arguably not the real cause of the trespass action—you had to say "with force and arms" to signal that this was a bodily injury action.

The second liability action to develop was "trespass on the case" ("in" the case makes more linguistic sense, but it is "on" the case). This was negligence, bodily harm for lack of due care, but advertised as still occurring with force and arms, even though it was recklessness that caused the harm.

In the early seventeenth century, Coke, who knew more about the common law than anyone before or since, explained the difference between trespass with force and arms (battery) and trespass on the case (negligence) this way: In the first kind of trespass action, someone has broken into your house wielding a sword and cut you on the arm. In the second the driver of an open cart filled with swords has driven wildly and far too fast down your street; the cart has hit a bump, swords have flown through the air, and one is projected through an open window and cuts your arm. Same injury, different reason or tort.

By the early sixteenth century the third form of trespass, called "action on the case," had emerged, This referred to any other kind of personal injury that was not obviously caused by battery or negligence. In action on the case the plaintiff did not obtain a formalized writ with the words already prepared. Unusual for the old common law, the plaintiff stated specifically what had happened and what the injury was. It certainly helped to get a lawyer to prepare the text of the writ for action on the case. Otherwise the defendant's attorney would try to point to gaps and inconsistencies in the wording of the story and plead an exception to have the case dismissed.

Action on the case—or simply "case," as it was called—was very popular with the bar. It made their services more necessary and it presented a rare opportunity for imaginative drafting of a writ starting an action. It might be said that case was the foundation of modern liability law. On any given business day in the Supreme Court of New York in Manhattan, you can hear horror stories graphically narrated, before bug-eyed juries, of mayhem inflicted on the body of the plaintiffs (or the plaintiff's deceased kin) in the grand tradition of sixteenth-century case.

A particular category of case actions was brought for "nuisance" or neighbors-from-hell misconduct. Nuisance was infringing on someone's normal expectation to enjoy hearth, home, air, and property without a neighbor befouling the environment with sound or smell. Allowing a company of actors to rehearse the Battle of Agincourt from Shakespeare's *Henry V* on your front lawn at 3:00 A.M. within earshot of your neighbor's domicile (but how about 3:00 P.M.?), or letting your backyard cesspool overflow and stink up the neighborhood—these are obvious actions on the case for nuisance. Of course it could get more complicated than that, and sometimes it was hard to distinguish between nuisance and negligence, trusting the ingenuity of attorneys and the wisdom of the judges to make the distinction.

Action on the case for nuisance exhibits the same weakness as oral contract and many actions for debt, namely excessive judicialization, or using the cumbersome and expensive adversarial system to deal with petty matters that would be more readily handled by community boards or lay arbitrators, a situation that might be called legal overdetermination. But there was a much more fundamental problem with the development of liability or trespass than that, namely the wide range of possible decisions on what actually constituted negligence. Tort doctrine remains a critical issue to the present day.

Looking at the whole period from the fifteenth century to today, there are three very distinct periods in the history of negligence, representing markedly significant shifts in the courts' views. From the fifteenth century down to the Industrial Revolution around 1850, the common law adhered to a principle of strict liability. When something wrong happened, especially in a way that could be construed as remotely falling under the rubric of someone's negligence, the court took a formalistic stand even if the defendant had taken reasonable care; even if the plaintiff had suffered no visible hurt, the finding was for the plaintiff. Trespass or tort had occurred, and the defendant had to pay damages, even if the penalty was trivial.

The landmark *Thorns Case* of 1466 set the pattern of strict liability. Even though the defendant in that case had no intention of invading the plaintiff's property in a hurtful or even insulting manner, when the former stepped over the boundary line to pick up thorns cut from a hedge dividing the properties, he had formally been negligent and had to pay at least token damages.

The coming of factories, with workers on assembly lines in front of dangerous machines, and railroads that were long notorious for inflicting injury on their employees and passengers alike, changed the law of liability in both England and the United States at around the same time, from about 1850 into the first decade of next century. Strict liability would quickly ruin the owners of factories and railroads and wipe out the investments of stockholders and bankers in the new, heavily capitalized enterprises, and the Industrial Revolution would grind to a halt if huge judgments were gained by victims of machinery.

The courts therefore allowed the introduction of amending principles that greatly eroded strict liability in negligence cases.

Two such innovative nineteenth-century doctrines became notorious for letting the bosses off the hook: the master-servant rule, by which, for instance, if you were mangled in a train wreck you could only sue the humble driver of the train but not the directors and stockholders of the company; or the doctrine of adhesion, by which limited liability warnings in fine print were stuck on back of railroad tickets (a strategy still pursued by airlines, and with some success on international flights).

Yet strict liability had not been forgotten, and it could reemerge like a ghostly vision under special circumstances, as it did in the famous case of *Rylands* v. *Fletcher* (1868). The case was decided for the plaintiff, a mining enterprise whose shafts had been flooded by a burst reservoir on the lands of the lord from whom the mining company had leased the right to sink mine shafts.

The case was decided for the plaintiff in Exchequer Chamber and confirmed in the House of Lords. The decision in Exchequer Chamber was based on the general principle of strict liability (someone had to pay). The confirming decision in the House of Lords also referred specifically to negligence.

Brian Simpson has shown that what lay behind the decision were notorious instances of burst water reservoirs in the two decades previous to *Rylands* v. *Fletcher*, which had caused much loss of life and gained hysterical public attention. Thus, in the interests of public welfare and as a reminder of threat from a well-known menace, the Victorian courts' proclivity to abandon strict liability to protect business enterprise could suddenly be reversed, showing an underlying nervousness about the move away from the old common law's tort doctrine.

In the early decades of the twentieth century, beginning with an opinion rendered by Benjamin Cardozo, then chief justice of the New York State Court of Appeals (*Macpherson* v. *Buick Motor Car Company*, 1916) there was a partial return to the old common-law doctrine of strict liability, but without the fusty formalism. An intermediate doctrine of care was enunciated by which—as in the Buick case—when you bought a car from a Buick dealer, you had reasonable expectation its wheels would not soon fall off, causing a dreadful accident, and you could sue the Buick Company as well as your local Buick dealer. Or when you bought a box of Kellogg's new Corn Flakes, there shouldn't be rat turd inside— the cereal makers had to observe the due care in manufacturing their product that a reasonable person would assume.

In England, under the close scrutiny of cautious judges without a jury, the doctrine of care has worked quite well. In American courts—with juries wanting to sock it to big corporations with seemingly infinitely deep pockets, and lax or populist or incompetent judges letting the liability bar run riot—anything can happen. When the liability bar stimulated suits against corporations and then combined thousands into a class action suit, businesses accused of having put out a popular product that later seemed possibly tortious began in the 1980s to hide behind bankruptcy laws—as in cases involving asbestos building materials and silicone breast implants. The confused results made many lawyers very rich.

The shift from the old common-law doctrine of strict liability to the limited liability that protected mid-nineteenth-century industrialists and railroad magnates forms the theme of the bestselling work on American legal history of the past three decades, *The Transformation of American Law, 1780–1860*, by Morton Horwitz of Harvard Law School, which has gone through at least ten printings since its publication in 1977. Ignoring the similar judicial trend occurring in England (and Canada and Australia) at the same time, Horwitz conjured up a nightmare plot of American capitalists and lawyers setting out to screw the common man:

> As political and economic power shifted to merchant and entrepreneurial groups in the postrevolutionary period, they began to forge an alliance with the legal profession to

advance their own interests through a transformation of the legal system. By around 1850, the legal transformation was complete. . . . The legal system had almost completely shed its eighteenth century commitment to regulating the substantive fairness of economic exchange. . . . Law once conceived of as protective, regulative, paternalistic and above all, a paramount expression of the moral sense of the community, had come to be thought of as facilitative of individual desires and as simply reflective of the existing organization of economics and political power.

Horwitz's book was awarded the Bancroft Prize by Columbia University, the most prestigious academic award for a work in American history. There is some validity to his thesis, but it is debatable.

Using a characteristic ploy of Marxist historiography, Horwitz views the old common law through a screen of romantic myth in order to make more stark the capitalist severity of nineteenth-century law. He sentimentalizes the old common law and makes it much more ethical, equitable, and hospitable to the needs of ordinary people than it actually was.

The common law's tendency to strict liability did have a paternalistic effect, but at its core the judicial system had served the interests of the gentry since the thirteenth century.

If common law was impelled by "the moral sense of the community," it was the community of the gentry for which the common law operated as an instrument. Before the Industrial Revolution of the early nineteenth century, capitalism had already transformed rural society and economy, and England had furthermore experienced a commercial revolution involving huge expansion of overseas trade in the period from 1450 to 1750.

The gentry and merchant class were the agents and beneficiaries of these economic developments. Insofar as ordinary people benefited, it was not because of paternalism or social ethics; it was a trickle-down effect from the prosperity of the upper middle class.

Horwitz's thesis on the transformation of liability can also be challenged along economic lines. How could industrialization have proceeded if the old common-law doctrine of strict liability had continued to be applied in the nineteenth-century courts? Strict liability would have severely impeded, possibly prevented industrialization in both England and the United States. When industrialization occurred in the Stalinist USSR, from 1930 to 1970, it also was at the cost of injuring the workforce, mistreating consumers, and ravaging the environment.

Could greater care have been taken in the nineteenth-century United States and England? Yes, somewhat. But giving priority to such a policy would have impeded technological change. The early phase of industrialization anywhere was tough on workers and consumers.

A significant degree of erosion of strict liability had to occur if society was to cross the threshold into mass production and the transportation revolution, represented by railroads. Once the economic and technological threshold was passed and mechanization was in place, there could be a partial reversion to strict liability, an intermediate position represented by the doctrine of reasonable care.

Industrialization occurred with the most benign side effects in nineteenth-century Germany and twentieth-century Japan. This was because these countries were tightly ruled by aristocratic-military elites that subjected industrialists to tight discipline. It was a matter of a different social structure from those existing in England and the United States. With relatively open societies and unlimited freedom and power vested in the upper middle class, industrialization was bound to be more reckless and draconian in England and the United States than in Germany and Japan. The latter two countries in the hands of aristocratic-military elites somewhat mitigated the effects of industrialization, but they also led their countries—and mankind—into ruinous wars. That's better?

Horwitz should have considered the implications of *Rylands* v. *Fletcher*, and what it shows about the nervousness of the courts, at least in Victorian England, at abandoning strict liability and the possibility of a sudden visceral return to strict liability when reminded of a sensationalized issue of general welfare.

Three centuries before the Industrial Revolution, liability law had already been affected, in the sixteenth century, by technological change—the introduction of the printing press. Gutenberg's movable-type kind of printing machine began to be used in London in the 1480s. Although extremely crude by modern standards, since each letter had to be set by hand and a copy of a single page so composed and locked in, individually produced, the printing press represented an enormous mechanical advance on manuscript, the production of an individual copy of a book by hand, which could take a year or more. In four months a book of equal size could be produced in as many as five hundred copies on sturdy rag paper and bound into a codex.

Initially the printing press was used to produce versions of the Bible and popular literature, such as Arthurian stories. It soon became evident that the printing press could also be used to disseminate rapidly any kind of information or opinion. The new Tudor government imposed never-effective licensing laws on printing presses (which did not lapse until the 1690s). The printing press also meant that the common law had to give attention to the problem of written defamation or libel.

Before the printing press, libel was a very small problem. How could someone's reputation be damaged by the sparse number of expensive handwritten copies? Five hundred copies, however, or even one hundred, produced on the creaking movable type-printing press in the form of a book, pamphlet, broadside, or poster could be damaging to a government official or private individual alike, especially when distributed in urban or heavily settled rural areas.

Hitherto written defamation, like oral defamation, had been something left to church courts. It was conjoined to ecclesiastical laws against blasphemy. Defamation arose from maliciously accusing someone of being a blasphemer (John accuses Henry of using the name of Jesus or Mary colloquially in an oath).

Another form of defamation that engaged the attention of church courts was the ruining of a woman's reputation by gossiping that an unmarried woman was promiscuous and that a married woman was cheating on ("cuckolding") her husband. The social historian Anthony Fletcher believes that such talk was a serious matter. It hurt the marriage prospects of young women of the gentry, who were supposed to enter marriage in a virginally chaste condition. Gossip that a married gentleman wore the horns of the cuckold, claims Fletcher, brought dishonor on the family and damaged its status in the county.

By the 1540s, as a result of greatly improved communication via the printing press, the common-law courts had brought libel and defamation mostly under their jurisdiction.

There were two kinds of libel, criminal and civil. Criminal libel was bringing a public official into disrepute by writing nasty things about him. It is still part of English law, although it is obsolete. There has been no action for criminal libel in Britain since the 1940s, and it has rarely been used since the late eighteenth century, when it was used so often by the Crown to pick on critics of its ill-fated American policy that criminal libel itself fell into disrepute.

Civil libel became part of the law of liability, personal injury, or tort—an action on the case. It consisted of harming someone by writing bad things about him or her. (Don't buy from John the butcher, his meat is rotten.) From the 1540s until the introduction of radio broadcasts in the 1920s, civil libel normally meant defamation in writing by using the printing press.

Just as the courts formalistically decided that injury was done by certain physical acts irrespective of intention, the English law of libel, as classically formulated by Coke at the end of the sixteenth century, applied strict liability to postulate that truth was not a defense in an action for civil libel. Libel was textual publication injuring someone by bringing him or her into disrepute even if the statement was true and was therefore subject to damages. John the butcher might sell rotten meat but if you published the fact and it hurt his business, he had an action for libel against you. The saving grace was that while a jury might find for libel when the statement was true, it might then assess only token damages. (We don't want to eat rotten meat; damages for libel, one farthing.)

Coke's "be it never so true" standard of liability, with truth not a defense, is still essentially the English law of libel. The saving grace of nominal damages has been joined in recent years by another mitigation—the public's right to know. If the prime minister is keeping a mistress in an upscale flat in the suburbs and a newspaper publishes it, and it is true (here is a photo of him stumbling out at 5:00 A.M. with his fly unzipped), did the public need to know in order to make a judgment at the next election, or is this irrelevant? A good question for attorneys to jawbone over, juries to consider, and media to go ballistic about.

The shadow of Sir Edward Coke nevertheless still lies heavily on the British press, which frequently pays out libel damages. The reported libelous sensation may, however, have skyrocketed the circulation of the paper, so a libel payout becomes just another way of doing business.

A common trick of London papers and other media is to get a member of Parliament to ask a saucy question, since MPs have since the seventeenth century had unlimited freedom of speech in Commons. (Is it true, Mr. Speaker, that Prince Charles said he wanted to be his mistress's tampon? Is it true, Mr. Speaker, that the Princess of Wales is disporting with her riding instructor? Headline: M.P. ASKS IN COMMONS. . . .)

The United States was spared all this nonsense by the First Amendment of 1791, prescribing freedom of the press. There was a feint toward criminal libel in the very early years of the Republic, but that has been inconceivable since then.

In 1964 the U.S. Supreme Court swung in the other, more liberal direction, making it extremely difficult for a "public figure" to win a libel action (*Sullivan* v. *New York Times*) even if the published statement is blatantly false. The plaintiff has to prove "actual malice"—that is, that the newspaper or other media knew it was false at the very time of publication but recklessly went ahead anyway, something that is very difficult and extremely expensive to prove. At first it seemed that a public figure was simply a government official (in the landmark *Sullivan* case, an obscure Louisiana sheriff) but later court decisions made a public figure anyone well known to the public, such as a film actress or rock star or even, in a 1996 New York case, an obscure individual who had been written about unfavorably in a tabloid newspaper column after she made a rape complaint.

While in recent years in practical terms the libel situation in the two countries' law has been getting somewhat closer together, there is still a significant gap. Anyone who publishes a book in both New York and London saying hostile things about a living person (even that an Oxbridge professor writes bad history books), will inevitably get a fax from her editor in London: "Our solicitors advise . . . ," and at least a line or two will have to be watered down. There is no point arguing about this; the spirit of Coke lives on in Britain.

In both England and the United States, it is impossible to libel the dead, so the first thing a libel defense lawyer will ask someone sued for civil libel is the age and health of the plaintiff.

The history of libel law captures in a nutshell the up- and downside extremes of liability law. There is a genuine social problem of defamation, to which inevitably and reasonably the courts and the legal profession feel impelled to respond. But in practice this judicial frontier is jagged and mushy, hard to define in precise terms. So a great deal is left to the skill of counsel, the temperament of juries, and the willingness of judges to give or not to give precise and clear instructions to juries and to rein in the rhetoric of counsel. In an American libel action the court has to make the very difficult, perhaps impossible distinction between a statement of fact and an opinion.

England in the matter of newspaper conduct actually has a press council that renders professional opinions on journalistic behavior, but this does not seem to suffice. As long as damages await, libel actions in court also go on and on.

As result of the *Sullivan* decision, there is less judicial activity in one matter of liability (libel) in the United States than in England. Since the *Sullivan* case, it has transpired that it doesn't seem to make much difference after all to the careers of public officials and popular idols to get muddied in the press and TV with impunity, even in a mendacious manner. They still do very well, which raises the general question of whether the law of libel may be obsolete and no longer socially necessary.

If an American newspaper or TV network is determined to fight a libel action and is willing to put out the vast funds necessary to retain the best counsel, and if necessary to appeal the case through several levels, the media organization is very likely to win.

That is what the two most celebrated libel cases in recent decades appear to demonstrate. In one case the prestigious *Washington Post* published an article accusing the president of a major oil company of arranging sweetheart contracts with a shipping company owned by his son. The trial court found for the plaintiff and assessed huge damages on the *Post*. But the newspaper appealed until the trial court was overruled. In another famous case a prominent general was accused by a TV network of falsifying mortality figures in the Vietnam War. The case never even reached a verdict, although the general seemed to have the winning argument. The general ran out of money and settled for a vague statement by the TV network upholding his integrity but not acknowledging error in this particular matter, and such libelous error very likely occurred.

The application of libel law has also been complicated by the emergence of the new networks of computer-based communication, just as the use of the printing press affected libel law in the sixteenth century. Statements on the Internet are not privileged communication like a telephone call, but fall into the category of publication as in a newspaper or book and are subject to the laws of libel. Many people using the Internet appear not to realize this. They make defamatory misstatements of fact about someone that are libelous. But there are so many websites and computer networks that many such defamatory remarks go unnoticed by their victims. Unlike buying a newspaper or book to follow up on hearsay that you have been libeled, defamation on the Internet is inaccessible to the computer illiterate or too time-consuming or expensive to pursue.

The Internet is being used in the 1990s to disseminate defamatory communications even more effectively and widely than in conventional printed formats, and it is a favorite medium for academics. In the early 1990s, a historian having published a provocative (and prizewinning), although libel-free book that many of his conservative colleagues in the field intensely disliked, the latter set some of their computer-literate graduate students to work, vilifying the controversial scholar through defamatory "flamings" on the Internet. Even if the victimized historian had cared enough to inaugurate libel actions, and could have afforded the expense of counsel and litigation, he only discovered that he had been libeled three years after the defamatory statement was posted, and the statute of limitation on libel is only one year.

Libel on the Internet shows how awkwardly and messily common law in some areas responds to technological change. This again raises the issue that liability might be better addressed by binding arbitration rather than by adversarial litigation that was invented in the fourteenth century.

12
Law and Power

THE GREAT DIFFERENCE BETWEEN the law and the
other prominent learned professions, medicine and academia, is
that the law is intertwined with the exercise of state power and for
the most part cannot be resisted by private persons.

One can decline to avail oneself of the attention of medical
doctors, and indeed down to the 1870s that refusal would more
likely have extended rather than shortened life; until the introduction of antibiotics in the 1940s, medical doctors could do little
to cure serious illnesses except engage in the amputation of
limbs. One can decline to attend colleges and universities and
still have a satisfying life and, indeed, still have a good chance for
personal wealth.

But it is not possible to resist the lawyers because they always
have the power of the state behind them. The common law was
the instrument of state power and its imposition on groups and
individuals in society.

Sometimes legal historians blithely talk about a high wall between public law and private law, implying that the latter deals with interpersonal relations and is outside the jurisdiction of state power. But this distinction is vulnerable because private law uses the power of the state to force people to pay attention and respond to its actions, and if they refuse to do so, to ruin them.

Obviously, treason, taxation, and criminal justice are matters of public law because they immediately reflect and demand the exercise of power by the government. But liability, for instance, the inner shrine of so-called private law, also depends on the exercise of state power. When you are sued in a civil action for injuring someone, the state gives sanction to the demand by the attorney for the plaintiff that you promptly respond. If you do not, the state court will declare you in default, and the resulting damages are likely to be ruinous. So the distinction between public and private law turns out to be a porous one.

This is a prime reason why the study and practice of law have since the crystallization of the common law in the later Middle Ages, and never more than in the United States today, appealed to bright, ambitious, and energetic young people of the affluent middle class. They are able to pursue a learned profession with all the intellectual, prestigious, fiscal, and behavioral advantages of that career, and even if they are not directly government lawyers—and it is usually more rewarding if they are not—and are engaged in private practice, they have the power of the state behind them.

That is perhaps also the prime reason why lawyers are so much hated in common-law countries, from the age of Shakespeare through the age of Dickens to today. Medical doctors cannot normally compel you to receive their biomedical remedies; professors cannot force you to listen to their interpretations of Plato and Dante. But lawyers can and do use the power of the state behind them, even in seemingly private quarrels.

Law and power are therefore symbiotically interrelated. Law is the prime means by which those who hold power in society—

whether in the central or regional government, or local communities, or in corporations, or in families—impose exploitation and ultimately control on everyone else. The common law provides the support of the state for those holding superior status and wealth in various social groups to discipline and punish other people living in their shadow. It is tempting to agree with Michel Foucault that seemingly humanitarian departures in the law—recognition of insanity as a distinctive behavioral condition, or imprisonment in place of execution or deportation were the two legal subjects Foucault wrote books about—are merely new forms of oppression dreamed up by the powerful to dominate the weak and many.

Yet without this vehicle of law, not only would a high degree of disorder occur, but the seeking of justice and equity by individuals and populations would become more difficult and require the exercise of strenuously political and possibly violent means.

Behind the phrases "due process of the law" and "rule of law" is the historical fact that some particular people control the process and exercise the rule. But the common law has also provided a venue for the weak, the marginal, and the many to gain a measure of personal if imperfect justice and to live in a context of satisfyingly stable order.

It is not a simple story, the history of the common law. Young people who say they want to become lawyers to do good, or veteran attorneys who claim to have cultivated high ethical principles, are not necessarily talking nonsense. Neither the sentimental praises of the bourgeois liberals nor the curses of the Marxists and Foucaultians tell the whole story.

Nor can it simply be said that the historical truth lies somewhere in between. There are instances of polarity, of the truth lying at or close to the extreme. It is necessary to look at the particular issue in which law and power are interacting. It is also worth remembering that historical judgment depends on the perspective of the particular historian and is always a relative and debatable matter. Stubbs, Maitland, Milsom, and Horwitz each views the common law from quite distinct perspectives. That does not delegitimize each historian's judgment on the relationship between law and power.

Between the late thirteenth and the late sixteenth centuries occurred the modernization of the jury; the gentrification of the land law; and the development of personal actions, especially liability. These can be regarded as the most important departure in the deepening of the structure of the common law and the widening of its judicial frontiers. But along with these developments were many others in which the exercise of power in society and the operations of the law were interactive and profoundly affected people's lives.

In the history of any society, the incidence of violent crime is not a constant but varies significantly from time to time. The priority given to suppressing crime and the level of state resources provided for this purpose are important variables. But sociological and demographic factors conducive to crime are also at work.

Another important variable is the percentage of the population who are postadolescent males. If that is on the rise, so will be the amount of crime. In mid-thirteenth-century England organized rural crime—gangs of young men preying on farming society—clearly was a growing problem.

Whether the historical source of the Robin Hood legends emerged from this context is debatable. It is also possible that the historical Robin Hood was among the disinherited gentry whose families were judicially dispossessed for supporting Simon de Monfort in the Barons' War against King Henry III in the 1260s. But the proliferation and popularity of the Robin Hood and other outlaw legends date from the late thirteenth and early fourteenth centuries—precisely when organized rural crime involving outlaw gangs of young men, disturbing the gentry manor houses and peasant villages alike and increasing the dangers of highway travel, was given special attention by royal justices.

Rural poverty engendered sexual frustration, which in turn contributed to the aggressive behavior of young men. Under the conditions of land shortage around 1300, it became the practice to marry late or not at all. One estimate from mid-fifteenth-century data is that astonishingly close to a quarter of the population of late medieval England never married.

Another persistent problem, not really faced until the mid-nineteenth century, was the lack of a policing system. In the cities the mayors and aldermen paid for some security forces, but in the countryside there was only the old-fashioned self-help system—going back to Anglo-Saxon days of the hue and cry and the frankpledge (or tithing)—which was now impotent in the face of gangs of young men with weapons in their hands.

The more heavily populated villages came to designate constables. But the effectiveness of this untrained and poorly armed official can be gauged by the constable being a stock figure of slapstick fun in Shakespeare's plays—his mere appearance on the scene being a signal for the theater groundlings to start catcalling and laughing in derision.

In the late thirteenth century, as the English population boom reached its painful medieval height, the villages were over-crowded, land was steadily inflating in value, and there was plenty of underemployment and unemployment in rural society, not only among the peasants but also among the poorer gentry families, whose desperate younger sons could give leadership to orga-nized rural crime.

During the late fourteenth century the demographic strain had been sharply alleviated by biomedical disaster, but by now a new social factor was driving organized crime. The Hundred Years' War recruited thousands of farm lads and younger sons of gentry to fight as mercenaries in the royal armies in France. After a decade or so of hostilities that ravaged the sweet countryside of western France, there was always a long truce, and demobilized, highly trained, battle-hardened veterans were sent home. Most of them probably adjusted well enough, but a large minority were not eager, after years of camaraderie and looting in France, to get behind the plow or into the sheep or cattle ranch. They took to organized crime.

A third factor productive of organized crime was the political and military conflicts within the royal family and among the aristocracy that began in the 1380s and reached their peak in what the Victorian writers called the Wars of the Roses between the Lancastrians and the Yorkists. Their civil war was not completely stilled until the upstart Tudor dynasty, distantly related to the Lancastrian group, gained the throne by force in 1485 and attempted to make an uneasy peace through Henry VII's political marriage with a Yorkist heiress and through a more centralized government.

In the disturbed political conditions of most of the fifteenth century, great lords and wealthier gentry recruited and paid for contingents of armed retainers, who engaged in "livery and maintenance." The former term meant that they wore a warlord's badge and enjoyed his protection; the latter that the boss "maintained" them in the courts, bribing and threatening judges and suborning juries to keep the law from interfering with the violent conduct of their retainers. It was a mafia kind of situation, as celebrated in many of Martin Scorsese's films.

As occurs in our society, the expansion of crime will be accompanied and to a marginal degree stimulated by dissemination of ideological justifications by discontented academics and other intellectuals. In the fourteenth and early fifteenth centuries this was provided by the radical wing of the Franciscan Order, which dreamed of a socialist church; by university graduates unhappily finding country vicarages beneath the level of their expectations and hence prone to radicalization; and by the Lollards, a group of itinerant heretical preachers, the followers of the heretical Oxford professor John Wycliffe.

"When Adam delved and Eve span, who was then the gentleman?" was the provocative question posed by these leftist agitators in rural society. Their Christian egalitarianism was used to justify crime as the righteous protest of the poor against exploitation by the rich. In pratice modest gentry and peasant families were more likely victims of the gangs than the nobility and the rich gentry, who could afford security guards.

As organized crime escalated because of these succeeding waves of causation—rural underemployment of testosterone-crazed males; demobilized soldiers; and armed retainers given livery and maintenance by warlords; socialist agitators—the criminal justice system responded in fits and starts with three sets of judicial innovations: trailbaston, justices of the peace, and Star Chamber.

Trailbaston was a special judicial commission given to a select panel of tough-minded justices to go suddenly into the villages, impanel blue ribbon grand juries, and wipe out gangs. This is a ploy still used from time to time in New York State. High-profile prosecutors like Tom Dewey in the 1930s or Rudolph Giuliani in the 1980s are close modern equivalents to late medieval justices on trailbaston.

Does it work? Marginally and temporarily it is bound to have an effect, but the underlying social causes of organized crime remain.

It is curious that the medieval justices had a close equivalent to modern techniques of breaking up gangs through use of a "stoolie," a gang member caught early and induced to "turn state's evidence," to testify against the other gang members and, latterly, to enter "the federal witness protection program."

In the late Middle Ages there was a similar system of "approvers." A gang member convicted early on by the justices accused the other members of his gang one by one and offered to prove his accusation through archaic trial by battle against each one. If he vanquished each defendant, he was ultimately pardoned. If he lost a judicial duel he was hanged—if he had not died in the combat.

The system of justices of the peace goes back to the days of Simon de Montfort in the 1260s, when they were called keepers of the peace. After sundry experiments, the JP system was fully established by legislation in the 1340s. This was another self-help approach to rural law and order, but with the burden and power falling on the wealthier gentry. In each county several dozen of this social elite were given royal commissions of peace to police their communities and repress crime and assist sheriffs. They were laymen, not lawyers, although many of the JPs had a year or two of study at the Inns of Court during their late teens.

In their quarter session courts, the JPs were authorized to deal with all manner of misdemeanors—drunken brawls, poaching, petty thievery—so as to alleviate the burdens on the grand juries and the county courts and circuit judges. They were also intermittently authorized to try felony cases in their quarter session courts, with a royal justice presiding. Essentially what the government was saying to the wealthier gentry was: It's your county; police it, maintain order, repress gangsterism, and reduce the pressure on the personnel of royal criminal justice in London.

The JPs were not paid, but receiving a justice of the peace commission was highly desired in gentry families by the fifteenth century. It was official recognition of favored status and ascending political importance, possibly leading eventually to election as MP or appointment as sheriff. It helped in the arranging of good marriages.

The JP system—which lasted in this form until the 1880s—did not do much to stem organized crime in the late Middle Ages, the social and political factors stimulating gangsterism being then too strong for such amateurish intervention. But in the sixteenth century, with prosperity at home and peace abroad (and therefore no recruitment and training of armies), and in combination with the work of the Court of Star Chamber, the JPs began to be highly effective in stabilizing the counties. They were also given additional power when the Tudors introduced unemployment (poor law) legislation, whose enforcement of which the JPs were authorized to carry out.

The commissioning of JPs from wealthy gentry families had the effect of adding judicial authority to their existing social and economic power and strengthening the hold of the top stratum of the gentry over county society. No small landowner, let alone a farm laborer, was likely to cross a prominent gentry family with boundless fiscal resources, access to prominent attorneys, and now holding a JP commission besides.

Thus the JP system became by 1600 a prime example of the way that the common law buttressed the already existing hierarchical nature of county society. Consequently modern leftist historians, beginning with Tawney in the early years of this century through E. P. Thompson in the 1960s, were unstinting in their scathing criticism of the JP system—and not without cause.

In defense of it, two things can be said. The origins of the JP system lie not in the Crown's deliberate effort to strengthen the power of the gentry, although that was a side effect that was entirely amenable to the royal government of the fourteenth century, but rather to improve the functioning of criminal justice and to enhance peace and order in a then disturbed and perilous countryside.

The other positive side to JP enhancement of gentry power was that it helped significantly to give England one of its most attractive qualities, celebrated alike in nineteenth-century fiction and later-twentieth-century film, namely the continuing of a stable countryside generation after generation. This is still a condition that Englishmen, foreign visitors, and filmmakers alike find satisfying. Tawney was right to remark around 1910 that behind the amenities of gentrified rural England darkly lay social polarity and economic inequity, but the beauty and order did prevail and shone brightly through the memory of many centuries.

*   *   *

The Court of Star Chamber was even more important than entrenchment of JPs in the late fifteenth and early sixteenth centuries in stopping gangsterism and improving peace in the countryside. The criminal court of Star Chamber was one of the two "conciliar" or "prerogative" courts that originated in the later years of the fifteenth century, the other being the civil Court of Chancery. The courts were called conciliar because they began as subcommittees of the royal council, some ten to twenty privy sworn councillors that governed the country for the king. They are called prerogative courts because they functioned under the king's prerogative, or residual authority, to maintain justice and repress crime.

For assurance Henry VII had Parliament pass a Star Chamber Act in 1487, but the court was already functioning by then. It was called Star Chamber because of a product of fifteenth-century interior design, a love of painted wooden ceilings (such as still survives in Duke Humphrey of Gloucester's library at Oxford University). The privy councillors committed to serving in this special criminal court initially met in a room with stars painted on its ceiling.

Star Chamber was originally created to deal with "overmighty subjects" ruining the criminal justice system through livery and maintenance, that is organized crime getting the support of wealthy and prominent people. The equivalent today would be a special court established to bring down drug lords.

As organized crime and gangsterism declined, there was still plenty for Star Chamber to do. It helped in the general pacification of society in the sixteenth century. Endemic violence was a characteristic of this early modern society:

> Men had weapons about them and were readily enough moved to use them. Arguments quickly became quarrels, and there were always daggers handy to draw blood. The records are full of such violence because too many men (and women)

believed in taking the law into their own hands. This was the rough, superstitious, excitable and volatile society which the king's government had to rule. (G. R. Elton)

Star Chamber made use of no jury of any kind but simply brought the accused before it under a bench writ, or subpoena—turn up or suffer punishment, or do or don't do something as soon as your receive this or you will be punished—for example, give that widow the money coming to her; stop stealing from the trust fund; stop ignoring that will. Pronto. Star Chamber made extensive use of paid informers as well as receiving petitions or bills of complaints from individuals in both rural and urban areas. The operative word in such bills was "riot." Use of "riot" as the trigger word vaguely implied organized disturbances that allegedly had the prospect of becoming political rebellion as well as criminal misconduct and therefore had to be dealt with immediately and severely.

There is a similarity between a Roman-law court and Star Chamber in that the latter like the former sought to get the accused to incriminate himself by a grilling in the presence of its judges, who were prominent servants of the Crown. Whether Star Chamber used torture to get at the truth is a matter of dispute (most of the court's records in its early decades have disappeared). Probably torture was used rarely, if at all; demanding inquiry under oath was its weapon.

Star Chamber could not impose a sentence of capital punishment. If the examination of the defendant turned up evidence of a capital crime, the defendant had to be indicted by a grand jury and the normal procedure of the common law had to take its course. Star Chamber otherwise punished by fine, by short-term imprisonment, and by public humiliation such as the cropping of ears, and then sending the perpetrator walking through the streets of London with a derogatory placard around his neck.

Star Chamber worked because it frightened people into realizing that the days of gangsterism were over, that the royal council would come down on dangerous anti-social behavior immediately and harshly, that even well-connected criminals would be dispatched. In consequence Star Chamber was popular through most of the sixteenth century. How the court operated is revealed in a delightful book, one of the best ever written about English law, *Star Chamber Stories*, by Geoffrey Elton.

Star Chamber ran into trouble when, in the closing years of the sixteenth century, it turned its attention to religious dissent, to evangelical Protestants who had "separated" from the Church of England and were thought to be subversive. By the 1630s Star Chamber had turned its awful engine against this humble but numerically large minority, dragging Puritan preachers before it, harassing them, throwing up claims of sexual misconduct against them, trying to force the dissenters to incriminate themselves for one misstep or another—unlicensed meetings, criminal libel, perjury, and so forth.

When a majority of the House of Commons sympathetic to these dissenting Protestant targets of Star Chamber got the upper hand in Parliament in 1642, they passed a statute abolishing the court and furthermore prohibiting an English court from trying to get a defendant to give testimony against himself. This exclusion of self-incrimination passed into the Fifth Amendment of the American Constitution.

Many critics have claimed that American congressional committees, using their ostensible power to obtain background information for legislation, especially in the Joseph McCarthy era of the 1950s, in effect revived Star Chamber proceedings under oath ("Are you now or have you ever been a Communist?") and was thereby unconstitutional, violating the Fifth Amendment. But the Supreme Court in deference to Congress, under the separation of powers within the federal government, declined to intervene.

In England police and prosecutors have frequently ignored the

Star Chamber Act of 1642 and assiduously sought to get investigated targets to incriminate themselves in pretrial interviews. Such aggressive conduct by police and prosecutors is now blatantly illegal in the United States, at the state as well as the federal level, as a long series of Federal civil rights cases decided in the 1960s, particularly *Gideon* v. *Wainright* (1963) and *Miranda* v. *Arizona* (1966). Not only can the defendant stand mute, but he has a right to counsel before and during interrogation.

When the radicalized Commons in 1642 abolished Star Chamber it suspended temporarily the other conciliar or prerogative court, that of Chancery, which also started operating in the late fifteenth century. But after a four-year hiatus Chancery resumed functioning and still operates today in England. Under the reform of the high courts by the Judicature Act of 1873, Chancery remained one of the principal central court jurisdictions. The American colonies and the new United States inherited chancery courts. These have now all but disappeared, but chancery—or equity—proceedings are still important in American as well as in English common law.

Maitland said that Chancery was not a real equity court, as in Roman law, but only "quasi-equity." The difference is that the continental judges in the Justinian tradition had the power, exercising their reason under natural law, to suspend and change law, so that justice was done. Common law would never recognize such an audacious principle.

Chancery was a civil court that had special responsibilities and instruments to provide justice for vulnerable populations—widows, heirs (if they were minors), heiresses, and lunatics—and in time to oversee the administration of trust and wills which were intended to protect such vulnerable groups.

These Chancery proceedings worked on the principle that the old common-law courts, particularly Common Pleas, where these matters would normally be tried, were too slow, cumbersome, and expensive—but especially slow—to protect these special populations and to deal with crucial, pressing matters. So a new court that could provide quick intervention was necessary.

Chancery intervention began when someone—the plaintiff personally or a guardian or attorney—petitioned the chancellor as the king's chief official to do something immediately to prevent injustice from being done. Chancery was a "court of conscience"—technically the king's. Chancellors had been receiving such petitions on behalf of the king for centuries. In a sense all that happened in the fifteenth century was that the chancellor regularized receiving and acting on such petitions for quick and effective equity by setting up a judicial board or separate court to focus on these problems.

Chancery having considered the petition and possibly interviewed the plaintiff, or her guardian or attorney, and possibly obtaining a quick response from the alleged defendant, if it was convinced that there was a prima facie (at least superficial) case for intervention, proceeded to do so by issuing a bench writ under subpoena.

There were and still are two kinds of Chancery injunctions: positive, called a writ of mandamus ("We command that . . ."); and negative, called a writ of prohibition ("We order you to stop . . ."). It should be stressed that a Chancery proceeding was technically meant to be only a short-term intervention. The case could and was often later heard at full length in Common Pleas. But lawyers who specialized in Chancery proceedings soon became skillful at putting all sorts of impediments to transferring the case to common pleas to resolve the dispute finally. Since the dispute was often about the disposal of liquid assets, such as land that could be mortgaged or sold, a Chancery lawyer would want to extend the case as long as possible knowing there was enough money available for him to be well rewarded. One of Dickens's novels involves a Chancery inheritance case that goes on interminably until the assets under dispute are entirely used up, mostly to pay the lawyers. Such things did happen in Victorian times—and still do.

Another debatable aspect of Chancery proceedings in modern times was the use of injunctions, in both England and the United States, to restrain strike activity or any kind of public demonstration. Injunctions are still issued to make pickets stand a prescribed number of yards from the entrance to a retail business so that the business can continue to operate in the face of picketing strikers or other demonstrators. Labor unions hate injunctions. But injunctions are also used to keep abortion clinics open in the face of protesting crowds.

In its first century or so of operation, Chancery acquired an aura of being the court that protected the rights of relatively vulnerable propertied women—widows and heiresses. The common law does not get high ratings in feminist histories, nor should it. It was conditioned by the patriarchal and masculine values of the people who created and administered it.

The principle in the common law, not entirely rooted out until the 1880s, that husband and wife were *una persona*, one person, and the husband spoke for that person is particularly offensive to feminist sensibility. Nor was it without consequence. A married woman could not participate in litigation of any kind without her husband's assent and at least normally he spoke and she kept quiet. A married woman's property (unless protected by prenuptial agreement) and wages, if she worked for wages, belonged to her husband to do with what he liked. When consumer banking began in the fifteenth century, a married woman could not open a bank account in her own name without her husband's approval. This was still the situation in mid-Victorian England.

The *una persona* doctrine fell most harshly on working-class and petit bourgeois women. Women of wealthy families received substantial protection from the common law, and Chancery was especially helpful in this regard through the medium of trusts.

A trust (called a "use" or "devise") was a legal mechanism by which the assets of a beneficiary were protected and managed by one or more trustees on behalf of the beneficiary in return for moderate or no remuneration. (Compare the board of trustees of a private American university today; they get lots of free partying and honorary degrees but no payment.)

In 1500 any wealthy woman or potential heiress did not, if the family had good counsel, enter marriage without elaborate trust arrangements so that most of her capital was shielded from her husband's disposal. He could not in a trust arrangement invade her assets without the approval of the trustees, who could be other family members and/or her attorneys.

A widow had special rights. During her lifetime she was supposed to receive her "dower," one-third of the income of her husband's estate until she died.

In practice these legal protections sometimes did not work smoothly. An heiress could be pressured or persuaded by her husband to participate in a scheme to break the trust, or the trustees could engage in collusion to do so.

Given the perils of medicineless childbirth, the widow of a rich man could be his second or third wife, and the stepmother, not the mother of the heir by primogeniture from his father's first marriage, with an underlying oedipal edge from the condition of the stepmother being of the same age or younger than the heir. The dower provision for widows was often therefore observed in the breach. The heir simply refused to recognize his stepmother's (or, even more cruelly, his own mother's) dower rights, left her impoverished, and sent over an attorney to get the widow to sign away her dower rights for a small pension.

It was to help heiresses and widows in these harsh situations that Chancery was especially created. Did it work? Sometimes. It was better than nothing. The problem was that husbands and stepsons could often afford better counsel than could the women they were abusing.

A problem that emerged when a trust or "use" was set up to protect the capital of a minor or a married woman was: Who payed the taxes on the income generated by the trust? Was it the trustees who were liable, or the beneficiary of the trust? In the early sixteenth century, Chancery became the forum of a huge expansion of uses or trusts, which were often designed simply as tax dodges. Finally the Act of Uses of 1536 specified that if no one else payed the tax on income from a trust, then the beneficiary was liable.

Who was the beneficiary—the heiress whose capital in trust was producing the income, or her husband who was enjoying the income while shielded from seizing the capital—was an interesting question. But since in law husband and wife were one person, it usually didn't matter.

The status of women in the propertied classes was also deeply affected by the development of marriage and divorce categories in the canon law of the church in the later Middle Ages.

In the twelfth and thirteenth centuries the papacy's compulsive zeal to legislate on and discipline all aspects of human behavior, given initial impetus by the Gregorian reform movement emanating from Rome 1070–1120, was articulated in the church's canon law. England was politically remote from Rome, and the material and human resources of the church in England were closely exploited and controlled by the monarchy. But by the mid-thirteenth century papal policy and resulting canon law stipulations on marriage and divorce penetrated England and were enforced in church courts there with the acquiescence of the royal government and the common-law judges.

This wave of church judicialization of marriage raised major issues for the propertied classes and significantly affected their behavior. Paradoxically, but on second thought not so surprisingly, the unmarried and in practice usually celibate men who comprised the legislating Catholic cardinals and the canon lawyers took highly idealistic views of marital unions.

Canon law took the romantic position that even without family consent a marriage freely entered into by a male and female was valid (same-sex unions were not validated in the Western Church, although they may have been in obscure Balkan regions, where anything could happen). The woman needed to be fourteen and the man sixteen, but their families did not have to give consent. The response of the English landed families was: Lock up your daughters, to prevent them from entering into clandestine marriages or eloping with unsuitable spouses. The church's view that two people of the minimum age of consent vowing their troth were validly married in face of family opposition meant that young women of wealthy families henceforth had to be kept in close confinement. The church's voluntarist and romantic view of marriage therefore had the effect of further constricting the lives of young women of the nobility, gentry, and merchant class.

In England by 1500, as a way of mitigating the church's recognition of free choice between parties irrespective of family approval, it became the practice to "proclaim the banns," to announce an engagement in the family's local church for several weeks previous to the actual union. Secrecy was the avenue of unfavorable marriage, publicity a defense against it, in the eyes of propertied families. But the banns system was not foolproof. As long as the lovers could find a priest, even a derelict wandering friar, to join them, it was a valid marriage. This loophole required ever closer watching of unmarried women in propertied families.

The second major change introduced by the celibate cardinals and the zealous canon lawyers facilitated getting around the controlling purposes of announcing the banns. Beginning with the Gregorian reform of the late eleventh century and confirmed by the Fourth Lateran Council of 1215 (the same busy council that sank ordeals by withdrawing clerical participation), the church decreed that marriage was a sacrament, like baptism, and had to be performed by a cleric. The old Germanic secular marriage of merely giving a ring and having intercourse was no longer acceptable to the church as the way of getting married, although it continued to be practiced for centuries among a huge segment of the peasant and artisan classes.

By 1400 the landed families had fully accepted the church's view that marriage was a sacrament and that a religious ceremony was necessary. This recognition, however, had the consequence of validating secret unions and elopements. If the church service was so important, once a wandering friar had joined the couple, even if it was Romeo and Juliet from mutually feuding families, it was a legal union.

In late medieval marriage law, clerical idealism and family interest thus were constantly at cross-purposes, contributing not a little to the rising anticlericalism of rich people.

The romantic, individualistic view of marriage—not requiring family consent—continued in England after the Reformation split with Rome in the sixteenth century. In response to the problems this presented to the landed classes, an attempt was made in the Hardwicke Marriage Act of 1753 (named after the lord chancellor who put through the parliamentary legislation) to give authority over marriage to families. All marriages had to take place in an Anglican church, even those involving the third of the population who were not Anglicans, and the banns had to be posted. The intention was to prevent clandestine marriages in which an heiress married without her family's permission or a middle-class woman from a respectable family ran off and married someone beneath her station, such as an impecunious soldier. The Hardwicke Act partly but by no means entirely closed the legal loophole. Certain parishes, particularly one in North London, became famous as places where quick marriages, no questions asked, were still possible. Love triumphed over property and propriety, leaving Jane Austen with one of her favorite plot devices intact.

The turning of marriage into a sacrament by 1400, and the acceptance of this legal principle by the establishment, meant that it was harder now for nobility, gentry, and bourgeoisie to effect divorce. Spouses could not be so readily ditched by husbands. Marriage was in the eyes of God and the canon law an indissoluble union: What God has joined together let no man break asunder.

Of course for the Catholic Middle Ages there was a loophole, a pretty big one. There was no divorce because that would cancel a sacrament, but an annulment of the marriage on grounds that it was somehow invalid was still possible. Church courts could still determine that a marriage was void.

Obviously if there was no consummation, marriage had not occurred. In this instance women experts were called in to examine vaginas and look for broken maidenheads, and the celibate canon lawyers solemnly recorded these clinical details. But there were other reasons that an annulment could be ordained—marrying too close a relative (even as distant as a third cousin) remained the favorite. It was tricky judicial theory how the children of an annulled marriage could still be legitimate and could legally inherit, but the church courts managed to squirm through that one.

In practice divorce law affected only propertied people like gentry, merchants, nobility, and the royal family. In fact, the greatest divorce case involved King Henry VIII himself, who wanted to rid himself of his first wife, sourpuss Catherine of Aragon, and marry his vivacious and pregnant mistress Anne Boleyn. For political reasons the pope could not give Henry an annulment (the queen's nephew, the German emperor, was occupying Rome at the time and he was protective of Aunt Kate's interests). Finally the archbishop of Canterbury and some other royal councillors advised the king to declare himself—by act of Parliament so it would be unquestionably legal—the head of the Church of England and grant himself a divorce. Henry proceeded to do just that. Thus was the Church of England born in Anne Boleyn's eyes.

The separation from Rome under these peculiar circumstances made divorce no easier in England. In fact, with the rise of Calvinist Protestantism within and outside the Church of England in the closing decades of the sixteenth century, Puritan spiritual commitment to the idea of the sanctity of the family made marriage bonds even more indissoluble and even annulments difficult to obtain. Popular sentiment by 1650 was against divorce of any kind in England. The old Catholic gimmick of securing an annulment because—horrors!—you belatedly discovered that you had married your cousin no longer obtained.

By the eighteenth century dissolution of a marriage except in very unusual circumstances (kidnapping and rape; bigamy) was only possible by a private act of Parliament, an extremely awkward and immensely expensive procedure, virtually impossible for anyone who did not sit in the House of Lords. By 1750 only very rich lords got divorced in England. Everyone else, if they were propertied, even the upper stratum of the gentry, suffered on in unhappy marriages. Of course the unpropertied simply walked away from marriage and started new cohabitations. In some parts of rural England husbands of the lower classes even sold wives at county fairs, as graphically described in Thomas Hardy's novel *The Mayor of Casterbridge*, set in the 1860s.

The situation on divorce in common law did not change until the parliamentary legislation of 1857, which allowed divorce on grounds of adultery (which was often faked), followed by long-term desertion as grounds for divorce in 1884. But until the 1960s divorce remained a difficult matter in England. Certain hotels in the seaside resort of Brighton as late as the 1950s did a thriving business as the scenes of faked adultery incidents, complete with house photographer.

It is ironic that the conservative views on sex and marriage held by the male chauvinist and patriarchal church lawyers turned out to have consequences highly protective of married women. Because the dissolution of marriages was so difficult, it was a problem for husbands in the propertied classes to get rid of their wives as the latter grew old (that is, about thirty-five in this society) and disfigured by frequent childbirth.

This protection of rich wives compares with the early medieval situation, before 1150, when lords divested themselves of spouses almost as often as they changed horses, when the only protection from being abandoned (or shunted off to a nunnery) that a married woman of the upper class had was the threatened outbreak of a blood feud against the erring husband by her outraged kin.

The law of marriage and divorce as it developed between 1200 and the early nineteenth century involved all sorts of restrictions on the private lives of even wealthy people. They chafed under this restrictive regime, but they accepted it, because they could not articulate a common political and ideological response that would have liberated them to behave as they wished in their personal and family lives.

They could not define a political demand for legislation to liberate themselves for two reasons. One was that Christian ethics, as much or more in a post-Reformation Protestant context as in medieval Catholic culture, was extremely hostile to freedom of sexual behavior and encased it in the severe judicial restrictions of pre–1857 marriage and divorce law. The second reason why the gentry continued to live under a set of marriage and divorce laws that made them anxious and unhappy, the males perhaps even more than the females of the landed classes, was that marriage was inextricably involved with the acquisition, transference, and exploitation of land gained in the "jointure" of marriage, the coming together in one form or another through marriage vows of inherited estates.

The enjoyment of real estate was immensely more important to these people—and of course plenty of rich people today—than the enjoyment of sexual unions and happy marriages, so they were prepared to endure severe limitations on the latter to facilitate the former.

The common law, and those who shaped it in the royal government, the courts, and the legal profession, accommodated the gentry wishes. As trusts or uses became a central vehicle for the judicial administration of land, the Crown in the Statute of Uses of 1536 insisted that appropriate taxes be paid on lands held in trust, but confirmed the legality of these "devises" or legal instruments. The common lawyers working in the Court of Common Pleas were jealous that so much lucrative litigation about land had passed to Chancery, and they in turn invented various mechanisms to bring such litigation back into Common Pleas, resulting in procedural awkwardness, and in confusion and conflict within the legal profession between the Chancery lawyers and the more traditional kind of common pleas attorneys.

In accordance with the wishes of landed families and the visceral behavior patterns of rich men, who wanted more freedom to dispose of landed assets in a system in which entails and trusts constrained them, the Crown provided the Statute of Wills of 1540. Some historians have seen this liberal parliamentary act as quid pro quo for the tax-restrictive Statute of Uses of four years before.

Wills disposing of assets after death were very old legal instruments, going back to the Anglo-Saxon era, but they could dispose only of movable property (such as jewels, swords, horses) not land. The Statute of Wills of 1540 allowed as much as two-thirds of a landlord's estate to be devised or granted by the document after his death. This was an important transition away from primogeniture, but not as big a step as it might seem. The eldest son was already protected by entail, which legally decreed the passing of the income of the greater part of the family land to the eldest son generation by generation. Other land, such as that gained in marriage, was often already allocated in the next generation by use or trust. There was normally precious little land free to allocate by will.

The disposal of an estate was thus already rigidly stipulated by legal instruments before the death of the landlord. But there was some enhanced flexibility and enunciation in 1540 of an important principle of moving toward freedom of disposal of landed assets. A century later all land not tied up in entail and trusts, not just two-thirds, could be allocated by will. If a landlord died intestate (without a will), rules of primogeniture prevailed.

Therefore the drafting and periodical revising of a will to the point of the landlord's expiration was a major occupation for the head of a gentry family, as time-consuming as foxhunting. Estate (inheritance) lawyers gained in status and wealth.

After someone with a will died, the will had to be "probated," that is, approved as a genuine last will and testament by the courts. This could take some time and if a disgruntled scion contested the validity of the will for one reason or another (it was fake, it wasn't the very last will, the deceased was of infirm mind when it was drawn up, and so on), probate could be complex and very expensive in lawyer's fees as well as court costs.

That is why probate law is a very lucrative kind of legal practice today, as it has been for many centuries. Since so much, in a contested probate case, depends on the personal decision of the judge, probate judges in New York City are treated as gods by the bar and by wealthy people. I have heard William Zabel, one of the leading probate lawyers in New York City today, tell a class of prelaw students that every night he, Zabel, says a prayer of thanks to the shade of Henry VIII for the Statute of Wills of 1540.

The male head of an eighteenth-century gentry family often could not marry the woman he wanted to: The family usually made that decision for him. Later he couldn't get rid of his wife and take another one, hoping for a better marriage. But after 1540 he became marginally free to dispose of his assets after death, even some of his land by will. He could take some satisfaction from that.

In relatively open societies such as England had become by the sixteenth century, the established classes normally get what they want over time. Landed wealth was the highest object of gentry desire, not sexual freedom and affective satisfaction. The institutions of judicial power went along with these sorts of priorities.

The common law would have found it immensely more difficult to respond to an organized upper-middle-class demand for sexual freedom and benign divorce laws. The big difference between the Tudor gentry and upper class of today is that the latter wants it all—property, sex, *and* easy divorce.

Until the twentieth century, rich people accepted the Christian doctrine that you can't have it all, easing pressure on the legal system. This conclusion accords with the view of the leading historical theorist of the critical legal studies group, Robert Gordon, in 1984: "The power exerted by a legal regime consists less in the force that it can bring to bear against violators of its rules than in its capacity to persuade people that the world described in its images and categories is the only attainable world in which a sane person would want to live." In other words, in a relatively free society, law expresses the values of the culture in which it functions.

13
Law and Revolution

FROM THE LATE THIRTEENTH to the late eighteenth century, England like other Western European states was in the process of transition from a medieval to a modern society; from a world dominated by kings, lords, churchmen, and peasants, and a condition in which Western Europe was turned inward upon itself to a world in which urbanization, secularization, democracy, and overseas colonialism were making inroads into the old regime. A process of transformation, still ongoing today, to modern industrial, high-tech, urban, mass society and global integration was under way.

Political and social upheavals, some extending themselves into structural change, some merely dramatic and noisy and largely abortive or ephemeral in consequence, accompanied these seismic shifts from aspects of the medieval to the modern world in the half millennium between the accession of King Edward I in 1272 and the accession of King George III in 1760.

There were revolutions or attempted revolutions in the condition and status of the working class; in affiliations between church and state; and in the relationship between monarchy and Parliament. These may be called in turn the social revolution, the political revolution, and the liberal revolution.

The lawyers and judges in the common law went about their daily business, drawing up entails, getting juries to indict and convict criminals, defining liability, fumbling with family law, and other such immediate judicial issues and mechanisms. The lawyers pursued the stuff of the law. But they did so in the context of the social, political, and liberal revolutions, the great upheavals and conflicts that were the conduits, the rites of passage, from the medieval to the modern world.

The common law, operating in the context of revolutions, provided instruments for shaping the outcomes of revolutions. Particularly in a country where an elaborated and distinctive judicial system presses diurnally on the lives of individuals and families, the use of judicial forms to affect positively or negatively the outcomes of the social, political, and liberal revolutions was going to be a ready and frequent recourse.

The lawyers could not, even if they wanted to, and they were ambivalent about this, wall themselves off from the macro-transformations and conflicts that surrounded them. As members of the upper middle class, they had ideological and emotional responses to the revolutionary issues of the time and place in which they lived. As important members of the power elite, they participated in the great debates and struggles and brought from these exertions and anxieties, attitudes, concepts, and ambitions that were integrated back into the development of the law.

The common law was not walled off from the great transformative passions and causes of the revolutions that were the means of transition from medievalism to modernity. On the other hand, the law and the legal profession were not crude instruments of revolutionary interest. The common law retained, as it still does, a high degree of autonomy and identity. It remained a culture and profession that pursued its own way of doing things and of understanding the world.

In their image of themselves, the common-law lawyers believed that the judicial system exhibited an aura of integrity and separateness from political and social contexts. They thought that in all the changes and conflicts between Edward I and George III, the common law preserved its own identity and was not just the instrument of class and power. They held their heads high as professionals, as men of probity, learning, and public education, as special role players even in revolutionary times and places.

This kind of identity and sense of honor remain characteristic of the legal profession everywhere in common-law countries, from the Inns of Court, to the corridors of the NYU School of Law, to corporate law firms in Dallas or Chicago, to a two-person law firm in Winnipeg, Canada.

The social revolution in England from the late thirteenth to the mid-eighteenth century comprised efforts to give the working class in country and town a greater share of worldly goods, to give them a greater sense of solidarity and personal moral worth, to protect the working class from the ravages of the business cycle and harsh rationality of market criteria for economic change, and to give the working class a voice in political decision making.

The social revolution along these lines failed overwhelmingly in the half millennium after 1272, though not for lack of trying and ideological expression or activist demonstration. These expressions of working-class aims and discontents occurred, but with nowhere near the persistence and well short of the massive pressure and of the success that developed in the nineteenth century.

The lawyers were not supporters of the social revolution in this period. There was no Legal Aid Society. Barristers did not engage in pro bono (charitable) representation of indigent clients. There were no lawyers taking roles as political or agitational spokesmen for the masses.

The lawyers, insofar as they encountered the social revolution, did so as its enemies, as agents of established classes and ruling groups. They were hired to forestall and push back the social revolution, and they did so skillfully and with equanimity. Hence twentieth-century socialists among historians of the period, like Tawney and Thompson, were unscathing in their criticism of the behavior of the legal profession.

In fiction, drama, and films about the period, the lawyer is stereotyped as a hawk-nosed, wily, obfuscating, ruthless agent of privilege. There are grounds for this kind of stereotype. It is a feature of the no-longer-much-read novels of Sir Walter Scott, writing between 1810 and 1830, and the still-much-read fiction of Charles Dickens, written in the next two decades.

In the early seventeenth century there were 2,500 nonecclesiastical lawyers in England, of whom 500 were barristers. None took it as their mission—as do perhaps 5 percent of the bar in the Anglo-American world today—to help laboring and poor people. On the contrary, since the rise of the legal profession in the fourteenth century, the lawyers were actively engaged in helping the established classes repress working people.

In the late 1340s the Black Death produced a very critical labor shortage and inaugurated a grave problem for gentry landlords. In the previous century they had invested heavily in a demesne kind of farming, the intensive exploitation of as much arable and ranchland as they could acquire by using the cheap labor available in a glutted rural population. Now there was a rapid reversal, as surviving laborers took advantage of the tight employment market to demand higher wages.

The gentry response was to turn to their attorneys to draft legislation to put before Crown and Parliament fixing wages at the pre–Black Death level and also restricting the physical mobility of labor looking for better jobs. This is an example of rich people using lawyer lobbyists to get legislation highly favorable to their fiscal interests—still a prime business conducted in Washington today.

The working-class response to the Statute of Laborers of 1351 was extremely violent, the major proletarian rebellion of the Middle Ages. Urged on by radical preachers advocating Christian socialism, there were a series of peasant risings in 1381 through most of the central and southern part of the eastern third of the country (East Anglia and Kent).

The rebels' first target was always the legal and administrative records kept by gentry in their manor houses. Burning these records was at least symbolically a way of eliminating the judicial framework of the peasants' oppressed and exploited status. Then judges, royal officials, and prominent ecclesiastics were waylaid and murdered. Then the peasants marched on London and put the royal government temporarily in a fearful position. With better leadership the apocalyptic commune the radical preachers dreamed about would have been possible.

But the peasant rebels congregated in many thousands in a London suburb professed hysterical loyalty to the person of the king, a minor, Richard II. He was programmed by his councillors to promise them justice, and after the most outspoken of the peasant leaders was struck down in the king's presence by a courtier with no outbreak from the mob, they were persuaded to go home.

Commissions of trailbaston, waving the new Statute of Treason from the busy legislative year of 1351, fanned out in the countryside. Many hundreds of the peasants were hung as traitorous rebels who had conspired against the king.

On a much smaller scale there was another rural rebellion in Kent in 1451, possibly led by a disaffected member of the lower gentry, with similar results.

The Statute of Laborers was not enforced, however. The peasants won on that score. Rural wages rose to the point that demesne farming—maximal direct exploitation of gentry estates—could no longer be pursued. The fifteenth century was therefore the golden age of leasehold or "farming" lands to peasant proprietors. The more hardworking, skillful, and lucky of them became prosperous yeomen, and in some instances their descendants squirmed into the gentry class in the sixteenth century.

The administration of leasehold tenure by attorneys for gentry families was therefore a service provided by the bar for the more resourceful of the peasant class, allowing their upward mobility. This is the most positive action that the legal profession provided to the rural working class in the entire half millennium after 1272. Though not impelled by any ideological sympathy for the peasants—it was a product of market pressures and was intended to assist the lawyers' gentry clients—leasehold gave the more affluent and ambitious peasants a great opportunity.

In the next phase of rural history, the first enclosure movement from about 1490 to about 1570, the lawyers in fact treated the peasantry with exceptional severity. There was a steadily growing market for agricultural products, especially wool and meat, in the late fifteenth and early sixteenth centuries, brought about by peace and population growth, reurbanization after city decline in the fifteenth century, and after 1520 by skyrocketing inflation due to incessant continental wars and importation of silver into Europe from the Americas.

Under these market conditions, landlords were impatient now about collecting rents at outmoded modest medieval levels from copyholders (peasants whose families had been emancipated from serfdom long before and who had received a copy of the charter of freedom indefinitely setting the rent levels for their lands). Landlords also were no longer happy with cheap leaseholds established decades before, when they had been satisfied to get any return on their vacant lands. They had no use for tenants at will, who had no documents at all, but merely lived on the lords' lands for modest rents or as sharecroppers.

What the gentry wanted to do was to terminate these various peasant arrangements, dispossess the peasantry, and enclose the old arable strips for sheep and cattle runs—using planted hedges for fencing, the wonderful green hedges of rural England still visible today. It was the lawyers' role to assist the gentry landlords in the enclosure movement. Historians dispute how widespread was the enclosure movement of the early sixteenth century. Perhaps 20 percent of the arable land in the southern half of the country was involved.

The lawyers did their job. Copyholds were challenged in the courts as fraudulent. Leases were claimed to have run out, or were voided for some technical reason. Tenants at will were treated as squatters without any rights.

A favorite tactic was for the attorney to advise his landlord client simply to usurp the peasant family's lands, turning them out on the byways (to become what were called "sturdy beggars," or the physically able unemployed, who in turn had to be dealt with by welfare legislation, the poor laws). The attorney also advised his client to plant hedges as quickly as possible. Then, should the villagers invade the fences and demonstrate to get their land back, the lawyers would file a bill of complaint in Star Chamber for riot, and the peasants would be hauled before the court and get their ears cropped (an idiosyncratic form of Star Chamber punishment) for their efforts.

There were a few years in the 1520s when a chancellor who was a cardinal archbishop, Thomas Wolsey, soft on social justice and not overly impressed by market rationality, swayed the Chancery to receive petitions from peasant communities (the petitions were probably prepared by radical clergy, not lawyers) and to issue injunctions against enclosures. But the cardinal soon fell from office, and his successors were more fully attuned to the demands of the market economy and the interests of the gentry, and furthermore were personally friendly with the barristers in the Inns of Court who represented the enclosing landlords.

The legal profession played a key role in providing the judicial mechanism for dispossessing many thousands of peasants from their ancestral lands in the sixteenth century. The lawyers provided the same kind of severe service to landlords in the second wave of the enclosure movement in the eighteenth century.

There is a close parallel between the legal profession's role in the capitalist agrarian revolution in early modern England and what happened later under the British in India. There too the common law meant that customary rights of peasants would be swept away by a judicial steamroller:

> The new English legal system was incomprehensible and too expensive to be of any use to the poor. . . . [Occasional] triumphs of justice were of little consolation to the peasant who lost his land to the moneylender or the landlord. The intricacies of the land tenure system and the incomprehensible laws enmeshed the agrarian population in ruinous law suits.

This sober assessment of the impact of the application of English common law to the raj in the nineteenth century, made by P. J. Marshall in the authoritative *Cambridge Illustrated History of the British Empire* (1996), is also a perfect summary of what the common law and the legal profession meant in the life of the English peasantry between 1500 and 1800.

There is here indeed not just a dramatic parallel but a causal connection: The common lawyers learned their techniques of oppression against peasantry on the home country and then subsequently applied them in India.

In addition to the unemployed and homeless created by enclosure evictions, there was increased working-class poverty after the great sixteenth-century boom ended in the 1570s. England had like the rest of Western Europe been riding the upside of the business cycle since around 1490. Now would come close to a century of severe business depression and unemployment.

The Crown instructed its lawyers to prepare legislation addressing the problem of poverty and the unemployed. The royal councillors were moved partly by classical and Christian ideas of a commonwealth that ethically encouraged taking care of the unfortunate. But for the most part the motivation behind the Tudor poor laws, which received their first draft as early as 1540 and their definitive version around 1580, was fear that discontented proletarians could coalesce into another peasants' revolt (there had been a dreadful uprising in Germany in 1525) or provide the military personnel for a dissident aristocrat aiming to seize the throne.

The Tudor poor laws were artfully constructed by brilliant lawyers. There was no amending legislation on this subject until the 1830s, and the system remained in force until the 1880s and in some respects until the coming of the English welfare state in the late 1940s.

The Tudor poor laws worked on four principles. First, special local taxes that came to be called "rates" should be levied for unemployment relief. Second, the unit of collecting and dispersing the taxes and the administration of poor relief ought to be the smallest local existing political unit, namely the parish.

What inspired this provision was the intelligent belief that the more local the way poor relief was taxed for and administered, the tougher on the poor would be the administrators, because the recipients of relief would be their own neighbors: We are more likely to have contempt for and be harsh on unemployed people we know personally. On the other hand, the national state is inclined to be generous toward the poor. The money comes out of the general tax base and is grandly dispensed by sympathetic administrators to the faceless poor as their constituents. The poor law authors, like conservative American Republicans today, wanted to force poor law administration to the local level so it would be handled as meanly as possible. It was.

The third principle of the Tudor poor law—still operative everywhere today in Western society—is that a distinction had to be made between the able-bodied unemployed ("sturdy beggars") and those who couldn't work—the old, the infirm, nursing mothers, and so on. The latter got "outdoor relief"—that is, direct aid, although a very modest amount. The former were put to work in parish poorhouses, Bastille-like factories, making brooms, potholders, and the like to earn their keep. Next to debtor's prison and even more than Chancery courts, what rankled Charles Dickens most about the early-nineteenth-century common law was its establishment of poorhouses. In the era before bankruptcy laws, unfortunate or incapable businessmen could end up there and nothing could seem worse to middle-class people.

The fourth principle of the Tudor poor law was that within the counties, overseeing the parish wardens' immediate governance of the system, were placed the JPs—very rich gentry implementing the relief system for the unemployed and impoverished. They were not inclined to be charitable. Perhaps nothing angers modern leftist historians about the poor law system so much as the fact that the JPs were put in charge of it—about as far as you can get from the temperament of the welfare state. This system inevitably enhanced the power and status of the JPs in county life.

One may hate it and hold it in contempt, but what has to be admired as a skilled piece of legislation is the work of the Crown lawyers on poverty law in the sixteenth century. From the point of view of conservative social policy it was a brilliant piece of work and it endured unchanged for many centuries. Again it was the lawyers sticking it to the working class and keeping them down.

Lawyers did not change their hostile attitude toward the working class during the seventeenth and eighteenth centuries (actually there was no significant change until the second half of the twentieth century). Barristers and solicitors formed the bulwark against social revolution and a mighty fortress on behalf of the interest of the gentry, who paid them and from whose ranks they came.

In the tumultuous radicalized era between the 1630s and 1660, there were in England groups that took a positive attitude toward allowing working-class participation in political life, the Levellers; or were active communists wanting to seize village lands for "the people," the Diggers; or who anticipated the imminent inauguration of a Christian utopia, the Fifth Monarchy Men. These democratic groups were all rooted in the evangelical wing of seventeenth-century Protestantism. They had no sympathy from the lawyers, who were their implacable enemies.

During the Cromwellian military dictatorship of the 1650s, there was demand in radical circles for reform of the common law, meaning at least codification to make it more accessible to the layman, and reduction in lawyers' fees. Henry Parker, on the more radical wing of the House of Commons, and himself a barrister, criticized the legal profession for its conservatism and dullness. Law was "to be improved by policy." Cromwell appointed a commission of lawyers and others to consider judicial reform. Nothing happened; it had a few desultory meetings and never reported before Cromwell died in 1658.

By abolishing the House of Lords, the Cromwellian republic removed the latter's role as the highest court of appeal. But the Lords came back with the restored Stuart monarchy in 1660. The lawyers welcomed the Restoration of the monarchy in 1660 and with it, that of the old common law (except for Star Chamber, permanently abolished in 1642) untrammeled. The lawyers favored parliamentary abolition of the vestiges of feudal wardship in 1662 but that was because this legislation helped the gentry, their clients.

In the early eighteenth century, as the crime rate began to rise again on par with a rapid increase in population, and particularly of adolescent and postadolescent males, the criminal-prone groups, the legal profession gave renewed attention to the problem of crime. There was one significant effort to institute a more effective police system, resulting in the appearance in London's streets of a group that anticipated Sir Robert Peel's Victorian

"Peelers," the protomodern public police force. The novelist Henry Fielding and his brother, who were both London magistrates, organized a court-managed security force, "the Bow Street Runners," and sent them out to apprehend perpetrators and bring in indicted criminals. It was a step forward but too negligible to make much of a difference.

The other way in which the eighteenth-century legal profession proposed to countervail increasing crime was a tactic much favored in the United Staes today—more and more severe sentences for petty crime, elevating these incidents to hanging felonies. From this policy came between 1720 and the end of the century, the "Black Acts," parliamentary legislation designed to frighten people into refraining from crimes by the severity of the sentences.

Poaching a rabbit, stealing a pocket handkerchief, or blackening one's face at night (allegedly preparatory to theft) now became hanging offenses, even for apprehended children.

Much condemned by leftist historians, the Black Acts and similar severe legislation showed a judicial system, again like ours, feeling desperate and impotent to combat crime. What the leftist historians have failed to notice is that for the most part the Black Acts remained dead letters. Juries refused to convict if it meant execution under extremist laws, or judges plea-bargained felonies down to misdemeanors, or simply issued discharges, especially to the customary favored classes—children, young women, clergy, and the old and the feeble. Reading the texts of the Black Acts conjures up an image of criminal justice of the utmost severity. In practice it was on the lax side.

Along with multiplying the numbers of crimes that were nominally accorded capital punishment, the masses were supposed to be frightened by elaborate spectacles, mainly in London, of public executions.

Condemned criminals had always been hanged publicly, but in eighteenth-century England the executions were carried out as ritualized spectacles that attracted crowds in the size and frenzied demeanor of Super Bowl proportions. Newspapers whipped up public excitement. Some of the condemned, especially professional robbers, were hailed as popular heroes and the condemned frequently cooperated in the hanging as spectacles by making speeches from the gallows.

Whether public executions as spectacles ever discouraged anyone from a criminal act nobody knows. It is significant, however, that the executed criminals were scarcely ever from the gentry or merchant class. Thousands of London's poor people went into sadomasochistic ecstasy witnessing the execution of another member of the humble classes.

Public executions continued in London and elsewhere until the 1860s, although Victorian propriety resulted in measures reducing the size of crowds after 1820. Thomas Hardy, who died in 1928 in his eighties, remembered witnessing as a young boy in remote rural southwest England the execution of a young woman, an image that helped to inspire him to write his great psychosexual novel, *Tess of the D'Urbervilles*, which ends with the public hanging of Tess, a hapless farm girl.

The Black Acts had an important positive consequence in the late eighteenth century. Since capital punishment was now prescribed even for petty crimes, and juries and judges refused to apply these stringent laws, legal reformers adjusted the punishment, finding alternatives to capital punishment.

Beginning in the 1730s there was a frequently exercised substitution for capital punishment, at the discretion of the judges: deportation at hard indentured labor for a term of years or for life; first to America, and later, after the American Revolution, to Australia, which continued as a penal colony down to about 1820. "We left our country for our country's good," went a favorite Australian music-hall song of the mid-nineteenth century.

The other substitution for capital punishment that was a reaction to the idiotic severity of the Black Acts was put forward by Quakers and other Protestant humanitarian groups, which believed that long prison sentences would provide opportunity to reform prisoners through prayer and education. (They are still hoping.) For the first time by 1800 imprisonment for more than a few months was intended as a redeeming punishment.

A new frightening building, accompanying the poorhouse, rose on the English landscape—the penitentiary. It was supposed to represent a triumphant advance of liberal humanitarianism, like the abolition of the English participation in the slave trade by act of Parliament, which the same religious humanitarian groups gained in 1803.

In the period between 1720 and 1780, the legal profession again served the gentry by helping them implement the second phase of the enclosure movement, which affected at least 30 percent of England's arable land. This time the legal vehicle was the private bill, artfully prepared by lawyers and quietly pushed through Parliament. Because of the sovereign character of Parliament legislation, there was no way to contend against these bills in the courts, even if the dispossessed tenant farmers could have afforded counsel.

So hundreds of thousands of rural folk were driven off their ancestral lands by legal intervention. But this time there was a place for them to go, to the rapidly expanding industrial cities. The adult males were not considered good workers in the regimented conditions of factory assembly lines. They had to go into the coal mines, whose product was needed to drive the steam engines of the factories, or sit in the tavern and get blindly drunk on gin. But children and women of the dispossessed farm families were ideally malleable personnel for the highly disciplined factory workforces, ready to respond at dawn to the bells signaling the start-up of the machinery that frequently mangled them. The women also found urban occupation as whores. In the mid-nineteenth century, one-sixteenth of women in London between sixteen and twenty-five were prostitutes.

In the early years of the nineteenth century Scottish lawyers also prepared private bills so that the lairds, the landlords of lowland Scotland, could belatedly implement the enclosure movement there. This had the effect of driving the "crofters," the Scottish peasants, to seek new homes in Ontario and Manitoba in Canada—aided by rich philanthropists such as Alexander Galt and Lord Selkirk. The lawyers of the old common law are therefore ultimately responsible for the Scottish lilt ("oat and aboat") in the Canadian Anglophone accent to this day.

No chapter in the history of the common law is in a way bleaker than the one describing how the barristers and solicitors played key roles from 1350 to 1800 in the oppression of the working class and thus in forestalling the social revolution at every turn.

But this conclusion is only a bleak one to those believing in modern welfare liberalism. If you are an adherent of the Ricardian-Friedmanite-Thatcherite school of market economics and its satellite, the Law and Economics group at the University of Chicago Law School, you will conclude that the lawyers rendered a very positive service to the English economy and made the Industrial Revolution of the late eighteenth century possible. Good wages and generous benefits and preservation of rural tenures for the working class would have greatly limited, these economists' argument goes, the accumulation of capital by the gentry through half a millennium. Oppressive treatment of the peasantry through legal instruments meant the vast accumulation of capital in gentry families and the availability of this capital, deposited in county banks, for the financing of the Industrial Revolution in the late eighteenth century, which in turn put England a half century or more ahead of its European rivals in technological and economic development.

While the English landlords with judicial assistance were downsizing the laboring force in the countryside, the conservative thesis goes, the foolish democratic French Revolution in the 1790s broke up great estates and created a nation of small proprietors, which constituted a drag on the French economy until the 1950s, although it did a lot for French cuisine.

Leftist historians will immediately deride this thesis of gentry-serving lawyers as farsighted capitalist handmaidens of the English Industrial Revolution. Granting that industrialization required huge amounts of investment capital, they will point to overseas British imperialism as the source of liquid capital—the African slave trade, which the British dominated in the eighteenth century; to the slave-driven sugar plantations in the West Indies; and to the capital the British "nabobs" looted from India in the eighteenth century. These other sources of capital appear to have been drawn upon, but the capital acquired by the gentry over many centuries from the dispossessed and lacerated peasantry, with the indispensable aid of the legal profession, probably remained most important of all as the source of financing the Industrial Revolution.

Lawyers and judicial concepts were also critical in a second kind of revolution that was an avenue from the medieval to the modern world—the assertion of state sovereignty over the church in the sixteenth century.

In sixteenth-century Western Europe, whether a country remained within the Roman Catholic Church, as Spain did, or adhered to one or the other forms of Protestantism, such as Lutheranism or Calvinism, the trend was toward enhanced state control over ecclesiastical institutions and religious life.

This politicization or nationalization of the territorial churches by royal government in many Catholic as well as Protestant territories had been advocated in the early fourteenth century by Parisian philosopher Marsilio of Padua in his treatise *Defender of the Peace*. It had been also propounded by the radical Oxford theologian John Wycliffe in the late fourteenth century and less categorically in the early sixteenth century by the Florentine writer Niccolò Machiavelli. In the first three-quarters of the sixteenth century, this statist approach to religion and ecclesiastical institutions was advocated by a wider variety of thinkers in Western Europe, variously called *politiques,* Erastians (after a certain philosopher Erastus), and proponents of "sovereignty," a newly fashionable term. Some were Catholic, some were Protestant.

It was the view of Cambridge University historian Geoffrey Elton in three highly influential books published in the late 1950s and early 1960s that the key figure in the "Tudor Revolution in government" as Elton called it, was Thomas Cromwell, Henry VIII's chancellor in the 1530s. It was Cromwell who put into operation in England the new political ideas circulating in early-sixteenth-century Europe.

Of obscure bourgeois background, Cromwell studied in Italy, where he imbibed Roman law and the ideas of Marsilio of Padua and Machiavelli. Although he was secretly a committed Protestant, Cromwell's attitude to the church was based mainly on ideas of state sovereignty fashionable in his generation in both Catholic and Protestant countries. The confusing pluralism and lax division of authority of the previous century had to be replaced by the vesting of all legal and political decision making in the royal government if there was to be social stability in an era of expanding commercial capitalism and overseas colonialism and the maximization of the use of social resources within national territory.

In 1540 Henry VIII had Cromwell removed from power and executed because the king had grown jealous of his chief minister's power in the royal administration and suspicious of Cromwell's Protestant religious commitment. But between 1532 and 1540, as described by Elton, Cromwell carried out a political revolution, involving the use of parliamentary statutes to separate the English church from Rome, to make the king the head of the English church, and to begin the dissolution of the monasteries and the expropriation of their immensely rich lands by the Crown, as well as carrying out internal restructuring of the royal administration to make it more efficient and faster acting.

In Elton's view Cromwell's revolution went far beyond the general control over and exploitation of the church in England that had existed since the Norman Conquest. The English political system now moved to a new level.

In the late 1960s the Oxford medievalist G. L. Harris attacked Elton's view of the Tudor revolution in government, and argued for strong continuity between fifteenth- and sixteenth-century political systems and church-state relations, rather than perceiving a rupture in the 1530s.

It was Harris's view, held by many medievalists, that nothing significant changed in the 1530s. This interpretation points to rising anticlericalism in late medieval England, on which the monarchy built to clarify legally its position in relation to the church. The Statute of Provisors of 1351 severely cut back on papal appointments in the English church. The Statute of Praemunire of 1353 prohibited appeals to Rome without royal permission. These statutes, along with the Statute of Treason of 1351, were part of the new policy of firming up discipline in the country, according to Robert C. Palmer, after the catastrophe of the Black Death.

The vision of a secular government exercising full control over the church and expropriating ecclesiastical property was in line with an idea of sovereignty, the medievalist thesis maintains, that Wycliffe enunciated in the 1370s, in his doctrine of dominion arguing for state authority over the church. Wycliffe worked under the patronage and protection of the Lancastrian royal family.

What then was different in the early sixteenth century that allows identification of a political revolution and reflects lawyerly involvement in these changes?

The work of Eamon Duffy, Christopher Haigh, and Euan Cameron during the late 1980s and early 1990s on the meaning of the Reformation supports Elton's view. The Reformation—in England and Europe-wide—was the imposition of a new cultural and political order on the European masses, according to Duffy, Haigh, and Cameron. This order was the construct of a small learned elite, invigorated by Renaissance classicism and philosophy, who held in contempt the masses' devotion to popular Catholicism with its focus on saints, relics, constant repetitions of the Eucharist and imbibing of Christ's body, and the faith healing to which these rituals led.

It is possible to regard the common-law lawyers as part of this revolutionary elite, imposing changes from the top, subjugating and nationalizing the church. As a result of the Reformation and the separation from Rome and expropriation of monastic property, the lawyers deflated the power and social leadership of the only competing learned profession, the clergy. The way the Reformation worked itself out in England, beginning with Thomas Cromwell, friend of and large-scale employer of lawyers, himself well read in both common and Roman law, the lawyers in royal government advanced their own profession at the expense of the clergy. The revolutionary lawyers also imposed much greater social discipline on the lower middle class and working class by stripping them of their Catholic altars.

The Reformation in England was based on both Roman and common law. On the Roman side, the key piece of parliamentary legislation, the Act in Restraint of Appeals to Rome of 1534, went judicially far beyond the Act of *Praemunire* of 1353, by asserting that "this realm of England is an empire." Thereby Henry VIII and Cromwell were not making reference to the British Empire, which at the time consisted of a handful of fishing villages in Newfoundland, but to the Justinian code: The king was claiming the *imperium*, the sovereign power in the country.

The English Reformation also made use of the common law, especially the Treason Act of 1351, slightly modified and expanded. Those who opposed the split with Rome and Henry's divorce from Catherine of Aragon and therefore regarded his union with Anne Boleyn and its issue as illegitimate, were guilty of "imagining and encompassing the death of the king" in the words of the Treason Act. It was a stretch, but it was used to remove Thomas More, distinguished humanist and former chancellor and to convict him—along with several other opponents among the magnates—of treason and to frighten most of the common people into silence and compliance. A northern rising of devout gentry against the Reformation, the Pilgrimage of Grace of 1536, was put down with the vigor suitable to the suppression of high treason.

In *Policy and Police* (1972), Elton stressed the judicial enforcement of the Reformation, how the common law was employed to carry out the political revolution:

> The law, especially that of treason, was severe, reached far, and could punish even casual utterances with savagery. Its administration, though governed by comprehensive rules which imposed limits on the exercise of mere power, was intensive and precise. Police activity [that is, the use of informants] in discovering and communicating [oppositional] suspects, was energetic and continuous.

The common law stymied the social revolution in England. But just as forcefully it was a prime instrument in the political revolution against the church.

With regard to religion, what happened in England in the 1530s was only the first, statist phase of the English Reformation. Henry VIII, after the split with Rome and making himself head of the Anglican Church by act of Parliament, remained Catholic in his own theological outlook and hostile to the intrusion of the ideas of the continental Protestant reformers into England. The Tudor state eliminated the leading English Protestant reformer of the 1530s, William Tyndale, whose biblical translations were in the early seventeenth century heavily used by the authors of the canonical King James or Authorized version.

But the Henrician strictly political act against the Roman church opened the way for the intrusion of continental Protestantism into England in the following half century, partly by way of dissemination of printed literature, partly by English Protestants studying on the Continent, especially at the Calvinist center in Geneva.

The political revolution of the 1530s also opened the way for a native English dissenting tradition, derived from late medieval heretical Lollardy, to surface again. Although Lollardy was suppressed by the royal government in the early fifteenth century because of its radical political overtones and its alarming intrusion into the ranks of the wealthier gentry, it had been perpetuated as an underground church, especially in the north of the country, where royal scrutiny was relatively weak.

Queen Elizabeth I's church settlement in the 1560s and 1570s combined her father's political sovereignty over the church (and the establishment and governance of the Church of England as a department of the state) with the heavy intrusion of Calvinist theology into the Anglican Church and tolerance of separatist Protestant groups like Presbyterians and Baptists, the heirs of the Lollards, operating outside the Church of England.

In 1600 about 75 percent of the population of England and Wales were members of the Church of England, which itself was a relatively latitudinarian, multicultural institution, including a majority Protestant Calvinist wing and a minority group still inclined to traditional Catholicism (without the pope) in theology and ritual. Twenty percent of the population were one kind or another of Protestant separatist outside the Anglican Church, functioning in their own religious communities. Five percent of the English people, including some nobility and gentry, were still Roman Catholic.

As long as the separatist Protestants and the Roman Catholic "recusants" remained politically quiet and accepted the queen as the head of the Church of England, even while they were not members of it, the royal government, ever watchful and suspicious but without strong ideological commitments, left them alone.

The point of tension in this Elizabethan system became evident in the two decades before the queen's death in 1603. The more ideologically Calvinist group in the Church of England, led by Cambridge University academics, wanted to press on to "reformation without tarrying"—to further cleansing of the Church of England of Catholic ritual and tradition. This was opposed by the queen and her ministers, partly because they temperamentally liked the compromise status quo, partly because continental Calvinism, centered in Switzerland and Holland, had strong republican tendencies, as did the Calvinist Presbyterianism in Scotland.

Moving in more of a Calvinist direction would mean closer intellectual affiliation with the English Presbyterians outside the established national Anglican Church, and these Presbyterians, congregated in London and other large cities, had a tone of middle-class radicalism about them and, in the eyes of the queen and her ministers, were not in the long run to be trusted.

In the first four decades of the seventeenth century as the unmarried and childless Elizabeth I was succeeded on the English throne by her Scottish cousins, the Stuarts, religious development became intertwined with a resurgent and radicalized variant of judicial liberalism.

This potent combination of religious activism and constitutional liberalism, placed in an inflammatory context of persistent economic depression and ineptitude on the part of the Stuart government, ignited in the 1640s into what has been variously called the Civil War, the English Revolution, and the Puritan Revolution. It resulted in the trial and execution of King Charles I and the military dictatorship from 1648 to 1658 of Oliver

Cromwell, who was descended from Thomas Cromwell's brother, before the old regime was restored in 1660.

The political revolution by which the English state asserted its judicial sovereignty over the church had a long-range intellectual outcome, contributing directly to seventeenth-century England being the major player in the emergence of modern science. The judicial background was indicated in Harold Berman's *Law and Revolution* (1984) and further developed in Toby E. Huff's *The Rise of Early Modern Science* (1993).

The canon law of the Roman Catholic Church as it developed by the early thirteenth century sustained papal claims to a high degree of centralization in the church—the papal plenitude of power. But within this formal facade of papal centralization, canon law accorded to corporate bodies within the church, like universities and religious orders, a high degree of autonomy. Within this corporate pluralism intellectual inquiry of an innovative and speculative kind, from the tradition of Aristotelian philosophy to protomodern science, could occur.

In asserting legal authority over the Church of England, the royal lawyers of the sixteenth century allowed the continuation of this corporate semiautonomy. It meant that cathedral clergy continued to administer and exploit their substantial property as celebrated in Anthony Trollope's Victorian novels. It also meant that corporate status remained with the colleges of Oxford and Cambridge universities. Particularly at Cambridge this corporate identity allowed for intense cultivation of Calvinist doctrine in the late sixteenth and early seventeenth centuries. But by the second half of the seventeenth century, it was mathematics and physics that were the avant-garde subjects in the Cambridge colleges.

The corporate status of the colleges gave them sufficient independence to invest their resources in scientific thought, leading to the Newtonian revolution in physics at the beginning of the eighteenth century. It provided a legal shell that protected freedom of inquiry into highly controversial subjects.

According to Berman and Huff, then, the foundations of modern science lie in the corporate pluralism of the late medieval church, which was absorbed into the national church of the sixteenth century and perpetuated by the Tudor lawyers.

The political revolution made possible the scientific revolution. The church was nationalized, but in the process the corporate pluralism of the late medieval church was transferred into the judicial and political culture of the seventeenth century.

A civil society in which the autonomous pursuit of learning and research enjoys privileged legal status was a characteristic of eighteenth-century England. The judicial basis for this intellectual freedom lay in the absorption by the monarchical state of the medieval church's recognition of semiautonomous units pursuing education and learned inquiry.

14
The Rise of Liberalism

THE ENGLISH CIVIL WAR (or the English Revolution) began in 1642 and resulted in the defeat of the Stuart monarchy, the execution of King Charles I in 1649, and the setting up of a republican military dictatorship headed by Oliver Cromwell, which lasted until his death in 1658. In the following two years another general negotiated with the son of Charles I on terms for allowing the restoration of the Stuart monarchy. About the only novel thing they could agree on was the provision of a dukedom for the general, who was of petit bourgeois origin. Otherwise the constitutional and political clock in 1660 was set back to the time when the Civil War began, in 1642.

In 1689 another upheaval occurred. The overwhelming majority of the landed and merchant classes decided that James II, Charles II's Roman Catholic brother, who had succeeded him in 1685, had to leave the throne and country and be succeeded by his Protestant daughter, Mary, and her husband, the Dutch prince William of Orange. This change was called the Glorious Revolution, because it was popular and peaceful.

Except for the abolishing of Star Chamber in 1642, the temporary four-year suspension of Chancery at that time, and the abolition of the vestiges of the Crown's feudal wardship over members of the landed classes in 1662, did these dramatic events have any significance for the development of the common law? The courts and the legal profession functioned in 1700 about the same as they functioned in 1640, Chancery having been fully restored.

There was, however, significance for the common law in the Civil War and the Glorious Revolution because both happenings were carried out in the name of the rule of law and the preservation of legal due process. Both upheavals were effected in the name of constitutional liberalism that had been articulated in the thirteenth century and strengthened and reinforced thereafter.

The Civil War was fought over the House of Commons' assertion on May 27, 1642, that the key principle of the English constitution was the king's two bodies, his political body and his natural one; his public will, which was king in Parliament, and his personal will. The political body, king in Parliament, was superior to the king's natural body, his personal will. If king and Parliament could not agree on a major issue, then Parliament spoke for the king's political body, his public personality, and could legally use force against his natural body.

This is the doctrine of judicial and political liberalism suggested by Bracton, which became the theory and practice of constitutional monarchy that has been the center of English government since 1689.

The Glorious Revolution of 1689 confirmed the Commons's declaration of May 27, 1642. James II claimed and acted that he had prerogative or reserved or residual royal right to suspend laws he didn't like (in this case the harsh laws limiting the political and civil rights of fellow Catholics). The Bill of Rights of 1689 declared that the king had no power to suspend the laws by his own will. Since James had behaved illegally as though he had such a prerogative authority, he had to leave.

The Civil War and the Glorious Revolution were preceded by constitutional issues that emerged in late medieval common law. What was already beginning to happen in the later years of Edward I around 1300 was confirmed and highlighted in the seventeenth century, namely the bonding together of the doctrine that the law was superior to the king, jointly with the idea of parliamentary power to make law that the king personally had to observe.

From 1272 to 1689 the rule of law came to mean the rule of Parliament. This was a derogation from the idea of the rule of law in a pure and abstract sense. It represented a politicization of legal supremacy to mean parliamentary sovereignty if Parliament chose to legislate clearly on an important matter.

There was, therefore, some theoretical difficulty with this idea of the bonding of law and Parliament. In theory it could be claimed that the rule of law is not compatible with the doctrine of the sovereignty of Parliament. But this theoretical problem does not detract from the importance of the bonding of law and Parliament, and of this fusion becoming the core of the English constitutional settlement of the eighteenth century.

The doctrine of judicial liberalism that Bracton propounded in the mid-thirteenth century, that law was superior to the king, that the rule of law and due process made royal power possible rather than the reverse, sat uneasily with many people in Bracton's own time and in the following century.

The king was universally regarded as the anointed of the Lord "and he is Christ," an archbishop had boldly proclaimed in Henry I's reign. The law was in his mouth, in his breast, said the Roman lawyers. And he was at least in theory the feudal overlord, the direct successor of William the Conqueror, who had stood victorious on the battlefield of Hastings and declared: This land is my land.

Bracton's liberalism threatened all that, and angry royalists wrote nasty comments in the margin of the manuscripts of his treatise *On the Laws and Customs of England*, comments derived from the common law to make their conservative point all the more sharply against the esteemed chief justice of the Common Pleas: "No writ runs against the king.... There is no assize against the king." The king is below the law? Then try suing him and see what happens.

For all the opposition to judicial liberalism, it still gained ground in the two centuries after Bracton, so that another chief justice of the Common Pleas, a supporter of the Lancastrian dynasty that was slowly but steadily losing its grip on the throne, Sir John Fortescue, could assert around 1460 that there were two kinds of government—regal and political. Regal government is absolutist, irresponsible monarchy, above the law, for the boors of France and Germany, said Fortescue, people born to bend the neck. Upstanding Englishmen, solid gentry, have "political government," government by consent, government that takes account of the community, government in which the king is bound by the laws along with his subjects.

That the Lancastrians by this time were too weak and unpopular to rule without Parliament, having been ignominiously driven out of France by the Witch of Orleans, Joan of Arc, indicates why Bracton's judicial liberalism prevailed in spite of much doubt about it: It fitted in with the political correctness of the time. It could be used for propaganda and political maneuvering in the civil conflicts of the later Middle Ages.

The Lancastrian family, established by the charismatic third son of Edward III, John of Gaunt, and holding the throne from 1399 to 1461, were much like the Kennedy family in the United States in recent times. Fabulously rich, insatiably ambitious, internationally minded, often sexually vigorous, they burnished their glamorous image and held the visceral loyalty of millions of people, in France and Spain as well as England, and they reinforced this loyalty by taking liberal positions.

Especially under the Lancastrian aegis the idea of rule of law and due process became tied to parliamentary centrality in the constitution. It became a code word for strong limitation on royal government by any faction that dominated the House of Lords and the House of Commons, one aristocratic group or another headed by a royal duke who wanted to place himself or his son on the throne.

Just as "welfare liberalism" in our and recent decades in the United States is a code word for the supremacy of the Democratic Party and those who manage its fortunes, so the rule of law and due process came to have strong political overtones and to be used in the often fierce politics of the fourteenth and fifteenth centuries, usually on the Lancastrian side.

In the third quarter of the fourteenth century, Parliament was divided into two distinct corporate bodies that met separately, the Lords and the Commons. The Commons chose a Speaker who "spoke for," or represented, the MPs from the shires and towns to the king, his council, and the Lords. The shifting aristocratic factions maneuvered to control the Commons and the first Speaker chosen in 1376 was in fact the steward or estate manager for a leading political earl. No Commons independence here, but the constitutional mechanisms giving the Commons greater power—which could then be used in the struggle between aristocratic factions—were being implemented.

In the same year that the first Speaker was chosen, the institution of impeachment was first used. It was designed to make the king's ministers responsible to the dominant party in Parliament, and failing that, to remove them for high crimes in a show trial. In impeachment—still used in the American Congress and the threat of which forced President Richard Nixon's resignation in 1974—the lower house acts as the prosecutor, and the upper house acts as jury and votes guilty or not guilty. The political propaganda of the time brought in judicial liberalism to give credibility to this political strategy. The king's ministers, because of their corruption or other serious misbehavior, have violated the law and are rightfully to be removed by Parliament. So said the militant "Good Parliament" of 1376, and the mechanism of impeachment endured.

Another mechanism invented in the early fifteenth century was even more rough and ready—the bill of attainder. In the attainder procedure, there was not even a show trial: A bill was simply passed through both houses of Parliament declaring someone an enemy of the king and the kingdom. Not only did the passing of this bill (when it received royal signature) mean that the victim was summarily executed for high treason but that his blood was attainted, permanently corrupted, so that his heir could not inherit. The family immediately lost all its lands.

Not surprisingly in the mid-fifteenth century, the loser of a battle in the aristocratic, internecine Wars of the Roses much preferred summary battlefield execution under the laws of chivalry to attainder under the common law: The defeated lord lost his head under chivalry, but his family retained his lands, able and willing to continue the fight on a better day.

The American Constitution prohibits bills of attainder—although very few Americans know what Madison and Jefferson saved them from—but they are still on the books in England. If Hitler's Operation Sea Lion plan for invading England in the summer of 1940 had been successfully carried out, there was a perfectly legal mechanism in a Nazi-dominated Parliament to carry out political and racial cleansing. First Churchill and then Lord Rothschild and other rich Jews could have been attainted. All quite legal, no need for the Gestapo rough stuff.

Judicial liberalism came into its own with the deposition of Richard II by his Lancastrian cousin, John of Gaunt's son, who became Henry IV in 1399. In 1327 Edward II had been forced to abdicate by his French queen, her aristocratic lover, and a group of great lords who did not like Edward's sexual preferences and his lavish patronage of his gay lovers. After abdication Edward was hauled away and murdered with a red-hot poker up his anus.

The termination of Richard II was much more within the scope of the common law and artfully arranged so as to advertise the doctrine of judicial liberalism that the Lancastrians favored, and to enshrine Henry IV in constitutional legitimacy.

Feckless, impetuous, bad-tempered, homoerotic, unlucky Richard II, having been militarily overcome, abdicated in favor of his Lancastrian cousin and was hauled off to miserable confinement in Pontefract Castle, where he was eventually murdered. But first, as Shakespeare phrased it, how was the balm to be washed off an anointed king? By Parliament, citing the rule of law—that was a powerful solvent.

Having already abdicated, poor Richard was now also deposed by a hastily summoned Parliament. At a combined special session of the Lords and Commons, Henry of Lancaster sat modestly among the MPs, still uncrowned. Then a long list of Richard's alleged crimes was read off, headed by his alleged devotion to the political doctrine of the Justinian code, the absolutist theory of monarchy.

It was shockingly reported that Richard had said the law was in his own mouth and breast. Therefore he could not rule England any longer. Only a king who affirmed Bracton's judicial liberalism had the legitimacy to rule. And so Henry modestly stood up and in robust native English, not effete aristocratic French, publicly affirmed adhesion to politically correct liberal doctrine. Only then was Henry crowned.

Judicial liberalism had received a huge boost, and Fortescue's anodyne political treatise along those lines followed a half century later. The Commons, manipulated by the Lancastrians and other royal and aristocratic factions, had done what it was told, but in the 1450s and 1460s it alarmingly began to assert "the liberties and privileges of the House of Commons," which went beyond the convenience of any royal or aristocratic group that had massaged them.

Three liberties were now claimed for the Commons. First, an MP should have freedom of speech in the House of Commons—to speak in the Commons without later being called to account for what was said there, even if it was critical of the policy and behavior of the royal administration. Second, MPs should be free from arrest for any reason while Parliament was sitting and while the MPs were going to and returning from Westminster. In other words they demanded immunity from harassment while they were doing their job.

Third, the Commons and not the Crown or the courts should determine the outcome of disputed elections of MPs, of which there were a goodly number. In at least half the elections of MPs there were no contests. The leading gentry families (or merchant families of the towns) simply got together and decided among themselves which of them should this time send forward the two MPs to Westminster. Over a ten-year period the coveted position of MP would thus by consensus circulate among four or five very wealthy gentry families in the shire.

But in a quarter of the cases when the sheriffs received writs telling them to oversee elections and return the names of the successful candidates, the top families could not reach agreement and an actual poll had to take place. Many times the sheriff manipulated the results in deference to one of the great families, and a noisy controversy broke out. Only the Commons itself, stressing its standing as a corporate entity could, said those demanding the liberties of the Commons, decide in the disputed elections.

No aristocratic faction felt easy with this show of independence by the Commons, and no king of whatever dynasty was prepared to concede the liberties. The Yorkist rivals of the Lancastrians, who ruled from 1461 to 1485, were uneasy about Parliament in general and tried to summon it as seldom as possible. The same was the case with Henry VII, the first of the new Tudor dynasty, which supplanted the Yorkists in 1485 (but took care to heal the rift by marrying a Yorkist princess of ancient lineage).

The fashion was now for direct rule by king and a privy (sworn) council. Parliament had a bad image of uncontrollable interventions from Lancastrian days.

The issue of the Commons's liberties, therefore, remained moot and was not pressed again until late in the sixteenth century. But far from continuing to ignore Parliament, Henry VIII used the common law more assiduously than any previous king in order to carry out the break with Rome, making himself head of the Church of England, and expropriating the monastic lands in the 1530s and 1540s, as well as deciding the royal succession among progeny from three different wives.

The mechanism of statute was used to carry out the political revolution over the church and to stop a prospective social revolution in its tracks with the poor law. This compulsive Tudor use of Parliament was not due to ideology but to pragmatic necessity. Thomas Cromwell, the royal chancellor, convinced Henry VIII that an act of the state mandated by statute could not be challenged in the courts, and that to resist it implied traitorous conduct.

Cromwell had actually wanted to begin the dissolution of the monasteries on grounds of public morality—that the monks and nuns had proved to be sexually licentious, and the Crown had reluctantly had to intervene to get rid of the discredited monastic houses. But his investigating commissioners advised him that they could only find masturbation, not cohabitation, in the monasteries and convents. So in the end it was a simple parliamentary statute that declared the monastic establishments dissolved.

The abbots were mostly happy because they were allowed a piece of the monastery's land and often the fine stone house in which the monks lived. They became founders of new gentry families. The monks were initially well treated, like long-tenured professors, with comfortable pensions—until wild inflation sharply reduced the value of their pensions if they lived long enough.

It was the abbesses and nuns who were shabbily treated in this male chauvinist society. They were returned to inhospitable family hearths to live out disappointed lives in a mean and impoverished ambience.

Meanwhile the gentry in the Commons, who had unflinchingly accepted the dissolution of the monasteries with no questions asked, were well rewarded. The dissolution allowed the Crown to seize 20 percent of the best arable land in the country. Within a quarter of a century the Crown had sold off most of it at knockdown prices to the delighted gentry.

No wonder the strange doings of the Tudor dynasty in the decade after Henry VIII's death in 1547 were accepted so quietly—bouncing under Edward VI in the direction of unequivocal Protestantism, then under his sister Mary (the daughter of Catherine of Aragon) back to Roman Catholicism, then with Elizabeth I in 1558 back to something close to where the Church of England had been on the death of her father.

Why worry about the next world when the gentry were doing so well in this one? What a wonderful sovereign institution statute was, with its capability of keeping greed entirely within the confines of the common law!

By working on the assumption that a parliamentary statute could not be contested in the courts, the Tudors in a kind of oblique way were confirming the principle of the rule of law and the practice of satisfying material ambition through the use of due judicial process. They greatly strengthened the symbiotic union of greed and law. The Tudors were proud forerunners of today's American billionaire entrepreneurs and their corporate lawyers.

When, in the last two decades of the sixteenth century, the liberties of the House of Commons were again propounded by some MPs, it was against this background of the greatly increased visibility of the Commons in English political and social life that the Tudor governments themselves had created. If the Commons served king and people so well with their great statutes, then the MPs ought to have freedom of speech, immunity from arrest, and freedom to decide their own elections, it was claimed.

The Privy Council, which initiated all significant legislation, remained firmly in control of Parliament. Elizabeth's chief ministers were all gentry. They sat on the front bench of the Commons, managed legislation, and dominated its proceedings. The queen's ministers each controlled several boroughs, with small or negligible franchises, that had been mostly given representation in the fifteenth and sixteenth centuries. Along with the MPs who were civil servants or royal pensioners, these MPs from the nominated boroughs meant there was no danger in Elizabeth's reign that the Crown would not control the proceedings in the House.

But there was a small and slowly growing group of obstreperous MPs, some of whom indeed sat for boroughs controlled by members of the royal government, who raised difficult policy questions and put forward again the issues of the liberties of the House. These policy issues were the succession to the throne after the death of the Virgin Queen, and the condition of the Church of England, from which—as we have seen—the MPs wanted to eliminate any remaining vestiges of Catholic liturgy and ritual.

What made for potential difficulties for the royal government was an increasing restlessness among the gentry, even some of the wealthiest ones, as well as among the merchant class, as the century and Elizabethan era drew to a close. The restlessness was partly inspired by concern about the international political situation, focused on the power of the Spanish Hapsburg Catholic rulers, who made one great effort to invade England in 1588 that failed, but that could recur. It was harder to take a moderate stand on religion in face of this Catholic military presence.

The gentry's restlessness, reflected in the views of oppositional and vocal MPs, was also inspired by the worsening economic situation, the bewildering downturn in the business cycle, after more than a half century of boom. The Tudors, for all their family eccentricities, had benefited greatly from the economic expansion. Now they were losing popularity because of business contraction.

Sixteenth-century economic theory was mercantilistic. It associated business conditions directly with the outcomes of state policy, and this view was embarrassing for any government during the downside of the business cycle.

The common lawyers went about their business as they had for centuries. Being dependent on the royal courts and eager for the government's judicial business, the lawyers were a thoroughly loyal and politically conservative group. But the gentry families from which they came were buffeted by the winds of religious and economic change. In time this affected the intellectual and political outlook of the lawyers as well.

The more intransigent Protestants within the Church of England and the Calvinist separatists without—the Puritans as they came to be called—produced lawyers among their sons as well as landlords, merchants, theologians, and preachers. The kind of legal outlook popular among the Puritan gentry intermixed professional knowledge and technical competence with a high degree of ethical content that made them ultimately vulnerable to radicalizing political ideology.

Since the time of Bracton and Fortescue, the lawyers had given a strongly moralistic edge to their judicial behavior. The penetration into English secondary education at the end of the fifteenth century of the classical humanistic curriculum devised in Renaissance Italy meant that reading Cicero was central to the education of adolescents who within ten years of completing their secondary schooling had been called to the bar. They brought with them a view of the world that was narrow but intensely moralistic.

The law is a word profession. Lawyers are retailers of the spoken and written word in certain lucrative markets. If the word count they are familiar with is heavily laced with ethical terms, in a certain ambience this can have an impact on the mind-set and behavior pattern of lawyers. It happened in the United States from the late 1930s to the mid–1970s, when lawyers were in the front ranks of the New Deal and civil rights movement. It happened in England in the late sixteenth and early seventeenth centuries.

Lawyers became immersed in a liberal culture that overlaid the facilitation of greed and power with a gloss of ethical mandates about commonweal, community, and doing God's work in one's calling in life. Precisely because they were so self-righteous, the lawyers were vulnerable to being affected by religious trends, which in turn impacted on their image of themselves as attorneys.

This shift, which would have momentous political significance, was just beginning to happen at the end of Elizabeth's reign. It would sharply accelerate thereafter. Historians have debated endlessly why and how this occurred, how the intensely conservative and royalist attorneys and judges began to be affected by a more radical culture that was centered in Puritan theology and homiletics. But happen it did, eventually. This produced a schism in the political nation and led finally to civil war.

Elizabeth I would not give in to the small minority of dissident MPs in her day. But the actions her government took against them—a few hours or at most days of honorable confinement—were so trivial that it was obvious that the Crown was afraid of the oppositionists or, in the case of some privy councillors, ideologically sympathetic to them.

Finally, two years before her death in 1603, the aged queen put on her pancake makeup and her red fright wig and personally addressed the Commons. She talked about her love for them and their loyalty to her, and by the time she finished her short but eloquent address, there was probably not a dry eye in the House. But all this show meant nothing. The MPs were just waiting for Elizabeth to die.

When Elizabeth's chosen successor, her eccentric Scottish cousin, finally meandered down to London in 1604 to receive by his coronation the kingdom as James I, the first of the Stuart dynasty on the English throne, he discovered that ideological tensions had broadened and intensified.

The opposition MPs had drawn up an elaborate document called *The Apology of the House of Commons*, which—beyond demanding further reform of the established church and making other provocative assertions—had now identified the liberties of the Commons with the liberties of Englishmen. What had started as corporate privileges had now become universal rights.

Historians now question whether the *Apology* was ever formally presented to James. The MPs may not have had enough courage for such a symbolically provocative act. But the new king certainly knew what was in the manifesto circulating among political and religious dissidents, and he was not happy.

James I (1603–25) was a highly literate man who wrote third-rate treatises on political theory that communicated a high sense of the royal prerogative with a low sense of the Commons oppositionists, who reminded him of the hillbillies in Edinburgh who had driven his vivacious mother, Mary, from the Scottish throne to her death in England at the hands of the Elizabethan government.

James had all sorts of advanced ideas: that peace was much better than war; that smoking tobacco poisons the lungs; that it was all right to play football on Sunday afternoons; that a well-turned male leg in the silk stockings of a courtier was enough to merit a dukedom.

But judicial liberalism? He was not buying into that. He saw through the Commons's opposition, he thought. They were really radical Protestants, contemptible Puritans, who wanted to make the Church of England Presbyterian ("no bishop, no king," he wisely remarked) and were just using judicial and political liberalism as a weapon to advance their interests, make trouble, and broaden their narrow political support.

In the first decade of James's reign, the greatest obstacle to the Puritan party and affiliated discontented gentry broadening out into a "country party" in the Commons, in opposition to the Crown party of privy councillors and their dependents, was the greatest common lawyer of the time, Sir Edward Coke.

As long as Coke served the king as a pit-bull attorney general and then as chief justice, the wish of the oppositionists to affiliate the Puritans and lawyers in a united country party that could take over direction of the Commons would not be realized. Until then judicial liberalism would not be fully politicized.

It was when Coke broke with the king and joined the Commons opponents of the royal administration that the political scene underwent a rapid change and the way was open for the confrontation that developed into the Civil War.

It was Coke who fully realized and activated what Bracton had long ago suggested—that the common law could be a political force against the monarchy. Therefore, after Bracton, Coke was the most important lawyer involved in the rise of liberalism.

15
The Age of Coke

Sɪʀ Eᴅᴡᴀʀᴅ Cᴏᴋᴇ (pronounced Cook, 1552–1634) knew more about the common law than anyone in or before his era or, with the possible exception of F. W. Maitland, even since his time. There is no definitive biography of Coke nor perhaps will there ever be one, because when he died in 1634, agents of the Stuarts seized all his personal papers at his country estate, and they have disappeared. A Cambridge legal historian has been looking for Coke's papers for a quarter of a century, believing that they will yet turn up.

If Coke's papers are eventually discovered, it could very well be in an air-conditioned library in San Remo, California; Austin, Texas; or New Haven, Connecticut—American repositories specializing in collecting English manuscripts—rather than romantically in some dank manor house in the Home Counties.

Coke came from middling gentry. His father was a lawyer. Pursuing the law was a career necessity as well as a personal choice for him. Coke got wealthy and well connected early on by marrying an heiress. The circumstances of the marriage were extraordinary—they eloped when she was underage. Technically Coke had committed kidnapping and rape, and he could have been punished as a felon as well as losing his legal career. But his wife's family decided that the impetuous young barrister was a rising star and a good match for their daughter.

This story foreshadows what happened again and again in Coke's life—his tendency to take great risks and defy authority. There was a self-destructive streak in him. He reached the pinnacle of the political and social as well as judicial establishment, but he was not the kind of establishment figure who acts conventionally and prudently; quite the contrary. He was a big risk taker, an outrider.

Coke is best understood as a Renaissance figure, both temperamentally and intellectually. He believed in greatness of soul, the pursuit of "virtue" (excellence) and reliance on "fortune," like Machiavelli, although he came to identify fortune with divine providence. He thought that only the strenuous life was worth living. He could have been a lead character in a play by Shakespeare—who was almost his contemporary, just a little older.

Intellectually, too, Coke was very much a man of the Renaissance, which reached its full force as a dynamic cultural movement in England only in the closing years of the sixteenth century. As a Renaissance man Coke was fascinated by language; obviously he relished writing. He rose to the task of articulating the principles and procedures of the common law in sturdy English prose in his four-volume *Institutes* of the common law, which remains along with Maitland's work the greatest single study of the common law.

Coke began his treatise modestly, as a commentary on Littleton, a drab fifteenth-century textbook on land tenure, but he warmed to the task and his mastery of words carried him forward. He relished putting complex and hoary concepts into the learned English of his day, but not so learned that it could not be read by any educated person.

Maitland complained about Coke's uncontrollable urge to lay out great gobs of learning. That too was a trait of the Renaissance intellectual. Learning per se—history, philosophy, literature—was a good thing that would bring enlightenment and refinement. You could never get enough of it.

It was his love of learning as well as his image of himself as a leading barrister that led Coke early in his career to get involved in editing and publishing what are now called *The English Reports*, an annual publication of the extensive recording of important trials, which in the late sixteenth century replaced the now defunct series of anthologized *Year Books*.

Coke's prose style reflects someone well educated as an adolescent in the Latin classics. By Coke's time the curriculum of secondary education for boys of gentry family had been well settled and would remain so until well into the twentieth century. It was strictly humanistic schooling. Aside from a little mathematics, the "public" (private prep) school student thoroughly studied the Greek and Latin classics, among whom Cicero stood out.

The influence of Cicero on Coke is substantial. Certainly Cicero reinforced Coke's disposition to see law as connected to an ethical continuum. This encouraged belief in right and wrong, rather than the seeking of accommodation and compromise. It augmented a sense of the special quality and of the high degree of desirable autonomy of the law.

Cicero served for Coke as a role model for combining advocacy and politics. Reading Cicero also pushed Coke to try, as Cicero had, to write about law in a humanistic vein, accessible to the educated public.

Finally Coke was something of a romantic. His eyes moistened over as he thought of the beauty of the English countryside and the quiet, happy life of the yeoman and farmer. His sensitivity to nature was not Wordsworthian, however, but classical—it is reminiscent of Virgil writing about the Roman countryside.

Coke had a developmental perception of the law. He was aware of its changes over time, but he was not historically minded. There was an ancient constitution whose laws over time "by the wisdom of the most excellent men, in many succession of ages, by long and continual experience, the trial of right and truth [were] fined and refined." That was the history of English law, in Coke's capsule version. Coke's vision is spatially rather than temporally directed. There is the space of rural and urban England. There is the structure of the law, which overlays it and maximizes the functioning of human relationships and group interactions.

Coke was not a historian because he had little sense of the developmental character of institutions. But he was an antiquarian who collected old legal manuscripts, easily and cheaply available at the time, and enjoyed reading and studying them closely. In this antiquarian pursuit Coke was not unusual in his era. The seventeenth century was the first great age of English antiquarianism, and since the government did not value its boundless inherited deposit of manuscripts in the Tower of London and elsewhere, there was a very active London market in medieval legal and political manuscripts. The dissolved monasteries were another prime source of old manuscripts.

John Selden was both politically active on the parliamentary side and an assiduous collector and explicator of ancient legal texts, with the purpose of supporting by historical evidence the claims of the House of Commons against the monarchy. Later in the century Sir Robert Cotton's immense collection of medieval manuscripts, mostly derived from the dissolved monasteries, became the nucleus of the manuscript collection of the British Museum when it was founded in the mid-eighteenth century. Around 1700 Thomas Maddox wrote a history of the medieval Exchequer from manuscript sources that comes close to meeting modern scholarly standards, including footnote apparatus.

Coke's antiquarian pursuits provided part of the database for his treatise on the common law, and his superior erudition made it hard for anyone to challenge his interpretations.

Coke rose as a Crown legal official to be a particularly aggressive attorney general. Some of his summations are extant—he was himself principally responsible as editor of the *English Reports* of important trials for their publication. In these cases he is masterful and brutal; he shows no mercy; he denigrates defendants in court even when they are prominent gentry. He wants the death penalty without reservation—and he gets it.

For his assiduous and highly visible work as a state prosecutor, Coke was raised to the bench and became chief justice of the Common Pleas, then and now the most important judgeship in England. Among his other achievements in this capacity was establishing the formalistic English law of libel—the doctrine that truth is not a defense against a claim of libel.

But Coke began to be restless and to quarrel first with his colleagues on the bench, then with the lord chancellor and the Court of Chancery, and finally with the king.

Coke found himself in a minority of one when, in *Bonham's Case* (1610), he asserted the power of judicial review by Common Pleas not only over earlier decisions, the lower courts, and the marking out of undefined judicial frontiers, but over parliamentary legislation: "And it appears in our books that in many cases the common law will control acts of Parliament and sometimes adjudge them to be utterly void: for when an act of Parliament is against common right or reason, or repugnant or impossible to be performed, the common law will control it and adjudge such act to be void."

As a result of the extensive Tudor use of statute and the trend of sixteenth-century political thinking to posit sovereignty as much as possible in one place, the English courts had come to accept even more firmly than before the supreme position of Parliament relative to the judiciary. An unambiguous clause in a statute could not be weakened, eroded, or undermined by judicial review.

The English were well on their way to according absolute sovereignty to king in Parliament—as classically articulated in the Resolution of the House of Commons of May 27, 1642—the constitutional position that still prevails. Coke held a different view, which favored the giving of power to courts, and especially Common Pleas, over statute. In accordance with learning and reason, Coke held that the courts could review an act of Parliament and could reject its legality.

Coke's advocacy of supremacist judicial review might have flown in the fourteenth century, but it could not in the seventeenth. Coke wanted to reopen a door that was already firmly shut. His colleagues on the bench would not support his position.

Coke's ideas of supremacist judicial review conform to the tradition of the U.S. Supreme Court rather than to the subsequent history of the common law in England. In *Marbury* v. *Madison* (1803), Chief Justice John Marshall wrote the opinion declaring an act of Congress to be unconstitutional and therefore void. It was a relatively trivial matter, but Marshall wanted to use the opportunity to get on the record the assertion of the power of the federal Supreme Court to review and strike down not only acts of state legislatures and courts but those of the federal Congress itself. There was an outcry against Marshall's Coke-like position, not least from President Thomas Jefferson, a relative of Marshall, who disliked him intensely on both personal and political grounds.

Nevertheless the supremacist position on judicial review was asserted again—disastrously, from a political point of view—in Chief Justice Roger Taney's *Dred Scott* slavery decision in 1857, and has frequently been practiced in the twentieth century, notably in the early 1930s by a conservative Court against the New Deal and then in the liberal Court, under Chief Justices Earl Warren and Warren Burger, from 1954 to 1973.

When the U.S. Supreme Court reviews and endorses acts of Congress, there is no problem. Controversy erupts when the Court declares acts of Congress illegal, which is what Coke wanted the English high courts to have the power to do with parliamentary legislation.

Historians are divided on the question of whether Coke's opinion in *Bonham's Case* migrated across the Atlantic and influenced Marshall, or whether Marshall arrived at the same principle independently. Characteristically, Marshall's opinion in *Marbury* is devoid of citations or references. But those legal historians, like Barbara Black, who see the giant figure of Coke lurking behind the U.S. Supreme Court, have a plausible argument.

By putting forward his hard line on judicial review, Coke disturbed his colleagues on the bench. It also did not make him popular with the activist House of Commons. He appeared to be a political maverick, not the future leader of the Commons against the Stuart monarchy. The leaders of the Commons in the early seventeenth century were building on the medieval doctrine of the king's two bodies to identify the rule of law with parliamentary sovereignty. Coke's devotion to the common law around 1610 made him a dissenter from this extreme politicization of the common-law tradition. He wanted to uphold the common law as superior equally to king and Parliament, and therefore to sustain the position of the high-court judges as interpreters of the constitution.

In that respect Coke anticipated the American definition of liberalism rather than the modern English one. While A. V. Dicey and other Victorian juristic authorities talked about the rule of law as England's way, they actually meant the rule of Parliament. In the American Republic, as it developed, the Constitution and the Supreme Court's authority to interpret it were held to be superior to the executive and the legislative branches—the constitutional system Coke envisaged in *Bonham's Case* but could not get anyone to support.

Coke's view of the high autonomy of the common law (before he became a leader of the House of Commons in the 1620s) appears to have been strongly influenced by a treatise written by an early-sixteenth-century barrister, Christopher St. German. The latter "believed English law to be a rational law. It contained *within itself* the principles of reason rather than being subject to external measures of its rationality" (Glenn Burgess). Similarly Coke in his preparliamentary days regarded the common law as the embodiment of rational truth refined over time and therefore unchallengeable.

He said in another opinion, *Calvin's Case*, that the common law was an ethical and material substance superior to "the wisdom of all the men in the world [that] in any age could ever have effected or attained." On the one side this is a conservative doctrine, substantially freezing the inherited common law in place. But it also is a radical one, elevating the judges and barristers, who alone master the legitimate legal text, above the executive and legislature.

Whatever damage Coke's legal supremacism in *Bonham's Case* and *Calvin's Case* did to his reputation and his legitimacy among the political elite, it was in fact his conflict with the lord chancellor and his persistent attacks on the Court of Chancery that brought about his break with James and the royal government.

Coke insisted that Chancery was not a court of record, not a common-law high court. Therefore any decision in Chancery could not be cited as *stare decisis*, as precedent, severely limiting its judicial standing. If Coke got his way, the Chancery judges would no longer be able to cite their own previous decisions in a case before them, nor could a case in Chancery be appealed *certiorari* to Common Pleas, discouraging the bringing of cases to Chancery in the first place—as Coke well knew.

Coke also denigrated the Chancery judges as not being of the quality of judges in Common Pleas and King's Bench. A Chancery judge who had a doctorate in civil Roman law from Oxford, as some by this time did, was doubly suspect in Coke's view: They were likely to be ideological subverters of the common law, lovers of continental despotism.

Coke made his quarrel with Chancery an issue of jurisprudence, an intellectual matter. To some degree it probably was, but it was also a professional matter. The attorneys and judges in Common Pleas, not for the first time, believed that Chancery had far exceeded its original mandate. From being a special court set up to give quick but temporary relief to certain vulnerable groups, it had become a regular common-law court in assiduous competition with Common Pleas. Its jurisdiction over trusts and uses rankled, because this was a lucrative practice that was being lost by Common Pleas to the Chancery judges and lawyers.

In Coke's view Chancery not only threatened to unbalance the whole court system of the common law, but, what was worse, it threatened the livelihood of the Common Pleas lawyers—the backbone of the legal profession.

Coke, unlike most of the common lawyers of his day, disliked entails. He thought that binding future generations on distribution of family property was an invasion of freedom, a point that the courts agreed with in the late seventeenth century, when they enunciated the doctrine against perpetuities and limited entails to one generation. But there was a professional matter involved for Coke as well: It was part of his hostility to Chancery, since Chancery obtained a lot of entail business.

After giving plenty of warning that he regarded the lord chancellor and the Court of Chancery as far exceeding their allotted powers and as destabilizing the common law, Coke began to take direct action from the bench against Chancery. He refused to hear appeals from Chancery and, what was most provocative, started to issue bench writs stopping Chancery cases and transferring them to Common Pleas. As a matter of fact, it was probably legal for him to pursue these guerrilla judicial tactics, but it made the lord chancellor, a favorite royal minister, very angry—as expected—and precipitated a tremendous row between Coke and the king.

At the chancellor's urging James transferred Coke from the Court of Common Pleas to the head of King's Bench, where he would be much less likely to be in competition for cases with Chancery. Coke regarded the transfer as a demotion, which it was. Now he got into nasty public quarrels with James I.

The crunch came when James requested judges to consult privately with the king if a current or impending case seemed likely to affect the monarchy in some way. Specifically James propounded the view that if the king for any reason had an interest in a case, he had a right to discuss it with the presiding judge before and during trial. James's position was provocative but not unconstitutional; there were many centuries of precedent for it. But Coke insisted that James's view invaded the independence of the judiciary and undermined its integrity.

James then got on his theoretical and rhetorical high horse—which he mounted—not always fortunately, when he was troubled and angry—and insisted that the judges were "lions under the throne" and responsible to him. Coke thought that judges, once appointed, served for life; and could be removed only for gross misbehavior, such as taking bribes; and were responsible only to the common law as their mind and conscience instructed them, or to God.

Neither James nor Coke was adept at, or inclined to, cool down difficult situations. A bitter debate ensued, which garnered much public attention, and when the smoke cleared in 1616 James had dismissed England's greatest lawyer from the bench.

James Stuart came from Scotland, a country that was firmly committed in the early seventeenth century to Roman law. In the fourteenth century the Scottish kings and lords helped their successful resistance to English invasion by an alliance with the

English king's traditional enemy, the French monarchy. A consequence of the Scottish-French alliance was the wholesale importation of Frenchified civil law into Scotland and its teaching at the University of Edinburgh.

Only later on, in the eighteenth century, after the Union of England and Scotland in 1707, did the English common law penetrate to a modest extent into Scotland, resulting in a hybrid legal system that distinctively combined ingredients of both Roman and English law, still with a preponderance in Scottish law of the civil-law tradition going back to the Justinian code.

So it could be said that James encountered in England a common law with which he was not familiar and in whose procedures and political implications he ran counter to the Roman-law system with which he was cognizant. But James was a well-educated and intelligent man. He would have no difficulty in understanding common law. He simply didn't like it, not only for its consensual political implications but perhaps even more for its tradition of a highly autonomous legal profession and a relatively independent bench of judges.

In early Stuart England, from 1603 to 1642, there was a large measure of consensus among courtiers, nobility, and the wealthy gentry on the major dimensions of politics and culture. If there were occasional flareups of disputes, from the point of view of the king and his government these irritations seemed relatively modest or of no consequence compared to the general community of values that prevailed. They could not conceive of a rupture that would polarize the landed classes and lead to some great political upheaval. Indeed, it has been the fashion of important recent historians writing about early-seventeenth-century England, such as Conrad Russell, similarly to stress political consensus and cultural community rather than conflict and polarization.

Yet in 1642 a great upheaval did occur, and it was not only about religion and the church. Aggravating as were these ecclesiastical disputes, Coke was the key figure in laying the groundwork, articulated initially in terms of the common law, for the rupture within the political nation and elite cultural community that finally led to the Civil War.

Where James and his son and their ministers and courtiers gravely miscalculated was in not imagining the capacity of this socially conservative, establishmentarian, and affluent legal profession to become radically activist and oppositional if it felt its status and income were threatened by the monarchy, and if it found a suitably prestigious leader who would legitimate this unaccustomed oppositional stance on the part of the common lawyers. Coke served the latter role very well.

The fiery conflict between Coke and James I is usually presented in ideological and political terms, and of course that is in a sense a valid perspective on their falling out. But there is another way to look at it, which is psychological. They appear to have been men of similar disposition—learned, egotistical risk takers who liked to stir things up. Both would today be regarded as highly aggressive personalities. It was hard for two such men whose paths crossed to get along with each other.

There was something else involved. At least in his mature years (after he had married and fathered a child) James became openly gay. Coke on the other hand seems to have been aggressively heterosexual. Gay behavior was fully acceptable in court and high aristocratic circles, but it was alien to gentry and middle-class behavior and mores. This contrast may account for the deep psychological tensions that prevailed in the relationship between the two men. They had intense personal hatred for each other, not just strong differences on jurisprudence.

Coke believed that he had been not only unjustly but illegally dismissed, since he felt that the judiciary should be independent of the Crown and once appointed should serve for life (except for proof of gross professional misconduct). James thought that judges served at the pleasure of the king and could be dismissed for policy reasons.

Coke could do nothing about his dismissal. At this point he had no tangible support in the Commons. He retired to his beloved country estate and worked quietly for several years on his massive treatise on the common law. It seemed to the king and his ministers that Coke had been well handled. The old lawyer would rummage endlessly among his musty lawbooks and manuscripts, pursue scholarship, publish esoteric legal works, and stay out of trouble and the limelight. In the short run they were right; in the long run—a period of five years—they were calamitously wrong.

What the king should have done was to offer Coke a peerage, get him into the House of Lords, and prevent him from sitting in the Commons and using it as a mighty weapon of revenge against royal government. Another recourse (a favorite way of getting rid of political troublemakers in the nineteenth and twentieth centuries) would have been to offer Coke an ambassadorship to a far-away country, like Prussia or Turkey. Coke would probably have rejected the ambassadorship, but his vanity would have precluded his rejecting a peerage.

Instead James's government did nothing, and in 1621 Coke entered the House of Commons and very soon advanced into the leadership cohort of MPs trying to form a country party in opposition to the Crown supporters. Coke provided the missing link they had long needed, not only through his personal prestige and capacity to invent clever and novel tactics, but by bringing with him a nucleus of barristers from Common Pleas, for whom he was a god.

Coke showed greater political skills than anyone could have anticipated. To firm up the country party, in which devout Puritans loomed large, he avowed his deep commitment to the Protestant faith, not noticeable previously. By the time James died in 1625 and was succeeded by his son, Charles I, from his earlier heterosexual days, the united front in the Commons of Puritans, lawyers, and generally discontented gentry anxious about their falling incomes during continued economic depression was in place.

Historians in recent decades, lovers of power and haters of liberal Protestantism, have put most of the blame for the political deadlock and crisis of the years 1625–29 on the allegedly unreasonable and obstreperous Commons. But Charles I was all wrong to be king of England, at least in the strained ambience of the early seventeenth century. Charles was married to a devout French Roman Catholic princess, always a warning sign to the Puritan gentry. He gave lavish parties for gay friends and other courtiers while the government was strained for funds. He thought that the Commons's oppositionists were vulgar troublemakers and that Coke was an uncouth madman.

Strangely Charles seemed more self-conscious than his father about being a Scottish alien in unfriendly England, perhaps because the English gentry were becoming intensely chauvinistic and even objected to Scottish subjects getting English citizenship on easy terms.

The best thing about Charles, and perhaps the prime reason he has received a good press among historians recently, is that he was a well-educated aesthete. He was an astute patron of painters, whom he imported from the Continent when he could afford their services. He put together Europe's finest collection of Renaissance and Baroque paintings. Some of this collection is still in the National Gallery in London, huge explosions of glorious color depicting biblical and classical themes, leaving modern painters and critics in awe of their craftsmanship.

After Charles's execution in 1649, the Cromwellian dictatorship, which detested the visual arts as pagan and un-Christian, sold off the greater part of Charles's art collection at cheap prices. Much of this segment of Charles's collection is now in the Louvre in Paris.

Coke built up support among the common lawyers against Charles and his ministers by instilling fear that the legal profession was being undermined by the Crown. Whatever their political views, and their natural disposition to caution, the lawyers had to pay attention when the greatest lawyer in their country and the former chief justice portrayed the common law as being in grave political danger.

By favoring Chancery the Crown was ruining barristers' practices and drastically cutting their incomes, said Coke. By dismissing judges, the autonomous and corporate nature of the courts and the legal profession was shredded. Oxford doctors of civil (Roman) law were now getting the best jobs, claimed Coke, not the graduates of the Inns of Court.

Certainly Coke was exaggerating the threat to common law. Perhaps he cynically made up his complaints, but he was convincing. A hitherto passionate, loyal, and intensely conservative legal profession was being radicalized. The government should have seen the worrisome political implications of this great fear among the barristers. They saw what Coke was doing and they didn't like it, but they did not extrapolate the political consequences of what was happening.

Unquestionably things would have been different in an expanding economy, when it was easy—as in the mid-sixteenth century—for lawyers as well as landlords and merchants to make money. Now times were difficult; money was tight. An atmosphere of gloom ran through upper-middle-class society, which contrasted starkly with the revels and balls sponsored by the royal court.

In the late 1620s Shakespeare's plays were losing their audience in favor of a new dramatic genre, the revenger's tragedy (although *Hamlet* is itself an early but still moderate example of this genre), in which the dramatist killed off all the characters in the most cruel way imaginable, like Hollywood movies in the 1990s, another sign of a sick culture.

All the social and cultural downers were aggravated by the weather. England had become colder, especially during winter;

England was going through the "Little Ice Age," a severe deterioration of the climate, making daily life harsher, shortening the growing season, and decreasing crop yields for the gentry landlords. There are paintings from the 1620s showing people skating on the Thames. That was not possible in the Middle Ages, a period of unusual warmth in England, nor would it be advisable today.

Historians do not know the cause of the Little Ice Age; some think it was part of the normal weather cycle; others that volcanic eruptions in Indonesia threw huge clouds of dust into the atmosphere that eventually filtered out sunlight in western Europe. Whatever the cause, the colder climate made life all the more miserable, and short tempers ever more furious.

By 1628 Coke was one of the two or three leaders of the country party in the House of Commons. These opposition MPs were mostly elected on the basis of what they advocated, usually in contested elections, and not placed in the Commons by privy councillors controlling the delimited franchise of nominated boroughs. These oppositionist MPs used caucuses, legislative committees, and public agitation to pursue their goals.

Therefore the country party of the late 1620s is the first modern political party in English history. Coke's special contribution to its activity was dredging up obscure medieval judicial instruments (for example, *The Petition of Right*, 1628) and entrapping the royal government in this maze of hoary expedients from the old common law.

By 1629 it was clear that the Commons would never vote a subsidy (general tax) without major policy concessions by the Crown. Therefore Charles dissolved Parliament and determined to rule without it and only through his appointed council. The most visibly successful monarchs in Europe—in France, Spain, and Austria—ruled without a legislature. Why should England be different and use apparently obsolete medieval assemblies?

Parliament was not summoned again for another decade. One

of the leaders of the country party was held in prison, but Coke was free to return to his beloved country home, finish the *Institutes*, and die peacefully in 1634, at which time royal agents impounded all his manuscripts. The Crown's action was legally doubtful and not returning the papers to Coke's family certainly was illegal. Ironically the Crown by its posthumous action against Coke seemed to verify his claim that the Stuart government was bent on tyrannical subverting of the law.

Coke's heart and soul lay with the common law. His political career came late and seems to have been inspired by a sense of personal grievance and a wish for revenge. But these are persistent motivations toward political activity at any time and place. By his ideas and his political career, Coke strengthened the affiliation between judicial liberalism and parliamentary and particularly Commons power, and augmented the politicization of the common law.

Charles I's experiment in nonparliamentary government worked for a decade, but at the price of having to resort to extreme strategies to raise money from nonparliamentary sources. The Stuarts had already raised the customs rate without parliamentary approval, resulting in the *Bates Case* in 1606, in which the bench sustained the Crown's argument that the mixed medieval precedents gave them the power to impose the increased rates unilaterally. Bates was a London merchant importing currants from the Levant, who refused to pay the increased customs as a test case.

Another test case involved the legality of ship money. This obscure late medieval tax, imposed on some port towns to raise money for ships to combat piracy, levied under the royal prerogative, was now applied to the whole country as an arbitrary tax. A leader of the country party, John Hampden, a very wealthy landowner who lived far inland in 1637, refused to pay ship money, producing a constitutional test case.

In *King* v. *John Hampden*, a panel of twelve judges meeting as the Exchequer Chamber, the special high court in important appeals cases, heard good presentations by highly skilled counsel for both sides. Unfortunately the Crown attorney at the end of his oral presentation launched into a provocative soliloquy on the glories of the royal prerogative. The court found for the Crown but narrowly—seven votes to five. This was a grim warning to the royal government that their hold on gentry support was slipping away.

But Charles paid little attention to politics, and he allowed his archbishop of Canterbury, the neoconservative William Laud, to pursue extremely controversial measures to make the Church of England more Catholic in ritual and liturgy at a time when there was a strongly Puritan group within the church wanting to push it in a more Calvinist direction. This bitter dispute occurred at a time when religious conflict in Central Europe had exploded into the Thirty Years' War, whose troubling events were given a sharply ideological and sensational cast by the newspapers sold in London's streets.

In 1638 Charles and Laud tried to impose the Anglican Prayer Book on the Calvinistically inclined Church of Scotland. The result was revolution in Edinburgh. This was soon followed by rebellion of the Catholics in Ireland. Charles's government had immediate need of raising large armies to put down these upheavals in the outer regions and could no longer scrape by on indirect taxation such as increased customs and ship money, controversial as that had been.

Charles called Parliament for the first time in a decade to get a general subsidy. The gentry, lawyers, and devout Protestants who led the country party in the Commons were Coke's political heirs and had imbibed his style of confrontation. They wouldn't begin to consider a tax unless a long list of political and religious reforms was made. Charles sent the Short Parliament home.

Matters got worse in Scotland and Ireland. The king summoned a new Parliament, in which the country party in the

Commons was even more determined and seemed to have more support than before. This Parliament came to be called the Long Parliament, because it sat for a dozen years.

This Long Parliament was the revolutionary assembly. Charles, never keen for tough politics, surrendered to the MPs, passively accepting the impeachment of Laud and the passing of a bill of attainder against another chief minister. Star Chamber was abolished, Chancery temporarily suspended, and various strategies entered into to make the Church of England more Protestant.

After two years of frenetic activity and royal lassitude, the Commons passed a resolution stating that the county militias—England's only armies—were now directly responsible to the Commons, stripping the king of his one remaining power, that of commander of the armed forces. When Charles in response proclaimed his authority over the militias, the Commons passed the Resolution of May 27, 1642, which stipulated the fundamental principle of the English constitution and brought four hundred years of political and legal history to a climax.

The resolution stated that king in Parliament was superior to the king alone, and if king and Parliament couldn't agree, then Parliament (and for practical purposes the Commons) could act on behalf of the king. The political body of the king was superior to his natural body. Law stood above his personal will.

Bracton was thus confirmed, and the tradition of judicial liberalism originating in the thirteenth century was cemented forever to that of parliamentary, and especially of Commons, supremacy. Coke's vision of the 1620s was vindicated.

Charles I reasonably took the Commons resolution as a declaration of war against him. He went to Oxford, raised the banner of Saint George, called for universal support, and prepared for civil war. Around 70 percent of the House of Lords rallied to the king. Twenty-five percent went home and did nothing. Five percent stayed with the Commons—these were devout Puritan nobility. Slightly more than 50 percent of the Commons stayed in

London and prepared to fight the king on behalf of God and the common law. Around 20 percent supported the king, including some who had previously adhered to the country party, which they now viewed as having gone too far and having threatened the constitution. About 30 percent of the Commons went home and did nothing. What could not be decided in the law courts and Parliament would now be determined on the battlefield.

The age of Coke was the age of "liberty." Liberty was the code word, the term of art of political correctness on which diverse anti-Stuart groups and interests coalesced and fused. Coke played perhaps the leading role in making possible this fusion of the three distinct meanings of liberty into one powerful expression.

There were first the liberties of the House of Commons—freedom of speech, immunity from arrest, freedom to decide on its own elections—that not only made the Commons an autonomous corporate entity but which in the age of Coke became advertised as the bulwark of, and eventually expressive of, the liberties of Englishmen.

There was a second strain to the liberties of Englishmen. This was due process of the common law, which, it was asserted, in civil and criminal matters protected individual citizens from oppressive authority and insecurity and defended their lives and their property. This idea had been clearly enunciated down through the centuries, ever since King John in Magna Carta was made to promise that he would observe the law of the land. Due process was symbolized by the writ system, the juries, the right to be represented by an attorney in civil actions, and by adversarial pleading in court.

There were people in the age of Coke, or at least within a decade of his death, who sharply pointed out that the liberty promised by the common-law due process was class biased, that it was much more likely to help the rich and well connected than the poor and friendless. But for Coke and the gentry and the MPs in the Commons, this argument was inconsequential. It did not detract from the importance of due process as liberty.

The third meaning of liberty was grounded in the Protestant religion and the radical Catholicism of the late Middle Ages, from which Protestantism emerged. It went back to a pamphlet written by Martin Luther around 1520, called *The Liberty of the Christian Man*. As it wound its way through the Calvinism that was the foundation of Protestantism in England, it evolved into the radical Puritanism that in Coke's time came—in most cases only momentarily, but it was a critical moment—to affect a large segment of the gentry. Christian liberty became a kind of individualism, a belief in the capacity of each devout or born-again Protestant to communicate directly with God, to become part of what Luther had called the priesthood of all believers.

By the time Coke died in the mid–1630s it was becoming fashionable to talk about an "inner light" in the mind and soul of every committed Protestant. There was plenty that was debatable in this concept from a theological or psychological point of view, and both Luther and Calvin would have found it dangerously anarchistic. But it came to be widely held and was the intellectual foundation of the doctrines of the Congregationalists, Baptists, and Quakers (Society of Friends), not to speak of fringe eschatological sects like Fifth Monarchy Men.

Spiritual individualism lives on in modern liberal Protestantism and was boldly admired by three great historians of the age of Coke: Samuel R. Gardiner in the nineteenth century and G. M. Trevelyan and William Haller in the first half of the twentieth. It seems to have no appeal to the generations of historians writing about Coke's era since the late 1950s. They stress how disparate were the three ideas of liberty—the Commons's, due process of law, and Puritanism—actually were, and how vulnerable, badly thought out, and temporary was their fusion in the 1630s. Inner-light evangelical Protestantism does not get much empathy from historians writing about seventeenth-century England since 1960.

But the fusion of the three ideas of liberty was meaningful to Coke and his colleagues, and it was under the banner of liberty that the war against the Stuart monarchy was fought.

In 1603 both the monarchy and the country party in the House of Commons spoke respectfully of the custom of the common law that putatively provided a vast depository of guidelines for public behavior. It might be necessary to massage custom at the margin and apply "reason" to the inherited judicial culture, but such application was only, it was assumed, a marginal and occasional action.

By 1642 there had been a tremendous erosion of faith in the consensual utility of the inherited common law. First, the king in trying to rule without Parliament and devising eccentric fiscal expedients communicated a sense of pragmatic will driving the government's policy and behavior. By May 1642 the Commons were also talking in these pragmatic terms. In the Remonstrance of the Commons of May 26, 1642, the House declared that precedents cannot "be limits to bound our proceedings, which may and must vary according to the different conditions of men."

This expression of legal realism was followed a day later by the Commons resolution on the king's two bodies, which allegedly were rooted in the ancient constitution. The outbreak of civil war was therefore grounded in a bifocal judicial perception—an historical constitution and yet experiential expression of collective will unbounded by the past. This was to remain the paradox of English constitutionalism—a combination of rule of law with parliamentary sovereignty.

If Coke had still been in the House of Commons in the tempestuous revolutionary days of May 26 and 27, 1642, he probably would have voted both for the Remonstrance of May 26 and the Resolution of May 27, knowing, as J. G. Pocock has written, that "the common law argument was failing because it had reached the limits of its own strength. . . . A historical discourse had exhausted itself and was giving way to a discourse of another kind."

16
From Oliver Cromwell to William Blackstone

THE ENGLISH CIVIL WAR was, like most civil wars, fought with ferocity, even though (or perhaps because) England, having no standing army, was a country backward in military science, as compared to the bellicose days of the later Middle Ages. The royalists ("Cavaliers") initially did well in fighting against the Commons forces because the king's nephew had had some military experience in the Thirty Years' War on the Austrian side and raised a well-disciplined cavalry.

But the Commons ("Roundheads") had one great advantage from the start—the support of most of the London merchants and bankers, which meant deep pockets. If they could find a good general, the Commons were bound to win if they kept fighting long enough.

The necessary general who came forward in 1643 was an obscure member of the lower stratum of the gentry from East Anglia near Cambridge, Oliver Cromwell. He had no previous military experience or professional training whatsoever. Cromwell had broken into politics in the 1630s as a fanatical Puritan (something of a mystic in fact) and as the spokesman for the poor people of the east coast fenlands who were resisting land development, the draining of the fens that would deprive them of their wetlands and meager incomes.

Cromwell, with the Commons' approval, raised a New Model army of farmers and artisans, with very few gentry to serve as officers. Even the middle rank of officers were promoted from the troops. The army was well served by radical Puritan preachers and by "agitators," paid political commissars.

With this democratic army between 1643 and 1648 Cromwell fought two successful wars—first against the king and then against the Scots, who felt after Charles went down that England was falling into radical hands. Then Cromwell took some of his army to Ireland and carried out horrible massacres of Catholics in several towns.

In 1649 Cromwell was the military dictator ("lord protector") of England. He apportioned the country's civil administration among "majors-general," who did an excellent job. Aside from trying—and executing—the king for treason before a special high court when he still refused to accept parliamentary supremacy, the question was, What now?

Two solutions were proposed. One came from Thomas Hobbes, a political philosopher of hitherto royalist sympathies, in *Leviathan*, the first book of modern political theory. Hobbes was a judicial positivist, a political pragmatist, a follower of Marsilio of Padua, not a liberal, not a believer in combining ethics with law and politics. Power is power; the law is the law.

The holder of power makes law. Mankind is by nature violent and greedy, said Hobbes. Without the restraining power of the state, the life of man would be "nasty, brutish, and short." The state protects us from ourselves and we have no reserved rights against the power of the state. What this meant in the context of

1650 was that Cromwell had legitimacy to rule indefinitely as a military dictator, and to pass on power after his death by whatever means he chose, to another general or by setting up a new dynasty.

This was the right-wing realist solution. The other point of view came from the left, from a loose group called Levellers, who were well represented among the agitator-commissars in the army. They were petit bourgeois democrats. At a meeting of high and low army officers in a farmhouse in a little village called Putney in the winter of 1648, Cromwell listened intently to what the left had to say, and he undoubtedly read some of the many Leveller pamphlets that flooded the London streets.

The Levellers envisioned a democratic unicameral republic with the legislative franchise being extended to 60 percent (from less than 5 percent) of the adult male population. The executive should be responsible to the democratic legislature. There should be a written constitution and a bill of rights.

What the Levellers proposed was inspired by the middle-class republicanism that later influenced the American constitutional settlement of 1787–91. There was also a strand of social radicalism among these democrats. They wanted reform and codification of the common law. While the leader of the communist Diggers, Gerard Winstanley, speaking for the rural proletariat that had been dispossessed by the enclosures, simply denounced the common law as the instrument of property and tyranny, the Levellers' middle-class radicalism took a more complex attitude. They were people—small farmers, artisans, shopkeepers—who often had a bit of money and property, and they needed the protection of the law. But they wanted the law to be cheap and accessible. The law served them by being a principal means of conflict resolution, but it needed to be drastically reformed, said the Levellers, "that so [sic] the meanest commoner that can but read written hand in his own tongue may fully understand his own proceedings in the law."

The common law in the 1650s fell well short of this ideal. It was learned law, rife with French and Latin jargon, written down in old books, and expressed in a trail of difficult cases that required years of study to understand. Legal representation was expensive.

Therefore the Levellers' middle-class radicalism could take on an impatient air and sound a note of confrontation against the established order. One of the lower-ranked officers told Cromwell at Putney, "The poorest he that is in England has a life to live as the richest he."

We can speculate that if the Levellers had prevailed, the common law that would have emerged from their judicial reform would not have been merely less favorable to the affluent and more generous to those of modest circumstance. It would have been a highly politicized kind of law in which the traditional autonomy of the legal profession would have been erased by the authority of democratic legislators and commissars. From that day to this, the Levellers have been viewed through bifocal lenses, making them out to be alternatively benign progressives and radical revolutionaries. It is significant that the most detailed and enthusiastic treatments of Levellers' thought have come from the Oxford socialist don Christopher Hill.

It was probably because of this whiff of social revolution that Cromwell listened to his son-in-law, Henry Ireton, another high general, that the franchise must not be extended, because communist revolution could be next. Only those with a stake in society—that is, men of property—should vote. Reform of the law was given low priority by Cromwell's government.

The Putney debates were taken down stenographically but were not published; they were hidden away until 1885. Within two years of the Putney debates, Cromwell had gotten rid of both the king on the right and the Levellers on the left. He shot a few of the army agitator-commissars. Some of the Leveller leaders he exiled to imprisonment in the Channel Islands, which were Crown possessions but outside the writ of the common law.

Cromwell waited for his Calvinist God to tell him what to do about the future of the English constitution, but God chose to be mute.

Meanwhile Cromwell pursued a vigorous foreign and colonial policy. He took Jamaica, important for its slave-worked sugar plantations. He went to war against the equally devout Dutch Protestants in the interest of expanding English commercial capitalism. Cromwell admitted Jews into England for the first time since the reign of Edward I. Cromwell was a fanatical hater of Roman Catholics, but otherwise he was very tolerant in religion. Radical spiritual groups like the Baptists and Quakers flourished during his regime.

The lord protector made several efforts to establish an effective legislature that he could work with, but he never found one. His eruptions while dismissing what he regarded as uncooperative Commons became legendary.

To dismiss the Long Parliament's "Rump," or remnant, Cromwell burst into their chamber with an armed bodyguard and while his soldiers cocked their muskets, he shouted at the MPs: "You have sat here too long for the good that you have done. Begone, and let us have done with you. In the name of God, go!" They went.

Cromwell's words to the Long Parliament were quoted in the darkest day in British history in May 1940, by a Conservative MP seeking the resignation as prime minister of his own party leader, Neville Chamberlain. Chamberlain quit, Winston Churchill became prime minister, and humanity would ultimately be saved from the Nazis. Cromwell would have been delighted. Although Churchill came from the high aristocracy, the two men had similar personalities. On another occasion Cromwell exploded at a parliamentary group: "By the bowels of Christ, think that you are mistaken."

Not surprisingly the first modern biography of Cromwell was written in the nineteenth century by Thomas Carlyle, who believed that history was made by heroes. Also unsurprisingly, the best Cromwell biography, *God's Englishman* (1970), was written by a Marxist, Christopher Hill. Again, there are similarities between Cromwell and Lenin. They were bold, charismatic, ideologically fanatical men.

Even when he selected the MPs himself, Cromwell could not get together a group of legislators with whom he could work amicably. The problem was that he was on the far left wing in religion but relatively moderate in politics and social policy.

When Cromwell died in 1658, power passed—after momentary confusion—to another general, a sometime butcher. He immediately entered into negotiations with Charles I's son. The future Charles II was vegetating in penury on the Continent, but he turned out to be very tough in negotiations about the terms of restoring the monarchy. Aside from assuring the general of a dukedom, the only thing that could be agreed on was to turn the clock back to just before the Resolution of May 1642 and hope for the best.

Charles II came back to a wave of frenzied adulation, in no way deserved. But the long economic depression was waning at last. Prosperity had returned to country and town, and there was an overwhelming wish to cool down the political situation under the revived old monarchy and get on with private life.

The legal profession was in the forefront of hailing the Restoration of the Stuart monarchy in the person of devious, lazy, oversexed Charles II. Cromwell had been the lawyers' worst nightmare, as if Lenin had taken over New York City. His kind of government threatened the status of the lawyers and the continuation of the common law as they knew it. Fortunately he had not actually damaged the lawyers, but they wanted no further risk with a ruler like him. In response to the Levellers' demand for reform and codification of the common law, Cromwell had appointed a commission, dominated by lawyers, to look into the situation. After four years of desultory discussion, the commission disbanded without even rendering a final report.

Here again Cromwell did not know what he really wanted. If he had wanted to reform the common law, he would have done so, thoroughly and quickly. The lawyers knew that, and they did not want another hazard like that. The Cromwellian interlude thoroughly deradicalized the legal profession. The barristers and solicitors turned so far away from Coke that only one printing of Coke's *Institutes* was made after the Restoration, and it was in fact not reprinted again until the 1980s.

The Restoration left most problems unresolved, including the precise meaning of royal prerogatives, the relationship between king and Parliament, and how the king could gain a steady income for his government (Charles II resorted to taking secret handouts from the French king).

Some issues were settled. Star Chamber stayed dead. Chancery was restored. The vestiges of feudal wardship were extinguished. A few of the ad hoc judges who had condemned Charles I were hunted down and executed, but otherwise there were no reprisals. Cromwell's secretary, the poet John Milton ("Cromwell, thou chief of men. . . .") went home peacefully. Now blind, he dictated an almost endless epic poem, called (appropriately for the time) *Paradise Lost*, to his daughters.

The foremost consequence of the Restoration was that the ramshackle, incoherent Church of England would continue to be so. It would include both Protestants and Catholics (without the pope, of course) and the theology, ritual, and artwork of one local Anglican church could differ markedly from those to be found in one a few miles away. There would be (and still is) both a High Church (Anglo-Catholic) and a Low Church (Protestant) wing to the established church. Charles II was secretly a Roman Catholic; why should he care?

A consequence of the Cromwellian dictatorship and its Puritan blue laws (no theater, no football on Sunday, whitewashing over religious frescoes, smashing stained-glass windows) was a national majority's popular revulsion against Protestant separatists, now called Dissenters.

By the parliamentary Test Acts of the late 1660s, both the Dissenters and Roman Catholic "recusants" were deprived of political rights and lost some civil rights. You now had to be a member of the Church of England not only to vote or stand for Parliament, but to attend the universities or to be admitted to the Inns of Court and the bar as well.

As far as the Dissenters (about 20 percent of the population) were concerned, this invasion of political and civil rights, the way it worked for them in the eighteenth century, was not as severe as originally prescribed or intended. Membership in the Church of England meant only that you had to take communion there once a year. Many upper-middle-class Dissenters used "occasional conformity" in this nominal way to participate in politics, attend universities, and enter the legal profession. The Dissenters also founded their own colleges ("academies"), which in the mid-eighteenth century offered better education than the universities did. The Test Acts were abolished at the end of the 1820s. Full citizenship was not granted to the very small Jewish minority until the 1850s.

As in the case of the American Civil War for U.S. historians, British historians never cease to write at great length about the English Civil War, especially its causes. When all is said, the cause was simple: Charles I's government was both weak and unlucky. The reason why revolutions occur in any society in transition from medieval to modern conditions—France, Russia, China, Cuba, Iran—is that the government is both weak and unlucky.

Revolutions will not occur if the government is self-confident and tough, if it is willing physically to repress the opposition. But when it gets distracted by a budget crisis, a foreign war, a spiritual upheaval—or a combination of these—and becomes hesitant and freezes in place, then the opposition which has been around for a long time and is by no means invincible walks in and takes over. It is always thus, whether it is London in 1641, Paris in 1790, St. Petersburg in 1917, or more recently Beijing, Havana, or Teheran.

What is distinctive about the English Revolution is that it was so dramatically successful in a military sense and accomplished so little, in the long run, politically. Yet it brought to power Cromwell, England's greatest leader before Winston Churchill. It gave a boost to imperialism and commercial capitalism. It helped the proliferation of radical Protestant sects.

Its greatest consequence, however, was a negative one. It taught a majority of the English people to be conservative, to hold on somehow to their tattered monarchy, to their divided Church of England, and to their unreformed medieval common law.

Reluctantly in 1689 a revived and expanded aristocracy and an again prosperous gentry, as well as the great merchants, had to face once more and begin to resolve the problem of where supremacy actually lay in the constitution. Charles II, in spite of spawning an endless series of bastards, had no legitimate issue, and the Crown in 1685 passed to his Roman Catholic brother, James II, in spite of abortive efforts by political activists in the upper classes to prevent it. Three years later James suspended the deprivation of political and civil rights under the Test Acts to help the Catholic minority. He claimed he had the power of royal prerogative to suspend the laws.

The result was the Glorious (that is, peaceful) Revolution of 1689. After an almost unanimous rising of the landed classes against James, he fled the country, and his Protestant daughter Mary and her husband, the Dutch prince William of Orange, were summoned to take the throne.

Parliament passed the Bill (or Declaration) of Rights, which prohibited the monarch from suspending the laws by his own will and thereby confirmed the Resolution of the Commons of May 1642, placing sovereignty in England firmly in Parliament. The Declaration of Rights also prohibited a Roman Catholic from ever again sitting on the throne, a provision that remarkably is still in effect, although a good 20 percent of the population of England—due to Irish immigration, conversions, and natural increase—is now Roman Catholic.

The Bill of Rights of 1689 was drawn up by a coalition of conservative gentry. Gone were the days of enthusiasm among this kind of people, who sat in the Commons, for Puritan ideas of liberty as reflective of some mystical inner light. The authors of the Bill of Rights considered themselves Protestants, but they were Low Church, moderate Protestants of the Church of England, which for them was more an integrative, national social institution than a religious one.

Whereas in the age of Coke, Puritan fervor and born-again Christianity's idea of inner-light liberty were conjoined to the liberties of the House of Commons as the bulwark of the liberties of Englishmen, and due process of the common law was equivalent to liberty, now only the latter two (Commons and common law) of the threefold intertwined ideas of liberty of the 1630s were meaningful to the moderate, cautious landlords who controlled the House of Commons.

The mind-set of the Parliament of 1689, therefore, that set down the rights of Englishmen was cautious, conservative, concerned prosaically to prevent the state from bothering them. Most of the rights it stipulated were set down in negative fashion. The key word was "illegal," expecting the common law to protect the rights of citizens. The theoretical assumption was that Parliament could at any time alter the content of legality.

It was illegal for the Crown to levy a tax without consent of Parliament; illegal to prosecute someone for petitioning the king, said the Bill of Rights; illegal for the Crown to raise or keep a standing army in peacetime without consent of Parliament; "excessive bail ought not to be required, nor excessive fines imposed, nor cruel and unusual punishments inflicted" (words repeated wholesale in the American Bill of Rights of 1791).

To these were added in a more positive vein the right of

Protestants to bear arms (Catholics might use arms for rebellion or terrorism); the notion that "election of members of Parliament ought to be free" (that is, without government interference); and freedom of speech for MPs.

Juries should be "duly impanelled" (in other words, paneling of juries ought not to be manipulated by the Crown or the bench in their favor). But juries in cases of high treason should consist of "freeholders"; such importanct cases should be tried by blue-ribbon juries of propertied gentry.

To these stipulations in the Bill of Rights were added, as part of the Glorious Revolution's idea of liberty, the decision in *Bushell's Case* of 1670 that juries cannot be punished for nullification of the law; and the Habeas Corpus Act of 1679, by which the medieval writ of habeas corpus changed from being a privileged writ of grace to a writ of course. This meant in practice that anyone held in jail without indictment at the nearest court session (or without a detailed explanation by prosecutors to the bench of the special reason why not) had an automatic right to be brought before the judges and freed. Indict and try as soon as reasonably possible, or release. Habeas corpus meant the right to an early indictment and a speedy trial—so dramatically different from Roman law.

This set of rights aimed not to make men better or bring them closer to God. It simply meant that, as far as possible in a civil society, citizens had a right to be left alone by the government as long as they observed the laws and paid their taxes. In the 1650s under Oliver Cromwell there had been much talk of a New Jerusalem, of a "City on the Hill." Such idealism had passed completely out of political life and would not be revived until modern socialist movements expounded secular versions of it.

The men of 1689 were affluent property holders who wanted as little government as possible and the embedding of government within the due process of the common law to assure that quietude.

Since the late fourteenth century, England had gone through a series of political upheavals, culminating in the half century of revolution between 1642 and 1689. In 1714 instability threatened again when the Protestant (hence politically legitimate) line of the Stuart dynasty died out and the Stuarts' Hanoverian cousins were brought over from Germany to occupy the throne.

England was by now for the first time since the early fifteenth century a great European power, competing with France for hegemony in Western Europe. England was also now a great commercial and colonial power, contending with the French for rule over eastern North America. Constitutional specification and political settlement had to be fully worked out to achieve the stability suitable for a great international power.

The Glorious Revolution of 1689 and peaceful accession of the Hanoverian dynasty (known since 1914 as the Windsors, and still on the throne) were accompanied by five other developments that were the ingredients of the necessary political settlement.

First, there was the theory of legitimate revolution propounded by the philosopher John Locke in his *Second Treatise on Civil Government* in 1690. Against Hobbes's *Leviathan*, Locke argued that the entry into civil society from a state of nature did not mean the surrender of all rights of individuals to the state. On the contrary, everyone still retained natural rights to life, liberty, and the accumulation and enjoyment of property.

Hobbes took a pessimistic view of humanity as violent, vicious, and uncooperative, bad personality traits that were natural and could not be eliminated but could only be necessarily repressed by the authoritarian state. Against Hobbes, Locke propounded a psychological view that is the bedrock of modern progressive liberalism. Man's psyche at birth is a *tabula rasa*, a clean slate. The personality and behavior patterns that develop in each individual case depend on environment, education, and benign experience.

Men and women can be made good, responsible, cooperative citizens by favorable ambience and treatment. This auspicious prognosis for human nature, arising from good nurture, means a liberal state and civil society is possible, indeed necessary, to provide the suitable environment for personal development.

From the point of view of legal history, Locke's theory is a peculiar combination of ingredients from both common-law and Roman-law traditions. From common law came the emphasis on individual liberty and on the right to accumulate and enjoy property. From Roman law, with help from the Thomistic philosophical tradition—which had been reaffirmed in England around 1600 by the Anglican theologian Richard Hooker—came the principle that the needs of social order never overruled an inherent set of natural rights belonging to an individual and discoverable by exercise of reason.

In practice Locke knew the theoretical outcome that he wanted and cleverly combined ingredients from the common-law tradition on the one side and the Roman-law and Thomistic tradition on the other, the whole amalgam buttressed by his progressive psychology.

That Bracton, the founder of judicial liberalism, was himself drawing on both the procedural context of the common law and Thomistic philosophy made Locke's theory more persuasive and capable of being seen as within mainline legalistic tradition. Locke's theory is forward looking. It provides an intellectual base not only for judicial liberalism and recognition of natural rights but also for the later activist welfare state of modern times.

The second ingredient for the political settlement during the reigns of the first two Hanoverians, George I and II (1714–60), was cabinet government, a creation of the Whigs. The Whig political party was in power from 1721 to 1760. The party was led by a group of billionaire aristocrats who were especially interested in controlling nominated (or "pocket") boroughs, generating a nucleus of Commons seats and in real estate development in the West End of London, where Whig family names like Bedford and Russell are still prominent on street signs.

Alongside these high-living, hard-drinking, sexually active, religiously skeptical aristocrats, the backbone of the Whig Party was the wealthier and more sophisticated stratum of the gentry, prominent civil servants dependent on the Whig grandees for public office and private patronage, and merchants in the expanding international trade. They placed leadership and power in the hands of Sir Robert Walpole, who operated as the first modern prime minister.

Walpole devised the system of cabinet government, which bridged the king's ministry with leadership of the House of Commons. Under this system the king had to choose his ministers from the majority party in the House of Commons if he wanted his budget to be passed and his policies to be implemented.

In practice today the sovereign recognizes the leader of the majority party as the prime minister, who then forms a cabinet of ministers from among his own party (in Walpole's time there were only six ministers). The prime minister and the other cabinet ministers have to kiss the sovereign's hand—that is, become privy councillors—but it is the cabinet rather than the privy council that now runs the government. The privy council has become a mostly honorific body.

Centuries-old conflicts between executive and legislature were thus resolved by a symbiotic union of the former and latter. This means that when the ruling party loses its majority in a general election, the prime minister has to resign immediately and the sovereign chooses as the next prime minister the leader of the new majority party. The sovereign only has some freedom of choice when there is no majority party and the cabinet is made up of a coalition of parties.

George III in the late eighteenth century tried to break this system by boldly choosing a prime minister first and then letting him, by use of royal patronage and declaration of policy principles, find a majority in the House of Commons. This sometimes worked for Farmer George, as he was called, but only because by then the billionaire Whig aristocrats no longer had such firm control over the MPs as they had in the age of Walpole. The king's nineteenth-century successors did not emulate his bold moves and stuck with prime ministers who they knew beforehand had the confidence of the Commons.

When the drafters of the American Constitution met in a Philadelphia tavern during a heat wave in 1787, they chose not to follow the new English cabinet system and instead opted for the old separation of powers between the executive and legislative branches, so that deadlock was possible, in that the executive could come from a different party than the majority in one or both houses of Congress.

This American rejection of cabinet government has been variously explained: that the drafters did not realize that party bonds would become so strong in the new Republic; that they were influenced by a prestigious French theorist who idiosyncratically favored separation of powers. But the reason seems to be simply that Walpole's cabinet system made for a very strong executive as long as it controlled the majority of the Commons, and such an executive was unacceptable to the American states, which disliked the idea of a strong federal executive.

The third foundation for political stability was the way Walpole and his colleagues went about solving the age-old budgetary problems of the Crown. These had occurred mainly in wartime, when extraordinary expenditures were immediately necessary. With the help of the quasi-public Bank of England, Walpole's governments took loans and sold bonds guaranteed by the Bank to provide immediate funds for the Crown against future income.

This national-debt approach was also used for ordinary income and expenditure. Each year the government presented to Parliament estimates of its income and expenditures and got this budget approved. If income did not quite match the approved level of expenditure, the government could again dip into the national debt, borrow with the help of the Bank of England against the future.

The system worked well, up to a point. But when George III's ministers demanded that the American colonists help to pay the debt accumulated in colonial wars against the French in North America, reducing the tax burden on the home-country gentry, but would not give the colonists representation in Commons, the American Revolution was precipitated. When Winston Churchill's World War II government ran up the national debt to stratospheric levels and then the succeeding postwar Labour government introduced the extremely generous welfare state, the British government in effect went bankrupt, even with American aid, and had to abandon in a couple of decades most of the Empire that had taken two centuries of blood and toil to create. There was therefore from 1763 to 1965 a dialectical relationship between the elasticity of taxes to service the national debt and the feasibility of empire.

Walpole's political system incorporated what had been decided by a court case and a resolution of the House of Commons in 1710, that not only should any money bill originate in the Commons but that the Lords could only pass it or vote down, not amend it. In practice this meant that the Commons decided money matters and the Lords accepted the Common's decisions on taxes and expenditures.

When in 1911 the Lords rejected a money bill on the grounds that it sneakingly incorporated legislation inaugurating the welfare state, a constitutional crisis was caused, resulting in the effective demotion of the Lords to little more than a debating society. It could only hold up Commons legislation of any kind for two years and never reject money bills at all. In the late 1940s the Lords lost even this vestige of legislative power.

Today the House of Lords is known mainly as the highest appeals court in England, but this function is exercised by a panel of professional judges given non-inheritable lordships for life, not by a hereditary aristocracy. However, the latter are too busy working in advertising or real estate development to care.

A fourth source of political and social stability in the first half of the eighteenth century was the sacring, or glorification, of property—the identification of real estate with, as Locke had said, life and liberty. But more than this abstract proposition, the sacring of property for the aristocracy, gentry, and mercantile and banking groups involved an emotional and aesthetic association of personal well-being and divine order with lands and houses.

This manic, almost erotic regard for real estate fueled the second enclosure movement of the eighteenth century, which featured the dispossession of peasantry from their ancestral farms by private parliamentary bills and withdrawal of the courts from protection of the peasants. The sacring of property also churned the frenetic and elaborate development—principally by aristocratic families who inherited or obtained newly vacant fields there—of the West End of London into the fashionable district it still is.

"The Good Old Cause" of the ascendant Whig Party was grounded in the shaping of a stable political settlement that made possible real estate speculation and development untrammeled by any traditional reservation or ideological, environmental, or ethical concerns. This meant the forgetting alike of Cromwellian revolution and radical Puritan communalism on the one side and royal paternalism and Anglo-Catholic retromedieval idealism on the other.

The cultivation of property's opportunities for wealth, power, and creative managerial and business activity required the skilled and energetic services of legions of barristers and solicitors. The complex shadows of medieval land law were thoroughly reviewed and its somewhat musty instruments put to hyperactive use. Marriage settlements and probate law were drawn up as cognate bastions of the judicial shaping of property development.

The central support role of the legal profession not only to rural enclosures but also to the upscale urbanization of West End

London resembled closely the service of Wall Street lawyers to corporate takeovers and mergers in the New York City of the 1980s.

The pursuit of property and its encasement within the cage of morally unchallengeable real estate law contributed mightily to political stability in eighteenth-century England by focusing the energy of the propertied classes on material pursuits—part of which was the architectural beautification of London with imposing houses, spacious squares and parks, and paved streets.

The opportunity for legal work in connection with London's real estate development was a boon to the legal profession and made it even more ideologically conservative, narrowly engaged, materialistic, and politically conformist or inert.

Yet there were those in this archconservative legal profession who were marginally sensitive to further definition of civil rights. In the 1760s and early 1770s the chief justices of the King's Bench, Lord Camden and Lord Mansfield, rendered two landmark decisions in this judicial field.

Camden held in *Entick* v. *Carrington* (1765) that not only can government agents not engage in search and seizure within a private domicile without the previous obtaining of a court warrant on showing of probable cause for the search, but also that the state agents could individually be sued for trespass. Camden's decision is the basis for the Fourth Amendment to the American Constitution.

Mansfield's decision in *Somerset's Case* (1772) was that a black slave imported into England as a personal servant was automatically emancipated since the common law in England did not recognize the status of chattel slavery.

These famous civil rights decisions should not be excessively glorified, however. Mansfield's manumission of slaves in England dealt with a minuscule population. Although the common law also ran in Virginia and Jamaica, where there were many thousands of black slaves, Mansfield did not apply his liberating doctrine there, where it would have had momentous consequences. (Slavery was abolished in the British Empire by Act of Parliament in 1833, and this did have a devastating impact on the sugar plantations of the West Indies.)

Similarly Camden's landmark decision on search and seizure may well have been politically motivated—to embarrass government ministers he didn't like.

What counted with the bench and the bar of the eighteenth century was property, not liberty—property subsumed liberty. This was the juristic essence of the Whig Good Old Cause. It was a dominant political culture that powerfully contributed to the wealth and status of the legal profession.

The fifth and final aspect of the political settlement of mid-eighteenth-century England was a legal theory that integrated the common law with the modified political system and placed both the judicial and political systems in a historical perspective that gave moral sanction to the Whig settlement and to England's rise to world power and imperial hegemony.

This was the work of William Blackstone. Hitherto an obscure lawyer and political writer for the Whig Party, he was rewarded with a professorship of law at Oxford University in a patronage appointment. His lectures integrating law, politics, and history were popular with the students because of their humanistic clarity, and he published them in the early 1760s as his *Commentaries* on English law.

Blackstone was then further rewarded with a state pension and a seat in the Commons. He sat through the debates leading to the American Revolution and never said a word. Another MP backbencher, at the same time, was Edward Gibbon, author of *The Decline and Fall of the Roman Empire*, still regarded, as Blackstone's *Commentaries* are not, as a great work of historical literature. Gibbon also sat through the debates on the American Revolution and never spoke. Blackstone's and Gibbon's silence may indicate how important the debate on American Revolution appeared to intellectuals among the gentry in the 1760s and 1770s.

Blackstone's legal history of England, which takes up close to half of his four-volume *Commentaries*, owes much for its central paradigm to the antiquaries and radical Leveller polemicists of seventeenth-century England. They had popularized the "Norman myth," by which Anglo-Saxon society was a free one that was subverted by Norman French lordship.

Yet English freedom endured in the common law. The first clear statement of this paradigm of English constitutional history appears to have been made by Selden in the 1630s. He argued that while "the English Empire" was overthrown at the Norman Conquest, the new laws that became the common law "take their denomination from the English rather than the Normans."

Over the centuries government, through the instrumentality of the law, as described in detail by Blackstone, worked its way to a compromise between freedom and authority, achieving the political stability and judicial protection of liberty and property enjoyed by Englishmen in the mid-eighteenth century. In Blackstone's view this was a historically grounded, rationally commendable, and morally defensible legal and political system appropriate for a great power and a free people.

There is an echo in Blackstone of Coke's view of the development of the law, but worked out not only in much greater detail but also delicately, subtly, and with a certain kind of enlightenment, charm, and good humor.

Blackstone was genuinely a historian, with a narrative paradigm easily understood by the general reader. In that regard he was much more of a historian than Coke, for whom legal history was simply law that happened in the past. Similarly, Blackstone's work was a big advance on that of Sir Matthew Hale, a justice of Common Pleas under Cromwell, and chief justice of the King's Bench in the 1660s. Hale's two-volume history of the pleas of the Crown was in the Coke mode of legal history as law that happened in the past, immensely learned but lacking a general narrative paradigm. Blackstone, like his contemporary Gibbon, was a modern historical writer and thinker. He had internalized vast learning but communicated it in a way that was easily accessible and indeed pleasurable to the common educated reader.

Chief Justice Hale did have one positive impact on Blackstone. This was in Hale's style of writing about law, his effort to organize and systematize what he had to say about the pleas of the Crown. Hale was an educated jurist with a good knowledge of Roman law and French jurisprudence. He thought the common law, while maintaining its intrinsic and separate character, should aim at similar clear and orderly understanding and exposition. Hale was much more systematic, much more under control as a writer than was Coke.

It might be said that Coke represented the late Renaissance, with its love of deep learning and preciousness of detail. Hale represents the Newtonian era, the beginning of the Enlightenment, with its desire for clarity and order. This was the style of writing that Blackstone aimed at, and he also pursued the Enlightenment aim of communicating to the educated public at large and not just professional lawyers and students.

Legal history was for Blackstone a form of literature, transcending antiquarianism. No wonder his *Commentaries* were a huge and enduring publishing success. He was a historical structuralist who—like the German philosopher Hegel in the early nineteenth century—believed that a historical structure evolved dialectically over time (in this case through the polarity of Anglo-Saxon freedom and Norman French lordship) to result in a system that accorded with the highest principles of reason.

With Blackstone an intellectual trend that had been inaugurated in the Renaissance came to historical cognition. This may be termed a developmental sense, a realization that the law had significantly changed over time, that the medieval world exhibited differences from the modern one. Some historians think that it was the study of the law that drove this historicizing recognition. Blackstone may not have fully perceived the structural differences between the medieval world and that of his day, but he realized it sufficiently to make him the first modern historian of the common law.

From Cicero and the classical culture that was the basis of the secondary-school curriculum, Blackstone imbibed the assumption that the common law was surrounded by the penumbra of ethical standards and took on the sanction of morality determinable by rational understanding. So the common law and parliamentary and cabinet government conformed to and were shaped by history, ethics, and reason.

Blackstone's paradigm of common-law history—which was adopted and refined by Stubbs in his *Constitutional History of England* in the 1860s, still used as a history textbook at Cambridge and Harvard universities in the 1950s—provided the kind of historical theory that all imperialist powers require.

To justify their domination of other peoples, preferably overseas ones of different ethnicity, language, and religion, imperial cultures have to view their own countries' history as settled, as having resolved internal problems and ended contradictions, as having achieved a state of rational conclusion. This gives the imperial society the self-image of peace, security, and success needed to impose itself justifiably on other peoples and cultures, which putatively have not resolved their inner conflicts and mitigated their polarities. The imperial power will now take over and do just that for them.

This "white man's burden," as it was called at the end of the Victorian era, is grounded for the imperial power in a vision of the ending, the rational conclusion, of national history. Blackstone's history of the common law gave ideological and moral grounding to Britain's imperial ascent.

Similarly, the consensus view of American history propounded at Harvard and Columbia Universities in the 1940s made possible the American Cold War and Vietnam commitments. Blackstone prepared the way for great imperialists like Warren Hastings in India and Sir Guy Carleton (Lord Dorchester) in Canada. Samuel Eliot Morison, Allan Nevins, and Richard Hofstadter—the first a Harvard Brahmin and the latter two Columbia paragons—did the same for the American venture in Vietnam.

There was plenty of dissent in Blackstone's day from his optimistic view of the common law. The poet and critic Oliver Goldsmith said that the common law was rich man's law foisted on the poor. This was an obvious dissent. A more comprehensive attack was to follow. Twenty years after Blackstone published his *Commentaries*, his paradigm of legal history came under strenuous attack from utilitarian social philosopher, penal and judicial reformer, and radical polemicist Jeremy Bentham. He denounced Blackstone's work as "nonsense on stilts." It was, held Bentham, conservative mumbo-jumbo designed to defend a chaotic and archaic judicial system that was actually cruel, dysfunctional in many respects, uncodified, and harshly protective of the interests of the landed classes. A somewhat similar view of Blackstone was presented in *The Mysterious Science of the Law* (1941) by the young Daniel Boorstin, later famous as a cultural historian and as a Librarian of Congress.

Bentham was England's contribution to the ranks of the *philosophes*, those outspoken intellectuals and publicists who in the 1770s and 1780s put the old royal and aristocratic regimes in the transatlantic world to the test of reason and science, and found them wanting. Voltaire, the master French *philosophe*, himself visited England and distastefully dismissed it as a hopeless country of "a thousand religions and one sauce." Bentham had a stronger stomach.

He was influenced not so much by Voltaire and the French Enlightenment as by a middle-class disdain for aristocratic privilege and reckless consumption. Like his near-contemporary, the

Italian philosopher Cesare Beccaria (1738–94), subjecting the whole judicial and political system encased in the common law to the standard of "the greatest happiness of the greatest number," Bentham was particularly offended by the criminal justice system of the old regime as an inefficient combination of cruelty and laxity.

Bentham gained support from some upper-middle-class people who were affected by the new sensibility that would blossom into the romanticism of the early nineteenth century. But Bentham himself was a management theorist, not a new-wave sentimentalist. What judicial system was appropriate for the modern state? How could the old common law be made both more effective and more humane and equitable? These were the crucial issues as far as he was concerned, and they are still highly provocative ones for bar associations and law schools.

The bottom line was that Bentham saw in the common law neither the reserved laws of nature nor the historical wisdom of the ages, but a ramshackle, cumbersome set of practices that smacked of privilege, chaos, and obsolescence.

Bentham never held political office, but he gathered around him a group of brilliant disciples, one of whom, Sir Robert Peel, became prime minister. Among the Benthamites (also called the Utilitarians, the philosophical radicals) were the attorney and legal reformer Henry Brougham, the environmental engineer and public health official Edwin Chadwick, and the philosopher and economist John Stuart Mill. Bentham was also a leading founder of the University of London, aiming to make higher learning accessible to the middle class.

Bentham's impact on nineteenth-century England has been related many times, perhaps most persuasively by the French historian Elie Halevy in the 1920s.

Bentham wanted the whole common-law system to be scrapped in favor of a new system based on pragmatic reason and democratic needs, and taking accessible codified form. It is indicative of

American visceral conservatism that no prominent legal thinker in the history of the United States has ever come close to Bentham's program for dismantling and replacing the common law—certainly not such august judicial figures, with liberal reputations, as Oliver Wendell Holmes, Jr., and Louis D. Brandeis.

Between 1820 and 1860 the Benthamites carried out significant law reform, as they did in several other areas: the first publicly funded English urban police system; abolition of entails (but not of the strict settlement in marriages, which achieved much the same purpose); the drastic diminution of the Black Acts and extensive replacement of capital punishment and transportation in indentured servitude with prison sentences in penitentiaries (Bentham himself designed some of the early ones), which were supposed to reform criminals and return them to society; granting of full civil rights to Dissenters, Roman Catholics, and Jews; divorce actions in the courts on grounds of adultery; regulation of working conditions in mines and factories and of urban environments (particularly sanitation).

But the core of the judicial system that Blackstone believed represented the residue of history, reason, and ethics remained. The common law that was in place in 1760 was still 95 percent in place in 1860. Bentham's pet project, codification of the law, was not begun, even by cabinets that included some Benthamite ministers. The common lawyers remained a privileged and highly autonomous caste. Civil actions were beyond the income of eighty percent of the population. There was no effective legal aid for the indigent in English criminal trials until the Labour government of the mid-twentieth century.

The Benthamite reformers were able to modify Blackstone's legal culture at the margins, but they were unable to strike it from its historical and social foundations. The opportunity to do that was forgone in the revolutionary times of the 1650s and never came back.

Nor would subsequent waves of English legal reform (1873–1910;

since 1945) make more than marginal improvements. In the 1970s and 1980s former Chief Justice Lord Denning published a series of books extolling the common law in enthusiastic Blackstonian tones. Denning's books were very popular.

If he were brought back today, Blackstone would not be at all surprised by the common law in either Britain or the United States. He would applaud it. He never said that the common law was perfect, only that it was very good, a system filtered through history and conforming to reason. He did not deny that there was room for judicial improvement. For instance, he indicated his dislike of the Black Acts, the harsh criminal laws of his day. Nonetheless, Blackstone thought the core of the common law— land tenure, liability, probate, the jury, the adversarial system of pleading—was marvelous. So do most barristers in London and lawyers in New York today.

Blackstone's optimistic view of the common law included the expectation that in time the legal system's imperfections would be corrected. He sensed a very important character of the common law, that it was *common*; it had been since the thirteenth century national law. This meant that its critics had to engage in debate about reforming law by thinking of judicial changes in terms of the whole country. They had to focus on national institutions and propose reforms that operated at an ecumenic level. The common law thus intellectually co-opted its critics and challenged them to offer solutions of a general nature.

In Blackstone's day a democratic political movement was already important in England. It failed to achieve institutional change, but perpetuated by middle-class radicals like Bentham and by working-class radicalism as well, it became effective in the 1830s and 1840s. The impact of the common law is one way of explaining why England succeeded in making the modernizing transition to democracy without revolution. This situation justified Blackstone's faith in the benign character of the common law.

The law, like any other cultural facet, is affected by the social and cultural ambience in which it operates. For the peasantry dispossessed by the enclosure movement, and the urban as well as rural proletariat menaced by the Black Acts, the age of Blackstone did not offer a generous environment. But for someone of Blackstone's gentry status, it was a time of enhanced civility and comfort, and this influenced his optimistic view of the common law.

Certainly we are what we eat and drink, and in regard to drink, the eighteenth century offered—in addition to the new menace of cheap gin—the novel amenity of stimulating beverages that were hot and nonalcoholic. It was the age when drinking coffee and tea became central to the English diet. Unlike Glanville, Bracton, and probably Coke, Blackstone did not have to begin the day with beer.

By the late eighteenth century, tea was sought by the working class as well as the wealthy people; coffee remained a rich man's drink, and this distinction endured well into the twentieth century. Tea was so much in demand and consequently so expensive that the poor and those of modest means had for another century to satisfy themselves with reboiled tea leaves. Only someone of Blackstone's class or higher could enjoy the full fragrance of fresh Indian or Chinese tea.

By Blackstone's day as well, the smoking of tobacco—in a relatively healthy manner through long-stemmed clay pipes—had also become central to gentry life. Here was a narcotic to soothe away anxiety about lawsuits and also help calm the toothaches that had become common with the decay of English teeth from the remorseless ingesting of West Indian sugar.

There has been a spate of books in recent years trying to communicate a sense of the general pattern of eighteenth-century English history. Was it a dark or a light time? One book, by John

Brewer, is called *An Ungovernable People*. Another, by Paul Langford, is in the New Oxford History of England series, and therefore bears the stamp of establishmentarian legitimacy and will be closely studied by a generation of British school and college students. It is called *A Polite and Commercial People*, a quote in fact from Blackstone. The titles to the fine books by Brewer and Langford indicate the complexity of eighteenth-century English history and the different perspectives by which this world—which was creating empire and an industrial society and moving by fits and starts to modern democracy—can be perceived.

Langford stresses the bourgeoisifaction and commercialization of eighteenth-century England, something downplayed by historians in the 1950s, who, under the influence of the central European expatriate Lewis B. Namier, focused on the dominance in government and society of the Whig aristocracy and their machine politicians, like Walpole. In 1985 Jonathan Clark gained attention with a book contending that the burden of eighteenth-century English history lay with the monarchy, aristocracy, and especially the Church of England, a view well within the Namier conservative tradition. But Langford's book and its enthusiastic reception in the 1990s seems to signal a major historiographical shift in the general interpretation of eighteenth-entury England. Now the turn seems to be toward viewing the aristocratic mold as eroding in the mid-eighteenth century and being replaced by the middle-class ventures and values of an enterprise culture—a point of view actually suggested by the great Victorian historian of the eighteenth century, W. H. Lecky, whom Namier and his disciples despised.

In a developing middle-class and commercial society, the common law perpetuated a strong institutional, operational, and intellectual legacy from an earlier aristocratic world. The failure to reform the common law, let alone displace it, during the revolutionary movement of the mid-seventeenth century, meant that English society and economy would move into the modern world within a judicial structure founded in the temperament and discourse of the medieval landed classes and hence substantially conservative and restraining in its impact.

As England moved toward experiencing its first modern economy between 1770 and 1830, the impress of the old common law contributed to stability and social harmony. This was an important factor in England's ability to modernize without the traumas that occurred in other European countries, such as France and Russia.

The framework of the legal system, the idea and practice of due process, the law of property, and the high degree of autonomy of the legal profession and its independence from governmental dictates all shaped the preexisting public culture that made possible the growth of English commercial, industrial, and financial capitalism with a relatively moderate degree of social conflict and political strain.

Even though the enervating consequences of the two world wars negatively affected Britain's economy, exhausted its people for two generations, and made it fiscally impossible to maintain the empire while pursuing a commitment to the welfare state, London itself is still an immensely creative and beautiful metropolis and the City, its financial center, continues to thrive as a focus of international enterprise. London still exhibits characteristic English civility and amenity.

The law centers are still in Westminster, as they have been since the twelfth century, and still play a role, although a diminished one compared to the age of Blackstone, in sustaining the English economy and society.

17
American Lawyers and the Common Law

BETWEEN 1300 AND 1750 lawyers were the most important professional group in English society, and the common law was the structural framework for both economy and politics. This privileged position for lawyers and the common law began to wane in England in the late eighteenth century and certainly was no longer true after the passing of the great Reform Bill of 1832. Industrialists, bankers, politicians, and for a time colonial proconsuls were now the dynamic groups in English society. The importance of lawyers and the law declined.

Many accounts of the discourse of the American Revolution, most thoroughly that of John Philip Reid, have revealed how extensively the political ideas derived from English judicial liberalism were drawn on by the angry colonists in the late 1760s and 1770s. The potential conflict between the idea of the rule of law and due process on the one side, and the principle of parliamentary sovereignty on the other, was brought to the fore and never resolved by the Declaratory Act of 1766, which asserted the British Parliament's power to "bind" the colonies on all matters whatsoever. With the Americans already numbering one-third the population of the home country and containing a significant number of minorities and religious radicals, these were fighting words.

In the second British Empire of the nineteenth century, the same kind of constitutional conflicts emerged, beginning with abortive rebellions in Canada in 1837 and culminating in the miserable Boer War of 1899–1902 in South Africa and the Indian liberation movement of the 1930s. The issue that was broached in 1766 was never settled judicially but only superseded by piecemeal relinquishing of parliamentary sovereignty over the Empire between the 1850s and the 1960s.

After the American Revolution the activist torch of the common law was passed from England to the United States. Two eras, that of Marshall's chief justiceship on the Supreme Court in the first third of the nineteenth century, and the New Deal of the 1930s and its successor in the postwar civil rights period, put the legal profession into the forefront of American life just as contemporarily the importance of lawyers and law eroded in England from their peak in the seventeenth century.

The John Marshall era (1800–35) and the New Deal and civil rights era (1937–73), the age of federalism in the first instance and liberal nationalism in the second, augmented the role of lawyers and the common law in American life, which was already generally at a high level.

This was stressed by the first great work of political sociology about the United States, Alexis de Tocqueville's *Democracy in America*, published in the 1830s. Tocqueville commented that the United States was an extraordinarily litigious society, and that "scarcely any political question arises in the United States that is not resolved sooner or later into a judicial question." Tocqueville provocatively remarked of the American legal profession: "The lawyers of the United States form a part which . . . acts upon the country imperceptibly, but finally fashions it to suit its own interests."

Tocqueville's prescient comment encapsulates a good deal of American history. *The History of American Law* by Stanford Law School's Lawrence Friedman (1985) is mostly a fascinating account of the shaping of America by land lawyers and railroad attorneys in the nineteenth century. The civil rights revolution of the 1950s and 1960s was made possible by U.S. Supreme Court decisions much earlier, and by more than congressional legislation. The prohibition against state governments preventing abortion on choice was effected by the Supreme Court's *Roe* v. *Wade* (1973) decision, which would never have been possible by means of congressional legislation.

The surrender of the Supreme Court justices to threats from President Roosevelt in 1937, and the Court's acceptance of the doctrine that federal jurisdiction over interstate commerce meant that the federal government could legislate to regulate business, protect labor unions, and provide welfare to the poor, opened the way for the modern regulatory and welfare state.

Conversely when the Supreme Court was unable to resolve the slavery issue amicably—its *Dred Scott* v. *Sanford* decision of 1857 was a terrible dud—the country had to resort to civil war to solve the slavery question and make the emancipating Thirteenth and Fourteenth amendments (1863, 1868) possible.

The leaders of the American Revolution, such as John Adams and Thomas Jefferson, talked grandly about breaking with the European past and starting "a new order of the world." But when the Constitutional Convention met in a steamy summer in Philadelphia in 1787, it was with the assumption that English common law would continue unchanged in the United States.

A Constitutional Convention close to half of whose active members were attorneys could perhaps not be expected to do otherwise. Yet the leader of the radical Jacobin wing of the French

Revolution at about the same time (1789–93), Maximilien Robespierre, was also a lawyer, but one who had no hesitation in breaking with the judicial as well as political past of the ancien régime. Perhaps the fact that Robespierre was an underpaid provincial government official, and that the drafters of the American Constitution like James Madison were upper-middle-class landowners as well as lawyers, made a difference.

Even the American Bill of Rights, the first ten amendments of 1791 to the Constitution, drew heavily upon the common-law tradition. The Second Amendment, the right to bear arms, comes from the English Bill of Rights of 1689; the Fourth Amendment against arbitrary search and seizure is derived directly from a decision by Chief Justice Lord Camden in 1765; and the Fifth Amendment's prohibition of self-incrimination comes ultimately from the 1642 act abolishing Star Chamber.

The provision in the American Constitution of 1787 prohibiting any state in the Union from making any "law impairing the obligation of contracts" reflects a common-law tradition that goes as far back as Bracton and that was given vigorous affirmation in eighteenth-century Whiggery. It meant that the law protected property and sustained business transactions and as such stirred the imagination of fourteenth-century barristers and judges who identified the law with a burgeoning market economy.

The controversial and much disputed in judicial interpretation of the Fourteenth Amendment of 1868—"nor shall any state deprive any person of life, liberty, or property, without due process of law; nor deny to any person within its jurisdiction the equal protection of the laws"—also draws resonance from the centrality of the common-law tradition going back to Magna Carta and Bracton. The wording of the Fourteenth Amendment signifies a democratization of the common law, an opening up of its benefits beyond privileged classes, but that judicial universalization conforms to the Leveller ideology and would not have been rebuffed by Coke and Blackstone.

Part of the First Amendment of 1791, which specifies "the right of the people peaceably to assemble, and to petition the Government for a redress of grievances," is squarely within the tradition of eighteenth-century English Whiggery, and the same may be said, with only slightly less confidence, about the prohibition of a congressional law "abridging the freedom of speech, or of the press." These stipulations bear the coloration of the more liberal side of the common-law ethos as it had developed by 1700. With respect to the first clause of the First Amendment— "Congress shall make no law respecting an establishment of religion, or prohibiting the free exercise thereof," it may be said that the first provision cancels the English established church (often called for in England since 1800 but never consummated) while the latter provision on the free exercise of religion draws sustenance from the seventeenth-century radical Protestant tradition as well as from the eighteenth-century secular philosophy of the Enlightenment.

In the perspective of legal history, the United States is in some ways a more conservative country, closer to the common law in the age of Blackstone, than is modern England. Beginning with the Reform Bill of 1832, the English relied on legislation, not litigation and judicial review, to effect change and bring the country forward into the modern world. As Tocqueville's remarks indicate, the United States has relied at least as much on the legal profession and judicial review to carry out necessary changes.

The most respected and influential of American legal historians, the University of Wisconsin Law School's J. Willard Hurst, in his classic *Law and the Constitution of Freedom in the United States* (1956), ascribed to law in nineteenth-century America an indispensable role in the "release of creative energy," mainly in the economic but also in the political realm.

It was this judicial facilitating of the release of energy that transformed a continent and shaped American civilization, said this legal realist and social determinist:

The substance of what business wanted from law was the provision for ordinary use of an organization through which entrepreneurs could better mobilize and release economic energy. . . . It was natural to its buoyant optimism and its confidence in the release of energy that nineteenth-century law coupled concern for vested rights with a high regard for keeping open the channels of change [resulting in] . . . preference for dynamic rather than static property, or for property put to creative new use rather than property content with what it is.

Hurst's view of the common law and the legal profession in the United States is founded on the dramatic claim by Oliver Wendell Holmes, Jr., in his otherwise murky book *The Common Law* (1881), that "the life of the law has been experience," reflecting "the felt necessities of time," a proposition in turn inspired by the pragmatist philosophy of another Boston-Harvard Brahmin, Charles Saunders Peirce.

Influenced also by Maitland's social-contextualist view of early English legal history, Hurst's kind of legal history combines respect for the common law as a distinctive culture with commitment to early-twentieth-century midwestern progressivism and the New Deal of the 1930s. Except for Morton Horwitz's Marxist reductionism and occasional postmodernist suggestions from others in the critical legal studies group, American legal historiography is still cultivating Hurst's paradigm.

The institutional base of American legal historiography lies in law school faculties, and Hurst's approach to accounting for the development of American law established a sufficient framework for what they wanted to do, which was to provide illustration of and confirmation for a kind of liberal nationalism. Laura Kalman has called this mainline judicial-historical discourse "legal liberalism."

Lawrence Friedman was Hurst's student and devoted his career to detailing Hurst's vision of American legal history. Three other important American legal historians—William E. Nelson, Stanley Kutler, and G. Edward White—also accepted Hurst's assumption that an overlay of democratic nationalist and progressive ideology on the old common law was a good thing for the United States. Tocqueville clearly had his doubts as he witnessed the unfolding of American law and the shaping of the legal profession, but then he was a Frenchman whose culture had been indelibly affected by Robespierre's Jacobinism.

The great majority of nineteenth-century American lawyers learned law by interning in a lawyer's office or were self-taught. The spirit of Jacksonian democracy militated against an academic training for lawyers; it was widely held that the profession should be open to any literate male (women were not admitted to the bar until the 1880s and remained a small minority of the profession until the 1960s). The upgrading in the quality of Harvard Law School under deans Christopher Columbus Langdell and Roscoe Pound between 1885 and 1925, and their insistence on the case method in which law was learned by close reading of appeals court rulings as well as greater attention to relationship between legal study and cognate university disciplines such as history and philosophy, was a major turning point in the development of the American legal profession. Harvard was taken as the model, and other university-based law schools rushed to imitate the Langdell-Pound system. By the 1930s the majority of American lawyers were law school graduates. By 1960 all were.

Another major change in the first two decades of the twentieth century was the founding of corporate law firms, mainly in New York City—the Wall Street bar—precisely to serve as counsel to big business. The firm of Cravath, Swaine & Moore was the model in this development, including the sharing of profits by the partners and the severe exploitation of young law school graduates during a five-year probationary period as associates (closely resembling the draconian organization of the leading universities).

The establishment of public regulatory agencies in the New Deal of the 1930s and during World War II greatly expanded opportunities for dignified if modestly remunerated federal service for law school graduates, particularly welcomed during the Great Depression. This departure was also important for providing an avenue of mobility by which hitherto marginal ethnics like Jews and Italians found their way into major corporate law firms, who hired them in New York and Washington in the 1940s and 1950s to represent their clients' corporate interests vis-à-vis the regulatory agencies the young lawyers had previously served in with distinction.

Efforts made at Yale and Columbia University Law Schools in the 1930s and 1940s to integrate legal study with the leading edges of the social and behavioral sciences had a modest and mostly ephemeral impact. Except for market economics, social and behavioral theory has remarkably little impact on American law schools today.

The final big change in the American legal profession came in the three decades after the civil rights movement of the 1960s. Membership in the top stratus of the profession was ethnically diversified to a significant degree to include African-Americans, Hispanics, and Asians. Even more important, women had become heavily represented in the profession (as in no other country) by the 1990s.

Half of the students at Harvard and other major law schools were now women. Women were well represented in at least the lower echelons of the major corporate law firms, with reasonable promise of advancement to partnerships on a significant scale. The Chief Administrative Judge of New York State was now Judith S. Kaye, a graduate of the (now-defunct) night school division of NYU Law School. Two women were now among the nine U.S. Supreme Court justices. The feminization of the American legal profession portended for the early twenty-first century a gender shift in the American power elite of greater social significance than anything that occurred since in the 1830s Jacksonian democracy displaced the elite gentry.

In 1987 Stanford Law's Friedman turned up at William Nelson's colloquium on legal history at NYU Law School and read a paper—charming, witty, but serious—on a highly successful long-running TV series called *L.A. Law* and its significance for the legal profession, which in Friedman's view was mainly making the profession and practice of law seem so glamorous as to help recruit more and better college graduates.

L.A. Law self-destructed after its creators had the lead woman attorney in the L.A. law firm fall down an empty elevator shaft. It was succeeded in TV's fascination with the legal profession by the likewise long-running *Law and Order*, situated and produced in New York in the 1990s. This was an altogether more sober presentation of a key segment of the legal profession, the prosecuting attorneys. They were an assiduous but highly sensitive lot, in this portrayal. A young woman was number two prosecutor. The district attorney on the program exhibited an uncanny imitation of the speech and facial mannerisms of the long-standing, much-respected Manhattan district attorney.

American fiction and film have presented lawyers in critical but not inaccurate terms. Tom Wolfe's megaton-bestselling novel, *The Bonfire of the Vanities* (and the mediocre film adapted from it), gave a picture of the criminal courts in the Bronx, New York, that was distinctly unflattering in view of their chaotic and politicized condition, but the judge in the *Bonfire* was drawn from life and he came through favorably, fair and strong.

John Grisham's *The Firm*, written by a southern lawyer who became an extremely successful writer of popular fiction, both in its literary version and in the good film made from it, depicted greed and crookedness in a corporate law firm in Nashville, while also highlighting the glamorous lifestyle of a young Harvard law graduate.

A young teacher of writing at Stanford University, Scott Turow, quit that dead-end job to go to Harvard Law School and in 1977 published *One L*, a persuasive and troubling memoir of his student experience there. In the early 1980s, while working as a federal prosecutor in Chicago, Turow wrote a thriller, *Presumed Innocent*, which was both a runaway bestseller and a highly successful film. The picture of criminal justice presented here is neither glamorized nor critical, but coolly clinical, although the prosecution does indict the wrong man.

In the early 1980s a young New York lawyer named Steven Brill founded a monthly magazine, *American Lawyer*, devoted to describing the professional and personal lives of attorneys, especially in corporate law firms. His magazine was at first condemned by the legal profession as sensationalist and meretricious, then eagerly read as a guilty secret, then widely accepted as a communicator of valuable and authentic information. Brill went on to establish a cable TV network, Court TV, to take advantage of the novel televising of trials—mostly criminal cases but also some exciting liability and contract trials—in many state jurisdictions.

Court TV received a tremendous boost in its ratings in 1995 from the O. J. Simpson murder trial. Court TV was chosen to provide the camera feed to the other networks, and along with CNN it presented the most thorough and insightful analysis of the trial, which was also shown in edited form overseas.

The O.J. case became a long-running TV series on its own and provided an education on the workings of the criminal justice system, at least in California. The racism and general slovenliness of the LA Police Department, the confusion and ineptitude of the young, modestly paid prosecution attorneys, the skill and boldness of the all-star cast of highly paid defense attorneys, the endless array of putative professional experts of one sort or another, the difficulty of the hesitant and inexperienced presiding judge in controlling the course of the trial, were all powerfully communicated.

When the O.J. trial was over, New York publishers rushed to

sign the two leading prosecuting attorneys and the two leading defense counsels to book contracts for huge advances. In short order a whole new series of literature was offered to the American public: How I won/lost the Simpson case.

In the late 1980s and 1990s there also appeared several serious nonfiction accounts, varying in tone from descriptive to polemical, about key aspects of contemporary American law. Some of the authors were lawyers or judges, some journalists, and some lawyer-journalists, a proliferating new breed of writer. They focused on five themes:

- Aggressive and amoral lawyers were assisting entrepreneurial predators to take over companies without consideration of the deleterious social consequences of such mergers.

- Liability and regulatory law has gotten out of hand, flies in the face of reason, and hurts business.

- The criminal justice system, with its excessive concern for civil rights, is too soft on perpetrators.

- Jury nullification of the law has become a critical matter and has to be alleviated.

- Brilliant lawyers in their forties are suffering early burnout and career disappointment while still paying off huge mortgages and updating their luxury cars.

The functioning of the common law in the United States today certainly does not lack for public attention, critical review, and attentive dramatization. It now equals, perhaps surpasses, medicine as the most glamorous profession in the public eye. This attention and scrutiny accords with the reality of the importance of the profession and its ever-growing size in late-twentieth-century America.

There are in the closing years of the twentieth century three-quarters of a million licensed lawyers in the United States. This is per capita of general population more than three times the number in England, the homeland of the common law.

Per capita the American legal profession is also four times the number of attorneys of another thriving industrial country, Germany. It is not surprising that per capita the size of the American legal profession is twelve times what it is in Japan. That comparison with a thriving technological competitor of the United States is probably not significant, however, because Japanese culture is unfriendly to litigation.

There are 175 accredited law schools in the United States. They graduate around sixty thousand new lawyers a year, which is close to the size of the whole existing legal profession in England. The top ten American law schools get at least six qualified applicants for every new student admitted. Although in the early 1990s there was a bit of a deflation of the mania for going to law school that characterized the 1980s, because the job situation for graduating lawyers was not quite as good in the mid–1990s as it was in the mid–1980s, nevertheless American law schools continue to get a very high proportion of the best graduates in the humanities and social sciences from the top two hundred colleges in the country.

My own experience is typical. I teach 150 undergraduates a year in the undergraduate college of NYU, recognized to be one of the top two dozen colleges in the country by anyone's criteria. In the past seventeen years, of the dozen best students I have had, nine have gone on to law school; only three to seek a Ph.D. and to become college teachers.

Given the size, wealth, and prominence of the legal profession in the United States of the 1990s, it would not be hard to portray it as a Godzilla that is eating America. But the investment of human and other resources in lawyers can be explained on rational and defensible grounds:

First of all the United States is a continental country, and its vast space and large, incomparably diversified and increasingly multicultural population requires the services of an expansive legal profession.

A continental country with a diversified population requires something to bind the country together. To some extent this is provided by the federal political system, but much less so than in the heyday of the Democratic Party in the 1930s and 1940s. Bill Clinton was elected president in 1992 with only 43 percent of the popular vote.

The closest comparison to the United States as a continental country was the Soviet Union before 1990. It was bound together in an authoritarian manner from the top down, by a narrow bureaucracy, an exclusive political party, the secret police, and the army. This is obviously not the American way, and the Soviet system is held to have inhibited economic development because it lacked the Anglo-American kind of legal system.

The legal profession and the culture of the common law binds the United States together and provides for the framework of civil society that allows for economic and technological progress. This is a commonly held view, propounded by, among many others, the English political philosopher John Gray.

Another perception is that lawyers in the United States in the later twentieth century perform the integrative role that the clergy played in medieval Europe. Like the thirteenth-century clerics, the lawyers guard public ethics, provide for improving governmental functions, and stimulate social reforms in various ways. And they do this more cheaply in terms of social costs than did the clergy of medieval England. In a population of six million in 1300, 5 percent were clergy of one kind or another, which is more than five times the per capita representation of lawyers in the American population of the 1990s.

The size of the American legal profession can also be defended by pointing to its federal system, unlike England's unitary system, where all jurisdiction is directly under the government in London. There are two levels of American courts, federal and state, overlapping to a substantial extent in what they do, and this multiplies the number of lawyers and judges.

Functionally useful in the nineteenth century, the federal system now exists mostly for traditional and politically partisan reasons. In light of contemporary information and transportation technology, the federal two-tier judicial system does not make much sense, but it is inconceivable that it will be superseded, and this condition contributes to the bloating of the legal profession.

Americans have so many lawyers also because they inherited from the early days of the Republic, as noted by Tocqueville, a propensity to litigation, to belief that every hurt and injury must have a judicial remedy. This was a direct inheritance from the culture of the old common law. It is not surprising that as late as the 1830s Blackstone's *Commentaries* continued to be seriously studied as a legal textbook in the United States, while it had become a historical curiosity in England. The English in modern times have more signally departed from the ambience of the old common law, while the Americans have retained its litigious spirit and its passion for civil liberties. American courts still use the jury in liability cases, a practice abandoned several decades ago in England.

In the 1990s parliamentary legislation in Britain qualified the ancient right against self-incrimination. A defendant's silence in British courts can now be adversely taken into account by a jury in a criminal trial. While advocated by some hard-nosed judges and prosecutors, this change is unlikely to occur in the United States.

Beginning in the 1830s the English began to reform their society and government by parliamentary legislation rather than by litigation and judicial review. Especially since the coming of the full-fledged welfare state in 1945, the English like to resolve many disputes by arbitration, administrative agencies, and quasi-public organizations ("quangos") rather than by the courts, although legal reformers still claim that there are too many lengthy and expensive civil actions in Britain.

That the losing party in an English civil trial must pay the fees of the winning party—even though the latter could be a wealthy corporation—and expensive court costs, and that British lawyers cannot represent clients on a contingency basis (you don't pay unless you win your case), is a mighty discouragement to litigation. The medical profession in England (and in Canada) is less bothered by prodigious malpractice litigation than are doctors and hospitals in the United States.

The tendency of the American federal political system to deadlock, and the relatively underdeveloped nature of the American welfare state compared to England's, is another inducement to the American perpetuation of the old common law's love of litigation to solve all problems. Decisions of public administration agencies at every level are much more likely to be challenged in the courts in the United States than in England (or again in Canada). This certainly multiplies the American need for lawyers. It also means that civil liberties are more closely protected in the United States than in England. The modern English (and the Canadians), for whatever reason, are inclined to let constituted authority regulate their lives. Some historians believe that the United States has never shaken off the anarchic spirit of Jacksonian democracy or the frontier.

A difference between England and the United States, accounting for the much larger per capita legal profession in the latter, is that England does not have a written constitutional Bill of Rights as the Americans have had since 1791. Having civil rights specified in this manner increases the volume of litigation, as Canada has discovered since introducing its own written Bill of Rights in 1983.

Furthermore, England since the clear establishment of the sovereignty of Parliament in the eighteenth century has had little or no room for judicial review. Envisaged by Coke but rejected in England, taken up by the U.S. Supreme Court under John Marshall in 1803, and particularly by the Warren Court in the 1950s and 1960s, aggressive review by a supremicist court of the acts of the national legislature significantly increases the business of lawyers in the United States from the highest federal levels down to the most local.

The capacity of the American law schools since 1975 or so to suck up like a runaway vacuum cleaner the intellectual cream of a younger generation coming out of college is also partly due to the sharp decline of the academic profession in the same period. As jobs for new Ph.D.'s in any discipline, even the natural sciences, have greatly declined and in the humanities all but disappeared, any college graduate with a high grade-point average would be a fool not to pursue law if they can remotely see themselves in legal practice or teaching in law schools.

A favorite tactic of young people wanting to be historians or philosophers is to take both a law degree and a Ph.D., and thereby hope for a teaching job in legal history or jurisprudence in a law school. The dean of NYU Law School in the 1990s went this route.

The huge expansion of the American legal profession in the 1980s was also partly explained by corporate merger and takeover mania of that frenetic decade, which revived somewhat in the late 1990s. This kind of corporate activity used a lot of high-priced legal talent.

There are intrinsic problems in American law at the end of the twentieth century. But this book has shown that these problems have been integral to the common law for many centuries. Perhaps they have been a little aggravated on the American scene latterly. But anyone knowing the history of the common law knows also that the complaining talk is about fundamental aspects of the common law during or long before the eighteenth century, and not about radical innovations since then.

The first complaint is that law is now less of a profession and more of a business. But the practice of the common law has been both from the thirteenth century onward. Those American lawyers, mostly in the northeast, who say that the pace and tone of legal practice has been corrupted by entrepreneurial zeal, that the dignity of the law has suffered, are actually referring to general changes in the character of the learned professions and to upper-middle-class lifestyles, not specifically to the law. The medical and academic professions have changed too, and have lost some of their sheen of gentility. We are speaking here about a general shift in American culture, not a defect of the legal profession: Whatever its empirical validity, aside from anecdotal impression, the myth of the degradation of the legal profession from ethical community to atomized entrepreneurship is one that affected the image of the medical and academic professions as well as the lawyers' consciousness of themselves.

The legend of ethical decline seems to be particularly powerful in the culture of the legal profession, and so far as it is believed in, shapes behavior and affects morale. But in terms of actual behavior pattern, the legal profession has undergone only marginal change.

When computerized billing visibly accentuates professional service per quarter hour as distinct from rounded gentlemanly submission of made-up billing in the old days, the legal profession seems to have changed significantly in recent times. But it is more a matter of external accoutrement—from starched white collar to more comfortable and no less expensive shirting, for instance—than change in actual behavior pattern. If American big-city lawyers are greedy today, then the common lawyers have been greedy since the age of Bracton.

Another complaint is that the jury of verdict in criminal cases does not work well, that blatant jury nullification of the criminal law occurs when the jury has some ethnic, gender, or class reason to empathize with the defendant. The responses to this complaint are numerous. The jury never worked well as a rational way of determining guilt from innocence from its very inception. The jury of verdict was never planned or legislated. It came about as a hasty ad hoc need quickly to find some procedure to replace the ordeal.

The only juries that worked reasonably well were blue-ribbon panels, elite panels carefully selected. This is unconstitutional in the United States and is no longer employed in England. In English criminal law, juries may function with less nullification because they are more closely instructed than in American courts. But following the sometimes heavy-handed behavior of English judges would in the United States get the conviction thrown out on appeal if not stopped by declaration of a mistrial.

There is complaint that in American courts there has been abuse of liability, of tort law, resulting in imposition of fantastically high judgments by juries against corporations or wealthy individuals. But there are also those who think that American liability law is the glory of the American system, providing free representation for a contingency fee, giving the little man a chance against institutions, appropriately punishing corporations and institutions for negligence.

This opportunity for the ordinary person to take judicial action against institutions is much less possible in Britain and almost unthinkable in Roman-law countries.

Another response to the complaints about American tort law is that the history of liability has gone through cycles, applying principles at one time more favorable to plaintiffs, at another time to defendants, especially if the latter are corporations or employers. A century ago the complaint of critics was that the American liability law was too soft on the rich and powerful; now it is claimed that the courts are too harsh. This too will pass; the cycle will advance.

Another complaint is that the American judiciary contains many judges who by training, experience, and temperament are unsuitable for their positions, as compared especially with the bench in England or judges in Germany. That is probably true, but it is a product of the American democracy. Uneven judging in the United States is the price that is paid for democracy, resulting in recruitment of judges from the legal profession at large and appointing them with attention to their political clout or as a result of direct election on the ballot.

In England the quality of the judiciary still is affected by the social-class limitations on entry into the Inns of Court and the career of a barrister. It is from among the top stratum of barristers, the QCs, that the high-court judges are chosen in England by the lord chancellor, a member of the cabinet. Political affiliation also affects the choice of judges in England, but there has been an earlier social filtering of the pool from which the judges are eventually chosen.

The American situation is much more open and democratic. The state and national bar associations are supposed to review and certify candidates, but the minimal standards are set quite low. Yet the American system has the advantage of bringing forth people to high-level judgeships who would be thrown out by a high standard of evaluation of candidates. Hugo Black, before becoming a Supreme Court justice, was just another southern senator, with an unsavory early association with the Ku Klux Klan. He is generally regarded as having been a very good Supreme Court justice and famed as an upholder of civil liberties. Earl Warren was a right-wing politician and governor of California and, previous to that, an Oakland, California, prosecutor not known for his sensitivity to the civil rights of the accused. There is nothing in his earlier career to suggest that he would preside over the Supreme Court's civil rights revolution and be the most important chief justice since John Marshall.

The American system of choosing judges brings forth plenty of mediocre people but also some extraordinarily good ones. The system in Germany by which the career of judge is entirely separated by training and experience from that of attorney has much to recommend it, but it does not fit at all into the American democratic ambience.

There is complaint that the criminal courts are essentially dysfunctional, that less than 10 percent of criminal cases go to trial, that the whole system would grind to a halt without plea bargaining. But it is a fantasy to believe that plea bargaining was invented in New York or Los Angeles. Eighteenth-century English criminal law functioned, as it had since the thirteenth century, on something very much like plea bargaining, that of "pleading clergy," or giving soft treatment to wide categories of the population. As a matter of fact, plea bargaining was even used extensively in eighteenth-century French criminal law.

There is complaint that access to legal recourse is expensive, that having a good attorney in any criminal or civil case is exorbitant for most people, that the hard-pressed lawyers provided by legal aid, whatever their intrinsic quality, usually do not have the time or backup to give good representation to poor people, that even middle-class people find good attorneys beyond their means, that the law therefore greatly favors rich people. All this is unquestionably true, but it was true of the common law from its inception.

What is not sufficiently noticed is that the high cost of superior legal services is true also of other professions. Rich people in the United States get infinitely better medical care than poor people and usually even than middle-class people protected by health insurance (which is rapidly deteriorating in the 1990s). That is why rich people are so willing to endow hospital wings and medical research centers: It is their lives that are being extended.

Rich people also normally get better secondary and college education than people of ordinary means. Therefore, they are better prepared to enter graduate study for the academic profession. This isn't much noticed because the scions of wealthy families rarely choose to enter the academic profession.

But it is noticeable that professors with private means can inequitably much better afford the travel and leave that enables them to do more and better research and advance more readily and higher in academia. From the mid–1950s to about 1990, the ready availability of research grants mitigated this distinction between affluent and poor professors. Now that foundation and federal support for academic research is shrinking, the class difference among professors will stand out, as it did before the 1950s.

Complaints are vented that a significant number of lawyers burn out between 35 and 50, disappointed in their careers. There is more talk about this burnout situation than there was twenty years ago, probably because the legal profession has during those two decades drawn a higher proportion of the elite of the college age population than previously.

The response is threefold. First, disappointment with the legal profession is at least in part the consequence of unreal expectations. Most of the work of law is not an intellectual occupation, and it is highly repetitive, although it carries high social prestige and often provides very good incomes.

Secondly, burnout is common in all the learned professions, especially in academia. Ninety percent of the members of the American Historical Association never publish anything of value beyond their dissertations; at least half never publish anything further at all. Do they compensate by excellence in teaching? Nobody really knows, but there is plenty of anecdotal information that they do not. Burned-out lawyers who are partners in large law firms usually continue to draw high incomes from the firms, although layoff of unproductive partners has now become a possibility; it used to be almost unheard of. The burned-out college professor has tenure and cannot be fired, but his salary level declines quickly in real dollars. In other words, burned-out and disappointed lawyers usually maintain upper-middle-class incomes and status; burned-out professors slide down into the petit bourgeoisie from which they had barely emerged in the first place.

Third, the proportion of burned-out and disappointed lawyers may not really be greater today than it was twenty years ago, or two hundred or four hundred years ago. We hear more about it because vocalization of personal disappointment has become socially acceptable in our therapy-driven culture. Some people of high intellectual talent and great energy are going to enter the legal profession and eventually become unhappy. That is probably a very old story.

If there are important defects in American law today, they have nearly always been present in the common law and the legal profession. They are not mainly the product of these times and places.

American law at the end of the 1990s is not a deterioration from some golden age of the common law. The common law today is what it has been since it crystallized in the fourteenth century. A London barrister of 1500 would need only a few months of remedial education to step into an American courtroom today.

If legal reform is now needed, it is much less a matter of going back to the past than of breaking with the past. If change comes, it ought to be carefully devised by cooperation of the leading law schools, the state and national bar associations, the federal and state attorneys general, and the senior partners in the great corporate law firms. Chipping away at one or another alleged problem arbitrarily, by piecemeal legislation, could do more harm than good.

Deep knowledge and comprehensive analysis are the avenue to legal reform, not political demagoguery of either the right or the left.

The history of the common law is a record of remarkable adaptability and response sooner or later to changing social and cultural contexts while preserving a strong core of continuity. Some of this spirit of adaptability and willingness to meet social needs with structural modification of the judicial system and the legal profession is desirable today.

On the other hand, it should be stressed that Hurst and his disciples were right to maintain that the common law and the legal profession have served American society and economy very well for the past two centuries. Even unreformed they will continue to play a central and commendable role in American life.

The most admired figure in American legal history is Oliver Wendell Holmes, Jr., the Harvard Law School–educated U.S. Supreme Court justice in the early decades of this century. When Holmes's father, a Harvard Medical School professor and newspaper columnist, wanted to give a starting boost to young Oliver's legal career, he arranged for Junior to give a series of public lectures in Cambridge, Massachusetts, on English common law, and they were soon published (1881) as *The Common Law*. That young Oliver didn't actually know much about the old common law is not important. People thought he did, and his career skyrocketed.

This story illustrates the symbolic nature of English common law for American lawyers. The old common law has had a kind of totemic significance for the American legal profession. It is in many ways a very different profession now than it was in Holmes's day—much larger in relation to the size of the American population, much more diverse in the social provenance of the lawyers, much wealthier. But led by the prominent law schools, the symbolic and totemic recognition of English common law endures.

Perpetuating in some way the English common-law tradition is central to the intellectual culture of at least the leading American law schools. Therefore they see themselves as upscale centers for legal research and jurisprudence and not just as training schools for producing attorneys. This grounding of American law in

English common law was the main point Holmes made in 1881, and it remains a paradigmatic conviction of the leading American law schools today. While law schools in Britain have nothing consequential to say about American legal history, English legal history receives substantial and increasing attention in American law schools.

The most admired names in American jurisprudence that followed Holmes—Louis Brandeis, Roscoe Pound, Learned Hand, Alexander Bickel, William Brennan, and currently Ronald Dworkin, Richard Posner, and Bruce Ackerman, whatever the differences among them, continue to work within the tradition of common-law culture, however they may seek to amend or shape it at the margins.

The Marxist and critical legal studies people have raised questions and inspired reconsiderations, but they have come forward with no alternative set of concepts to the common law as the bedrock of jurisprudence and judicial culture. The great American law schools are even less inclined than they were in the thirties and forties—when there were radical flickers at Yale and Columbia law schools—to engage in systems analysis, to rethink in applied terms the nature of law in postindustrial, late-capitalist society.

The intellectual conservatism of the American law schools in the 1990s can be gauged from the praise heaped on Yale Law School's Bruce Ackerman for his paradigm of American constitutional history, *We the People* (1991), in which the three creative moments of American constitutionalism are held to be the 1780s and early 1790s, the 1860s, and the period from 1937 onward. This plausible thesis was, however, presented in the early 1940s in a popular history of the United States written by two Columbia University professors of liberal Democratic mien, Allan Nevins and Henry Steele Commager, and distributed free in paperback to every member of the U.S. armed forces along with free cartons of that other elixir of the time, Lucky Strike cigarettes.

The exclusive paradigm taught in American law schools remains that of the common law updated and democratized to a greater or lesser degree. From time to time a prominent American attorney undertakes to write a popular book about the heritage of the common law. Charles Rembar's *The Law of the Land* (1980) and Alfred Knight's *The Life of the Law* (1996) are good examples of this discursive genre. But meanwhile in the faculties of leading American schools, close scholarly attention through teaching, research, and writing is being paid to the old common law.

English legal history is persuasively dealt with by the faculty of American law schools. It is a way of perceiving what the old common law means for the legal profession in the United States. It was a Harvard Law School professor, Samuel Thorne, who established a reliable text and superb translation of Bracton's treatise. Thorne was obviously drawn to his lifetime of labor on Bracton's text by its place at the head of a tradition of judicial liberalism that produced the American Constitution. Morris Arnold, then a University of Pennsylvania Law School professor, now a federal judge in Arkansas, has edited and explicated important fourteenth-century court rolls, and demonstrated unusual capabilities for reading medieval cases.

Tom Green of the University of Michigan Law School has written a history of jury nullification from the Middle Ages to the eighteenth century. This is the most detailed account of jury development in the old common law that has ever been published.

An American legal historian who writes in the Maitland mode of focusing on contingencies, on particular cases within a broad social context, is the University of Houston Law School's Robert C. Palmer. His *The Whilton Dispute* is a fascinatingly detailed and dramatic account of a great land inheritance case in which much of late-thirteenth-century civil law is illuminated. Palmer doesn't tell us what the common law is, he shows us.

American law schools consider the old common law of sufficient importance to import some of the best British legal historians to teach full-time or part-time to their students. Brian Simpson, whose *Leading Cases in the Common Law* (1994) will achieve the classic status of his earlier history of the land law, teaches at the University of Michigan Law School. J. H. Baker, a Cambridge don whose *English Legal History* (3rd ed., 1990) is a standard textbook for English barristers and solicitors, teaches part-time at NYU School of Law.

Perceiving the American legal system in the broader context of the old common law will help to focus on challenging issues that the mighty cohort of American lawyers faces at the end of the 1990s. This utility of longitudinal historical perception was the main point of Holmes's *The Common Law,* and he was right.

Also useful is the theme stressed by Maitland. The common law was the product of thousands of contingencies, of choices made by individuals and interests expressed by groups. In the Maitland view nothing in the common law was inevitable, organic, or predetermined. Everything in the common law was the outcome of the exercise of options, said Maitland. Bearing in mind this experiential lesson of history may make easier the reform of American law now and in the future.

The common law is sometimes hailed as a kind of fixed heavenly firmament, its procedures and principles shining down like beautiful and remote stars, infinitely set apart from the anxieties, confusions, and passions of particular human lives. That is not what legal history teaches. On the contrary, contingency, relativity, malleability, institutional change in response to modification in context and ambience—this is what the history of the common law teaches. It is a good frame of mind to be in when consideration of significant legal reform may be called for.

The conventional way of reading common-law cases is to find in each one an example of the exercise of universal reason. The case may involve adventitious circumstances, idiosyncratic, highly unusual behavior, and deconstructive language, but the reader posits the general issue that is obviously embedded in the complex text.

In order to practice law and especially to engage in litigation it may be necessary to exercise this unilateral rationalist way of reading a common-law case and for law schools to teach this issue-finding. But if the case narrative is closely scrutinized and background investigation into the case and its time and circumstances are pursued, the case can look different and the judicial idea of extrapolation from it may be modified. The beauty of Brian Simpson's *Leading Cases in the Common Law* is that he demonstrates how deeper knowledge of the time and place can give a variant perspective on the significance of a case from that conventionally taught in law schools.

Reading a case for historical purposes broadens the implications of the legal text and joins it with social, political, and cultural trends. This may not be what the lawyer always wants; it is what the historian always needs to explain judicial change or to use law cases for social history.

As the second millennium of the Common Era draws to a close, the practical contribution that legal historians can make to social policy increases. As both the intermittently strengthening bonds of the European Union become activated, and as the United States becomes increasingly involved in international economic and environmental regulatory agencies, the two great legal traditions of Roman law and English common law find themselves in active juxtaposition.

The initial interplay between common law and Roman law occurred first in admiralty law, as it developed between the seventeenth and nineteenth centuries during the proliferation of the oceanic trade by continental European powers like Spain, France, and Germany and the intensely ambitious and enterprising imperialistic peoples of Britain. A nineteenth-century case of shipwreck could involve courts meeting simultaneously in Portsmouth and

Hamburg and complex insurance findings that had to be resolved by international tribunals cognizant of both common and Roman law. On the whole the English judiciary gave way and admiralty law was developed mostly on Roman juristic lines.

Now, in the late 1990s, in some respects the highest court of the United Kingdom lies not in the House of Lords but in Strasbourg, where judges sitting in the European Union's tribunals hold partial overview on English legislation and judicial practice. The more the United States becomes committed to international trade compacts like GATT and NAFTA and recognizes the legitimacy of agencies that regulate world communications, ocean fisheries, global banking and space exploration, the same meeting of Roman- and common-law traditions occurs, and lawyers and judges drawn from the two great juristic traditions find themselves in close conversation and intense negotiation.

Legal history is not going to solve all the problems arising from confrontation of the two legal systems. That is to be determined by politicians and bureaucrats tied to democratic decision making within states. But legal history illuminates the two judicial cultures that are involved, sharpens understanding of the mind-sets that the two legal cultures have created, and places the increasingly necessary dialogue between the two judicial cultures in a historical perspective that makes negotiation, accommodation, and settlement easier and more effective.

It has long been thought that schooling in the structure of language, religion, and social mores makes for greater tolerance and understanding among nations and facilitates the bonding of multicultural and international entities. But the differences in law are also important and increasingly so, and therefore legal history's utility as well as its intrinsic humanistic value is visibly accentuated.

The primary lesson of English legal history is that the common law is a culture, like Renaissance humanism, Protestantism, Roman Catholicism, or secular liberalism. It is also the most important means in Anglophone countries of dispute resolution, and it is a necessary framework for the functioning of a market economy.

But the common law is still and most basically of all things a culture, which means that it is a superstructure by which all lives are lived and faiths affirmed. Like all cultures, common law was structured in formations of institutions and interest groups. Common law derived extraordinary strength and durability throughout its association with the operations of the sovereign national state.

Like all cultures common law was affected and at least on its periphery shaped by change, such as economic or political upheavals, spatial transference (such as from England to North America), and modification in values and lifestyles. But at the core the culture retains the operational structure and the value system that originally gave it integrity and power.

The intensification of the global economy and world information systems and the need to respond productively to Roman-law systems given new vitality and prestige in the European Union and other international bodies are but the latest in a series of challenges and ambient conditions that the old common law of Glanville and Bracton, of Coke and Blackstone, had to face over a long timespan. The common law is likely to function effectively in the newly changing environment. Deep cultures are durable; they are modified and developed but retain their core integrity and dynamic.

Bibliography

The Nature of Law

Altman, Andrew. *Critical Legal Studies: A Liberal Critique.* Princeton, N.J.: Princeton University Press, 1990.

Boyle, James, ed. *Critical Legal Studies.* New York: New York University Press, 1992.

Coleman, Jules L., and Anthony James Sebok, eds. *Jurisprudence.* New York: Garland Publishers, 1994.

Dworkin, Ronald M. *Taking Rights Seriously.* Cambridge, Mass.: Harvard University Press, 1978.

Feinberg, Joel, and Hyman Gross, eds. *Philosophy of Law.* 5th ed. Belmont, Calif.: Wadsworth Publishing Co., 1995 [1st ed., 1975].

Fuller, Lon L. *The Morality of Law.* Rev. ed. New Haven: Yale University Press, 1969 [1964].

Geldart, William. *Introduction to English Law.* 11th ed. Revised by David Yardley. 1911. Reprint, New York: Oxford University Press, 1995.

Goodrich, Peter. *Oedipus Lex: Psychonalysis, History, Law.* Berkeley: University of California Press, 1995.

Grossman, George S. *Legal Research. Historical Foundations of the Electronic Age.* New York: Oxford University Press, 1994.

Harris, J. W. *Legal Philosophies.* London/Boston: Butterworths, 1980.

Hart, Herbert Lionel Adolphus. *The Concept of Law.* 2d ed. With a postscript edited by Penelope A. Bulloch and Joseph Raz. Oxford, England: Clarendon Press/New York: Oxford University Press, 1994.

————. *Essays in Jurisprudence and Philosophy.* Oxford, England: Clarendon Press/New York: Oxford University Press, 1983.

Honoré, Tony. *About Law: A Short Introduction.* New York: Clarendon Press, 1995.

Kelly, John Maurice. *A Short History of Western Legal Theory.* Oxford, England: Clarendon Press/New York: Oxford University Press, 1992.

MacCormick, Neil. *H. L. A. Hart.* London: Edward Arnold/Stanford, Calif.: Stanford University Press, 1981.

Posner, Richard A. *Overcoming Law.* Cambridge, Mass.: Harvard University Press, 1995.

Radzinowicz, Leon, and Joan King. *The Growth of Crime: The International Experience.* New York: Penguin, 1979.

Twining, William L. *Legal Theory and Common Law.* Oxford, England/New York: B. Blackwell, 1986.

Ward, Ian. *Law and Literature.* New York: Cambridge University Press, 1995.

Roman Law

Primary Sources

Justinian. *The Code.* In *The Civil Law,* translated by Samuel Parsons Scott. 3 vols. Cincinnati: Central Trust Co., 1932.

Marcus Tullius Cicero. *De re publica: De legibus.* Translated by Clinton Walker Keyes. Vol. 16 of the Loeb Classical Library's *Cicero in Twenty-Eight Volumes.* London: W. Heinemann/Cambridge, Mass.: Harvard University Press, 1988.

SECONDARY SOURCES

Allison, J. W. F. *A Continental Distinction in the Common Law: A Historical and Comparative Perspective on English Public Law*. Oxford, England: Clarendon Press, 1996.

Bellomo, Manlio. *The Common Law Legal Past of Europe, 1000–1800*. Translated from the 2nd ed. by Ludia J. Cochrane. Washington, D.C.: Catholic University of America Press, 1995.

Berman, Harold Joseph. *Law and Revolution: The Formation of the Western Legal Tradition*. Cambridge, Mass.: Harvard University Press, 1983.

Brundage, James A. *Law, Sex, and Christian Society in Medieval Europe*. London/Chicago: University of Chicago Press, 1987.

Crook, John Anthony. *Legal Advocacy in the Roman World*. London: Duckworth/Ithaca, N.Y.: Cornell University Press, 1995.

———. *Law and Life of Rome*. London: Thames & Hudson; Ithaca, N.Y.: Cornell University Press, 1984.

Dawson, John Philip. *The Oracles of the Law*. Buffalo, N.Y.: W. S. Hein, 1986.

Harries, Jill, and Ian N. Wood, eds. *The Theodosian Code*. Ithaca, N.Y.: Cornell University Press, 1993.

Honoré, Tony. *Emperors and Lawyers*. Rev. ed. Oxford, England: Clarendon Press/New York: Oxford University Press, 1994.

Jolowicz, Herbert Felix. *Historical Introduction to the Study of Roman Law*. 1932. Reprint, Holmes Beach, Fla.: William W. Gaunt & Sons, 1994.

Kuttner, Stephan. *Harmony from Dissonance: An Interpretation of Medieval Canon Law*. Latrobe, Pa.: Archabbey Press, 1960.

Lewis, A. D. E., and David J. Ibbetson, eds. *The Roman Law Tradition*. Cambridge, England/New York: Cambridge University Press, 1994.

Nicholas, Barry. *An Introduction to Roman Law*. Oxford, England: Clarendon Press, 1962.

Spiller, Peter. *A Manual of Roman Law*. Clearwater, Fla.: D & S Publishers, 1986.

Stein, Peter. *The Character and Influence of the Roman Civil Law: Historical Essays*. London/Ronceverte, West Va.: Hambledon Press, 1988.

Van Zyl, Deon Hurter. *Cicero's Legal Philosophy*. Roodepoort, South Africa: Digma Publications, 1986.

Vinogradoff, Paul. *Roman Law in Medieval Europe*. 1909. Reprint, with a foreword by Peter Stein, Holmes Beach, Fla.: William W. Gaunt & Sons, 1994.

Watson, Alan. *The Spirit of Roman Law*. Athens: University of Georgia Press, 1995.

———. *Roman Law and Comparative Law*. Athens: University of Georgia Press, 1991.

English Common Law, 600–1272

PRIMARY SOURCES

Anglo-Saxon Wills. Edited and translated by Dorothy Whitelock. Cambridge, England: Cambridge University Press, 1930.

Anglo-Saxon Writs. 2nd ed. Edited by Florence Elizabeth Harmer. Stamford, England: P. Watkins, 1989 [1st ed., 1952].

Die Gesetze der Angelsachsen. Edited by Felix Liebermann. 3 vols. Halle an der Saale: M. Niemeyer, 1903–16.

English Historical Documents. Vol. 1 (c. 500–1042). 2nd ed. Edited by Dorothy Whitelock. London: Methuen/New York: Oxford University Press, 1979.

English Historical Documents. Vol. 2 (c. 1042–1189). 2nd ed. Edited by David Charles Douglas and G. W. Greenaway. London: Methuen/New York: Oxford University Press, 1979.

English Lawsuits from William I to Richard I. 2 vols. Edited by R. C. van Caenegem. London: Selden Society, 1990–91.

Henry de Bracton. *On the Laws and Customs of England*. Translated with revisions and notes by Samuel E. Thorne. Cambridge, England: Published in association with the Selden Society by the Belknap Press of Harvard University Press, 1968.

The Laws of the Earliest English Kings. Edited and translated by Frederick Levi Attenborough. New York: Cambridge University Press, 1922. New York: AMS Press, 1974.

Ranulf de Glanville. *The Treatise on Laws and Customs of the Realm of England, Commonly called Glanvill.* 1965. Reprint, with an introduction, notes, and translation by G. D. G. Hall and with a guide to further reading by Michael T. Clanchy, Oxford, England: Clarendon Press/New York: Oxford University Press, 1993.

SECONDARY SOURCES

Bartlett, Robert. *Trial by Fire and Water: The Medieval Judicial Ordeal.* Oxford, England: Clarendon Press/New York: Oxford University Press, 1986.

Brand, Paul. *The Making of the Common Law.* London/Rio Grande, Ohio: Hambledon Press, 1992.

————. *Origins of the English Legal Profession.* Oxford, England/ Cambridge, Mass.: B. Blackwell, 1992.

Caenegem, R. C. van. *Legal History: A European Perspective.* 1976–88. Reprint, London/Rio Grande, Ohio: Hambledon Press, 1991.

————. *The Birth of the English Common Law.* 2d ed. Cambridge, England; New York: Cambridge University Press, 1988 [1st ed., 1973].

————. *Royal Writs in England from the Conquest to Glanvill: Studies in the Early History of the Common Law.* London: B. Quaritch, 1959.

————. *An Historical Introduction to Western Constitutional Law.* New York: Cambridge University Press, 1995.

Cantor, Norman F., ed. *William Stubbs on the English Constitution.* New York: Crowell, 1966.

Clanchy, Michael T. *From Memory to Written Record, England 1066-1307.* 2nd ed. Oxford, England/Cambridge, Mass.: B. Blackwell, 1993 [1st ed., 1979].

Douglas, David Charles. *Feudal Documents from the Abbey of Bury St. Edmunds.* London: Published for the British Academy by Humphrey Milford, Oxford University Press, 1932.

Grant, Alexander, and Keith J. Stringer. *Uniting the Kingdom: The Making of British History.* London: Routledge, 1995.

Harding, Alan. *The Law Courts of Medieval England.* London: Allen & Unwin/New York: Barnes & Noble, 1973.

Hogue, Arthur R. *Origins of the Common Law.* Indianapolis: Liberty Press, 1985 [1966].

Holt, James Clarke. *Magna Carta.* 2nd ed. Cambridge, England/New York: Cambridge University Press, 1992 [1st ed., 1965].

Hudson, John G. H. *Land, Law and Lordship in Medieval England.* Oxford, England: Clarendon Press, 1994.

———. *The Formation of the English Common Law.* New York: Addison-Wesley Longmans, 1996.

Hudson, John G. H., ed. *The History of English Law: Centenary Essays on "Pollock and Maitland."* London: British Academy, 1996.

Hyams, Paul R. *King, Lords, and Peasants in Medieval England: The Common Law of Villeinage in the Twelfth and Thirteenth Centuries.* Oxford, England: Clarendon Press, 1980.

Jolliffe, John Edward Austin. *The Constitutional History of Medieval England: From the English Settlement to 1485.* 4th ed. New York: Norton, 1961.

———. *Angevin Kingship.* 2nd ed. London: A. & C. Black, 1963.

Kantorowicz, Ernst Hartwig. *The King's Two Bodies: A Study in Medieval Political Theology.* Princeton, N.J.: Princeton University Press, 1981.

Kern, Fritz. *Kingship and Law in the Middle Ages: Studies.* Translated and with an introduction by S. B. Chrimes. Westport, Conn.: Greenwood Press, 1985 [1939].

Maddicott, John Robert. *Simon de Montfort.* Cambridge, England/New York: Cambridge University Press, 1994.

Maitland, Frederic William. *The Collected Papers of Frederic William Maitland.* Edited by H. A. L. Fisher. 3 vols. Cambridge, England: Cambridge University Press, 1911. Reprint, Buffalo, N.Y.: W. S. Hein, 1981.

Meekings, Cecil Anthony Francis. *Studies in Thirteenth-Century Justice and Administration.* London: Hambledon Press, 1981.

Milsom, Stroud Francis Charles. *Studies in the History of the Common Law.* London; Ronceverte, West Va.: Hambledon Press, 1985.

———. *Historical Foundations of the Common Law.* 2nd ed. London/Boston: Butterworths, 1981.

———. *The Legal Framework of English Feudalism* (The Maitland Lectures Given in 1972). Cambridge, England/New York: Cambridge University Press, 1977.

Painter, Sidney. *The Reign of King John.* Baltimore, Md.: Johns Hopkins University Press, 1966 [1949].

———. *Studies in the History of the English Feudal Barony.* Baltimore, Md.: Johns Hopkins University Press, 1943.

Palmer, Robert C. *The County Courts of Medieval England, 1150–1350.* Princeton, N.J.: Princeton University Press, 1982.

———. *The Whilton Dispute, 1264–1380: A Social-Legal Study of Dispute Settlement in Medieval England.* Princeton, N.J.: Princeton University Press, 1984.

Pollock, Frederick, and Frederic William Maitland. *The History of English Law Before the Time of Edward I.* 2nd ed. 1898. 2 vols. Reprint, with an introduction and select bibliography by Stroud Francis Charles Milsom, London: Cambridge University Press, 1968.

Razi, Zvi, and Richard Smith, eds. *Medieval Society and the Manorial Court.* New York: Oxford University Press, 1996.

Reynolds, Susan. *Fiefs and Vassals: The Medieval Evidence Reinterpreted.* Oxford, England: Clarendon Press, 1994.

Richardson, Henry Gerald, and George Osborne Sayles. *The Governance of Mediaeval England from the Conquest to Magna Carta.* Edinburgh, Scotland: Edinburgh University Press, 1963.

Southern, Richard William. *Scholastic Humanism and the Unification of Europe.* Vol. 1. Oxford, England/Cambridge, Mass.: B. Blackwell, 1995.

Stenton, Doris Mary Parsons. *English Justice between the Norman Conquest and the Great Charter, 1066–1215.* Philadelphia, Pa.: American Philosophical Society, 1964.

Stenton, Frank Merry. *The First Century of English Feudalism, 1066-1166.* 2nd ed. Oxford, England: Clarendon Press, 1961. Reprint, Westport, Conn.: Greenwood Press, 1979.

Stubbs, William. *The Constitutional History of England in its Origin and Development.* 3 vols. 1897. Vol. 1, 6th ed.; vol. 2, 4th ed.; vol. 3, 5th ed. Reprint, New York: Barnes & Noble, 1967.

Treharne, Reginald Francis. *The Baronial Plan of Reform, 1258–1263*. Rev. ed. Manchester, England: Manchester University Press/New York: Barnes & Noble, 1971.

Turner, Ralph V. *The English Judiciary in the Age of Glanville and Bracton, c. 1176–1239*. New York: Cambridge University Press, 1985.

———. *Judges, Administrators and the Common Law in Angevin England*. London/Rio Grande, Ohio: Hambledon Press, 1994.

English Common Law, 1272–1547

PRIMARY SOURCES

Select Cases in the Court of King's Bench under Edward I, 1273–1307. 3 vols. Edited for the Selden Society by George Osborne Sayles. London: B. Quaritch, 1936–39.

Select Cases of Trespass from the King's Courts, 1307–1399. 2 vols. Edited for the Selden Society by Morris S. Arnold. London: Selden Society, 1985–87.

Wilkinson, Bertie. *Constitutional History of England in the Fifteenth Century (1399–1485): With Illustrative Documents*. New York: Barnes & Noble, 1964.

———. *Constitutional History of England, 1216–1399: With Select Documents*. 3 vols. London: Longmans, Green, 1948–58.

SECONDARY SOURCES

Abel, Richard L. *The Legal Profession in England and Wales*. Oxford, England/New York: B. Blackwell, 1988.

Baker, John Hamilton. *An Introduction to English Legal History*. 3rd ed. London/Boston: Butterworths, 1990.

Bellamy, John G. *Criminal Law and Society in Late Medieval and Tudor England*. Gloucester, England: A. Sutton/New York: St. Martin's Press, 1984.

———. *The Tudor Law of Treason: An Introduction*. London: Routledge & Kegan Paul/Toronto, Canada–Buffalo, N.Y.: University of Toronto Press, 1979.

———. *The Law of Treason in England in the Later Middle Ages.* Cambridge, England: Cambridge University Press, 1970.

Blatcher, Marjorie. *The Court of King's Bench, 1450–1550: A Study in Self-Help.* London: Athlone Press/Atlantic Highlands, N.J.: Distributed by Humanities Press, 1978.

Brady, Thomas A., Jr., Heiko A. Oberman, and James D. Tracey, eds. *Handbook of European History, 1400–1600: Late Middle Ages, Renaissance and Reformation.* 2 vols. Leiden, Netherlands/New York: E. J. Brill, 1994–95.

Chrimes, Stanley Bertram. *English Constitutional Ideas in the Fifteenth Century.* New York: AMS Press, 1978.

Cockburn, J. S., and Thomas Andrew Green, eds. *Twelve Good Men and True: The Criminal Trial Jury in England, 1200–1800.* Princeton, N.J.: Princeton University Press, 1988.

Doe, Norman. *Fundamental Authority in Late Medieval English Law.* Cambridge, England/New York: Cambridge University Press, 1990.

Du Boulay, F. R. H. *An Age of Ambition: English Society in the Late Middle Ages.* London: Nelson/New York: Viking Press, 1970.

Duffy, Eamon. *The Stripping of the Altars: Traditional Religion in England, c. 1400–c. 1580.* London/New Haven, Conn.: Yale University Press, 1992.

Elton, Geoffrey Rudolph. *Star Chamber Stories.* London: Methuen/New York: Barnes & Noble, 1974 [1958].

———. *Policy and Police: The Enforcement of the Reformation in the Age of Thomas Cromwell.* Cambridge, England: Cambridge University Press, 1972.

Fifoot, Cecil Herbert Stuart. *History and Sources of the Common Law: Tort and Contract.* New York: Greenwood Press, 1970.

Fletcher, Anthony. *Gender, Sex, and Subordination in England 1500–1800.* New Haven, Conn.: Yale University Press, 1995.

Graves, Michael A. R. *The Tudor Parliaments: Crown, Lords, and Commons, 1485–1603.* London/New York: Longmans, 1985.

Green, Thomas Andrew. *Verdict According to Conscience: Perspectives on the English Criminal Trial Jury, 1200–1800.* Chicago: University of Chicago Press, 1985.

Guy, John. *Tudor England.* New York: Oxford University Press, 1988.

Haigh, Christopher. *English Reformations: Religion, Politics, and Society Under the Tudors.* Oxford, England: Clarendon Press/New York: Oxford University Press, 1993.

Hastings, Margaret. *The Court of Common Pleas in Fifteenth-Century England: A Study of Legal Administration and Procedure.* Ithaca, N.Y.: Published for the American Historical Society by Cornell University Press, 1947.

Helmholz, R. H. *Marriage Litigation in Medieval England.* Holmes Beach, Fla.: William W. Gaunt & Sons, 1986.

Hilton, Rodney Howard. *Bond Men Made Free: Medieval Peasant Movements and the English Rising of 1381.* London/New York: Methuen, 1977 [1973].

Holt, James Clarke. *Robin Hood.* Rev. ed. London: Thames & Hudson, 1989 [1982].

Ives, Eric William. *The Common Lawyers of Pre-Reformation England: Thomas Kebell, A Case Study.* Cambridge, England/New York: Cambridge University Press, 1983.

Keen, Maurice Hugh. *The Laws of War in the Late Middle Ages.* Aldershot, England: Gregg Revivals, 1993.

————. *English Society in the Later Middle Ages, 1348–1500.* London: Penguin Books; Allen Lane, 1990.

————. *The Outlaws of Medieval Legend.* New York: Dorset Press, 1989.

Kermode, Jenny, and Garthine Walker, eds. *Women, Crime and the Courts in Early Modern England.* Chapel Hill: University of North Carolina Press, 1994.

Lander, Jack Robert. *English Justices of the Peace, 1461–1509.* Gloucester, England/Wolfeboro, N.H.: A. Sutton, 1989.

Leyser, Henrietta. *Medieval Women: Social History of Women in England, 450–1500.* London: Weidenfeld & Nicolson, 1995.

MacCaffrey, Wallace T. *Elizabeth I.* London; New York: E. Arnold, 1993.

Maitland, Frederic William. *English Law and the Renaissance: The Rede Lecture for 1901.* 1901. Reprint, Littleton, Colo.: F. B. Rothman, 1985.

Myers, Alec Reginald. *Crown, Household, and Parliament in Fifteenth-Century England*. London/Ronceverte, W. Va.: Hambledon Press, 1985.

Neale, John Ernest. *The Elizabethan House of Commons*. Harmondsworth, England: Penguin Books, 1963.

Ormrod, W. M. *The Reign of Edward III: Crown and Political Society in England, 1327–1377*. New Haven, Conn.: Yale University Press, 1990.

———. *Political Life in Medieval England, 1300–1450*. New York: St. Martin's Press, 1995.

Palmer, Robert C. *English Law in the Age of the Black Death, 1348-1381: A Transformation of Governance and Law*. Chapel Hill: University of North Carolina Press, 1993.

Plucknett, Theodore Frank Thomas. *Legislation of Edward I*. The Ford Lectures delivered in the University of Oxford, 1947. Oxford, England: Clarendon Press, 1962 [1949].

———. *A Concise History of the Common Law*. 1929. Reprint, Boston: Little, Brown, 1956.

Powell, Edward. *Kingship, Law and Society. Criminal Justice in the Reign of Henry V*. Oxford, England: Clarendon Press, 1989.

Powicke, Frederick Maurice. *King Henry III and the Lord Edward: The Community of the Realm in the Thirteenth Century*. 2 vols. Oxford, England: Clarendon Press, 1947.

Prestwich, Michael. *Edward I*. London: Methuen, 1988.

Rigby, Stephen Henry. *English Society in the Later Middle Ages: Class, Status, and Gender*. New York: St. Martin's Press, 1995.

Simpson, Alfred William Brian. *A History of the Land Law*. 2nd ed. Revised edition of *An Introduction to the History of the Land Law* [1961]. Oxford, England/New York: Clarendon Press, 1986.

———. *A History of the Common Law of Contract: The Rise of the Action of Assumpsit*. 2 vols. Oxford, England: Clarendon Press, 1975.

Steel, Anthony Bedford. *Richard II*. With a foreword by G. M. Trevelyan. 1941. Reprint, Cambridge, England: Cambridge University Press, 1962.

English Common Law, 1547–1780

PRIMARY SOURCES

Bentham, Jeremy. *A Bentham Reader.* Edited by Mary Peter Mack. New York: Pegasus, 1969.

Blackstone, Sir William. *Commentaries on the Laws of England.* With notes and additions by Edward Christian. 4 vols. 15th ed. Abingdon, Oxford, England: Professional Books, 1982.

Coke, Sir Edward. *The Institutes of the Laws of England.* Part 1 published as *The First Part of the Institutes of the Laws of England.* 2 vols., 1823. Reprint, Birmingham, Alabama: Legal Classics Library, 1985. Parts 2, 3, and 4 published as *Institutes of the Laws of England.* 4 vols. Buffalo, N.Y.: W. S. Hein, 1986.

Hale, Sir Matthew. *The History of the Common Law.* 5th ed. 2 vols. Edited by Charles Runnington. Holmes Beach, Fla.: William W. Gaunt & Sons, 1993.

Sources of English Legal History: Private Law to 1750. Compiled by John Hamilton Baker and Stroud Francis Charles Milsom. London: Butterworths/St. Paul, Minn.; Stoneham, Mass.: Butterworth Legal Publishers, 1986.

Tracts on Liberty in the Puritan Revolution, 1638–1647. Edited with a commentary by William Haller. 1934. Reprint, New York: Octagon Books, 1965.

SECONDARY SOURCES

Beattie, J. M. *Crime and the Courts in England, 1660–1800.* Princeton, N.J.: Princeton University Press, 1986.

Bonfield, Lloyd. *Marriage Settlements, 1601–1740: The Adoption of the Strict Settlement.* Cambridge, England/New York: Cambridge University Press, 1983.

Boorstin, Daniel Joseph. *The Mysterious Science of the Law.* Boston: Beacon Press, 1941.

Bowen, Catherine Drinker. *The Lion and the Throne: The Life and Times of Sir Edward Coke (1552–1634).* Boston: Little, Brown, 1990 [1957].

Brewer, John, and John Styles, eds. *An Ungovernable People: The English and their Law in the Seventeenth and Eighteenth Centuries*. London: Hutchinson/New Brunswick, N.J.: Rutgers University Press, 1980.

Burgess, Guy. *The Politics of the Ancient Constitution: An Introduction to English Political Thought 1603–1642*. University Park: Pennsylvania State University Press, 1992.

Burke, S. M., and Saum al-Din Quraishi. *The British Raj in India*. New York, Oxford University Press, 1995.

Cain, P. J., and A. G. Hopkins. *British Imperialism*. 2 vols. New York: Longmans, 1993.

Carswell, John. *The Old Cause: Three Biographical Studies in Whiggism*. London: Cresset Press, 1954.

Coquillette, Daniel R. *Francis Bacon*. Edinburgh, Scotland: Edinburgh University Press; Stanford, Calif.: Stanford University Press, 1992.

Cromartie, Alan. *Sir Matthew Hale, 1609–1676: Law, Religion, and Natural Philosophy*. Cambridge, England/New York: Cambridge University Press, 1995.

Cross, Claire, David Loades, and J. J. Scarisbrick, eds. *Law and Government under the Tudors: Essays Presented to Sir Geoffrey Elton, Regius Professor of Modern History in the University of Cambridge, on the Occasion of his Retirement*. Cambridge, England/New York: Cambridge University Press, 1988.

Dickens, Arthur Geoffrey. *The English Reformation*. 2nd ed. London: B. T. Batsford, 1989.

Douglas, David Charles. *English Scholars, 1660–1730*. 2nd rev. ed. Westport, Conn.: Greenwood Press, 1975.

Elton, Geoffrey Rudolph. *England under the Tudors*. 3rd ed. London/ New York: Routledge, 1991.

———. *The Parliament of England, 1559–1581*. Cambridge, England/ New York: Cambridge University Press, 1986.

Foucault, Michel. *Discipline and Punish: The Birth of the Prison*. Translated by Alan Sheridan. New York: Vintage Books, 1979.

Gardiner, Samuel Rawson. *History of England from the Accession of James I to the Outbreak of the Civil War, 1603–1642*. 10 vols. 1883. Reprint, New York: AMS Press, 1965.

————. *History of the Great Civil War, 1642–1649.* 4 vols. 1893. Reprint, London: Windrush Press, 1987.

————. *History of the Commonwealth and Protectorate, 1649–1656: In Four Volumes.* 4 vols. 1894. Reprint, Adlestrop, England: Windrush Press, 1988–89.

Gatrell, V. A. C. *The Hanging Tree: Execution and the English People, 1770–1868.* Oxford, England/New York: Oxford University Press, 1994.

Halevy, Elie. *England in 1815,* 2d rev. ed. Translated by E. I. Watkin and D. A. Barker, with an introduction by R. B. McCallum. London: E. Benn/New York: P. Smith, 1949.

Haller, William. *The Rise of Puritanism: Or, the Way to the New Jerusalem as Set Forth in the Pulpit and Press from Thomas Cartwright to John Lilburne and John Milton, 1570–1643.* 1938. Reprint, Philadelphia: University of Pennsylvania Press, 1972.

————. *Liberty and Reformation in the Puritan Revolution.* New York: Columbia University Press, 1963.

Helmholz, R. H., and Thomas Andrew Green. *Juries, Libel and Justice: The Role of English Juries in Seventeenth- and Eighteenth- Century Trials for Libel and Slander.* Papers read at a Clark Library seminar, Feb. 28, 1981. Los Angeles: William Andrew Clark Memorial Library, University of California, 1984.

Hill, Christopher. *God's Englishman: Oliver Cromwell and the English Revolution.* New York: Harper & Row, 1972 [1970].

————. *The World Turned Upside-Down: Radical Ideas in the English Revolution.* New York: Penguin, 1984.

————. *Liberty Against the Law.* New York: Penguin, 1996.

Holdsworth, William Searle. *A History of English Law.* 17 vols. London: Methuen, 1903–77. London: Sweet and Maxwell, 1982.

Holmes, Geoffrey S., and Daniel Szechi. *The Age of Oligarchy: Pre-Industrial Britain, 1722–1783.* London/New York: Longmans, 1993.

Holmes, Geoffrey S., ed. *Britain after the Glorious Revolution, 1689–1714.* London: Macmillan/New York: St. Martin's Press, 1969.

Jones, W. J. *Politics and the Bench: The Judges and the Origins of the English Civil War.* London: Allen & Unwin/New York: Barnes & Noble, 1971.

Kemp, Betty. *King and Commons, 1660–1832*. Westport, Conn.: Greenwood Press, 1984.

Landau, Norma. *The Justices of the Peace, 1679–1760*. Berkeley: University of California Press, 1984.

Langford, Paul. *A Polite and Commercial People. England, 1727–1783*. New York: Oxford University Press, 1989.

Lemmings, David. *Gentlemen and Barristers: The Inns of Court and the English Bar, 1680–1730*. Oxford, England: Clarendon Press/New York: Oxford University Press, 1990.

Levack, Brian P. *The Formation of the British State. England, Scotland and the Union, 1603–1707*. Oxford: Clarendon Press, 1991.

Linebaugh, Peter. *The London Hanged: Crime and Civil Society in the Eighteenth Century*. Cambridge, England/New York: Cambridge University, 1992.

Marshall, Peter J. *The Cambridge Illustrated History of the British Empire*. New York: Cambridge University Press, 1996.

Mendle, Michael. *Henry Parker and the English Civil War*. New York: Cambridge University Press, 1995.

Namier, Lewis Bernstein. *The Structure of Politics at the Accession of George III*. 2 vols. 1929. Reprint, 1 vol., London: Macmillan/New York: St. Martin's Press, 1963.

Plumb, John Harold. *Sir Robert Walpole: The King's Minister*. 2 vols. Boston: Houghton Mifflin, 1961.

Pocock, John Greville Agard. *The Ancient Constitution and the Feudal Law: A Study of English Historical Thought in the Seventeenth Century*. Cambridge, England/New York: Cambridge University Press, 1987.

Porter, Roy. *London, A Social History*. Cambridge, Mass.: Harvard University Press, 1995.

Postema, Gerald J. *Bentham and the Common Law Tradition*. Oxford, England: Clarendon Press/New York: Oxford University Press, 1986.

Prest, Wilfrid R. *The Rise of the Barristers: A Social History of the English Bar, 1590–1640*. Oxford, England: Clarendon Press/New York: Oxford University Press, 1986.

———. *The Inns of Court Under Elizabeth I and the Early Stuarts: 1590–1640*. London: Longmans, 1972.

Reid, John Phillip. *Constitutional History of the American Revolution.* Abridged ed. Madison: University of Wisconsin Press, 1995.

Rowse, Alfred Leslie. *The England of Elizabeth: The Structure of Society.* New York: Macmillan, 1951 [1950].

Russell, Conrad. *The Causes of the English Civil War: The Ford Lectures Delivered in the University of Oxford, 1987–1988.* Oxford, England: Clarendon Press/New York: Oxford University Press, 1990.

———. *Unrevolutionary England, 1603–1642.* London; Ronceverte, West Va.: Hambledon Press, 1990.

———. *The Crisis of Parliaments: English History, 1509–1660.* 1971. Reprint, with corrections, Oxford, England/New York: Oxford University Press, 1974.

Sharpe, Kevin. *The Personal Rule of Charles I.* New Haven: Yale University Press, 1992.

Simpson, Alfred William Brian. *Leading Cases in the Common Law.* Oxford, England: Clarendon Press/New York: Oxford University Press, 1995.

Stone, Lawrence. *Uncertain Unions and Broken Lives: Marriage and Divorce in England, 1660–1857.* Oxford/New York: Oxford University Press, 1995.

Stoner, James Reist Jr. *Common Law and Liberal Theory: Coke, Hobbes, and the Origins of American Constitutionalism.* Lawrence, Kans.: University Press of Kansas, 1992.

Tawney, Richard Henry. *The Agrarian Problem in the Sixteenth Century.* With an introduction by Lawrence Stone. London: Longmans, Green, 1912. Reprint, New York: Harper & Row, 1967.

Thompson, Edward Palmer. *Whigs and Hunters: The Origins of the Black Acts.* Harmondsworth, England: Penguin Books, 1990.

Tobias, John Jacob. *Crime and Police in England, 1700–1900.* Dublin: Gill and Macmillan, 1979.

Trevelyan, George Macaulay. *The English Revolution, 1688–1689.* New York: H. Holt, 1939.

Tuck, Richard. *Hobbes.* New York: Oxford University Press, 1989.

Underdown, David. *Revel, Riot, and Rebellion: Popular Politics and Culture in England, 1603–1660.* Oxford, England/New York: Oxford University Press, 1987.

————. *Pride's Purge: Politics in the Puritan Revolution.* London/Boston: Allen & Unwin, 1985.

White, Stephen D. *Sir Edward Coke and "The Grievances of the Commonwealth," 1621–1628.* Chapel Hill: University of North Carolina Press, 1979.

American Law

This is an introductory list only. There is a detailed annotated bibliography in Kermit L. Hall, *The Magic Mirror: Law in American History,* listed below. The notes to Laura Kalman, *The Strange Career of Legal Liberalism,* listed below, also comprise a valuable annotated bibliography.

Abramson, Jeffrey. *We, the Jury: The Jury System and the Ideal of Democracy.* Paperback ed., with additions, New York: Basic Books, 1995.

Ackerman, Bruce A. *We the People.* Cambridge, Mass.: Belknap Press of Harvard University Press, 1991.

Bork, Robert A. *The Tempting of America. The Political Seduction of the Law.* New York: Free Press, 1990.

Dworkin, Ronald M. *Law's Empire.* Cambridge, Mass.: Belknap Press of Harvard University Press, 1986.

Ely, John Hart. *Democracy and Distrust: A Theory of Judicial Review.* Cambridge, Mass.: Harvard University Press, 1980.

Friedman, Lawrence Meir. *A History of American Law.* 2nd ed. New York: Simon & Schuster, 1985.

Friedman, Lawrence Meir, and Harry N. Scheiber, eds. *American Law and the Constitutional Order: Historical Perspectives.* Enlarged ed. Cambridge, Mass.: Harvard University Press, 1988.

Hall, Kermit L. *The Magic Mirror: Law in American History.* New York: Oxford University Press, 1989.

Herget, James E. *American Jurisprudence, 1870–1970: A History.* Houston, Texas: Rice University Press, 1990.

Horwitz, Morton J. *The Transformation of American Law, 1870–1960: The Crisis of Legal Orthodoxy.* New York: Oxford University Press, 1992.

———. *The Transformation of American Law, 1780–1860.* Cambridge, Mass.: Harvard University Press, 1977.

Hurst, James Willard. *Law and the Conditions of Freedom: In the Nineteenth-Century United States.* Madison: University of Wisconsin Press, 1956.

———. *The Growth of American Law: The Law Makers.* Boston: Little, Brown, 1950.

Kalman, Laura. *Legal Realism at Yale, 1927–1960.* Chapel Hill, N.C.: University of North Carolina Press, 1986.

———. *The Strange Career of Legal Liberalism.* New Haven: Yale University Press, 1996.

Kutler, Stanley I. *Privilege and Creative Destruction: The Charles River Bridge Case.* Philadelphia, Pa.: Lippincott, 1971.

Nelson, William Edward. *Americanization of the Common Law: The Impact of Legal Change on Massachusetts Society, 1760–1830.* 2nd ed. Athens: University of Georgia Press, 1994.

Presser, Stephen B., and Jamil S. Zainaldin. *Law and American History: Cases and Materials.* 2nd ed. St. Paul, Minn.: West Publishing Co., 1989.

Schwartz, Bernard. *Main Currents in American Legal Thought.* Durham, N.C.: Carolina Academic Press, 1993.

White, G. Edward. *Justice Oliver Wendell Holmes: Law and the Inner Self.* New York: Oxford University Press, 1993.

———. *The Marshall Court and Cultural Change, 1815–1835,* abridged ed. New York: Oxford University Press, 1991.

———. *The American Judicial Tradition: Profiles of Leading American Judges.* Expanded ed. Oxford, England/New York: Oxford University Press, 1988.

Good Reading

For those who want the pleasure of good writing plus deep knowledge, here are the most enjoyable yet learned books ever written on the common law (full publishing information may be found above):

Pollock, Frederick, and Frederic William Maitland. *A History of English Law Before the Time of Edward I.* 2nd ed. Vol. 1.

Palmer, Robert C. *The Whilton Dispute.*

Elton, Geoffrey R. *Star Chamber Stories.*

Bowen, Catherine Drinker. *The Lion and the Throne.*

Simpson, A. W. Brian. *Leading Cases in the Common Law.*

Thompson, Edward P. *Whigs and Hunters.*

Friedman, Lawrence W. *A History of American Law.* 2nd ed.

Index

Brougham, Henry, 346
Brundage, James, 42
Burger, Warren, 306
Burgess, Glenn, 308
burnout, in legal profession, 362, 372–73
Bushell's Case 199, 333
Byzantium, 27–28, 29

cabinet government, origin of, 335–37
Caenegem, R. C. van, xiv, 43, 116
Caesar, Augustus, 21, 30
Caesar, Julius, 21
Cain, P. J., 185
Calvin's Case, 308
Calvinism, 256–57, 282–83. *See also* Protestant separatism
Cam, Helen Maude, 144
Cambridge Illustrated History of the British Empire (Marshall), 269
Cambridge University, importance of corporate status of, 284
Camden (Lord), 340, 341, 355
Cameron, Euan, 278–80
Canada, 1837 rebellions in, 353; Bill of Rights in, 366
canon law: codification of, 39, 119; divorce in, 256–57; and Justinian code, 30; marriage in, 253–55
capital punishment, 273–75
capitalism, rise of, and common law, 10
capitalist land market, liberation of, 202, 204–207, 218
capitalist theory, conservative, 10, 11
Cardozo, Benjamin , 226
care, doctrine of reasonable, 226–27, 229
careers in law, thirteenth century, 39–40
Carleton, Sir Guy, 345
Carlyle, Thomas, 327–28
case method, 78, 193–94, 358
Catherine of Aragon, 256
Catiline, 21'

Cavaliers, 323
central courts: in Angevin era, 112–14; appeals procedure in, 136–37; description of, 135; development of, 130–134
Chadwick, Edwin, 346
Chain, Ernest, 193
Chamberlain, Neville, 327
Chancery, Court of: Coke's attack on, 308–10; functions of, 41, 130–31, 249–53; restoration of, 287, 329; suspension of, 246. *See also* equity
chantries, proliferation of, 203
Charles I, 283, 286, 313, 314, 316–20
Charles II, 136, 328
charter, in Anglo-Saxon law, 81–82
Chaucer, Geoffrey, 136
Christian egalitarianism, 242–43
Church of England, 256, 282–83, 327
Church of Scotland, 318
church-state relations, 118, 203–204, 277–85, 282–83
Churchill, Winston, 19, 327, 338
Cicero, Marcus Tullius: 15–26; class and lineage of, 20; legacy of, 18–19, 20, 297, 303, 344; legal practice of, 17–18, 19, 25; and natural law, 33–34
circuit judge system, political importance of, 109–111
civil law, defined, 2, 30
civil libel, defined, 231–32
Civil War, English: 286, 323–24; causes of, 283–84, 300, 330–31; outbreak of, 322; precursors of, 312
Clanchy, Michael, xiv, 114
Clark, Jonathan, 350
clergy: benefit of, 60–61; celibacy of, 86; in House of Commons, 158; integrative role of, 364; loss of credibility of, 213; and ordeals, 66
Clinton, Bill, 364

elections, disputed and House of Commons, 293

Elizabeth I, 282–83, 295, 298

Elton, Sir Geoffrey, vii, 246–47, 248, 278–79, 281

enclosure movements, 267–69, 275–76, 339

England, periphery status of in medieval era, 119

English common law, in American law schools, 374–77

English constitution: liberalism of, 141–63, 287, 289–90; popular element in, 68, 70

English Law in the Age of the Black Death (Palmer), 181–82

English Reports, The, 180, 303

Enlightenment, 343

entails, abolition of, 347

Entick v. *Carrington*, 340

entry, writ of, 111–12, 128

equity, 41, 249. *See also* Chancery, Court of

Erastus, 278

esquires, 166–67

essoins (excuses), 56

estates, retention of, 202

European Union, 32–33, 378–79, 380

evangelical Protestantism and Star Chamber, 248

Exchequer Chamber, 134

Exchequer Court, 130, 131–32, 318

federal commercial law, codification of, 35

federalism, in United States, 5, 353, 365, 366

Federalist party, American, 24

fee entail, 206–207

fee simple, 206

fee tail, 206

felony, trials for, 104–105

feminist legal historiography, 9

feudal wardship, 106–107

feudalism, structure of Norman, 93

Fielding, Henry, 273

Fifth Amendment, United States constitution, 248

Fifth Monarchy Men, 272

Firm, The (Grisham), 360

First Amendment, United States constitution, 233, 356

Fitz Neal, Richard, 51

Fleischer, Lawrence, xiv

Fletcher, Anthony, 231

folkright, 79, 80, 82

force and arms, trespass with, 223

Fortescue, Sir John, 289, 292

Foucault, Michel, 9, 11, 13–14, 239

Fourteenth Amendment, United States constitution, 355

Fourth Amendment, United States constitution, 340

Fourth Lateran Council of 1215, 66, 254

Franciscan order, liberalism of, 142, 150, 242

Frank, Jerome, 13

frankpledge, 77

free market land law, birth of, 205

free speech, 212

freemen, legal status as, 51–52

Freudian psychology, 13, 141

Friedman, Lawrence, xiv, 354, 357, 360

Friedman, Milton, 10

From Memory to Written Record (Clanchy), 114

Fuller, Lon, 2, 147

Gaius, 30

Galt, Alexander, 276

Gardiner, Samuel R., 321

GATT (General Agreement on Tariffs and Trade), 379

gavelkind. *See* parage

gentry: family organization of, 167; and higher education, 168–69; importance of common law to, 169–70, 182, 184, 185; medieval, described, 164–69; rise of, 164–66, 168; wealth of, 166

George I, 335

Norman Conquest, 74–75, 85–86
Norman kings, attitude toward law of, 96
Norman/Anglo-Saxon integration, 89–90
Normans, origin of, 75
novel disseisin, assize of, 54, 128, 208–209
nuisance, as cause of action, 224

Oedipus Lex (Goodrich), 10
On the Laws and Customs of England (Bracton), 120–21, 288–89. *See also* Bracton
One L (Turow), 361
Ong, Walter, 115
oral contracts, validation of, 216–18
ordeal, proof by, 63–65, 66
outdoor relief, 271
outlawry, sentence of, 91
Oxford University, corporate status of, 284
oyer and terminer. *See* pleas of the Crown
Palmer, Robert C., 170, 181, 217, 279, 376
Paradise Lost (Milton), 329
parage, 79
Paris, as medieval academic center, 122, 150
parlement, in France, 157
Parliament: birth of, 153–54; contemporary use of questions in, 232–33; Cromwell, Oliver, and, 327–28; dissolution of, 316; ecclesiastical representation in, 158; Edward I's use of, 156–59; medieval functions of, 157–58; organization of, 290; Tudor use of, 294
parole evidence rule, 179–80
Passport to Pimlico (film), 144
Pearl (poem), 166
Peel, Sir Robert, 272–73, 346
Peelers, 273
peine fort et dure, 129–30
Peirce, Charles Saunders, 357
penitentiaries, 275, 347

Penn, William, 199
penumbra doctrine, 22–24, 144
periphery status of medieval England, 119
personal actions: adjudication of, 212, 216–30; development of, 209–10
personal liability, law of, 3, 220–30. *See also* torts; trespass
Petition of Right, The (1628), 316
Petrarch, 19
petty assizes, 54–55, 128, 208
petty (petit) jury. *See* jury of verdict
Philip IV the Fair, 155–56
philosophes, in eighteenth century England, 345
Pilgrimage of Grace of 1536, 281
Pipe Rolls, 131
Plantagenet. *See* Angevin
Plato, 23
plea bargaining: overuse of, 371; in Roman law, 37
pleaders. *See* barristers
pleas of the Crown, 160
Pliny the Younger, 25
pocket boroughs, 335
Pocock, J. G., 322
police force, first public, 272–73, 347
police system, lack of in thirteenth century, 241
Policy and Police (Elton), 281
Polite and Commercial People, A (Langford), 350
political parties, origin of modern, 316
Pollock, Frederick, 180
poor laws, Tudor, and justices of the peace, 245, 270–71
poor relief, local administration of, 270
poorhouses, 271
population: boom in thirteenth century England, 240–241; distribution in twelfth century, 93–94
Posner, Richard, 10, 375

possessory assizes, unwieldiness of, 208. *See also* petty assizes

post-adolescent males, in thirteenth century, 240

postglossators, 32, 45

Pound, Roscoe, 13, 358, 375

poverty in seventeenth century, 269–71

poverty law, birth of, 212

power and the law, 237–61

praecipe, writ of, 111–12, 148

Praemunire, Statute of (1353), 278, 280

praetor, 18

Presbyterians, in Scotland, 283

presentment of Englishry, 90

press council, English, 234

press, freedom of the, 212

Presumed Innocent (Turow), 361

Pride and Prejudice (Austen), 207

prime minister, role of, 336

primogeniture, 79, 81, 82

printing press, introduction of, 230

private law: articulation of, 212; contrasted with public law, 238; defined, 6; state sanctions in, 238

private life, restrictions on, 258

Privy Council, 296

probate law, 260, 339

Procopius, 35

professions, innate conservatism of, 215–16

prohibition, writ of, 250

property, sacring of, 339–40

prosecution, American and British compared, 177–78

Protestant separatism in Britain, 282–83, 329–30. *See also* Calvinism

Provisors, Statute of (1351), 279

public executions, 273–74

public law: compared with private law, 236; defined, 6

Puritan blue laws, 329

Puritan party, 298–300. *See also* country party

Puritan theology and homiletics, influence of, 298

Putney debates, 325–26

quare impedit, writ of. *See* force and arms

Queen's Counsel (QC), 177

Quia Emptores, Statute of (1290), 204–205

quo warranto proceedings, 155–56

Ralegh, Walter, 123–24

Raoul de Cambrai (poem), 105

Rattigan, Terence, 180

reasonable care, doctrine of, 226–27, 229

rebellion, right of, 149

Reform Bill of 1832, 352, 356

reform party, medieval, 153–54

reform via legislation in England, 365–66

Reformation, in England, 203–204, 280–82

regulatory agencies, public, 359

regulatory law in United States, 362

Reid, John Philip, xiv, 352

relief, Angevin, 106

religion, statist approach to, 278

religious individualism, thirteenth to sixteenth centuries, 191, 321, 332

Remains of the Day, The (Ishiguro), 168

Rembar, Charles, 376

Remonstrance of the Commons of May 26, 1642, 319, 322

replevin, writ of, 220

Republic (Plato), 23

Republican party, American, 24

Requests, Court of, 217

Restoration, 286, 328, 329

revolution: impact on common law of, 194; incidence of, 262–63; liberal, 286–300; political, 263, 277–85; social, 263, 264–77; theory of legitimate, 334–35

Ricardo, David, 10

Richard I the Lionhearted, 107